CHAPTER 1   LESSON 5

Objectives: Study, Test, Writing (journal), and Check.

STUDY TIME

Have students study the vocabulary words in their vocabulary notebooks. Remind students that any vocabulary word in their notebook could be on their test.

TEST TIME

Have students turn to page 97 in the Test Section of their book and find Chapter 1 Test *(Exercises 1 –3)*. Tell them that grammar is not tested yet. Go over the directions to make sure they understand what to do. After students have finished, check and discuss their test papers. Make sure they understand why their answers are right or wrong. *(For total points, count each required answer as a point.)* *(Chapter 1 Test keys are given below.)*

Chapter 1 Test

Exercise 1: Identify each pair of words as synonyms or antonyms by putting parentheses ( ) around *syn* or *ant*. For number 5, write two synonym words and identify them with *syn*. For number 6, write two antonym words and identify them with *ant*.

| 1. often, seldom | syn **(ant)** | 3. master, servant | syn **(ant)** | 5. **(Answers will vary.)** |
| 2. friendly, amiable | **(syn)** ant | 4. small, minute | **(syn)** ant | 6. **(Answers will vary.)** |

Exercise 2: Write *a* or *an* in the blanks.

1. We rode __a__ train.
2. I saw __an__ eagle.
3. Monday is __a__ holiday.
4. He found __an__ empty bottle.
5. It was __an__ easy test.
6. He is __a__ good friend.
7. __an__ acorn
8. __a__ telephone
9. __an__ otter
10. __a__ hat
11. __an__ oven
12. __a__ ring

Exercise 3: In your journal, write a paragraph summarizing what you have learned this week.

CHECK TIME

After students have finished, check and discuss their test papers. Make sure they understand why their answers are right or wrong. *(For total points, count each required answer as a point.)*

(End of lesson.)

© SHURLEY INSTRUCTIONAL MATERIALS, INC.

S0-DVG-839

CHAPTER 2 LESSON 1

Objectives: How to Get Started, Jingles (Noun, Verb), Grammar (Noun, Verb), Activity, and Vocabulary #1.

HOW TO GET STARTED

1. The word *students* will be used throughout the text in reference to the child/children you are teaching. The adult teaching this program will be referred to as *teacher*.

2. Stay one lesson ahead of your students. Study the entire lesson thoroughly before you present it. Then, read each lesson like you read a storybook: word-for-word. Your teacher's manual will give you teaching scripts to read out loud to your students. It will give you teacher's notes, and it will tell you when your students are to participate with you. Do not skip anything, and do not jump ahead. In just a few days, you will be in a comfortable routine that will help your students develop a love of learning.

3. All jingles and references are found in the **Jingle and Reference Section** in the front of the student book. A **Practice Section** is located after the Jingle and Reference Sections to give students practice on the skills they are learning. A **Test Section** is located after the Practice Section to test students on the skills taught.

4. The lessons in this book are divided into chapters. Each lesson takes approximately twenty to fifty minutes to complete. For best results, you should do one lesson everyday.

5. Your Shurley kit contains a teacher's manual, a student workbook, and an audio CD which demonstrates the Jingles and the Question and Answer Flows for the Introductory Sentences.

Read the six *Jingle Guidelines* below before you teach jingles to your students. These guidelines will give you ideas and help you establish procedures for the recitation of jingles.

Jingle Guidelines

1. **Jingles are used** to learn English definitions. Jingle Time should be fun as well as educational.

2. **Knowing English definitions** makes learning English concepts easier because children can use the definitions to remember how to classify words used in sentences.

3. **Approach Jingle Time** as a learning time. Most of the jingles are presented as choral chants with enough rhythm to make them easy to remember, but you can also sing, rap, or just read them. Learning definitions in jingle form makes this necessary practice more fun. Listen to the CD for an example of one way the jingles can be done.

4. **Jingles are more fun** if you make up motions for each jingle. Motions use the kinesthetic learning style of students and help them learn faster. Motions should be incorporated for several of the jingles. Relax and have fun. Have your children help make up motions they enjoy.

5. **You only need** to spend a short time on jingles (five to ten minutes) because you will be working with the jingles every day.

6. **Demonstrate each new jingle** for your students and then lead them in reciting the jingles. Let your students lead the jingles as soon as they are ready.

© SHURLEY INSTRUCTIONAL MATERIALS, INC.

CHAPTER 2 LESSON 1 CONTINUED

 JINGLE TIME

Have students turn to page 2 in the Jingle Section of their books. The teacher will lead the students in reciting the new jingles (*Noun and Verb*) below. Practice the jingles several times until students can recite the jingles smoothly. Emphasize reciting with a rhythm. Students and teacher should be together! (*Do not try to explain the jingles at this time. Just have fun reciting them. Add motions for more fun and laughter.*)

Jingle 1: Noun Jingle
This little noun Floating around Names a person, place, or thing. With a knick knack, paddy wack, These are English rules. Isn't language fun and cool?

Jingle 2: Verb Jingle		
A verb shows action, There's no doubt! It tells what the subject does, Like sing and shout.	Action verbs are fun to do. Now, it's time to name a few. So, clap your hands And join our rhyme; Say those verbs in record time!	Wiggle, jiggle, turn around; Raise your arms And stomp the ground. Shake your finger and wink your eye; Wave those action verbs good-bye.

 GRAMMAR TIME

TEACHING SCRIPT FOR THE NOUN AND VERB

The purpose of studying English is to learn the vocabulary and skills that will help you become effective in speaking and writing. We will begin our study of English with nouns and verbs.

The noun jingle that you learned today says a **noun** names a person, place, or thing. The noun is also known as a naming word. Words like **child** and **Bob** name people. Can you tell me two more nouns that name people? (*Give students time to respond.*) Words like **lions** and **tigers** name animals. Can you tell me two more nouns that name animals? (*Give students time to respond.*)

Words like **zoo** and **jungle** name places, and words like **fan** and **toy** name things. Can you tell me two more nouns that name places and things? (*Give students time to respond.*) (*Then, give students time to identify several nouns in the room.*) We use the abbreviation **N** for the word **noun** when we do not spell it out.

© SHURLEY INSTRUCTIONAL MATERIALS, INC.

CHAPTER 2 LESSON 1 CONTINUED

You have already learned several things about the verb from the verb jingle. A word that shows action is a verb. The **verb** tells what a person or thing does. Words like **play** and **wiggle** tell what children do. Children **play**, and children **wiggle**. Can you tell me two more verbs that tell what children do? (*Give students time to respond. Have students repeat the noun <u>children</u> with each verb.*) Can you tell me two verbs that tell what puppies do? (*Give students time to respond. Have students repeat the noun <u>puppies</u> with each verb.*) Can you tell me two verbs that tell what snakes do? (*Give students time to respond. Have students repeat the noun <u>snakes</u> with each verb.*) We use the abbreviation **V** for the word **verb** when we do not spell it out.

ACTIVITY / ASSIGNMENT TIME

For independent practice, have students take out a sheet of paper, make three columns, and write one of these titles above each column: kitchen, living room, and bedroom.   Then, have students list on their paper as many nouns as they can identify in each room. (*Example: Kitchen: stove, spoons, cabinets, etc.*) To add a higher level of complexity, give students a time limit in each room (*about five or six minutes in each room*). (*Check and discuss students' noun lists after they have finished.*)

VOCABULARY TIME

Assign Chapter 2, Vocabulary Words **#1** on page 8 in the Reference Section for students to define in their Vocabulary notebooks. Tell students they are to use a dictionary or thesaurus to look up the meanings of the vocabulary words. After they write each word and its meaning, students are to write a sentence using the vocabulary word.

Chapter 2, Vocabulary Words #1
(apt, suitable, certain, doubtful)

(End of lesson.)

© SHURLEY INSTRUCTIONAL MATERIALS, INC.

CHAPTER 2   LESSON 2

Objectives: Jingle (Sentence), Grammar (Introductory Sentences, Question & Answer Flow, classifying, labeling, subject noun, verb), Skill (five parts of a complete sentence), Activity, and Vocabulary #2.

 JINGLE TIME

Have students turn to the Jingle Section in their books and recite the previously-taught jingles. Then, lead students in reciting the new jingle (*Sentence*) below. Practice the new jingle several times until students can recite it smoothly. Emphasize reciting with a rhythm. Students and teacher should be together! (*Do not try to explain the new jingle at this time. Just have fun reciting it. Remember, add motions for more fun and laughter.*)

Jingle 3: Sentence Jingle

A sentence, sentence, sentence	Add a capital letter, letter
Is complete, complete, complete	And an end mark, mark.
When 5 simple rules	Now, we're finished, and aren't we smart!
It meets, meets, meets.	Now, our sentence has all its parts!
It has a subject, subject, subject	REMEMBER
And a verb, verb, verb.	Subject, Verb, Com-plete sense,
It makes sense, sense, sense	Capital letter, and an end mark, too.
With every word, word, word.	That's what a sentence is all about!

Teacher's Note: Do not spend a large amount of time practicing the new jingles. Students learn the jingles best by spending a small amount of time consistently, **every** day. (*Lead your students as they jiggle, wiggle, and jingle! Everyone should enjoy Jingle Time.*)

 GRAMMAR TIME

Put the introductory sentences from the box below on the board. Use these sentences as you go through the new concepts covered in your teaching scripts. For the greatest benefit, students must participate orally with the teacher. (*You might put the introductory sentences on notebook paper if you are doing one-on-one instruction with your students.*)

Chapter 2, Introductory Sentences for Lesson 2

1. Children played.
2. Mice ran.
3. Helicopters flew.

© SHURLEY INSTRUCTIONAL MATERIALS, INC.

CHAPTER 2 LESSON 2 CONTINUED

TEACHING SCRIPT FOR THE QUESTION & ANSWER FLOW

Understanding how all the parts of a sentence work together makes writing sentences easier and more interesting. Learning how to ask the right questions to get answers will help you identify the parts of a sentence. The questions you ask and the answers you get are called a **Question and Answer Flow**.

You will use a Question and Answer Flow to find what each word in a sentence is called. This method is called **classifying** because you classify, or tell, what each word in a sentence is called. After you classify a word, you will write the abbreviation above it. This is called **labeling** because you identify the words by writing abbreviations above them.

TEACHING SCRIPT FOR SUBJECT NOUN AND VERB IN A SENTENCE

I am going to show you how to use the noun and verb definitions and the Question and Answer Flow to find the subject noun and verb in a sentence. The subject of a sentence tells who or what a sentence is about. Since a noun names a person, place, or thing, a subject noun tells who or what a sentence is about. **The abbreviation *SN* is used for the words *subject noun* when we do not spell them out.** We ask a subject question to find the noun that works as the subject of the sentence. The subject questions are **who** or **what**. We ask *who* if the sentence is **about people**. We ask *what* if the sentence is **not about people,** but about an animal, a place, or a thing.

Look at Sentence 1: Children played.
Who played? children - subject noun (*Write SN above children.*)
Since the word *children* refers to people, we ask the subject question *who*.
The subject noun *children* tells *who* the sentence is about.

Now, let's learn the Question and Answer Flow to find the verb. The verb definition says the verb shows action. The verb tells what the subject is doing. To find the verb, ask **what is being said about** the subject. Let's say **what is being said about** five times. Go. (*Have your students recite "what is being said about" with you at least five times. This will help them remember this important verb question.*)

What is being said about children? children played - verb (*Write V above played.*)

Remember, the questions you ask and the answers you get are called a Question and Answer Flow. I will classify Sentence 1 again, but this time you will classify the sentence with me. After we finish Sentence 1, you will classify Sentences 2 and 3 with me.

Teacher's Note: Make sure students say the Question and Answer Flows correctly.

Question and Answer Flow for Sentence 1: Children played.

1. Who played? children - subject noun (Trace over the SN above *children.*)
   (Since *children* are people, we begin the subject question with *who*.
   The subject noun *children* tells *who* the sentence is about.)

2. What is being said about children? children played - verb (Trace over the V above *played.*)

Classified Sentence:
                 SN   V
                Children played.

© SHURLEY INSTRUCTIONAL MATERIALS, INC.

CHAPTER 2 LESSON 2 CONTINUED

Question and Answer Flow for Sentence 2: Mice ran.

1. What ran? mice - subject noun (Write SN above *mice*.)
   (Since *mice are animals*, we begin the subject question with *what*.
   The subject noun *mice* tells *what* the sentence is about.)

2. What is being said about mice? mice ran - verb (Write V above *ran*.)

Classified Sentence: SN   V
                            Mice ran.

Question and Answer Flow for Sentence 3: Helicopters flew.

1. What flew? helicopters - subject noun (Write SN above *helicopters*.)
   (Since *helicopters* are things, we begin the subject question with *what*.
   The subject noun *helicopters* tells *what* the sentence is about.)

2. What is being said about helicopters? helicopters flew - verb (Write V above *flew*.)

Classified Sentence: SN   V
                            Helicopters flew.

TEACHER INSTRUCTIONS

Have students recite the Question and Answer Flows for the first two sentences with you again, but this time they are to trace the labels on their desks with the first three fingers of their writing hand as they classify. This is excellent practice to develop dexterity and to learn at a faster pace.

Have students write the third sentence on a piece of paper. Then, students should go through the Question and Answer Flow with you again, but this time they are to write the labels above the words they classify. This will give them practice writing the labels before they are tested on them.

The key to success is to keep students constantly saying the Question and Answer Flows until they know them automatically. Follow the suggestions below for your students to get the greatest benefits from the grammar lessons.

1. Be sure to have the students read each sentence with you, in unison, before classifying it.
2. Make sure students are saying the **questions** and the **answers** with you as each Question and Answer Flow is recited.

SKILL TIME

TEACHING SCRIPT FOR THE 5 PARTS OF THE COMPLETE SENTENCE

Let's recite just the Sentence Jingle again. As you recite the Sentence Jingle, listen for the five parts that make a complete sentence. (*Recite the Sentence Jingle.*) Did you hear the five parts that make a complete sentence when we recited the Sentence Jingle? Of course, you did. Listen carefully as I go over the definition and the crucial parts of a complete sentence.

© SHURLEY INSTRUCTIONAL MATERIALS, INC.

CHAPTER 2 LESSON 2 CONTINUED

A **complete sentence** is a group of words that has a subject, a verb, and expresses a complete thought. A complete sentence should also begin with a capital letter and end with an end mark. Since you will be required to know the five parts of a sentence on a definition test later, you will learn the five parts of a sentence the easy way: by reciting the Sentence Jingle during Jingle Time. Now, listen for the five parts of a sentence as you recite the Sentence Jingle one more time. (*Recite the Sentence Jingle again.*) I want you to recite only the five parts of a sentence. (*Have students recite the section under REMEMBER several times.*)

REMEMBER
Subject, Verb, Com-plete sense,
Capital letter, and an end mark, too.
That's what a sentence is all about!

 ACTIVITY / ASSIGNMENT TIME

For the first part of your skill activity, you will need a white sheet of drawing paper. (*Construction paper or regular writing paper will do if you do not have drawing paper.*) You will fold the bottom of your paper to the top. You now have half a page. You will fold your paper again. This time, fold the left side of your paper to the right side. Crease your folds until they are very flat and smooth. Cut the bottom folds to make a little book. Staple the left side of the book to keep it together.

For the second part of your activity, you will follow several steps to complete your book. Turn to page 13 in your Reference Section and look at Reference 5. First, you will make a title page. Look at the information given for the title page in Part A. Center this information on the title page of your booklet. (*Make sure students are following and completing the directions correctly.*) Leave the back of the title page blank. Write a small number 1 in the bottom right-hand corner of the first page after the title page. Number each page. The back page should be page 6.

Reference 5: My Sentence Book Series, Book 1	
Part A	**Part B**
My **Sentence Book** **Series** **Book #1** **By:** (*Write your name.*) **Date:** (*Write the date.*)	Page 1: Horse runs. Page 2: Horse jumps. Page 3: Horse walks. Page 4: Horse eats. Page 5: Horse sleeps. Page 6: The End.

© SHURLEY INSTRUCTIONAL MATERIALS, INC.

CHAPTER 2 LESSON 2 CONTINUED

Your next step is to decide on a subject that you can use throughout the book. Look at Part B in Reference 5. We will use a horse for the subject in our sample. At the bottom of each page, you will print or write the story of a horse. Part B gives you a sample that you can use for each page. Remember, you can only use subjects and verbs for Book 1. (*Discuss the samples with your students.*)

If you would rather use something different for your first book, you may choose another set of subjects and verbs. (*Sun shines, ship sails, car races, etc.*) After you have written the subject/verb sentences at the bottom of each page, check each sentence carefully for the five parts of a sentence.

After you have checked to make sure your sentences are written neatly and correctly, you will illustrate each sentence at the top of the page. Illustrations can be drawn and colored, or they can be pictures cut out of magazines, old books, etc.

Read and discuss your first book with other family members. Decorate a shoebox or other small box to make a small library shelf designed specifically for your Sentence Book Series.

 VOCABULARY TIME

Assign Chapter 2, Vocabulary Words **#2** on page 8 in the Reference Section for students to define in their Vocabulary notebooks. Tell students they are to use a dictionary or thesaurus to look up the meanings of the vocabulary words. After they write each word and its meaning, students are to write a sentence using the vocabulary word.

Chapter 2, Vocabulary Words #2
(clear, vague, tired, weary)

(End of lesson.)

© SHURLEY INSTRUCTIONAL MATERIALS, INC.

CHAPTER 2   LESSON 3

Objectives: Jingle (Adverb), Grammar (Introductory Sentences, Adverb), Activity, and Writing (journal).

 **JINGLE TIME**

Have students turn to the Jingle Section in their books and recite the previously-taught jingles. Then, lead students in reciting the new jingle (*Adverb*) below. Practice the new jingle several times until students can recite it smoothly. Emphasize reciting with a rhythm. (*Do not try to explain the new jingle at this time. Just have fun reciting it. Remember, add motions for more fun and laughter.*)

Teacher's Note: Again, do not spend a large amount of time practicing the new jingles. Students learn the jingles best by spending a small amount of time consistently, **every** day.

Jingle 4: Adverb Jingle
An adverb modifies a verb, adjective, or another adverb. An adverb asks *How? When? Where?* To find an adverb: **Go, Ask, Get**. Where do I **go**? To a verb, adjective, or another adverb. What do I **ask**? How? When? Where? What do I **get**? An ADVERB! (Clap) (Clap) That's what!

 GRAMMAR TIME

Put the introductory sentences from the box below on the board. Use these sentences as you go through the new concepts covered in your teaching scripts. For the greatest benefit, students must participate orally with the teacher. (*You might put the introductory sentences on notebook paper if you are doing one-on-one instruction with your students.*)

Chapter 2, Introductory Sentences for Lesson 3
1. Children played happily today. 2. Mice ran away. 3. Helicopters flew around.

© SHURLEY INSTRUCTIONAL MATERIALS, INC.

CHAPTER 2 LESSON 3 CONTINUED

TEACHING SCRIPT FOR THE ADVERB

You are learning that jingles give you a lot of information quickly and easily. I will review several things that the Adverb Jingle tells us about the adverb. Listen carefully. **The Adverb Definition:** An adverb modifies a verb, adjective, or another adverb. **The Adverb Questions:** How? When? Where?

The adverb definition uses the word *modifies*. The word **modify** means to describe. When the adverb definition says that an adverb modifies a verb, it means that an adverb describes a verb. The abbreviation you will use for an adverb is *Adv*.

You will now learn how to use the adverb definition and the Question and Answer Flow to find the adverbs in sentences. But first, we will classify the main parts of a sentence, the subject and verb, before we find the adverbs.

Classify Sentence 1: Children played happily today.
Who played happily today? children - subject noun (*Write SN above children.*)
What is being said about children? children played - verb (*Write V above played.*)

The adverb jingle tells you the adverb definition and the adverb questions. Look at the Adverb Jingle in the Jingle Section on page 3 and repeat the Adverb Jingle with me. (*Repeat the Adverb Jingle with your students again.*) I am going to ask you some questions that will show you how to use the Adverb Jingle to find adverbs. You may look at the Adverb Jingle in your book so you can answer my questions about adverbs.

1. Where do you go to find an adverb? (*to the verb, adjective, or another adverb*)

2. Where do you go **first** to find an adverb? (*to the verb*)

3. What is the verb in Sentence 1? (*played*)

4. What do you ask after you go to the verb *played*?

   (*one of the adverb questions: how? when? where?*)

5. How do you know which adverb question to ask?

   Look at the words around the verb: (happily, today). (*Let these words guide you.*)

6. Which adverb question would you use to find the first adverb in this sentence? (*how?*)

This is how you would ask an adverb question and give an adverb answer in the Question and Answer Flow: **played how? happily - adverb** (*Write Adv above the word **happily**.*)

Look at the sentence again. As you can see, there is another word that needs to be classified. In order to classify this word, you must again ask the questions that you have learned. You will continue this question and answer procedure until all words in the sentence have been identified. That is why we call it the Question and Answer Flow.

Let's go back to the verb and do the Question and Answer Flow for another adverb:
Played when? today - adverb (*Write Adv above the word **today**.*)

I will classify Sentence 1 again, but this time you will classify it with me. I will lead you as we follow the series of questions and answers that I have just demonstrated. Then, we will classify Sentences 2-3.

© SHURLEY INSTRUCTIONAL MATERIALS, INC.

CHAPTER 2 LESSON 3 CONTINUED

Question and Answer Flow for Sentence 1: Children played happily today.

1. Who played happily today? children - subject noun (Trace over the SN above *children*.)
2. What is being said about children? children played - verb (Trace over the V above *played*.)
3. Played how? happily - adverb (Trace over the Adv above *happily*.)
4. Played when? today - adverb (Trace over the Adv above *today*.)

Classified Sentence:
SN   V   Adv Adv
Children played happily today.

Question and Answer Flow for Sentence 2: Mice ran away.

1. What ran away? mice - subject noun (Write SN above *mice*.)
2. What is being said about mice? mice ran - verb (Write V above *ran*.)
3. Ran where? away - adverb (Write Adv above *away*.)

Classified Sentence:
SN V Adv
Mice ran away.

Question and Answer Flow for Sentence 3: Helicopters flew around.

1. What flew around? helicopters - subject noun (*SN*)
2. What is being said about helicopters? helicopters flew - verb (*V*)
3. Flew where? around - adverb (*Adv*)

Classified Sentence:
SN V Adv
Helicopters flew around.

TEACHER INSTRUCTIONS

If this is the first year for Shurley English, have students recite the Question and Answer Flow for the first sentence with you again, but this time they are to trace the labels on their desks with the first three fingers of their writing hand as they classify. This is excellent practice to develop dexterity and to learn at a faster pace.

Have students write the second sentence on a piece of paper. Then, students should go through the Question and Answer Flow with you again, but this time they are to write the labels above the words they classify. This will give them practice writing the labels before they are tested on them.

© SHURLEY INSTRUCTIONAL MATERIALS, INC.

CHAPTER 2 LESSON 3 CONTINUED

ACTIVITY / ASSIGNMENT TIME

You will make Book 2 of the Sentence Book Series in your activity today. First, you will use another white sheet of drawing paper. (*Construction paper or regular writing paper will do if you do not have drawing paper.*) I will go through the directions again with you. You will fold the bottom of your paper to the top. You now have half a page. You will fold your paper again. This time, fold the left side of your paper to the right side. Crease your folds until they are very flat and smooth. Cut the bottom folds to make a little book. Staple the left side of the book to keep it together. Now, you have Book 2 ready to complete.

Look at Reference 6 on page 14. To make your title page, use the information in Part A. Center this information on the title page of your booklet. (*Make sure students are following and completing the directions correctly.*) Leave the back of the title page blank. Write a small number 1 in the bottom right-hand corner of the first page after the title page. Number each page. The back page should be page 6.

Reference 6: My Sentence Book Series, Book 2	
Part A	**Part B**
My **Sentence Book Series** **Book #2** **By:** (*Write your name.*) **Date:** (*Write the date.*)	Page 1: Horse runs fast. Page 2: Horse jumps high. Page 3: Horse walks slowly. Page 4: Horse eats quickly. Page 5: Horse sleeps soundly. Page 6: The End.

Next, you must decide to use the same subject/verb sets or choose a different subject/verb set. We will continue to use a horse for our sample. At the bottom of each page, print or write the new sentences about a horse. For Book 2, you are using only these three parts of a sentence: subject, verb, and an adverb.

After you have written the new sentences at the bottom of each page, check each sentence carefully for the five parts of a sentence. After you have checked to make sure your sentences are written neatly and correctly, you will illustrate each sentence at the top of the page. Illustrations can be drawn and colored, or they can be pictures cut out of magazines, old books, etc.

Read and discuss your second book with other family members and friends. Put Book 2 on the library shelf designed specifically for your Sentence Book Series.

WRITING TIME

Have students make an entry in their journals.

(End of lesson.)

© SHURLEY INSTRUCTIONAL MATERIALS, INC.

CHAPTER 2   LESSON 4

Objectives: Jingles (Adjective, Article Adjective), Grammar (Introductory Sentences, Adjective, Article Adjectives), Practice Exercise, Activity.

 **JINGLE TIME**

Have students turn to the Jingle Section in their books and recite the previously-taught jingles. Then, lead students in reciting the new jingles (*Adjective and Article Adjective*) below. Practice the new jingles several times until students can recite them smoothly. Emphasize reciting with a rhythm. Students and teacher should be together! (*Do not try to explain the new jingles at this time. Just have fun reciting the jingles. Remember, add motions for more fun and laughter.*)

Jingle 5: Adjective Jingle

An adjective modifies a noun or pronoun.
An adjective asks *What kind? Which one? How many?*
To find an adjective: **Go, Ask, Get**.
Where do I **go**? To a noun or pronoun.
What do I **ask**? What kind? Which one? How many?
What do I **get**? An ADJECTIVE! (Clap) (Clap) That's what!

Jingle 6: Article Adjective Jingle

We are the article adjectives,
Teeny, tiny adjectives:
A, AN, THE - A, AN, THE.

We are called article adjectives and noun markers;
We are memorized and used every day.
So, if you spot us, you can mark us
With the label A.

We are the article adjectives,
Teeny, tiny adjectives:
A, AN, THE - A, AN, THE.

© SHURLEY INSTRUCTIONAL MATERIALS, INC.

CHAPTER 2 LESSON 4 CONTINUED

GRAMMAR TIME

Put the introductory sentences from the box below on the board. Use these sentences as you go through the new concepts covered in your teaching scripts. For the greatest benefit, students must participate orally with the teacher. (*You might put the introductory sentences on notebook paper if you are doing one-on-one instruction with your students.*)

Chapter 2, Introductory Sentences for Lesson 4
1. The two small children played happily today.
2. The three mice ran away.
3. Several military helicopters flew around.

TEACHING SCRIPT FOR THE ADJECTIVE

Remember, jingles give you a lot of information quickly and easily. I will review several things that the Adjective Jingle tells us about the adjective. **The Adjective Definition:** An adjective modifies a noun or pronoun. **The Adjective Questions:** What kind? Which one? How many?

The adjective definition also uses the word *modifies*. The word **modify** means to describe. When the adjective definition says that an adjective modifies a noun, it means that an adjective describes a noun. The abbreviation you will use for an adjective is *Adj.*

You will now learn how to use the adjective definition and the Question and Answer Flow to find the adjectives in sentences. But first, we will classify the subject, verb, and adverb before we find the adjectives.

Classify Sentence 1: The two small children played happily today.
Who played happily today? children - subject noun (*Write SN above* **children**.)
What is being said about children? children played - verb (*Write V above* **played**.)
Played how? happily - adverb (*Write Adv above the word* **happily**.)
Played when? today - adverb (*Write Adv above the word* **today**.)

We will use the same procedure to find the adjectives. The Adjective Jingle tells you the adjective definition and the adjective questions. Look at the Adjective Jingle in the Jingle Section on page 3 and repeat the Adjective Jingle with me. (*Repeat the Adjective Jingle with your students again.*)

I am going to ask you some questions that will show you how to use the Adjective Jingle to find adjectives. You may look at the Adjective Jingle in your book so you can answer my questions about adjectives.

© SHURLEY INSTRUCTIONAL MATERIALS, INC.

CHAPTER 2 LESSON 4 CONTINUED

1. Where do you go to find an adjective? *(to a noun or pronoun)*
2. Where do you go **first** to find an adjective? *(to the subject noun)*
3. What is the subject noun in Sentence 1? *(children)*
4. What do you ask after you go to the subject noun *children*?
   (one of the adjective questions: what kind? which one? how many?)
5. How do you know which adjective question to ask?
   (Look at the word or words around the noun: (two, small)   These words will guide you.)
6. Which adjective questions would you use to find an adjective in this sentence?
   (What kind? How many?)

This is how you would ask an adjective question and give the adjective answer in the Adjective Question and Answer Flow: **What kind of children? small - adjective** *(Write Adj above the word **small**.)*

Look at the sentence again. As you can see, there is another word that needs to be classified. In order to classify this word, you must again ask the questions that you have learned. You will continue this question and answer procedure until all words in the sentence have been identified. That is why we call it the Question and Answer Flow.

Let's go back to the noun and do the Question and Answer Flow for another adjective:
How many children? two - adjective *(Write Adj above the word **two**)*

TEACHING SCRIPT FOR THE ARTICLE ADJECTIVE

We have another adjective to identify. This new adjective is known as the article adjective. There are only three article adjectives. Let's recite the Article Adjective Jingle to learn more about the article adjectives. *(Recite the Article Adjective Jingle with your students.)*

Article Adjectives are the three most commonly-used adjectives. The three article adjectives are *a, an,* and *the*. Everyone recite the words *article adjective* three times. *(article adjective, article adjective, article adjective)* Article adjectives are sometimes called noun markers because they tell that a noun is close by. The article adjectives must be <u>memorized</u> because there are no questions in the Question and Answer Flow to find the article adjectives. Article adjectives are labeled with an **A**.

This is how you would identify an article adjective in the Question and Answer Flow: **The - article adjective** *(Write **A** above the word **The**.)*

I will classify Sentence 1 again, but this time you will classify it with me. I will lead you as we follow the series of questions and answers that I have just demonstrated. Then, we will classify Sentences 2-3.

Question and Answer Flow for Sentence 1: The two small children played happily today.

1. Who played happily today? children - subject noun *(Trace over the SN above children.)*
2. What is being said about children? children played - verb *(Trace over the V above played.)*
3. Played how? happily - adverb *(Trace over the Adv above happily.)*
4. Played when? today - adverb *(Trace over the Adv above today.)*
5. What kind of children? small - adjective *(Trace over the Adj above small.)*
6. How many children? two - adjective *(Trace over the Adj above two)*
7. The - article adjective *(Trace over the A above The.)*

Classified Sentence: A   Adj   Adj   SN   V   Adv   Adv
                         The two small children played happily today.

© SHURLEY INSTRUCTIONAL MATERIALS, INC.

CHAPTER 2 LESSON 4 CONTINUED

Question and Answer Flow for Sentence 2: The three mice ran away.

1. What ran away? mice - subject noun (Write SN above *mice*.)
2. What is being said about mice? mice ran - verb (Write V above *ran*.)
3. Ran where? away - adverb (Write Adv above *away*.)
4. How many mice? three - adjective (Write Adj above *three*.)
5. The - article adjective (Write A above *The*.)

Classified Sentence:

      A   Adj SN V Adv

      The three mice ran away.

Question and Answer Flow for Sentence 3: Several military helicopters flew around.

1. What flew around? helicopters - subject noun (*SN*)
2. What is being said about helicopters? helicopters flew - verb (*V*)
3. Flew where? around - adverb (*Adv*)
4. What kind of helicopters? military - adjective (*Adj*)
5. How many helicopters? several - adjective (*Adj*)

Classified Sentence:

     Adj   Adj   SN   V Adv

     Several military helicopters flew around.

 PRACTICE TIME

Have students turn to page 61 in the Practice Section of their book and find Chapter 2, Lesson 4, Practice *(1-2)*. Go over the directions to make sure they understand what to do. Check and discuss the Practices after students have finished. (*Chapter 2, Lesson 4, Practice keys are given below.*)

Chapter 2, Lesson 4, Practice 1: Match the definitions. Write the correct letter beside each numbered concept.

F	1. sentences should begin with	A.	verb, adjective, or adverb
H	2. article adjectives	B.	who
I	3. adjective modifies	C.	what is being said about
C	4. verb question	D.	person, place, or thing
J	5. tells what the subject does	E.	what
E	6. subject-noun question (thing)	F.	capital letter
K	7. article adjectives can be called	G.	subject, verb, complete sense
G	8. parts of a complete sentence	H.	a, an, the
D	9. noun	I.	noun or pronoun
B	10. subject-noun question (person)	J.	verb
A	11. adverb modifies	K.	noun markers

Chapter 2, Lesson 4, Practice 2: Write *a* or *an* in the blanks.

1. We searched for **a** key.
2. James is **an** author.
3. Pam ate **an** ear of corn.
4. She served **a** bowl of soup.
5. Noah built **an** ark.
6. That is **a** great idea!
7. **a** letter
8. **a** wrinkle
9. **an** ostrich
10. **a** store
11. **an** index
12. **an** apricot

© SHURLEY INSTRUCTIONAL MATERIALS, INC.

CHAPTER 2 LESSON 4 CONTINUED

 ACTIVITY / ASSIGNMENT TIME

You will make Book 3 of the Sentence Book Series in your activity today. First, you will use another white sheet of drawing paper. (*Construction paper or regular writing paper will do if you do not have drawing paper.*) I will go through the directions again with you. You will fold the bottom of your paper to the top. You now have half a page. You will fold your paper again. This time, fold the left side of your paper to the right side. Crease your folds until they are very flat and smooth. Cut the bottom folds to make a little book. Staple the left side of the book to keep it together. Now, you have Book 3 ready to complete.

Look at Reference 7 on page 14. To make your title page, use the information in Part A. Center this information on the title page of your booklet. (*Make sure students are following and completing the directions correctly.*) Leave the back of the title page blank. Write a small number 1 in the bottom right-hand corner of the first page after the title page. Number each page. The back page should be page 6.

Reference 7: My Sentence Book Series, Book 3	
Part A	**Part B**
My **Sentence Book Series** **Book #3** **By:** (*Write your name.*) **Date:** (*Write the date.*)	Page 1: The beautiful horse runs fast. Page 2: The excited young horse jumps very high. Page 3: An old horse walks slowly away. Page 4: The hungry horse eats quickly. Page 5: The tired horse sleeps soundly. Page 6: The End.

Next, you must decide to use the same subject/verb sets or choose a different subject/verb set. We will continue to use a horse for our sample. At the bottom of each page, print or write the new sentences about a horse. For Book 3, you are using only these five parts of a sentence: subject, verb, adjective, article adjective, and adverb. You can add more adjectives and adverbs as long as they make sense.

After you have written the new sentences at the bottom of each page, check each sentence carefully for the five parts of a sentence. After you have checked to make sure your sentences are written neatly and correctly, you will illustrate each sentence at the top of the page. Illustrations can be drawn and colored, or they can be pictures cut out of magazines, old books, etc.

Read and discuss your third book with other family members and friends. Put Book 3 on the library shelf designed specifically for your Sentence Book Series.

(End of lesson.)

© SHURLEY INSTRUCTIONAL MATERIALS, INC.

CHAPTER 2   LESSON 5

Objectives: Jingles, Grammar (Practice Sentences), Skill (additional Article Adjective information), Activity, Study, Test, and Writing (journal).

 **JINGLE TIME**

Have students turn to the Jingle Section of their books. The teacher will lead the students in reciting the previously-taught jingles.

 GRAMMAR TIME

Put the Practice Sentences from the box below on the board. Use these sentences as you practice the concepts that have been taught. For the greatest benefit, students must participate orally with the teacher. (*You might put the Practice Sentences on notebook paper if you are doing one-on-one instruction with your students.*)

> ### Chapter 2, Practice Sentences for Lesson 5
>
> 1. The timid little girl sat alone.
> 2. A large fish swam briskly away.
> 3. The full moon shines brightly tonight.

TEACHING SCRIPT FOR CLASSIFYING PRACTICE SENTENCES

We will now classify three different sentences to practice the Question and Answer Flows. We will classify the sentences together. Begin.

Teacher's Note: At this time, your manual will no longer have the entire name written out for each part of speech used in the Question and Answer Flow. Instead of *adverb*, you will see *Adv*. You will continue to say *adverb* even though you see only the abbreviation *Adv*. You will say *subject noun* whenever you see the abbreviation *SN*. Always say *verb* whenever you see the abbreviation *V*, etc.

> **Question and Answer Flow for Sentence 1: The timid little girl sat alone.**
>
> 1. Who sat alone? girl - SN
> 2. What is being said about girl? girl sat - V
> 3. Sat how? alone - Adv
> 4. What kind of girl? little - Adj
> 5. What kind of girl? timid - Adj
> 6. The - A
>
> **Classified Sentence:**   A   Adj   Adj SN   V   Adv
>   The timid little girl sat alone.

© SHURLEY INSTRUCTIONAL MATERIALS, INC.

CHAPTER 2 LESSON 5 CONTINUED

Question and Answer Flow for Sentence 2: A large fish swam briskly away.

1. What swam briskly away? fish - SN
2. What is being said about fish? fish swam - V
3. Swam how? briskly - Adv
4. Swam where? away - Adv
5. What kind of fish? large - Adj
6. A - A

Classified Sentence: A Adj SN   V   Adv   Adv
                              A large fish swam briskly away.

Question and Answer Flow for Sentence 3: The full moon shines brightly tonight.

1. What shines brightly tonight? moon - SN
2. What is being said about moon? moon shines - V
3. Shines how? brightly - Adv
4. Shines when? tonight - Adv
5. What kind of moon? full - Adj
6. The - A

Classified Sentence: A Adj SN   V   Adv   Adv
                              The full moon shines brightly tonight.

Teacher's Note: Options Available for Classifying Sentences:

- Option 1 is recommended if this is your students' first year in Shurley English. Students will classify all *Introductory*, *Practice,* and *Test* Sentences orally with you to reinforce the concepts they are learning. As you progress through the program and see that your students are experiencing no difficulty, you might go to Option 2 for more student independence.

- Option 2 is recommended for second-year students or for strong first-year students. In this option, students could classify the Practice Sentences independently on notebook paper. You can check students' Practice Sentences from those provided in your teacher's manual. Since the Introductory Sentences are used to introduce new concepts, you should continue putting them on the board or on notebook paper for your students. Introductory Sentences are also provided in your Teacher's Manual.

- Option 3 is recommended if you choose to use the supplemental materials that are available. These materials include a Practice Booklet and two CDs for the Practice Sentences. The Practice Booklet contains all the Introductory and Practice Sentences that are located in your teacher's manual. The two Practice CDs can be used for independent work with the Practice Sentences. (The CD for the Introductory Sentences is included in your kit.)

I want you to look at Reference 8 on page 14 in the Reference Section of your book. You are given a Question and Answer Flow as an example so it will be easy for you to study. Let's read it together. Remember, we always begin by reading the sentence. (*Read and discuss the Question and Answer Flow in the reference box on the next page with your students.*)

© SHURLEY INSTRUCTIONAL MATERIALS, INC.

CHAPTER 2 LESSON 5 CONTINUED

Reference 8: Question and Answer Flow Sentence
Question and Answer Flow Sentence: The happy young man whistled cheerfully.
1. Who whistled cheerfully? man - SN
2. What is being said about man? man whistled - V
3. Whistled how? cheerfully - Adv
4. What kind of man? young - Adj
5. What kind of man? happy - Adj
6. The - A
Classified Sentence: A Adj Adj SN V Adv
The happy young man whistled cheerfully.

SKILL TIME

TEACHING SCRIPT FOR ADDITIONAL ARTICLE ADJECTIVE INFORMATION

You have seen how the article is used in the Question and Answer Flows to classify sentences. Now, I will give you more information about article adjectives. Turn to Reference 9 on page 14 in the Reference Section of your book. (_Have students follow along as you read the information in the reference box below._)

Reference 9: Additional Article Adjective Information
The article _The_ has two pronunciations:
a. As a long **e** (_where the article comes in front of a word that begins with a vowel sound_) the egg, the igloo, the excellent meal
b. As a short **u** (_where the article comes in front of a word that begins with a consonant sound_) the dance, the shoe, the green trees

ACTIVITY / ASSIGNMENT TIME

On a sheet of paper, write five nouns that begin with a vowel sound. Write the letter (**e**) in parentheses after each word to indicate that the article would be pronounced with the long e sound. Next, write ten nouns that begin with a consonant sound. Write the letter (**u**) in parentheses after each word to indicate that the article would be pronounced with the short **u** sound. After you have finished, we will say the words aloud with the proper pronunciation of the article **t-h-e** after each word. (_After students have finished, listen to them as they pronounce the article correctly for each word they have written on their paper._)

© SHURLEY INSTRUCTIONAL MATERIALS, INC.

CHAPTER 2 LESSON 5 CONTINUED

STUDY TIME

Have students study the vocabulary words in their vocabulary notebooks. Remind students that any vocabulary word in their notebooks could be on their test.

TEST TIME

Have students turn to page 97 in the Test Section of their book and find Chapter 2 Test *(Exercises 1 - 4)*. Go over the directions to make sure they understand what to do. After students have finished, check and discuss their test papers. Make sure they understand why their answers are right or wrong. *(For total points, count each required answer as a point.)* *(Chapter 2 Test keys are given below.)*

Chapter 2 Test

Exercise 1: Identify each pair of words as synonyms or antonyms by putting parentheses ( ) around *syn* or *ant*.

| 1. small, minute | **(syn)** ant | 3. servant, master | syn **(ant)** | 5. apt, suitable | **(syn)** ant |
| 2. clear, vague | syn **(ant)** | 4. doubtful, certain | syn **(ant)** | 6. weary, tired | **(syn)** ant |

Exercise 2: Write *a* or *an* in the blanks.

1. We saw __a__ clown today.
2. It was __an__ amazing idea.
3. We have __an__ unusual house.
4. It is __a__ clever trick.
5. It was __an__ easy job.
6. We want __a__ new car.
7. __an__ ostrich
8. __a__ siren
9. __an__ estimate
10. __a__ gnu
11. __an__ elf
12. __a__ book

Exercise 3: Match the definitions. Write the correct letter beside each numbered concept.

__F__	1. sentences should begin with	A.	verb, adjective, or adverb
__H__	2. article adjectives	B.	who
__I__	3. adjective modifies	C.	what is being said about
__C__	4. verb question	D.	person, place, or thing
__J__	5. tells what the subject does	E.	what
__E__	6. subject-noun question (thing)	F.	a capital letter
__K__	7. article adjective can be called	G.	subject, verb, complete sense
__G__	8. parts of a complete sentence	H.	a, an, the
__D__	9. noun	I.	noun or pronoun
__B__	10. subject-noun question (person)	J.	verb
__A__	11. adverb modifies	K.	noun marker

Exercise 4: In your journal, write a paragraph summarizing what you have learned this week.

(End of lesson.)

© SHURLEY INSTRUCTIONAL MATERIALS, INC.

CHAPTER 3 LESSON 1

Objectives: Jingles, Grammar (Introductory Sentences, Adverbs that modify Adjectives and Adverbs), Skill (Four Kinds of Sentences), Practice Exercise, Activity, and Vocabulary #1.

 **JINGLE TIME**

Have students turn to the Jingle Section of their books. The teacher will lead the students in reciting the previously-taught jingles.

 GRAMMAR TIME

Put the introductory sentences from the box below on the board. Use these sentences as you go through the new concepts covered in your teaching scripts. For the greatest benefit, students must participate orally with the teacher. (*You might put the introductory sentences on notebook paper if you are doing one-on-one instruction with your students.*)

> ### Chapter 3, Introductory Sentences for Lesson 1
>
> 1. The polite young singer sang exceptionally well.
> 2. The extremely loud music stopped abruptly.
> 3. Several brown ducks waddled awkwardly away.

TEACHING SCRIPT FOR IDENTIFYING ADVERBS THAT MODIFY ADJECTIVES AND ADVERBS

How do you find and classify adjectives? (*Go to the noun, ask an adjective question, and label the answer as an adjective.*) How do you find and classify adverbs? (*Go to the verb, ask an adverb question, and label the answer as an adverb.*)

The adverb definition tells you that an adverb modifies a verb, adjective, or another adverb. Today, I will show you how to find adverbs that modify adjectives and adverbs. To find these adverbs, you will go to an adjective or an adverb instead of the verb to ask an adverb question. Notice how these new concepts are demonstrated in the Question and Answer Flow. Begin.

Question and Answer Flow for Sentence 1: The polite young singer sang exceptionally well.

1. Who sang exceptionally well? singer - SN
2. What is being said about singer? singer sang - V
3. Sang how? well - Adv
4. How well? exceptionally - Adv

5. What kind of singer? young - Adj
6. What kind of singer? polite - Adj
7. The - A

Classified Sentence:

	A	Adj	Adj	SN	V	Adv	Adv
	The	polite	young	singer	sang	exceptionally	well.

© SHURLEY INSTRUCTIONAL MATERIALS, INC.

CHAPTER 3 LESSON 1 CONTINUED

Question and Answer Flow for Sentence 2: The extremely loud music stopped abruptly.

1. What stopped abruptly? music - SN
2. What is being said about music? music stopped - V
3. Stopped how? abruptly - Adv

4. What kind of music? loud - Adj
5. How loud? extremely - Adv
6. The - A

Note: "extremely" is an adverb that modifies an adjective in the complete subject. It is part of the complete subject.

Classified Sentence:

A	Adv	Adj	SN	V	Adv

The extremely loud music stopped abruptly.

Question and Answer Flow for Sentence 3: Several brown ducks waddled awkwardly away.

1. What waddled awkwardly away? ducks - SN
2. What is being said about ducks? ducks waddled - V
3. Waddled how? awkwardly - Adv

4. Waddled where? away - Adv
5. What kind of ducks? brown - Adj
6. How many ducks? several - Adj

Classified Sentence:

Adj	Adj	SN	V	Adv	Adv

Several brown ducks waddled awkwardly away.

Teacher's Note: Adverbs are classified in the order they appear after the verb because it is easier for the students. Only when an adverb modifies another adverb does the order change. The second adverb is classified first.

Example: *She sang extremely well.* Sang how? well - Adv; How well? extremely - Adv.

SKILL TIME

TEACHING SCRIPT FOR THE FOUR KINDS OF SENTENCES

There are four kinds of sentences. They are declarative, interrogative, imperative, and exclamatory. Let's recite the four kinds of sentences together five times. Go. (*Have your students recite "declarative, interrogative, imperative, and exclamatory" with you at least five times. This will help them remember the vocabulary necessary when discussing the kinds of sentences.*)

These sentences have four purposes: to tell, to ask, to request, or to show strong feeling. Now, you will learn more about the four kinds of sentences. Look at Reference 10 on page 15 in the Reference Section of your book. (*Read and discuss the information in the reference box on the next page with your students.*)

© SHURLEY INSTRUCTIONAL MATERIALS, INC.

CHAPTER 3 LESSON 1 CONTINUED

Reference 10: The Four Kinds of Sentences and the End Mark Flow	
1. A **declarative** sentence makes a statement. It is labeled with a *D*. Example: Jane ran every morning. (Period, statement, declarative sentence)	3. An **interrogative** sentence asks a question. It is labeled with an *Int*. Example: How many books did you read? (Question mark, question, interrogative sentence)
2. An **imperative** sentence gives a command. It is labeled with an *Imp*. Example: Take the students to class. (Period, command, imperative sentence)	4. An **exclamatory** sentence expresses strong feeling. It is labeled with an *E*. Example: The alligator snapped at us! (Exclamation point, strong feeling, exclamatory sentence)

Examples: Read each sentence, recite the end-mark flow in parentheses, and put the end mark and the abbreviation for the sentence type in the blank at the end of each sentence.

1. My dentist is a nice man **. D**
   (*Period, statement, declarative sentence*)

2. The strong wind shook our windows **! E**
   (*Exclamation point, strong feeling, exclamatory sentence*)

3. Take this medicine before noon **. Imp**
   (*Period, command, imperative sentence*)

4. Will you come to our party tonight **? Int**
   (*Question mark, question, interrogative sentence*)

Go to the examples listed at the bottom of your reference box and follow along as I identify each sentence by reciting the end-mark flow. Remember, the end-mark flow identifies the punctuation mark, the kind of sentence, and the name of that type of sentence. (*Read the examples with your students and recite the end-mark flow that is provided in parentheses.*)

 PRACTICE TIME

Have students turn to pages 61 and 62 in the Practice Section of their book and find the skills under Chapter 3, Lesson 1, Practice (*1-4*). Go over the directions to make sure they understand what to do. Check and discuss the Practices after students have finished. (*Chapter 3, Lesson 1, Practice keys are given below and on the next page.*)

Chapter 3, Lesson 1, Practice 1: Put the end mark and the abbreviation for each kind of sentence in the blanks below.

1. Put the vocabulary words in alphabetical order   **. Imp**

2. Are you working late tonight   **? Int**

3. They found the lost child   **! E**

4. We are moving to Florida   **. D**

5. Mow the lawn for Ms. Brown   **. Imp**

Chapter 3, Lesson 1, Practice 2: On notebook paper, write a sentence to demonstrate each of these four kinds of sentences: (1) Declarative, (2) Interrogative, (3) Exclamatory, and (4) Imperative. Write the correct punctuation and the abbreviation that identifies it at the end. Use these abbreviations: D, Int, E, Imp.

© SHURLEY INSTRUCTIONAL MATERIALS, INC.

CHAPTER 3 LESSON 1 CONTINUED

Chapter 3, Lesson 1, Practice 3: Write *a* or *an* in the blanks.

1. Jack blew out __a__ candle.
2. We built __a__ tree house.
3. He dressed up as __an__ Eskimo.

4. Tim caught __a__ fish.
5. She bruised __an__ elbow.
6. I want to be __an__ actor.

7. __a__ poem
8. __a__ bush
9. __an__ armadillo

10. __a__ temple
11. __an__ icicle
12. __an__ orchard

Chapter 3, Lesson 1, Practice 4: Match the definitions. Write the correct letter beside each numbered concept.

__F__	1. expresses strong feeling	A.	verb, adjective, or adverb
__E__	2. makes a statement	B.	noun markers
__I__	3. adjective modifies	C.	person, place, or thing
__B__	4. article adjectives can be called	D.	imperative sentence
__H__	5. subject question	E.	declarative sentence
__G__	6. asks a question	F.	exclamatory sentence
__D__	7. makes a request or gives a command	G.	interrogative sentence
__C__	8. noun	H.	who or what
__J__	9. tells what the subject does	I.	noun or pronoun
__A__	10. adverb modifies	J.	verb

ACTIVITY / ASSIGNMENT TIME

For your activity, you will make a sentence fan. First, you will fold a sheet of paper into a fan. (*If help is needed, show students how to fold their papers into a fan.*) Next, you will collect several sets of declarative, imperative, interrogative, and exclamatory sentences. Follow these directions:

1. For the first set, ask several people (*family members, friends, or other relatives*) to write one of the four types of sentences until you have collected all four.
2. For the second set, look in a newspaper or magazine and cut out an example for each of the four types of sentences.
3. For the third set, you must write an original sentence for each type of sentence: declarative, imperative, interrogative, and exclamatory.

You will label each of the twelve sentences that you have collected as a declarative, imperative, interrogative, or exclamatory sentence. Then, you will glue all the sentences on the different sections of your fan. Use the front and back of the fan if necessary. Color code your fan by coloring each type of sentence a different color. (*Discuss how the sentences are alike and how they are different.*) (*Note: This assignment could take several days. Work it in your schedule as time permits.*)

VOCABULARY TIME

Assign Chapter 3, Vocabulary Words **#1** on page 8 in the Reference Section for students to define in their Vocabulary notebooks. Tell students they are to use a dictionary or thesaurus to look up the meanings of the vocabulary words. After they write each word and its meaning, students are to write a sentence using the vocabulary word.

Chapter 3, Vocabulary Words #1
(kind, irreverent, curiosity, interest)

(End of lesson.)

Level 3 Homeschool Teacher's Manual

© SHURLEY INSTRUCTIONAL MATERIALS, INC.

CHAPTER 3   LESSON 2

Objectives: Jingles, Grammar (Introductory Sentences, Pattern 1 Sentences, end punctuation), Skills (introduce Skill Builder Checks and Noun Checks), Practice Exercise, and Vocabulary #2.

 JINGLE TIME

Have students turn to the Jingle Section in their books. The teacher will lead the students in reciting the previously-taught jingles.

 GRAMMAR TIME

Put the introductory sentences from the box below on the board. Use these sentences as you go through the new concepts covered in your teaching scripts. For the greatest benefit, students must participate orally with the teacher. (*You might put the introductory sentences on notebook paper if you are doing one-on-one instruction with your students.*)

Chapter 3, Introductory Sentences for Lesson 2
1. _____ The old dog howled quite loudly.
2. _____ A white shark swam very quickly away!
3. _____ The spirited racehorse ran swiftly today.

TEACHING SCRIPT FOR PATTERN 1 AND END PUNCTUATION

We will now classify Sentence 1. This time, there will be more information added to the Question and Answer Flow. You will classify the sentence with me until we get to the new part. The new part will be at the end of the Question and Answer Flow. Begin.

Sentence 1: The old dog howled quite loudly.
What howled quite loudly? dog - SN
What is being said about dog? dog howled - V
Howled how? loudly - Adv
How loudly? quite - Adv
What kind of dog? old - Adj
The - A

I will now explain the new parts and show you how to add them to the Question and Answer Flow. First, I will say the new parts in the Question and Answer Flow, and then I will explain each new part to you. Listen carefully as I repeat the two new parts.

1. Subject Noun Verb Pattern 1 Check. (*Write SN V P1 in the blank in front of the sentence. Be sure to say* **check***. You will use the check to identify any new skill that is added to the Question and Answer Flow.*)
2. Period, statement, declarative sentence. (*Write a D at the end of the sentence.*)

© SHURLEY INSTRUCTIONAL MATERIALS, INC.

CHAPTER 3 LESSON 2 CONTINUED

Note: Your sentence should look like this:

```
            A  Adj  SN /  V     Adv   Adv
SN  V       The old dog howled quite loudly.  D
P1
```

I will explain each new part, one at a time. Listen to the definition for a Pattern 1 sentence. The pattern of a sentence is the **order of the main parts** in that sentence. **Pattern 1** has only two main parts: the subject and the verb. Adjectives and adverbs add information to sentences, but they are not part of a sentence pattern. A **Pattern 1** sentence is labeled **SN V P1**. (*Put the SN V P1 on the board for your students to see.*) When you see or write the **SN V P1** labels, you will say, "Subject Noun, Verb, Pattern 1."

You will add a <u>*check*</u> to the sentence pattern to check for any additional skills to be identified. You will say, **"Subject Noun, Verb, Pattern 1, Check."** Remember these things:

1. The pattern of a sentence is <u>the order of its main parts</u>. <u>The subject and the verb are the main parts of a Pattern 1 sentence</u>.
2. Adjectives and adverbs are extra words that are not considered essential parts of a sentence pattern because they are used freely with all sentence patterns.
3. To identify a Pattern 1 sentence, you will write *SN V P1* on the line in front of the sentence.

The second new part is to identify the sentence as a declarative, imperative, interrogative, or exclamatory sentence. As soon as you say the pattern, you will immediately go to the end of the sentence, identify the end mark, the kind of sentence, and the name of that sentence. Look at Sentence 1. You will say, **"Period, statement, declarative sentence."** After you have identified the sentence as a declarative sentence, you will write a *D* after the period, but you will always say, "Period, statement, declarative sentence."

I will classify Sentence 1 again, and you will classify it with me this time. We will add the two new parts at the end of the Question and Answer Flow. Then, we will classify Sentences 2-3 together.

Question and Answer Flow for Sentence 1: The old dog howled quite loudly.

1. What howled quite loudly? dog - SN
2. What is being said about dog? dog howled - V
3. Howled how? loudly - Adv
4. How loudly? quite - Adv
5. What kind of dog? old - Adj
6. The - A

7. SN V P1 Check (Say: Subject Noun, Verb, Pattern 1, Check)
   (Write *SN V P1* in the blank beside the sentence.)
8. Period, statement, declarative sentence
   (Write *D* at the end of the sentence.)

Classified Sentence:

```
                   A   Adj  SN   V    Adv   Adv
       SN  V       The old dog howled quite loudly.  D
       P1
```

© SHURLEY INSTRUCTIONAL MATERIALS, INC.

CHAPTER 3 LESSON 2 CONTINUED

Question and Answer Flow for Sentence 2: A white shark swam very quickly away!

1. What swam very quickly away? shark - SN
2. What is being said about shark?
   shark swam - V
3. Swam how? quickly - Adv
4. How quickly? very - Adv
5. Swam where? away - Adv

6. What kind of shark? white - Adj
7. A - A
8. SN V P1 Check (Say: Subject Noun, Verb, Pattern 1, Check)
   (Write *SN V P1* in the blank beside the sentence.)
9. Exclamation point, strong feeling, exclamatory sentence
   (Write E at the end of the sentence.)

Classified Sentence:

                        A Adj SN   V Adv Adv Adv

       SN V   A white shark swam very quickly away! **E**
         P1

Question and Answer Flow for Sentence 3: The spirited racehorse ran swiftly today.

1. What ran swiftly today? racehorse - SN
2. What is being said about racehorse? racehorse ran - V
3. Ran how? swiftly - Adv
4. Ran when? today - Adv
5. What kind of racehorse? spirited - Adj

6. The - A
7. SN V P1 Check (Say: Subject Noun, Verb, Pattern 1, Check) (Write *SN V P1* in the blank beside the sentence.)
8. Period, statement, declarative sentence
   (Write D at the end of the sentence.)

Classified Sentence:

                        A   Adj   SN   V Adv Adv

       SN V   The spirited racehorse ran swiftly today. **D**
         P1

SKILL TIME

TEACHING SCRIPT FOR INTRODUCING SKILL BUILDER CHECKS AND NOUN CHECKS

Now that we have classified all three sentences, I am going to use them to do a Skill Builder Check. **A Skill Builder Check** is an oral review of certain skills. Skill Builder Checks are designed to make sure you keep basic skills sharp and automatic. The first skill that will be covered by the Skill Builder Check is the **Noun Check**. Even though a noun is only one part of speech, a noun can do many jobs or perform many functions in a sentence. The first noun job you have learned is that a noun can function as the subject of a sentence. The first noun job will be the subject noun.

Look at Sentences 1-3. In a Noun Check, we will identify the nouns in all three sentences by drawing circles around them. It will be easy today because we have only one noun job at this point. I will use Sentence 1 to demonstrate the four things that you say: **Number 1** (*You say the sentence number.*) **Subject Noun: dog** (*You say the noun job and the noun used for the noun job.*) **Yes** (*You say the word yes to verify that the word **dog** is a noun, not a pronoun.*) So it will not be confusing, I will repeat number 1 again. We will say, "Number 1: subject noun *dog*, yes." I will circle *dog* because we have identified it as a noun.

© SHURLEY INSTRUCTIONAL MATERIALS, INC.

CHAPTER 3 LESSON 2 CONTINUED

Let's start with number 1 again and do a Noun Check. Begin. (*Circle the nouns for all three sentences as your students recite the Noun Check with you: Number 1: subject noun **dog**, yes. Number 2: subject noun **shark**, yes. Number 3: subject noun **racehorse**, yes.*)

 PRACTICE TIME

Have students turn to pages 62 and 63 in the Practice Section of their book and find the skills under Chapter 3, Lesson 2, Practice *(1-3)*. Go over the directions to make sure they understand what to do. Check and discuss the Practices after students have finished. (*Chapter 3, Lesson 2, Practice keys are given below.*)

Chapter 3, Lesson 2, Practice 1: Put the end mark and the abbreviation for each kind of sentence in the blanks below.

1. Sit down when you tie your shoelaces   . Imp

2. Did you do well on your exam   ? Int

3. He won every race   ! E

4. I'm leaving on my trip tomorrow   . D

5. Cool down after the long race   . Imp

Chapter 3, Lesson 2, Practice 2: On notebook paper, write a sentence to demonstrate each of these four kinds of sentences: (1) Declarative, (2) Interrogative, (3) Exclamatory, and (4) Imperative. Write the correct punctuation and the abbreviation that identifies it at the end. Use these abbreviations: D, Int, E, Imp.

Chapter 3, Lesson 2, Practice 3: Write *a* or *an* in the blanks.

1. I ate **a** fresh strawberry. 4. She wore **a** bonnet. 7. **an** ear 10. **a** pillow

2. He is **an** architect. 5. Kate rode **an** elevator. 8. **a** nickel 11. **a** bike

3. We passed **an** old farm. 6. He owns **a** motorcycle. 9. **an** emerald 12. **an** oval

 VOCABULARY TIME

Assign Chapter 3, Vocabulary Words **#2** on page 8 in the Reference Section for students to define in their Vocabulary notebooks. Tell students they are to use a dictionary or thesaurus to look up the meanings of the vocabulary words. After they write each word and its meaning, students are to write a sentence using the vocabulary word.

Chapter 3, Vocabulary Words #2
(bland, tasty, cut, sever)

(End of lesson.)

© SHURLEY INSTRUCTIONAL MATERIALS, INC.

CHAPTER 3   LESSON 3

Objectives: Jingles, Grammar (Introductory Sentences, Complete Subject, Complete Predicate), Skills (review a Noun Check, Identifying Nouns as Singular or Plural), and Practice Exercise.

 **JINGLE TIME**

Have students turn to the Jingle Section of their books. The teacher will lead the students in reciting the previously-taught jingles.

 GRAMMAR TIME

Put the introductory sentences from the box below on the board. Use these sentences as you go through the new concepts covered in your teaching scripts. For the greatest benefit, students must participate orally with the teacher. (*You might put the introductory sentences on notebook paper if you are doing one-on-one instruction with your students.*)

Chapter 3, Introductory Sentences for Lesson 3
1. _____ The newborn baby cried rather weakly.
2. _____ The two girls sang so sweetly today.
3. _____ The inexperienced pilot landed safely.

TEACHING SCRIPT FOR COMPLETE SUBJECT AND COMPLETE PREDICATE

We will now classify Sentence 1. This time, there will be more information added to the Question and Answer Flow. You will classify the sentence with me until we get to the new part. The new part will be at the end of the Question and Answer Flow. Begin.

Sentence 1: The newborn baby cried rather weakly.
Who cried rather weakly? baby - SN
What is being said about baby? baby cried - V
Cried how? weakly - Adv
How weakly? rather - Adv
What kind of baby? newborn - Adj
The - A
SN V P1 Check (Subject Noun, Verb, Pattern 1 Check)
Period, statement, declarative sentence

I will now explain the new part and show you how to add it to the Question and Answer Flow. First, I will say the new part in the Question and Answer Flow, and then I will explain it to you. Listen carefully as I say the new part.

© SHURLEY INSTRUCTIONAL MATERIALS, INC.

CHAPTER 3 LESSON 3 CONTINUED

Go back to the verb - divide the complete subject from the complete predicate.
*(As you say **divide**, put a slash mark before your verb.)*

Note: Your sentence should look like this:

		A	Adj	SN	V	Adv	Adv	
SN V		The newborn baby / cried rather weakly.						**D**
P1								

Listen carefully as I repeat the new part again. **"Go back to the verb - divide the complete subject from the complete predicate."** Since this new part contains information about the complete subject and the complete predicate, I will go over these skills first. Listen carefully.

The **complete subject** is the subject and all the words that modify the subject. The complete subject usually starts at the beginning of the sentence and includes every word up to the verb of the sentence. The vertical line in front of the verb shows where the subject parts end and the predicate parts begin.

The **complete predicate** is the verb and all the words that modify the verb. The complete predicate usually starts with the verb and includes every word after the verb. The vertical line in front of the verb shows where the predicate parts start. The vertical line is a dividing line that divides or separates all the subject parts from all the predicate parts in the sentence.

Remember, the words you say in the Question and Answer Flow are these: **Go back to the verb - divide the complete subject from the complete predicate.** Then, you will put a slash mark in front of the verb to indicate that the verb and everything after the verb is the complete predicate, and everything in front of the verb is the complete subject. (*Exceptions to this general rule are addressed in Levels 4-6.*) This is an easy way to identify all the subject parts and all the predicate parts. I will classify Sentence 1 again, and you will classify it with me this time. Then, we will classify Sentences 2-3 together.

Teacher's Note: Make sure students are reciting each Question and Answer Flow orally, with you. They learn the concepts so much faster and retain them longer if they say the Question and Answer Flows orally!

Question and Answer Flow for Sentence 1: The newborn baby cried rather weakly.

1. Who cried rather weakly? baby - SN
2. What is being said about baby? baby cried - V
3. Cried how? weakly - Adv
4. How weakly? rather - Adv
5. What kind of baby? newborn - Adj
6. The - A

7. SN V P1 (Subject Noun Verb Pattern 1) Check
   (Write *SN V P1* in the blank beside the sentence.)
8. Period, statement, declarative sentence
   (Write *D* at the end of the sentence.)
9. Go back to the verb - divide the complete subject from the complete predicate.
   (As you say <u>divide</u>, put a slash mark before the verb.)

Classified Sentence:

		A	Adj	SN	V	Adv	Adv
SN V		The newborn baby / cried rather weakly. **D**					
P1							

© SHURLEY INSTRUCTIONAL MATERIALS, INC.

CHAPTER 3 LESSON 3 CONTINUED

Question and Answer Flow for Sentence 2: The two girls sang so sweetly today.

1. Who sang so sweetly today? girls - SN
2. What is being said about girls? girls sang - V
3. Sang how? sweetly - Adv
4. How sweetly? so - Adv
5. Sang when? today - Adv
6. How many girls? two - Adj

7. The - A
8. SN V P1 Check
9. Period, statement, declarative sentence
10. Go back to the verb - divide the complete subject from the complete predicate.

Classified Sentence:

            A   Adj SN   V Adv Adv   Adv
  __SN V__ The two girls / sang so sweetly today. D
     P1

Question and Answer Flow for Sentence 3: The inexperienced pilot landed safely.

1. Who landed safely? pilot - SN
2. What is being said about pilot? pilot landed - V
3. Landed how? safely - Adv
4. What kind of pilot? inexperienced - Adj
5. The - A

6. SN V P1 Check
7. Period, statement, declarative sentence
8. Go back to the verb - divide the complete subject from the complete predicate.

Classified Sentence:

            A   Adj   SN   V   Adv
  __SN V__ The inexperienced pilot / landed safely. D
     P1

I want you to look at Reference 11 on page 15 in the Reference Section of your book. You are given a Question and Answer Flow as an example so it will be easy for you to study. Let's read it together. Remember, we always begin by reading the sentence. (*Read and discuss the Question and Answer Flow in the reference box below with your students.*)

Reference 11: Question and Answer Flow Sentence

Question and Answer Flow: The three spirited horses ran quickly away.

1. What ran quickly away? horses - SN
2. What is being said about horses? horses ran - V
3. Ran how? quickly - Adv
4. Ran where? away - Adv
5. What kind of horses? spirited - Adj
6. How many horses? three - Adj

7. The - A
8. SN V P1 Check
9. Period, statement, declarative sentence
10. Go back to the verb - divide the complete subject from the complete predicate.

Classified Sentence:

            A   Adj   Adj   SN   V   Adv Adv
  __SN V__ The three spirited horses / ran quickly away. D
     P1

© SHURLEY INSTRUCTIONAL MATERIALS, INC.

CHAPTER 3 LESSON 3 CONTINUED

SKILL TIME

TEACHING SCRIPT FOR REVIEWING A NOUN CHECK

Now that we have classified all three sentences, I am going to use them to do a **Noun Check** during Skill Builder Time. Look at Sentences 1-3. We will identify the nouns in all three sentences by drawing circles around them. Let's start with number 1 and do a Noun Check. Begin. (*Circle the nouns for all three sentences as your students recite the Noun Check with you. Number 1: subject noun **baby**, yes. Number 2: subject noun **girls**, yes. Number 3: subject noun **pilot**, yes.*)

TEACHING SCRIPT FOR IDENTIFYING NOUNS AS SINGULAR OR PLURAL

We will now discuss two definitions that we will use as we learn more skills during Skill Builder Time. Find Reference 12 on page 16 in the Reference Section of your book. (*Reference 12 is located below.*) The next skill we will learn is identifying nouns as singular or plural. This is an easy skill, but you would be surprised at the number of people who have trouble with it. Follow along as I read the general definitions for singular and plural in your reference box.

A **singular noun** usually does not end in *s* or *es* and means only one. (*ring, cloud, star*) There are a few exceptions: Some nouns end in s and are singular and mean only one. (*mattress, bus*)

A **plural noun** usually ends in *s* or *es* and means more than one. (*rings, clouds, stars*) There are a few exceptions: Some nouns are made plural by changing their spelling. (*goose-geese, child-children*)

Reference 12: Definitions for a Skill Builder Check

1. A **noun** names a person, place, or thing.
2. A **singular noun** usually does not end in *s* or *es* and means only one. (*ring, cloud, star*)
   Exception: Some nouns end in s and are singular and mean only one. (*mattress, bus*)
3. A **plural noun** usually ends in *s* or *es* and means more than one. (*rings, clouds, stars*)
   Exception: Some nouns are made plural by changing their spelling. (*goose-geese, child-children*)
4. A **common noun** names ANY person, place, or thing. A common noun is not capitalized because it does not name a specific person, place, or thing. (*doctor, park*)
5. A **proper noun** is a noun that names a specific, or particular, person, place, or thing. Proper nouns are always capitalized no matter where they are located in the sentence. (*James, New York*)
6. A **simple subject** is another name for the subject noun or subject pronoun.
7. A **simple predicate** is another name for the verb.

We will now identify each circled noun in Sentences 1-3 as singular or plural. I will write *S* for singular or *P* for plural above each noun as we identify it. We will say "baby - singular," and I will write **S** above *baby*. Begin. (*baby – singular, girls – plural, pilot – singular. Mark the nouns with the letter "S" or "P" in all three sentences. Discuss why the nouns are singular or plural.*)

© SHURLEY INSTRUCTIONAL MATERIALS, INC.

CHAPTER 3 LESSON 3 CONTINUED

Let's review the general rules. A noun is usually singular when it does not end in s or es, and it means only one. That's easy, isn't it? A noun is usually plural when it ends in s or es, and it means more than one. As you can see, when you are identifying nouns as singular or plural, it is important to know a few simple rules.

 PRACTICE TIME

Have students turn to pages 63 and 64 in the Practice Section of their book and find the skills under Chapter 3, Lesson 3, Practice *(1-4)*. Go over the directions to make sure they understand what to do. Check and discuss the Practices after students have finished. (*Chapter 3, Lesson 3, Practice keys are given below*.)

Chapter 3, Lesson 3, Practice 1: For each noun listed below, write **S** for singular or **P** for plural.

Noun	S or P	Noun	S or P	Noun	S or P
1. houses	P	4. flights	P	7. children	P
2. gopher	S	5. calf	S	8. trees	P
3. men	P	6. building	S	9. automobile	S

Chapter 3, Lesson 3, Practice 2: Write *a* or *an* in the blanks.

1. Did you find _a_ penny?
2. Ben was dressed like _an_ elf.
3. The zoo had _an_ anteater.
4. We explored _a_ cave.
5. He plays _an_ organ.
6. I chased _a_ butterfly.
7. _a_ glove
8. _a_ helicopter
9. _an_ obstacle
10. _an_ iron
11. _a_ zebra
12. _an_ adult

Chapter 3, Lesson 3, Practice 3: Match the definitions. Write the correct letter beside each numbered concept.

D	1. tells what the subject does	A. verb, adjective, or adverb
H	2. subject question	B. noun markers
I	3. adjective modifies	C. person, place, or thing
B	4. article adjectives can be called	D. verb
C	5. noun	E. declarative sentence
G	6. asks a question	F. exclamatory sentence
J	7. makes a request or gives a command	G. interrogative sentence
E	8. makes a statement	H. who or what
F	9. expresses strong feeling	I. noun or pronoun
A	10. adverb modifies	J. imperative sentence

Chapter 3, Lesson 3, Practice 4: Put the end mark and the abbreviation for each kind of sentence in the blanks below.

1. Put the books on the shelf   . Imp

2. Do you have any pets   ? Int

3. They discovered the buried treasure   ! E

4. We will visit Grandma next week   . D

(End of lesson.)

© SHURLEY INSTRUCTIONAL MATERIALS, INC.

CHAPTER 3   LESSON 4

Objectives: Jingles, Study, Test, Check, and Activity and Writing (journal).

 JINGLE TIME

Have students turn to the Jingle Section of their books. The teacher will lead the students in reciting the previously-taught jingles.

 STUDY TIME

Have students study the vocabulary words in their vocabulary notebooks. Remind students that any vocabulary word in their notebooks could be on their test. Also, have students study any of the skills in the different sections that they need to review.

 TEST TIME

Have students turn to page 98 in the Test Section of their books and find Chapter 3 Test. Go over the directions to make sure they understand what to do. (*Chapter 3 Test key is on page 46.*)

 CHECK TIME

After students have finished, check and discuss their test papers. Make sure they understand why their answers are right or wrong. (*For total points, count each required answer as a point.*)

 ACTIVITY / ASSIGNMENT TIME

(Have a recipe box and a package of lined index cards ready for your children to use for the state activity in each chapter. Find a map of the United States that your students can use to draw or trace each state.)

General Directions: Starting with Chapter 3, you will have a state activity in each chapter until you have covered all 50 states. You will make an index card for each state. First, on the blank side of the index card, you will draw (or trace) and color the state assigned. Then, on the lined side of the index card, you will write some information about the state. The information you will use is listed on page 10 in the Reference Section of your book. Turn to page 10, and I will show you how this information is arranged. Look at number 1. The C3 means you have a state assignment in Chapter 3. The state is Alabama. The capital of Alabama is Montgomery. The postal abbreviation is AL, and Alabama was admitted to the Union in 1819.

State Information for the 50 States				
Chapter	**State**	**Capital**	**Postal Abbreviation**	**Admitted to Union**
1. C 3	Alabama	Montgomery	AL	1819

© SHURLEY INSTRUCTIONAL MATERIALS, INC.

CHAPTER 3 LESSON 4 CONTINUED

Now, I will show you how to put the State Information for Alabama on an index card. You will
Sample on page 11 in the Reference Section of your book. (*Have students turn to page 11 and
Sample with you.*)

You will use the questions that are in this sample for all 50 states, changing the name of the state and other
information each time. Remember, the first thing you must do is draw and color the state of Alabama on the
blank side of the index card. The first question will verify the state that you are recording on the index card.
The rest of the questions are answered from the information prepared for you on the State Information page.
(*Read and discuss the questions and answers on the Card Sample below. Tell students that they will use this sample and
the information provided on the State Information page to complete each assignment.*)

Last, look up an interesting fact about the state of Alabama and write it on the bottom of your card. You may
use your state cards to quiz family members, friends, and relatives.

Card Sample for State Information
1. What is the state on the front of this card? **Alabama**
2. What is the capital of Alabama? **Montgomery**
3. What is the postal abbreviation of Alabama? **AL**
4. What year was Alabama admitted to the Union? **1819**

TEACHER INSTRUCTIONS

Use the Question and Answer Flows below for the sentences on Chapter 3 Test on the next page.

Question and Answer Flow for Sentence 1: An inactive volcano erupted quite unexpectedly!

1. What erupted quite unexpectedly? volcano - SN
2. What is being said about volcano?
   volcano erupted - V
3. Erupted how? unexpectedly - Adv
4. How unexpectedly? quite - Adv
5. What kind of volcano? inactive - Adj

6. An - A
7. SN V P1 Check
8. Exclamation point, strong feeling, exclamatory sentence
9. Go back to the verb - divide the complete subject
   from the complete predicate.

Classified Sentence:

```
            A    Adj      SN        V    Adv      Adv
SN  V       An inactive volcano / erupted quite unexpectedly!  E
_____
     P1
```

Question and Answer Flow for Sentence 2: The very bright Christmas lights blinked rather slowly.

1. What blinked rather slowly? lights - SN
2. What is being said about lights? lights blinked - V
3. Blinked how? slowly - Adv
4. How slowly? rather - Adv
5. What kind of lights? Christmas - Adj
6. What kind of lights? bright - Adj

7. How bright? very - Adv
8. The - A
9. SN V P1 Check
10. Period, statement, declarative sentence
11. Go back to the verb - divide the complete subject
    from the complete predicate.

Classified Sentence:

```
            A   Adv  Adj      Adj      SN       V    Adv    Adv
SN  V       The very bright Christmas lights / blinked rather slowly.  D
_____
     P1
```

(End of lesson.)

© SHURLEY INSTRUCTIONAL MATERIALS, INC.

Chapter 3 Test
(Student Page 98)

Exercise 1: Classify each sentence.

              A   Adj   SN   V   Adv   Adv

1. <u>SN V</u>   An inactive volcano / erupted quite unexpectedly! **E**
   P1

              A   Adv Adj   Adj   SN   V   Adv   Adv

2. <u>SN V</u>   The very bright Christmas lights / blinked rather slowly. **D**
   P1

Exercise 2: Identify each pair of words as synonyms or antonyms by putting parentheses ( ) around *syn* or *ant*.

1. sever, cut	**(syn)** ant	4. apt, suitable	**(syn)** ant	7. curiosity, interest	**(syn)** ant
2. vague, clear	syn **(ant)**	5. tasty, bland	syn **(ant)**	8. friendly, amiable	**(syn)** ant
3. weary, tired	**(syn)** ant	6. seldom, often	syn **(ant)**	9. kind, irreverent	syn **(ant)**

Exercise 3: Put the end marks and the abbreviations for each kind of sentence in the blanks below.

1. Did you vote in the election   <u>**? Int**</u>

2. My uncle bought a new car   <u>**. D**</u>

3. I lost my new job   <u>**! E**</u>

4. Turn the heat on low   <u>**. Imp**</u>

Exercise 4: Write *a* or *an* in the blanks.

1. We rode <u>**an**</u> elk.   3. Did you see <u>**an**</u> elf?   5. <u>**a**</u> plate   7. <u>**an**</u> ant

2. He was <u>**a**</u> funny juggler.   4. I have <u>**a**</u> banjo.   6. <u>**a**</u> chimney 8. <u>**an**</u> ape

Exercise 5: For each noun listed below, write **S** for singular or **P** for plural.

Noun	S or P	Noun	S or P	Noun	S or P
1. books	P	4. children	P	7. shelves	P
2. door	S	5. planet	S	8. men	P
3. roads	P	6. star	S	9. car	S

Exercise 6: Match the definitions. Write the correct letter beside each numbered concept.

<u>G</u>	1. tells what the subject does	A.	verb, adjective, or adverb
<u>E</u>	2. article adjectives	B.	who or what
<u>F</u>	3. adjective modifies	C.	what is being said about
<u>C</u>	4. verb question	D.	person, place, or thing
<u>B</u>	5. subject-noun question	E.	a, an, the
<u>D</u>	6. noun	F.	noun or pronoun
<u>A</u>	7. adverb modifies	G.	verb

Exercise 7: On notebook paper, write the four kinds of sentences: Declarative, Interrogative, Exclamatory, and Imperative. Write the correct punctuation and the abbreviation that identifies it at the end. Use these abbreviations: D, Int, E, Imp.

Exercise 8: In your journal, write a paragraph summarizing what you have learned this week.

© SHURLEY INSTRUCTIONAL MATERIALS, INC.

CHAPTER 3   LESSON 5

Objectives: Writing (revising and editing) and Activity.

 WRITING TIME

TEACHING SCRIPT FOR REVISING AND EDITING

Before you start your writing assignments in another chapter, there are a few basic things I want you to know. First, writing is a process. You usually do not have a finished product the first time you write. When you write, you start out by writing a rough draft. A rough draft is a rough copy of your writing. It is not a finished piece of writing. In fact, you do not have to worry about errors as you write your rough draft. You will usually make changes in the rough draft to improve it. Today, we will learn the different terminology used as you go through the process of changing your writing to make it better.

Listen to the words **revise** and **edit**. Both revising and editing make your writing better. It's usually called revising when you find ways to make the content better. Look at Reference 13 on page 16 in your book. Let's read some of the things you need to know about revision. (*Read and discuss only the Revision Checklist on the next page.*)

After you have made revisions in your writing content, your next step is to check your paper for mistakes in spelling, grammar, usage, and punctuation. This called editing. It begins with careful proofreading. Look at the second part of Reference 13. It is called a Beginning Editing Checklist because it contains only some of the first skills necessary for you to know as you edit.

The editing list will continue to grow as more skills are introduced. We will go through the skills listed under "More Editing Skills" in later chapters. (*Teaching scripts for these additional skills will also be given to the teacher in later chapters.*) Eventually, you will have a regular editing checklist that will have most of the skills added. We will discuss only the beginning editing skills to make sure you understand each of them at this point. (*Read and discuss the Beginning Editing Checklist on the next page.*)

We will now study four paragraphs. Look at the four paragraphs in Reference 14. (*Your copy of Reference 14 is located on page 49 of this chapter.*) Nothing has been done to the first paragraph. It is a rough draft. Notice that the second paragraph has been revised, and the third paragraph has been edited. (*Read and discuss the differences in the first three paragraphs.*) Once you have revised and edited your rough draft, you will make a final copy of your work. Look at the third checklist. It is called "Final Paper Checklist." This will tell you what to expect as you write your final paper. (*Read and discuss the Final Paper Checklist on the next page.*) The last paragraph has gone through the "Final Paper Checklist" and is ready for publishing.

Let's review the procedure you should use for each writing assignment. This procedure is called the "Writing Process Checklist." Look at the last section of Reference 13. You will refer to this section to help you remember the writing procedures used in your writing assignments. (*Read and discuss the Writing Process Checklist on the next page.*)

Listen carefully as I repeat the writing process again. It is too important to forget. First, you gather information. Next, you write a rough draft. Then, you revise and edit the rough draft. Finally, you rewrite the rough draft and turn in a final paper. If your writing assignment takes more than one session, you will finish it in your free time. Make sure you refer to Reference 13 anytime you forget what to do.

© SHURLEY INSTRUCTIONAL MATERIALS, INC.

CHAPTER 3 LESSON 5 CONTINUED

Reference 13: Checklists

Revision Checklist

1. Eliminate unnecessary or needlessly-repeated words or ideas.
2. Combine or reorder sentences.
3. Change word choices for clarity and expression.
4. Know the purpose: to explain, to describe, to entertain, or to persuade.
5. Know the audience: the reader(s) of the writing.

Beginning Editing Checklist

1. Did you indent the paragraph?
2. Did you capitalize the first word and put an end mark at the end of every sentence?
3. Did you spell words correctly?

More Editing Skills

4. Did you follow the writing guidelines? (*located in Reference 19 on student page 20*)
5. Did you list the topic and two points (or three points) on separate lines at the top of the paper?
6. Did you follow the two-point (or three-point) paragraph pattern?
7. Did you use the correct homonyms?
8. Did you follow all other capitalization and punctuation rules?
9. Did you follow the three-paragraph essay pattern?

Final Paper Checklist

1. Have you written the correct heading on your paper?
2. Have you written your final paper in ink?
3. Have you single-spaced your final paper?
4. Have you written your final paper neatly?
5. Have you stapled the final paper to the rough draft and handed them in to your teacher?

Writing Process Checklist

1. Gather information.
2. Write a rough draft.
3. Revise the rough draft.
4. Edit the rough draft.
5. Write a final paper.

© SHURLEY INSTRUCTIONAL MATERIALS, INC.

CHAPTER 3 LESSON 5 CONTINUED

Reference 14: Drafts and Final Paragraph
Rough Draft
Before Dustin left for work, he shut Harvey his new puppy in the laundry room. Harvey whimpered wined and scratched at the door. Dustin ignored Harvey as he quickly headed out the door. On his lunch brake, he came back home to check on harvey. When he opened the laundry room door Harvey bolted out and ran through the house. Dustin looked at the big mess the puppy had made. Harvey had turned over his food and water bowl. Wet newspapers were shredded and spread all over the floor. Dustin sighed and began to clean up Harveys mess. Before he finished, Dustin heard a crash in the kitchen. Harvey had turned over the trashcan
Revision of Draft
Before Dustin left for work, he shut Harvey his new puppy in the laundry room. Harvey whimpered wined and scratched at the door. Dustin ignored **Harveys complaint as he rushed** out the door. On his lunch brake, he came back home to check on harvey. When he opened the laundry room door Harvey bolted out and **dashed** through the house. Dustin **stared** at the **huge** mess the puppy had made. Harvey had turned over his food and water bowl. Wet newspapers were shredded and **scattered** all over the floor. Dustin sighed **as he** began to clean up Harveys mess. Before he finished, Dustin heard a crash in the kitchen. Harvey had turned over the trashcan
Edit Draft
Before Dustin left for work, he shut Harvey**, [comma inserted]** his new puppy**, [comma inserted]** in the laundry room. Harvey whimpered**, [comma inserted]** whined**, [comma inserted]** and scratched at the door. Dustin ignored Harvey's **[apostrophe added]** complaint as he rushed out the door. On his lunch **break, [break, not brake]** he came back home to check on Harvey **[Harvey, not harvey]**. When he opened the laundry room door**, [comma inserted]** Harvey bolted out and dashed through the house. Dustin stared at the huge mess the puppy had made. Harvey had turned over his food and water bowl. Wet newspapers were shredded and scattered all over the floor. Dustin sighed as he began to clean up Harvey's **[apostrophe added]** mess. Before he finished, Dustin heard a crash in the kitchen. Harvey had turned over the trashcan! **[End mark]**
Final Paragraph
Before Dustin left for work, he shut Harvey, his new puppy, in the laundry room. Harvey whimpered, whined, and scratched at the door. Dustin ignored Harvey's complaint as he rushed out the door. On his lunch break, he came back home to check on Harvey. When he opened the laundry room door, Harvey bolted out and dashed through the house. Dustin stared at the huge mess the puppy had made. Harvey had turned over his food and water bowl. Wet newspapers were shredded and scattered all over the floor. Dustin sighed as he began to clean up Harvey's mess. Before he finished, Dustin heard a crash in the kitchen. Harvey had turned over the trashcan!

ACTIVITY / ASSIGNMENT TIME

Have students make and illustrate their own Checklist poster. Using Reference 13 on page 16 as a guide, have students divide a large poster board into the different checklist sections. After they have copied the information onto the poster board, have students color and decorate their Checklist poster in any design that pleases them. Students could use their Checklist poster to help them with their writing assignments.

(End of lesson.)

© SHURLEY INSTRUCTIONAL MATERIALS, INC.

CHAPTER 4   LESSON 1

Objectives: Jingles, Grammar (Practice Sentences), Skills (Skill Builder Check, Common and Proper Nouns, Complete Subject and Complete Predicate, Simple Subject and Simple Predicate, Oral Skill Builder Check), Practice Exercise, Vocabulary #1, and activity.

 **JINGLE TIME**

Have students turn to the Jingle Section of their books. The teacher will lead the students in reciting the previously-taught jingles.

 GRAMMAR TIME

First-Year Option: Put the Practice Sentences from the box below on the board or on notebook paper. Use these sentences as you practice the concepts that have been taught. For the greatest benefit, students must participate orally with the teacher. **Second-Year Option:** Have students classify the Practice Sentences independently on paper. Check students' sentences with the answers provided below. (*If you have the CDs for Practice Sentences, have students check their sentences with the CDs.*)

Chapter 4, Practice Sentences for Lesson 1
1. _____ The small mice scurried away quickly.
2. _____ The mosquito bite swelled immediately!
3. _____ A tremendously gifted scientist spoke briefly today.

TEACHING SCRIPT FOR PRACTICING PATTERN 1 SENTENCES

We will classify three different sentences to practice the Question and Answer Flows. We will classify the sentences together. Begin. (*You might have students write the labels above the sentences at this time.*)

Question and Answer Flow for Sentence 1: The small mice scurried away quickly.

1. What scurried away quickly? mice - SN
2. What is being said about mice? mice scurried - V
3. Scurried where? away - Adv
4. Scurried how? quickly - Adv
5. What kind of mice? small - Adj

6. The - A
7. Subject Noun Verb Pattern 1 Check
8. Period, statement, declarative sentence
9. Go back to the verb - divide the complete subject from the complete predicate.

Classified Sentence:

```
            A   Adj  SN   V     Adv   Adv
   SN V     The small mice / scurried away quickly.  D
   ----
   P1
```

© SHURLEY INSTRUCTIONAL MATERIALS, INC.

CHAPTER 4 LESSON 1 CONTINUED

Question and Answer Flow for Sentence 2: The mosquito bite swelled immediately!

1. What swelled immediately? bite - SN
2. What is being said about bite? bite swelled - V
3. Swelled how? immediately - Adv
4. What kind of bite? mosquito - Adj
5. The - A

6. SN V P1 Check
7. Exclamation point, strong feeling, exclamatory sentence
8. Go back to the verb - divide the complete subject from the complete predicate.

Classified Sentence:

	A	Adj	SN	V	Adv

SN V The mosquito bite / swelled immediately! **E**
P1

Question and Answer Flow for Sentence 3: A tremendously gifted scientist spoke briefly today.

1. Who spoke briefly today? scientist - SN
2. What is being said about scientist? scientist spoke - V
3. Spoke how? briefly - Adv
4. Spoke when? today - Adv
5. What kind of scientist? gifted - Adj
6. How gifted? tremendously - Adv

7. A - A
8. SN V P1 Check
9. Period, statement, declarative sentence
10. Go back to the verb - divide the complete subject from the complete predicate.

Classified Sentence:

	A	Adv	Adj	SN	V	Adv	Adv

SN V A tremendously gifted scientist / spoke briefly today. **D**
P1

SKILL TIME

TEACHING SCRIPT FOR A SKILL BUILDER CHECK

Now that we have classified all three sentences, I am going to use them to do a Skill Builder Check. We have already learned two skills that we can do during our Skill Builder Check. We will do a Noun Check, and then we will identify the nouns as singular or plural. Where do we go to find nouns? (_subject noun_) We know to go to the subject noun because we know that we can find nouns in the subject job. The subject noun is the first noun job that we have studied.

Remember, you say four things: the sentence number, the noun job, the noun used for the noun job, and the word _yes_ to verify that it is a noun, not a pronoun. I will circle the nouns as we identify them. Begin. (_Circle the nouns for all three sentences as your students recite the Noun Check with you: Number 1: subject noun_ **mice**, _yes. Number 2: subject noun_ **bite**, _yes. Number 3: subject noun_ **scientist**, _yes._)

We will now identify each noun as singular or plural. Before we begin, let's review the singular and plural skills. Look at Reference 12 on page 16 in the Reference Section of your book. We will read and discuss number 2 and number 3 about singular and plural nouns. (_Read and discuss the singular and plural nouns that are located in Reference 12 on the next page._)

We will identify each circled noun in Sentences 1-3 as singular or plural. I will write _S_ for singular or _P_ for plural above each noun as we identify it. Begin. (_mice – plural, bite – singular, scientist – singular. Mark the nouns with the letter "S" or "P" in all three sentences._)

© SHURLEY INSTRUCTIONAL MATERIALS, INC.

CHAPTER 4 LESSON 1 CONTINUED

Reference 12: Definitions for a Skill Builder Check
1. A **noun** names a person, place, or thing.
2. A **singular noun** usually does not end in *s* or *es* and means only one. (*ring, cloud, star*)   Exception: Some nouns end in s and are singular and mean only one. (*mattress, bus*)
3. A **plural noun** usually ends in *s* or *es* and means more than one. (*rings, clouds, stars*)   Exception: Some nouns are made plural by changing their spelling. (*goose-geese, child-children*)
4. A **common noun** names ANY person, place, or thing. A common noun is not capitalized because it does not name a specific person, place, or thing. (*doctor, park*)
5. A **proper noun** is a noun that names a specific, or particular, person, place, or thing. Proper nouns are always capitalized no matter where they are located in the sentence. (*James, New York*)
6. A **simple subject** is another name for the subject noun or subject pronoun.
7. A **simple predicate** is another name for the verb.

TEACHING SCRIPT FOR IDENTIFYING NOUNS AS COMMON OR PROPER

We will now discuss several new skills that we will use during Skill Builder Checks. Look at Reference 12 and follow along as I read the information in number 4 and number 5 about common and proper nouns. (*Read and discuss number 4 and number 5 in the reference box above with your students.*)

We will look at the nouns that are circled in the three sentences and tell whether they are common or proper. How do we recognize a proper noun? (*It begins with a capital letter no matter where it is located in the sentence.*) Do we have any proper nouns in our sentences? (*No.*) How do you know? (*None of the nouns that are circled begins with a capital letter.*) Since we do not have a proper noun in the three sentences that we have just classified, I want you to think of a proper noun. (*Get several responses and discuss why the nouns named are proper nouns.*)

Do we have any common nouns in our sentences? (*Yes.*) Are all the nouns common? (*Yes.*) How do you know? (*All the nouns that are circled begin with a lowercase, or small, letter.*)

TEACHING SCRIPT FOR MARKING THE COMPLETE SUBJECT AND THE COMPLETE PREDICATE

Since we have already discussed the **complete subject** and the **complete predicate**, we will only review them now. What is the definition of the complete subject? (*The complete subject is the subject and all the words that modify the subject. The complete subject usually starts at the beginning of the sentence and includes every word up to the verb of the sentence.*)

I want you to tell me the complete subject in Sentence 1, and I will underline it once. What is the complete subject? (*The small mice*) The reason I underlined the complete subject once is that, usually, anything dealing with the subject is indicated by only one line.

Level 3 Homeschool Teacher's Manual

© SHURLEY INSTRUCTIONAL MATERIALS, INC.

CHAPTER 4 LESSON 1 CONTINUED

Now, we will review the complete predicate. What is the definition of the complete predicate? (*The* ***complete predicate*** *is the verb and all the words that modify the verb. The complete predicate usually starts with the verb and includes every word after the verb.*)

I want you to tell me the complete predicate in Sentence 1, and I will underline it twice. What is the complete predicate? (*scurried away quickly*) The reason I underlined the complete predicate twice is that, usually, anything dealing with the predicate is indicated by two lines. (*Mark the answers for Sentences 2-3 in the same way. The mosquito bite swelled immediately! A tremendously gifted scientist spoke briefly today.*)

TEACHING SCRIPT FOR IDENTIFYING THE SIMPLE SUBJECT AND THE SIMPLE PREDICATE

We will now learn about the simple subject and the simple predicate. The **simple subject** is another name for the **subject** only. The simple subject is the subject noun or the subject pronoun. The simple subject is just the subject; it does not include the other words in the complete subject. The **simple predicate** is another name for the **verb**. The simple predicate is just the verb; it does not include the other words in the complete predicate.

Look at Sentence 1 again. Usually, I would draw one line under the simple subject and two lines under the simple predicate. But since I have already underlined the complete subject and complete predicate, I will just darken the lines under the concepts that need to be identified. To identify the simple subject, make sure you respond with the words "*the subject noun*" before you name the subject noun. **What is the simple subject?** (***the subject noun, mice***) I will darken the line under the simple subject **mice** so you can tell the difference between the simple subject and the complete subject.

To identify the simple predicate, make sure you say "*the verb*" before you name the verb. **What is the simple predicate?** (***the verb, scurried***) I will darken the lines under the simple predicate ***scurried*** so you can tell the difference between the simple predicate and the complete predicate. (*Mark the answers for Sentences 2-3 in the same way. The mosquito bite swelled immediately! A tremendously gifted scientist spoke briefly today.*)

TEACHER INSTRUCTIONS

From this time forward, the skills for an Oral Skill Builder Check and a short explanation will be listed in a Skill Builder box. As more skills are covered, they will be added to the skill box. These guidelines will help you know the skills you have covered.

Oral Skill Builder Check	
1. Noun check. (Say the job and then say the noun. Circle each noun.) **2. Identify the nouns as singular or plural.** (Write S or P above each noun.) **3. Identify the nouns as common or proper.** (Follow established procedure for oral identification.)	**4. Identify the complete subject and the complete predicate.** (Underline the complete subject once and the complete predicate twice.) **5. Identify the simple subject and simple predicate.** (Underline the simple subject once and the simple predicate twice. Bold, or highlight, the lines to distinguish them from the complete subject and complete predicate.)

© SHURLEY INSTRUCTIONAL MATERIALS, INC.

CHAPTER 4 LESSON 1 CONTINUED

Teacher's Note: During a Skill Builder Check, the teacher asks a series of questions designed to enhance students' knowledge and understanding of different skills on a regular basis. This exercise helps students identify sentence parts and types of nouns easily and also provides effective vocabulary work as concepts are added.

Look at Reference 15 on page 18 in your book to see how to use the skills you have been taught. This sample is set up in the same format as it will appear on your test. (*Read the directions to your students and then go through the sentence, showing them how to find the answers for the noun job chart. Reference 15 is located below.*)

Reference 15: Noun Job Chart

Directions: Classify the sentence below. Underline the complete subject once and the complete predicate twice. Then, complete the table.

```
            A      Adj     SN       V        Adv     Adv
1. SN V     The bewildered  hikers / stumbled desperately forward.  D
   P1
```

List the Noun Used	List the Noun Job	Singular or Plural	Common or Proper	Simple Subject	Simple Predicate
hikers	SN	P	C	hikers	stumbled

 PRACTICE TIME

Have students turn to pages 64 and 65 in the Practice Section of their book and find Chapter 4, Lesson 1, Practice (*1-5*). Go over the directions to make sure they understand what to do. Check and discuss the Practices after students have finished. (*Chapter 4, Lesson 1, Practice keys are given below and on the next page.*)

Chapter 4, Lesson 1, Practice 1: For each noun listed below, write **C** for common or **P** for proper.

Noun	C or P	Noun	C or P	Noun	C or P	Noun	C or P
1. babies	C	3. John	P	5. restaurant	C	7. truck	C
2. German	P	4. kitten	C	6. FedEx	P	8. Ford	P

Chapter 4, Lesson 1, Practice 2: Underline the complete subject once and the complete predicate twice.

1. The little puppies growled playfully.

2. Ten large fish swam away.

3. The big yellow bus honked loudly.

4. Four green frogs swam around slowly.

Chapter 4, Lesson 1, Practice 3: Underline the simple subject once and the simple predicate twice.

1. A tiny mouse squeaked.

2. The two yellow cars raced wildly.

3. The vegetable soup cooked slowly.

4. Several children swam yesterday.

© SHURLEY INSTRUCTIONAL MATERIALS, INC.

CHAPTER 4 LESSON 1 CONTINUED

Chapter 4, Lesson 1, Practice 4: For each noun listed below, write **S** for singular or **P** for plural.

Noun	S or P	Noun	S or P	Noun	S or P
1. trays	P	4. women	P	7. pond	S
2. oxen	P	5. truck	S	8. wolves	P
3. leaves	P	6. daisy	S	9. glass	S

Chapter 4, Lesson 1, Practice 5

Directions: Classify the sentence below. Underline the complete subject once and the complete predicate twice. Then, complete the table below.

```
             A   Adj  SN      V      Adv   Adv
  SN  V      The tiny duck / waddled slowly away.  D
  ───────
  P1
```

List the Noun Used	List the Noun Job	Singular or Plural	Common or Proper	Simple Subject	Simple Predicate
duck	SN	S	C	duck	waddled

VOCABULARY TIME

Assign Chapter 4, Vocabulary Words **#1** on page 8 in the Reference Section for students to define in their Vocabulary notebooks. Tell students they are to use a dictionary or thesaurus to look up the meanings of the vocabulary words. After they write each word and its meaning, students are to write a sentence using the vocabulary word.

Chapter 4, Vocabulary Words #1
(attempt, try, clean, soiled)

ACTIVITY / ASSIGNMENT TIME

This activity will help your understanding of singular and plural. Here is your assignment. Write the words on the board on a sheet of paper. (*Have the words below on the board for students to copy.*) You will go from room to room throughout the house to determine whether a singular or plural number of the items on your paper exists. Then, you will write the letter S or P beside each word.

1. ceiling fan	4. vacuum sweeper	7. television	10. fireplace
2. refrigerator	5. doorbell	8. computer	11. cabinet
3. closet	6. washing machine	9. bathroom	12. door

(End of lesson.)

© SHURLEY INSTRUCTIONAL MATERIALS, INC.

CHAPTER 4   LESSON 2

 **JINGLE TIME**

Have students turn to the Jingle Section in their books. The teacher will lead the students in reciting the previously-taught jingles.

 GRAMMAR TIME

First-Year Option: Put the Practice Sentences from the box below on the board or on notebook paper. Use these sentences as you practice the concepts that have been taught. For the greatest benefit, students must participate orally with the teacher. **Second-Year Option:** Have students classify the Practice Sentences independently on paper. Check students' sentences with the answers provided below. (*If you have the CDs for Practice Sentences, have students check their sentences with the CDs.*)

Chapter 4, Practice Sentences for Lesson 2
1. _____ Two beautiful horses grazed contentedly.
2. _____ The foolish duck quacked repeatedly.
3. _____ The five chimpanzees learned incredibly fast.

TEACHING SCRIPT FOR PRACTICING PATTERN 1 SENTENCES

We will classify three different sentences to practice grammar as we recite the Question and Answer Flows. We will classify the sentences together. Begin. (*You might have students write the labels above the sentences at this time.*)

Teacher's Note: Make sure students recite the **questions** and **answers** for each sentence. Be sure to lead them so they will say the Question and Answer Flows correctly.

Question and Answer Flow for Sentence 1: Two beautiful horses grazed contentedly.	
1. What grazed contentedly? horses - SN	5. How many horses? two - Adj
2. What is being said about horses? horses grazed - V	6. SN V P1 Check
3. Grazed how? contentedly - Adv	7. Period, statement, declarative sentence
4. What kind of horses? beautiful - Adj	8. Go back to the verb - divide the complete subject from the complete predicate.

Classified Sentence:

```
                        Adj   Adj    SN      V      Adv
           SN  V        Two beautiful horses / grazed contentedly.  D
           P1
```

CHAPTER 4 LESSON 2 CONTINUED

Question and Answer Flow for Sentence 2: The foolish duck quacked repeatedly.

1. What quacked repeatedly? duck - SN
2. What is being said about duck?
   duck quacked - V
3. Quacked how? repeatedly - Adv
4. What kind of duck? foolish - Adj

5. The - A
6. SN V P1 Check
7. Period, statement, declarative sentence
8. Go back to the verb - divide the complete subject
   from the complete predicate.

Classified Sentence:

	A	Adj	SN	V	Adv

<u>SN V</u> The foolish duck / quacked repeatedly. **D**
P1

Question and Answer Flow for Sentence 3: The five chimpanzees learned incredibly fast.

1. What learned incredibly fast? chimpanzees - SN
2. What is being said about chimpanzees?
   chimpanzees learned - V
3. Learned how? fast - Adv
4. How fast? incredibly - Adv
5. How many chimpanzees? five - Adj

6. The - A
7. SN V P1 Check
8. Period, statement, declarative sentence
9. Go back to the verb - divide the complete subject
   from the complete predicate.

Classified Sentence:

	A	Adj	SN	V	Adv	Adv

<u>SN V</u> The five chimpanzees / learned incredibly fast. **D**
P1

SKILL TIME

TEACHING SCRIPT FOR THE PARTS OF SPEECH

To have a keen understanding of different subject areas, you must understand the vocabulary used to communicate in any given area. English is no different. In fact, there are several areas in English where vocabulary is important. Knowing the vocabulary for grammar, mechanics, and usage will make it easier to communicate in writing and editing.

First, we must know why it is so important to have an excellent command of grammar. It is important to learn grammar well because it is the vocabulary for the sentences used in writing. We can talk to each other about writing and editing when we know how to talk about the sentences we write and how we put them together in paragraphs.

Second, we must gain mastery in the areas of grammar, mechanics, and usage to have a command of editing. Your study of English this year will help you in all these areas.

© SHURLEY INSTRUCTIONAL MATERIALS, INC.

CHAPTER 4 LESSON 2 CONTINUED

We will now discuss the eight parts of speech. Do you know that all words in the English language have been put into eight groups called the **Parts of Speech**? How a word is used in a sentence determines its part of speech. The sentences you have been classifying are made from four parts of speech. Do you know the names of these four parts of speech? *(noun, verb, adjective,* and *adverb)*

These first four parts of speech are easy to remember because you are using them every day. Make sure you remember them because you will also have them on your test. You will learn the other parts of speech later. *(Have students repeat the four parts of speech four or five times together, orally, and in a rhythmic fashion. Students will learn an Eight-Parts-of-Speech Jingle after all eight parts have been introduced.)*

TEACHING SCRIPT FOR ONLY ONE PART OF SPEECH IN A SENTENCE

(Note: Have the example below on the board or on a sheet of paper.)

Adjective(s): 1. The tall giraffe walked slowly away.

I am going to show you the steps to use whenever you need to identify only one part of speech in a sentence. No matter what part of speech you are looking for, always identify the subject and verb, first. This will give you the foundation from which to work. In the example on the board, we are looking for only one part of speech: the adjective.

1. Is Sentence 1 about a person, animal, place, or thing? animal
2. What is the sentence about? giraffe *(Write **SN** above giraffe.)*
3. What is being said about giraffe? giraffe walked *(Write **V** above walked.)*
4. What part of speech is listed to be identified? adjective
5. Where do we go to find adjectives? to nouns or pronouns
6. What is the noun in the sentence? giraffe
7. Are there any adjectives modifying the noun *giraffe*? yes
8. What are they? the, tall
9. We will do an adjective check to verify the adjectives:

> What kind of giraffe? tall - adjective (Underline the adjective *tall*.)
> The - article adjective (Underline the adjective *the*.)

Your finished sentence should look like this:

>   **SN**   **V**
> Adjective(s): 1. The tall giraffe walked slowly away.

If you follow this procedure, you should have no trouble finding a specific part of speech without having to classify the whole sentence. But if you are ever in doubt, classify the whole sentence to be sure of your answers.

© SHURLEY INSTRUCTIONAL MATERIALS, INC.

CHAPTER 4 LESSON 2 CONTINUED

You will now practice not only this skill, but you will also practice classifying a sentence and completing a noun job table.

 PRACTICE TIME

Have students turn to page 65 in the Practice Section of their books and find the skill under Chapter 4, Lesson 2, Practice *(1-2)*. Go over the directions to make sure they understand what to do. Check and discuss the Practices after students have finished. (*Chapter 4, Lesson 2, Practice keys are given below.*)

Chapter 4, Lesson 2, Practice 1: Classify the sentence below. Underline the complete subject once and the complete predicate twice. Then, complete the table.

SN V
P1

```
          A   Adj      SN        V      Adv   Adv
The loud motorcycles / thundered quickly away.  D
```

List the Noun Used	List the Noun Job	Singular or Plural	Common or Proper	Simple Subject	Simple Predicate
motorcycles	SN	P	C	motorcycles	thundered

Chapter 4, Lesson 2, Practice 2: Finding One Part of Speech. For each sentence, write *SN* above the simple subject and *V* above the simple predicate. Underline the word(s) for the part of speech listed to the left of each sentence.

```
                          SN        V
Adjective(s):   1. The crisp, crunchy granola crunched loudly.
                          SN    V
Adverb(s):      2. The injured gorilla limped very slowly around.
                          SN  V
Noun(s):        3. The new book fell open.
                      SN      V
Adjective(s):   4. The kittens played outside.
                      SN      V
Verb(s):        5. The cougar attacked quickly.
```

 VOCABULARY TIME

Assign Chapter 4, Vocabulary Words **#2** on page 8 in the Reference Section for students to define in their Vocabulary notebooks. Tell students they are to use a dictionary or thesaurus to look up the meanings of the vocabulary words. After they write each word and its meaning, students are to write a sentence using the vocabulary word.

Chapter 4, Vocabulary Words #2
(column, pillar, eager, indifferent)

(End of lesson.)

© SHURLEY INSTRUCTIONAL MATERIALS, INC.

CHAPTER 4   LESSON 3

Objectives: Jingles, Grammar (Practice Sentences), Skill (adding vocabulary check to skill builder, Oral Skill Builder Check, Practice and Improved Sentence).

 **JINGLE TIME**

Have students turn to the Jingle Section in their books. The teacher will lead the students in reciting the previously-taught jingles.

 GRAMMAR TIME

First-Year Option: Put the Practice Sentences from the box below on the board or on notebook paper. Use these sentences as you practice the concepts that have been taught. For the greatest benefit, students must participate orally with the teacher. **Second-Year Option:** Have students classify the Practice Sentences independently on paper. Check students' sentences with the answers provided below. (*If you have the CDs for Practice Sentences, have students check their sentences with the CDs.*)

Chapter 4, Practice Sentences for Lesson 3
1. _____ The school band played surprisingly well.
2. _____ Two small deer stood completely still.
3. _____ The ballet dancers performed very skillfully.

TEACHING SCRIPT FOR PRACTICING PATTERN 1 SENTENCES

We will classify three different sentences to practice grammar as we recite the Question and Answer Flows. We will classify the sentences together. Begin. (*You might have students write the labels above the sentences at this time.*)

Question and Answer Flow for Sentence 1: The school band played surprisingly well.

1. What played surprisingly well? band - SN
2. What is being said about band? band played - V
3. Played how? well - Adv
4. How well? surprisingly - Adv
5. What kind of band? school - Adj
6. The - A
7. SN V P1 Check
8. Period, statement, declarative sentence
9. Go back to the verb - divide the complete subject from the complete predicate.

Classified Sentence:

```
           A    Adj   SN    V      Adv    Adv
SN V  The school band / played surprisingly well.  D
P1
```

© SHURLEY INSTRUCTIONAL MATERIALS, INC.

CHAPTER 4 LESSON 3 CONTINUED

Question and Answer Flow for Sentence 2: Two small deer stood completely still.

1. What stood completely still? deer - SN
2. What is being said about deer? deer stood - V
3. Stood how? still - Adv
4. How still? completely - Adv
5. What kind of deer? small - Adj

6. How many deer? two - Adj
7. SN V P1 Check
8. Period, statement, declarative sentence
9. Go back to the verb - divide the complete subject from the complete predicate.

Classified Sentence:

<u>SN V</u>
P1

Adj Adj SN V Adv Adv
Two small deer / stood completely still. D

Question and Answer Flow for Sentence 3: The ballet dancers performed very skillfully.

1. Who performed very skillfully? dancers - SN
2. What is being said about dancers?
   dancers performed - V
3. Performed how? skillfully - Adv
4. How skillfully? very - Adv
5. What kind of dancers? ballet - Adj

6. The - A
7. SN V P1 Check
8. Period, statement, declarative sentence
9. Go back to the verb - divide the complete subject from the complete predicate.

Classified Sentence:

<u>SN V</u>
P1

A Adj SN V Adv Adv
The ballet dancers / performed very skillfully. D

SKILL TIME

TEACHING SCRIPT FOR ADDING A VOCABULARY CHECK TO SKILL BUILDER TIME

We will use the three sentences that we just classified to learn a new Skill Builder. We will add a Vocabulary Check to the Oral Skill Builder Check time. The Vocabulary Check will give me an opportunity to expand your vocabulary. I will select several words from the three sentences that we classify together for a Vocabulary Check. We will define the words, use them in new sentences, and name synonyms and antonyms for them.

TEACHER INSTRUCTIONS

Look over the words in the classified sentences. Select any words you think your students may not understand or words for which you want students to develop a broader understanding. Use the guidelines on the next page for a Vocabulary Check. (*For some words, you might use all the guidelines presented for a Vocabulary Check. For the reinforcement of other words, you might ask only for synonyms and antonyms. Talk about how synonym and antonym changes can affect the meaning of the original sentence. Show your students that synonyms and antonyms are powerful writing tools, and they must learn to use them well. It is very important that each child has a thesaurus of his/her own.*)

© SHURLEY INSTRUCTIONAL MATERIALS, INC.

CHAPTER 4 LESSON 3 CONTINUED

```
Guidelines for a Vocabulary Check
1. Give a definition for the word.
2. Use the word correctly in a sentence.
3. Think of a synonym for the word.
4. Think of an antonym for the word.
```

TEACHER INSTRUCTIONS

Use Sentences 1-3 that you just classified with your students to do an Oral Skill Builder Check. Use the guidelines below.

Oral Skill Builder Check	
1. Noun check. (Say the job and then say the noun. Circle each noun.) **2. Identify the nouns as singular or plural.** (Write S or P above each noun.) **3. Identify the nouns as common or proper.** (Follow established procedure for oral identification.) **4. Do a vocabulary check.** (Follow established procedure for oral identification.)	**5. Identify the complete subject and the complete predicate.** (Underline the complete subject once and the complete predicate twice.) **6. Identify the simple subject and simple predicate.** (Underline the simple subject once and the simple predicate twice. Bold, or highlight, the lines to distinguish them from the complete subject and complete predicate.)

Teacher's Note: A Vocabulary Check is an excellent way to enrich your students' writing vocabulary. There will be times when you may just ask for a synonym and an antonym for different words. This will give students a better command of the options they have when making word choices as they write sentences. Remind students of the power of words and give them plenty of practice as you utilize the three sentences they have classified. Again, it is very important that each student has a thesaurus of his/her own.

TEACHING SCRIPT FOR THE PRACTICE SENTENCE

Sentences are the foundation of writing; so, you must first learn how sentences are put together. Next, you will learn how to improve and expand sentences, and then you will learn to combine sentences into paragraphs.

The first two areas we will address are how sentences are put together and how to improve them. In order to talk about sentences, we must know the vocabulary that is used to build sentences. If you are building a house, you need to know about hammers and nails. You need to know the names of the tools and materials that you will be using.

© SHURLEY INSTRUCTIONAL MATERIALS, INC.

CHAPTER 4 LESSON 3 CONTINUED

In the same way, when you are building or writing sentences, you need to know the names of the parts you will be using and what to do with them. Your writing vocabulary will develop as you learn all the parts of a sentence. We will start by learning how to write a sentence from a given set of English labels. This is called a **Practice Sentence**.

A **Practice Sentence** is a sentence that is written following certain sentence labels (A, Adj, SN, V, Adv, etc.). The difficulty level of the sentence labels will increase as your ability increases. To write a Practice Sentence, you will follow the labels given to you in your assignment. You must think of words that fit the labels and that make sense.

Look at the Practice Sentence in Reference 16 on page 18 in your Reference Section. Since we have learned only four parts of a sentence so far, the Practice Sentence will demonstrate only these four parts. Notice that by using these sentence parts (*article adjective/adjective, subject noun, verb,* and *adverb),* we can make a seven-word sentence: **The shy young lady spoke very softly**.

Reference 16: Practice Sentence						
Labels:	A	Adj	Adj	SN	V	Adv	Adv
Practice:	**The**	**shy**	**young**	**lady**	**spoke**	**very**	**softly.**

There are three adjectives used in this sentence: *the, shy,* and *young.* There are two adverbs: *very* and *softly.* And, of course, there is the subject noun *lady,* and there is the verb *spoke.* We could just as easily have written a sentence with the bare essentials: *The lady spoke.* That is a correct sentence, but, by adding more parts, we are able to make the picture of the lady even clearer.

As you learn how to use more sentence parts to expand your sentences, you will use them automatically because they make your writing better.

Put these labels on the board: **A Adj SN V Adv**

Look at the sentence labels on the board: **A Adj SN V Adv**. Now, I am going to guide you through the process of writing a sentence using all the parts that you have learned thus far. Most of these steps will become automatic in a very short time.

Get out a sheet of notebook paper. On the top line of your notebook paper, write the title *Practice Sentence.* Copy the sentence labels from the board onto your notebook paper. Be sure to leave plenty of writing space between each label. Now, I will guide you through the process you will use whenever you write a Practice Sentence.

1. Go to the **SN** label for the subject noun. Think of a noun that you want to use as your subject. Write the noun you have chosen on the line *under* the **SN** label.

CHAPTER 4 LESSON 3 CONTINUED

2. Go to the **V** label for the verb. Think of a verb that tells what your subject does. Make sure that your verb makes sense with the subject noun. Write the verb you have chosen on the line *under* the **V** label.

3. Go to the **Adv** label for the adverb. Go to the verb in your sentence and ask an adverb question. What are the adverb questions? (*How? When? Where?*) Choose one adverb question to ask and write your adverb answer *under* the **Adv** label.

4. Go to the **Adj** label for the adjective. Go to the subject noun of your sentence and ask an adjective question. What are the adjective questions? (*What kind? Which one? How many?*) Choose one adjective question to ask and write your adjective answer *under* the **Adj** label next to the subject noun. Always check to make sure your answers are making sense in the sentence.

5. Go to the **A** label for the article adjective. What are the three article adjectives? (*a, an,* and *the*) You will choose the article adjective that makes the best sense in your sentence. Write the article adjective you have chosen *under* the **A** label.

6. Finally, check the Practice Sentence to make sure it has the necessary parts to be a complete sentence. What are the five parts of a complete sentence? (*subject, verb, complete sense, capital letter, and an end mark*) Does this Practice Sentence have all the parts necessary to make a complete sentence? (*Allow time for students' responses and for any corrections to be made on the board or on students' papers.*)

TEACHING SCRIPT FOR AN IMPROVED SENTENCE

Now that we have written a correct sentence using all the parts that we have studied, we must now concentrate on improving what we have written. The result is called an **Improved Sentence**. An **Improved Sentence** is a sentence made from the Practice Sentence that is improved through the use of synonyms, antonyms, or complete word changes. Writing Improved Sentences will help you make better word choices as you write because your writing vocabulary increases.

Look at the Improved Sentence in Reference 17 on page 18 in your Reference Section. The original English labels are on the first line. The sample Practice Sentence is on the second line. On the last line, you see an Improved Sentence made from synonyms, antonyms, and complete word changes. Knowing how to make improvements in what you have written means that you are beginning to revise and edit. (*Read the Practice and Improved Sentences in the box as your students follow along. Make sure students see the difference that improving sentences can make.*)

Reference 17: Improved Sentence							
Labels:	A	Adj	Adj	SN	V	Adv	Adv
Practice:	The	shy	young	lady	spoke	very	softly.
Improved:	**A**	**reserved**	**elderly**	**woman**	**chatted**	**quite**	**earnestly.**
	(word change)	(synonym)	(antonym)	(synonym)	(synonym)	(synonym)	(word change)

© SHURLEY INSTRUCTIONAL MATERIALS, INC.

CHAPTER 4 LESSON 3 CONTINUED

> Put these directions on the board or on notebook paper:
> **Make at <u>least</u> one synonym change, one antonym change, and one complete word change.**

The directions on the board tell you to make these changes in your Practice Sentence: **Make at <u>least</u> one synonym change, one antonym change, and one complete word change.** I am going to show you how to improve your Practice Sentence by making synonym, antonym, and complete word changes with some of the words.

The changed sentence will be called an **Improved Sentence** because you will make several improvements. Most of these steps will become automatic in a very short time. Now, on another line, under your Practice Sentence, write the title *Improved Sentence*.

1. Look at our Practice Sentence on the board. Let's find a word that can be improved with an antonym. *(Identify the word to be changed.)* Give me an antonym suggestion, and I will write your suggested antonym to improve, or change, the word.

   Remember, antonyms are powerful because they completely change the direction or meaning of your sentence. *(Discuss several antonym suggestions from students.)* Let's write the antonym we have chosen *under* the word we want to change in the Practice Sentence. *(Write the antonym choice on the board and have students write it on their papers.)*

2. Let's find a word in the Practice Sentence that can be improved with a synonym. *(Identify the word to be changed.)* Give me a synonym suggestion, and I will write your suggested synonym to improve the word. Remember, synonyms improve your writing vocabulary faster because they give you more word choices. *(Discuss several synonym suggestions from students.)* Let's write the synonym we have chosen *under* the word we want to improve in the Practice Sentence. *(Write the synonym choice on the board and have students write it on their papers.)*

3. Sometimes, you will think of a better word to use to improve your sentence that is not a synonym or antonym. We call this type of improvement a complete word change. It will give you more flexibility as you work to improve your sentences. Look at the Practice Sentence again. Is there another word that we want to change by simply making a complete word change? *(Discuss several complete word change suggestions from students.)* Let's write the complete word change we have chosen *under* the word we want to change in the Practice Sentence. *(Write the complete word change on the board and have students write it on their papers.)* If you cannot think of a complete word change, you can always use a synonym or antonym change.

4. Let's look at our Improved Sentence. Do you want to make any more improvements or changes? *(Discuss and then make extra improvements or changes as indicated by student participation.)*

5. Finally, let's check the Improved Sentence to make sure it has the necessary parts to be a complete sentence. Does our Improved Sentence have all the parts necessary to make a complete sentence? *(Allow time for students' responses and for corrections to be made on the board and on students' papers.)*

I want you to write your own Practice and Improved Sentences. You may use the same English labels that I listed on the board: **A Adj SN V Adv.** Make sure you follow the procedures we have just gone through. Remember, any time you write an Improved Sentence, you are actually editing your writing, and that's why it is so important that you learn to write Improved Sentences. *(Check and discuss students' Practice and Improved Sentences after they have finished. They will add more adjectives and adverbs to their Practice Sentence in the next chapter, but if they want to add them now, allow them to do so.)*

(End of lesson.)

© SHURLEY INSTRUCTIONAL MATERIALS, INC.

CHAPTER 4   LESSON 4
Objectives: Jingles, Study, Test, Check, Activity and Writing (journal).

 JINGLE TIME

Have students turn to the Jingle Section in their books. The teacher will lead the students in reciting the previously-taught jingles.

 STUDY TIME

Have students study the vocabulary words in their vocabulary notebooks. Remind students that any vocabulary word in their notebooks could be on their test. Also, have students study any of the skills in the Practice Section they need to review.

 TEST TIME

Have students turn to page 99 in the Test Section of their books and find Chapter 4 Test. Go over the directions to make sure they understand what to do. (*Chapter 4 Test key is on the next page.*)

 CHECK TIME

After students have finished, check and discuss their test papers. Make sure they understand why their answers are right or wrong. (*For total points, count each required answer as a point.*)

 ACTIVITY / ASSIGNMENT TIME

(Have a recipe box and a package of lined index cards ready for your children to use for this activity.) Find a map of the United States. Draw or trace the state of Alaska on the blank side of an index card. On the lined side of the card, write the following questions and answers.

1. What is the state on the front of this card? **Alaska**
2. What is the capital of Alaska? **Juneau**
3. What is the postal abbreviation of Alaska? **AK**
4. What year was Alaska admitted to the Union? **1959**

Color this state. Look up an interesting fact about this state and write it on your card. Use the card to quiz family members, friends, and relatives. You may want to time the responses to your questions.

(End of lesson.)

Level 3 Homeschool Teacher's Manual

© SHURLEY INSTRUCTIONAL MATERIALS, INC.

Chapter 4 Test
(Student Page 99)

Exercise 1: Classify each sentence.

        A   Adj   Adj   SN   V   Adv   Adv

1. <u>SN V</u>   The professional baseball player / pitched wildly today! **E**
   P1

        Adj Adj   Adj SN   V   Adv   Adv

2. <u>SN V</u>   Two feisty lion cubs / played vigorously together. **D**
   P1

        A   Adv   Adj SN   V   Adv   Adv

3. <u>SN V</u>   An exceptionally strong wind / blew fiercely yesterday. **D**
   P1

Exercise 2: Use Sentence 2 to underline the complete subject once and the complete predicate twice and to complete the table below.

List the Noun Used	List the Noun Job	Singular or Plural	Common or Proper	Simple Subject	Simple Predicate
1. cubs	2. SN	3. P	4. C	5. cubs	6. played

Exercise 3: Name the four parts of speech that you have studied. (*You may use abbreviations.*) **(The order may vary.)**

1. **noun**   2. **verb**   3. **adjective**   4. **adverb**

Exercise 4: Identify each pair of words as synonyms or antonyms by putting parentheses ( ) around *syn* or *ant*.

1. small, minute	**(syn)** ant	5. pillar, column	**(syn)** ant	9. apt, suitable	**(syn)** ant
2. master, servant	syn **(ant)**	6. soiled, clean	syn **(ant)**	10. curiosity, interest	**(syn)** ant
3. vague, clear	syn **(ant)**	7. sever, cut	**(syn)** ant	11. doubtful, certain	syn **(ant)**
4. attempt, try	**(syn)** ant	8. seldom, often	syn **(ant)**	12. eager, indifferent	syn **(ant)**

Exercise 5: For each noun listed below, write **S** for singular or **P** for plural.

Noun	S or P	Noun	S or P	Noun	S or P	Noun	S or P
1. trail	S	3. feet	P	5. playground	S	7. butterfly	S
2. pencils	P	4. puppies	P	6. mice	P	8. alleys	P

Exercise 6: For each noun listed below, write **C** for common or **P** for proper.

Noun	C or P	Noun	C or P	Noun	C or P	Noun	C or P
1. teacher	C	3. American	P	5. lamp	C	7. bicycle	C
2. Patsy	P	4. sky	C	6. Taco Bell	P	8. Honda	P

Exercise 7: Underline the complete subject once and the complete predicate twice.

1. <u>The two boys</u> <u>wrestled carelessly</u>.
2. <u>Ten large birds</u> <u>flew away</u>.
3. <u>The little brown bug</u> <u>scurried quickly</u>.
4. <u>Four lanky runners</u> <u>ran briskly</u>.

Exercise 8: Underline the simple subject once and the simple predicate twice.

1. A tiny <u>baby</u> <u>cried</u>.
2. The two yellow <u>flowers</u> <u>wilted</u> today.
3. The chicken <u>soup</u> <u>boiled</u> wildly.
4. Several <u>bees</u> <u>swarmed</u> yesterday.

Exercise 9: On notebook paper, write a Practice Sentence and an Improved Sentence. Use these labels: **A Adj Adj SN V Adv. (Answers will vary.)**

Exercise 10: In your journal, write a paragraph summarizing what you have learned this week.

© SHURLEY INSTRUCTIONAL MATERIALS, INC.

CHAPTER 4 LESSON 4 CONTINUED

TEACHER INSTRUCTIONS

Use the Question and Answer Flows below for the sentences on the Chapter 4 Test.

Question and Answer Flow for Sentence 1: The professional baseball player pitched wildly today!

1. Who pitched wildly today? player - SN
2. What is being said about player? player pitched - V
3. Pitched how? wildly - Adv
4. Pitched when? today - Adv
5. What kind of player? baseball - Adj
6. What kind of player? professional - Adj
7. The - A
8. SN V P1 Check
9. Exclamation point, strong feeling, exclamatory sentence.
10. Go back to the verb - divide the complete subject from the complete predicate.

Classified Sentence:

```
                        A    Adj      Adj   SN     V    Adv  Adv
              SN V    The professional baseball player / pitched wildly today!  E
              P1
```

Question and Answer Flow for Sentence 2: Two feisty lion cubs played vigorously together.

1. What played vigorously together? cubs - SN
2. What is being said about cubs? cubs played - V
3. Played how? vigorously - Adv
4. Played how? together - Adv
5. What kind of cubs? lion - Adj
6. What kind of cubs? feisty - Adj
7. How many cubs? two - Adj
8. SN V P1 Check
9. Period, statement, declarative sentence
10. Go back to the verb - divide the complete subject from the complete predicate.

Classified Sentence:

```
                        Adj Adj Adj  SN     V      Adv        Adv
              SN V    Two feisty lion cubs / played vigorously together.  D
              P1
```

Question and Answer Flow for Sentence 3: An exceptionally strong wind blew fiercely yesterday.

1. What blew fiercely yesterday? wind - SN
2. What is being said about wind? wind blew - V
3. Blew how? fiercely - Adv
4. Blew when? yesterday - Adv
5. What kind of wind? strong - Adj
6. How strong? exceptionally - Adv
7. An - A
8. SN V P1 Check
9. Period, statement, declarative sentence
10. Go back to the verb - divide the complete subject from the complete predicate.

Classified Sentence:

```
                        A      Adv      Adj  SN     V    Adv     Adv
              SN V    An exceptionally strong wind / blew fiercely yesterday.  D
              P1
```

© SHURLEY INSTRUCTIONAL MATERIALS, INC.

CHAPTER 4   LESSON 5

Objectives: Writing (Expository, writing definitions, two point paragraph) and Writing Assignment #1.

 **WRITING TIME**

Teacher's Note:
As students write their two-point paragraphs, it is very important that they follow the exact writing pattern that this lesson teaches. If this is done consistently, the students will learn to organize their writing by learning how to do these things: write a topic sentence for any given topic, write sentences that support the topic, and write a concluding sentence that summarizes their paragraph.

Teaching students how to write a two-point paragraph gives students several advantages:

1. It gives students a definite, concrete pattern to follow when asked to write a paragraph.
2. It gives students the practice they need in organizing their writing.
3. It gives students a chance to greatly improve their self-confidence because, as they advance in the program, they become stronger and more independent in all areas of their grammar and writing skills.

TEACHER INSTRUCTIONS

Put the following writing definitions on the board:

---

1. **Paragraph** - a group of sentences that is written about one particular subject or topic.
2. **Topic** - the subject of the paragraph; the topic tells what the paragraph is about.
3. **Expository writing** - the discussion or telling of ideas by giving facts, directions, explanations, definitions, and examples.

TEACHING SCRIPT FOR INTRODUCING EXPOSITORY WRITING AND WRITING DEFINITIONS

As a third grade student, you want to be prepared to be a good writer. As a part of that preparation, today, we are going to learn about expository writing and how to organize your writing by writing a two-point paragraph. First, let's look at some key definitions to be sure that we know what we are talking about.

Look at the first two definitions. A **paragraph** is a group of sentences that is written about one particular subject or topic. A **topic** is the subject of the paragraph; the topic tells what the paragraph is about.

Now, let's look at the last definition: **expository writing**. I want you to say "expository writing" with me so we can feel this type of writing on our tongues: **Expository writing**! Expository writing is the discussion or telling of ideas by giving facts, directions, explanations, definitions, and examples.

© SHURLEY INSTRUCTIONAL MATERIALS, INC.

CHAPTER 4 LESSON 5 CONTINUED

In other words, expository writing is informational. Its purpose is to inform, to give facts, to give directions, to explain, or to define something. Remember that expository writing is informational because it gives some type of information.

Since expository writing deals with information of some kind, it is very important to focus on making the meaning clear and understandable. The reader must be able to understand exactly what the writer means.

Now that we know what expository writing is, we must learn more about it because the first type of paragraph that we learn to write is an EXPOSITORY paragraph. What makes any type of writing easy is knowing exactly what to do when you are given a writing assignment. And the first thing you learn to do is organize your writing.

Expository writing may be organized in different ways. One of the most common ways to write an expository paragraph is by using a **two-point paragraph** format. The two-point paragraph format is a way of organizing the sentences in your expository paragraph that will help make your meaning clear and understandable.

Now, you will learn how to write a two-point expository paragraph. I am going to give you a topic about which you are to write your paragraph. Remember that a topic tells what the paragraph is about; it is the subject of the paragraph. In order to make sure you understand, we are going to write a two-point expository paragraph together, following specific steps.

TEACHING SCRIPT FOR SELECTING THE TWO POINTS OF THE PARAGRAPH

The first thing we learn is how to select and list the points that we are going to write about. Let's begin with our topic. Remember that a topic is a subject. The topic about which we are going to write our paragraph is "Favorite Colors." I will write this on the board under "Topic" (*Demonstrate by writing on the board.*)

Topic: My Favorite Colors

Do you have some favorite colors that you could write about? (*Discuss some of the students' favorite colors.*) Now, let's see how we are going to write this paragraph. Remember that I told you this paragraph is called a two-point paragraph. First, we are going to look at our topic, "My Favorite Colors," and see if we can list two favorite colors about which we can write.

Teacher's Note:
Even though students have named their favorite colors, the teaching sample will use green and yellow.

Level 3 Homeschool Teacher's Manual

© SHURLEY INSTRUCTIONAL MATERIALS, INC.

CHAPTER 4 LESSON 5 CONTINUED

Green and yellow: These are two good favorite colors. I will list these two colors on the board under "Two points about the topic." They will be the two points for our two-point expository paragraph. (*Demonstrate by writing on the board.*)

Two points about the topic:

1. _____green_____   2. _____yellow_____

Now, let's set them aside for a minute and begin our paragraph. We are going to use these two items shortly.

Teacher's Note: The simplified outline below will give you a quick view of what you will be covering with your students in your discussion of the two-point expository paragraph. Write each part on the board only as it is being discussed so that your students will not be overwhelmed by the amount of written work that they see on the board.

The Two-Point Expository Paragraph Outline

Topic
2 points about the topic
Sentence #1: Topic sentence
Sentence #2: A two-point sentence
Sentence #3: A **first**-point sentence
Sentence #4: A **supporting** sentence for the first point
Sentence #5: A **second**-point sentence
Sentence #6: A **supporting** sentence for the second point
Sentence #7: A concluding sentence

Teacher's Note: As you work through the steps, be sure to show students how the sentences are divided into three categories: the introduction (*topic and two-point sentence*), the body (*the two main points and their supporting sentences*), and the conclusion (*the concluding sentence*).

TEACHING SCRIPT FOR WRITING THE TOPIC SENTENCE

First, we must write what is called a topic sentence. A topic sentence is very important because it tells the main idea of our paragraph. We are going to let the topic sentence be the first sentence in our paragraph because it tells everyone what our paragraph is going to be about. In many paragraphs, it is not the first sentence. Later, we can learn to put the topic sentence in other places in the paragraph, but, for now, it is important that we make it the first sentence in our two-point paragraph.

© SHURLEY INSTRUCTIONAL MATERIALS, INC.

CHAPTER 4 LESSON 5 CONTINUED

The topic sentence for a two-point paragraph needs three things:
1. It needs to tell the main idea of the paragraph.
2. It needs to be general because the other sentences in the paragraph must tell about the topic sentence.
3. It needs to tell the number of points that will be discussed in the paragraph.

When you write a topic sentence for a two-point paragraph, follow these two easy steps:
1. You will use all or some of the words in the topic.
2. You will tell the number of points, or ideas, you will discuss in your paragraph.

Now, we are going to write a topic sentence by following the two easy steps we have just discussed. Look at our topic, "My Favorite Colors." Without actually listing the two specific points – green and yellow – let's write a sentence that makes a general statement about the main idea of our topic and tells the number of points we will list later.

How about using "I have two favorite colors" as the topic sentence? I will write this on the board under "Sentence #1: Topic sentence." (*Demonstrate by writing on the board. Read the sentence to the students.*)

Sentence #1. Topic sentence: I have two favorite colors.

Look at the topic sentence on the board. Notice that in this sentence, we have mentioned our topic, "My Favorite Colors," and we have stated that there are two of these colors; we will tell what the two are in the two-point sentence that follows.

Also, notice that we did not say, "I am going to tell you about my two favorite colors." We do not need to tell the reader we are going to tell him/her something; we simply do it. To say "I am going to tell you" is called "writing about your writing," and it is not effective writing. Do not "write about your writing."

TEACHING SCRIPT FOR WRITING THE TWO-POINT SENTENCE

Now that we have our topic sentence, our next sentence will list the two specific points our paragraph will discuss. Our next sentence could be, "These colors are green and yellow." I will write this on the board under "Sentence #2: A two-point sentence." (*Demonstrate by writing the information below on the board. Read the sentence to the students.*)

Sentence #2. A two-point sentence: These colors are green and yellow.

Look at the order in which I have listed the two subjects. You must always be aware of the order in which you put your points because that will be the order in which you discuss these points in your paragraph.

I have chosen to place these in this order: green and yellow. I did not have any particular reason for placing green first. Depending upon your two points as well as your purpose in writing, you will select the order of your two points.

Page 72   Level 3 Homeschool Teacher's Manual
© SHURLEY INSTRUCTIONAL MATERIALS, INC.

CHAPTER 4 LESSON 5 CONTINUED

Notice three things we have done here:

1. We have put our two items in the order we have chosen, remembering that we will be discussing these points in this order later in our paragraph. (*green and yellow*)

2. We have written our first sentence, and our first sentence tells us the number of points that will be discussed in the rest of the paragraph. (*I have two favorite colors.*)

3. We have started our listing sentence with words that helped us connect it to our first sentence. (*These colors are **green** and **yellow**.*)

Notice how we have used repetition to link our two sentences. Our first sentence mentions **"favorite colors"** by stating **"I have two favorite colors."** Sentence number two, **"These colors are green and yellow,"** refers to sentence number one by stating **"These colors,"** meaning the favorite colors just mentioned in sentence number one. Although you will not want to use repetition in every sentence to link sentences, repetition is a good device for making your paragraph flow smoothly.

TEACHING SCRIPT FOR DEVELOPING AND SUPPORTING THE POINTS OF THE PARAGRAPH

After you have stated the general topic sentence and then followed it by the more specific two-point sentence, you will begin to discuss each of the two points, one at a time. DO NOT FORGET: You are going to discuss them in the order in which you listed them in sentence number two. You will begin your third sentence by stating, "My first favorite color is green." This is your first listed point. I will write this on the board under "Sentence #3: A first-point sentence." (*Demonstrate by writing the information below on the board. Read the sentence to the students.*)

Sentence #3. A first-point sentence: My first favorite color is green.

Next, you will write one sentence about green. It can be a descriptive sentence about green. It can be a reason why you like green, but it must be about green being your favorite color. This is called a supporting sentence. I will now write a supporting sentence on the board under "Sentence #4: A supporting sentence for the first point." You can use this sentence or make up your own: "I like green because I love budding leaves after a long winter." (*Demonstrate by writing the information below on the board. Read the sentence to the students.*)

Sentence #4. A supporting sentence for the first point: I like green because I love budding leaves after a long winter.

When you keep your writing targeted to the topic you are assigned, your paragraph will have what we call "unity," or will be a "unified" paragraph. In a unified paragraph, all sentences work together to form one idea about the subject, or topic.

As you get more skilled at two-point writing, you may write two or more sentences about each of your listed points, but, for now, stay with one sentence for each point. Each of the sentences that you write following your points should support what you have stated in that point. Use only ideas that support. Discard non-supporting ideas.

© SHURLEY INSTRUCTIONAL MATERIALS, INC.

CHAPTER 4 LESSON 5 CONTINUED

So far, we have introduced our topic and listed our two specific points. We have begun to discuss our two points and have completed the first point along with a sentence that supports the first point. So far, we have four sentences.

Your fifth sentence will introduce the second point of the two-point paragraph. Your second point is "yellow." Since "yellow" is the second item you listed, your fifth sentence should state, "My second favorite color is yellow." I will write this on the board under "Sentence #5: A second-point sentence." (*Demonstrate by writing the information below on the board. Read the sentence to the students.*)

Sentence #5. A second-point sentence: My second favorite color is yellow.

Just as you wrote the sentence supporting the statement of your first point, so now you must write a sentence supporting your statement about yellow being your second favorite color. I will write the next supporting sentence on the board under "Sentence #6: A supporting sentence for the second point." (*Demonstrate by writing the information below on the board. Read the sentence to the students.*)

Sentence #6. A supporting sentence for the second point: Yellow reminds me of warm sunshine and summer days.

By now, you can begin to see a pattern to your paragraph. So far, you have written six sentences in your paragraph. Your seventh sentence will be your last or final sentence.

TEACHING SCRIPT FOR WRITING THE CONCLUSION OF THE PARAGRAPH

We have now introduced our topic, or subject, listed each of our two points, and made one supporting statement about each point. Now, we need to complete our paragraph, leaving the reader with the impression that he/she has read a finished product. In order to complete our paragraph, we need a conclusion, or final sentence.

There are different ways to write a concluding sentence, but one of the best and simplest is the summary statement. This means that the main points of the paragraph are stated again, briefly, in one sentence.

When you write a concluding sentence, follow these two easy steps:
   1. You will use some of the words in your topic sentence.
   2. You will add an extra, or concluding, thought about your paragraph.

You might try a good concluding sentence, such as, "My two favorite colors remind me of summer which has an abundance of green and yellow everywhere." I will write this on the board under "Sentence #7: A concluding sentence." (*Demonstrate by writing the information below on the board. Read the sentence again to the students.*)

Sentence #7. A concluding sentence: My two favorite colors remind me of summer, which has an abundance of green and yellow everywhere.

© SHURLEY INSTRUCTIONAL MATERIALS, INC.

CHAPTER 4 LESSON 5 CONTINUED

TEACHING SCRIPT FOR CHECKING THE FINISHED PARAGRAPH

It is good to get in the habit of checking over your writing after you have finished. Just reading your finished paragraph several times slowly will help you see and hear things that you may want to correct. It also helps to have a checklist that tells specific areas to check to make sure you do not lose points for careless mistakes.

Turn to page 19 and look at Reference 18 as I read what it tells you to do as you write each sentence of your two-point paragraph. (*Read and discuss each section of the two-point paragraph example in Reference 18. Tell students to use this reference page if they need it when they write a two-point paragraph. It will help them organize their writing, and it will help them see the pattern of a two-point expository paragraph.) (Reference 18 is reproduced for you on the next page.)*

Teacher's Note: There was neither discussion nor guidelines provided for writing a title for the paragraph. Single paragraphs are often written without titles; the decision is left to the teacher or writer. Remind students that this is an expository paragraph, which means that its purpose is to inform or explain. The two-point format is a way of organizing an expository paragraph.

TEACHER INSTRUCTIONS FOR WRITING ASSIGNMENT #1

Give Writing Assignment #1 from the box below. Remind students to use the two-point paragraph example in Reference 18 on page 19 in the Reference Section if they need it. **If this is their first year in the program, tell students that this writing assignment will be done on a writing page in their books.** The writing page is already set up in a two-point format that will help them follow the form of the two-point paragraph. Direct students to page 66 in the Practice Section of their books. (*The practice page is reproduced for you at the end of this lesson on page 78.*)

Writing Assignment Box

Writing Assignment #1: Two-Point Expository Paragraph

Writing topic choices: **My Favorite Colors** or **My Favorite Hobby** or **My Favorite Holiday**

After students have filled out the two-point practice page, have them transfer their paragraph to a sheet of notebook paper or type it on a computer. Before students begin, go over the Writing Guidelines on page 77 so they will know how to arrange their writing assignment on notebook paper or on the computer.

© SHURLEY INSTRUCTIONAL MATERIALS, INC.

CHAPTER 4 LESSON 5 CONTINUED

Reference 18: Two-Point Paragraph Example

Topic: **My favorite colors**
Two main points: 1. **green**   2. **yellow**

Sentence #1 – <u>Topic Sentence</u> (*Use words in the topic and tell how many points will be used.*)
I have two favorite colors.

Sentence #2 – <u>2-Point Sentence</u> (*List the 2 points in the order you will present them.*)
These colors are green and yellow.

Sentence #3 – <u>First Point</u>
My first favorite color is green.

Sentence #4 – <u>Supporting Sentence</u> for the first point.
I like green because I love budding leaves after a long winter.

Sentence #5 – <u>Second Point</u>
My second favorite color is yellow.

Sentence #6 – <u>Supporting Sentence</u> for the second point.
Yellow reminds me of warm sunshine and summer days.

Sentence #7 – <u>Concluding (final) Sentence</u> (*Restate the topic sentence and add an extra thought.*)
My two favorite colors remind me of summer, which has an abundance of green and yellow everywhere.

<u>SAMPLE PARAGRAPH</u>

My Favorite Colors

    I have two favorite colors. These colors are green and yellow. My first favorite color is green. I like green because I love budding leaves after a long winter. My second favorite color is yellow. Yellow reminds me of warm sunshine and summer days. My two favorite colors remind me of summer, which has an abundance of green and yellow everywhere.

© SHURLEY INSTRUCTIONAL MATERIALS, INC.

CHAPTER 4 LESSON 5 CONTINUED

TEACHING SCRIPT FOR WRITING GUIDELINES

Today, we will go through some guidelines for your writing. Turn to page 20 in your book and look at Reference 19. You will use these guidelines every time you are given a writing assignment. (*Read and discuss the Writing Guidelines with your students.*)

Reference 19: Writing Guidelines

1. Label your writing assignment in the top right-hand corner of your page with the following information:

    A. Your Name
    B. The Writing Assignment Number. *(Examples: WA#1, WA#2, etc.)*
    C. Type of Writing (Examples: Expository Paragraph, Persuasive Essay, Descriptive Paragraph, etc.)
    D. The title of the writing on the top of the first line.

2. Think about the topic that you are assigned.

3. Think about the type of writing assigned, which is the purpose for the writing.
   (Is your writing intended to explain, persuade, describe, or narrate?)

4. Think about the writing format, which is the organizational plan you are expected to use.
   (Is your assignment a paragraph, a 3-paragraph essay, or a letter?)

5. Use your writing time wisely.
   (Begin work quickly and concentrate on your assignment until it is finished.)

TEACHING SCRIPT FOR USING THE WRITING PROCESS FOR WRITING ASSIGNMENT #1

As you begin this writing assignment, you will use the writing process discussed in Reference 19. I will give you a quick review of that writing process. First, you will think about your topic and gather any information you might need in order to do the writing. Second, you will write a rough draft. Remember that it is called a rough draft because it will be revised and edited. You do not have to worry about mistakes as you write your rough draft. After you write the first draft, you will make revisions, using the Revision Checklist in Reference 13. After you revise your writing, you will edit it, using the Beginning Editing Checklist in Reference 13. Finally, after you are satisfied with your revising and editing, you will write a final paper, using the Final Paper Checklist in Reference 13. You will then give the finished writing assignment to me.

TEACHER INSTRUCTIONS FOR CHECKING WRITING ASSIGNMENT #1

Read, check, and discuss Writing Assignment #1 after students have finished their final paper. Use the editing checklist (*Reference 13 on teacher's page 48*) as you check and discuss students' papers. Make sure students are using the editing checklist correctly. In the beginning, you must also check students' papers carefully for <u>form</u> mistakes. This will ensure that students are learning the two-point format correctly.

Teacher's Note: It's okay for students to pattern their sentences after the examples. As they get stronger in this system and change topics, you will see more independent sentences. In fact, you will see a lot of variety in these paragraphs because students will probably choose at least two different subjects and write different supporting sentences. Remind students to add adjectives and adverbs to make their sentences more interesting.

© SHURLEY INSTRUCTIONAL MATERIALS, INC.

CHAPTER 4 LESSON 5 CONTINUED

Chapter 4, Lesson 5, Practice Writing Page: Use the two-point outline form below to guide you as you write a two-point expository paragraph.

Write a topic: _____

List 2 points about the topic:

1. _____ 2. _____

Sentence #1   Topic sentence (*Use words in the topic and tell how many points will be used.*)

_____

_____

Sentence #2   2-point sentence (*List your 2 points in the order that you will present them.*)

_____

_____

Sentence #3   State your first point in a complete sentence.

_____

_____

Sentence #4   Write a supporting sentence for the first point.

_____

_____

Sentence #5   State your second point in a complete sentence.

_____

_____

Sentence #6   Write a supporting sentence for the second point.

_____

_____

Sentence #7   Concluding sentence (*Restate the topic sentence and add an extra thought.*)

_____

_____

Student Note: Rewrite your seven-sentence paragraph on notebook paper. Be sure to indent and use the checklists to help you edit your paragraph. Make sure you re-read your paragraph several times, slowly.

(End of lesson.)

© SHURLEY INSTRUCTIONAL MATERIALS, INC.

CHAPTER 5   LESSON 1

Objectives: Jingles (Preposition, Object of the Prep, Preposition Flow), Grammar (Practice sentences), Skill (Oral Skill Builder Check, Expanded Practice Sentence), Vocabulary #1, and Activity.

JINGLE TIME

Have students turn to the Jingle Section in their books and recite the previously-taught jingles. Then, lead students in reciting the new jingles (*Preposition, Object of the Preposition, and Preposition Flow*) below. Practice the new jingles several times until students can recite them smoothly. Emphasize reciting with rhythm. Students and teacher should be together! (*Do not try to explain the jingles at this time. Just have fun reciting them. Remember, add motions for more fun and laughter.*)

Teacher's Note: Again, do not spend a large amount of time practicing the new jingles. Students learn the jingles best by spending a small amount of time consistently, **every** day.

Jingle 7: Preposition Jingle
A PREP PREP PREPOSITION Is a special group of words That connects a NOUN, NOUN, NOUN Or a PRO, PRO, PRONOUN To the rest of the sentence.

Jingle 8:   Object of the Prep Jingle
Dum De Dum Dum! An O-P is a N-O-U-N or a P-R-O After the P-R-E-P In a S-E-N-T-E-N-C-E. Dum De Dum Dum - DONE!

Jingle 9: Preposition Flow		
1. **Preposition, Preposition Starting with an A.** (Fast) aboard, about, above, across, after, against, (Slow) along, among, around, at.	2. **Preposition, Preposition Starting with a B.** (Fast) before, behind, below, beneath, beside, between, (Slow) beyond, but, by.	3. **Preposition, Preposition Starting with a D.** down (slow & long), during (snappy).
4. **Preposition, Preposition Don't go away. Go to the middle And see what we say. E-F-I and L-N-O** except, for, from, in, inside, into, like, near, of, off, on, out, outside, over.	5. **Preposition, Preposition Almost through. Start with P and end with W.** past, since, through, throughout, to, toward, under, underneath, until, up, upon, with, within, without.	6. **Preposition, Preposition Easy as can be. We're all finished, And aren't you pleased? We've just recited All 49 of these.**

© SHURLEY INSTRUCTIONAL MATERIALS, INC.

CHAPTER 5 LESSON 1 CONTINUED

 GRAMMAR TIME

First-Year Option: Put the Practice Sentences from the box below on the board or on notebook paper. Use these sentences as you practice the concepts that have been taught. For the greatest benefit, students must participate orally with the teacher. **Second-Year Option:** Have students classify the Practice Sentences independently on paper. Check students' sentences with the answers provided below. *(If you have the CDs for Practice Sentences, have students check their sentences with the CDs.)*

Chapter 5, Practice Sentences for Lesson 1

1. _____ The adorable little kittens purred contentedly.
2. _____ The new quarterback performed quite impressively.
3. _____ The dark storm clouds gathered threateningly overhead.

TEACHING SCRIPT FOR PRACTICING PATTERN 1 SENTENCES

We will classify three different sentences to practice grammar as we recite the Question and Answer Flows. We will classify the sentences together. Begin. (*You might have students write the labels above the sentences at this time.*)

Question and Answer Flow for Sentence 1: The adorable little kittens purred contentedly.

1. What purred contentedly? kittens - SN
2. What is being said about kittens? kittens purred - V
3. Purred how? contentedly - Adv
4. What kind of kittens? little - Adj
5. What kind of kittens? adorable - Adj
6. The - A
7. SN V P1 Check
8. Period, statement, declarative sentence
9. Go back to the verb - divide the complete subject from the complete predicate.

Classified Sentence:

```
              A     Adj   Adj   SN      V      Adv
  SN V     The adorable little kittens / purred contentedly.  D
  ―――――
   P1
```

Question and Answer Flow for Sentence 2: The new quarterback performed quite impressively.

1. Who performed quite impressively? quarterback - SN
2. What is being said about quarterback? quarterback performed - V
3. Performed how? impressively - Adv
4. How impressively? quite - Adv
5. What kind of quarterback? new - Adj
6. The - A
7. SN V P1 Check
8. Period, statement, declarative sentence
9. Go back to the verb - divide the complete subject from the complete predicate.

Classified Sentence:

```
              A   Adj    SN        V      Adv    Adv
  SN V     The new quarterback / performed quite impressively.  D
  ―――――
   P1
```

© SHURLEY INSTRUCTIONAL MATERIALS, INC.

CHAPTER 5 LESSON 1 CONTINUED

Question and Answer Flow for Sentence 3: The dark storm clouds gathered threateningly overhead.

1. What gathered threateningly overhead? clouds - SN
2. What is being said about clouds?
   clouds gathered - V
3. Gathered how? threateningly - Adv
4. Gathered where? overhead - Adv
5. What kind of clouds? storm - Adj

6. What kind of clouds? dark - Adj
7. The - A
8. SN V P1 Check
9. Period, statement, declarative sentence
10. Go back to the verb - divide the complete subject from the complete predicate.

Classified Sentence:

                       A Adj Adj SN   V   Adv   Adv

<u>SN V</u>   The dark storm clouds **/** gathered threateningly overhead. **D**
P1

SKILL TIME

Use Sentences 1-3 that you just classified with your students to do an Oral Skill Builder Check. Use the guidelines below.

Oral Skill Builder Check	
1. Noun check. (Say the job and then say the noun. Circle each noun.) **2. Identify the nouns as singular or plural.** (Write S or P above each noun.) **3. Identify the nouns as common or proper.** (Follow established procedure for oral identification.) **4. Do a vocabulary check.** (Follow established procedure for oral identification.)	**5. Identify the complete subject and the complete predicate.** (Underline the complete subject once and the complete predicate twice.) **6. Identify the simple subject and simple predicate.** (Underline the simple subject once and the simple predicate twice. Bold, or highlight, the lines to distinguish them from the complete subject and complete predicate.)

TEACHING SCRIPT FOR AN EXPANDED PRACTICE SENTENCE

Put these labels on the board: **A Adj Adj SN V Adv Adv**

In the previous lesson, I guided you through the process of writing a Practice Sentence and an Improved Sentence for the first time. Today, I am going to guide you through the same process again, but this time you will write an expanded sentence by adding a few more sentence labels. Look at the new sentence labels on the board: **A Adj Adj SN V Adv Adv**.

Get out a sheet of notebook paper and write the title *Practice Sentence* on the top line. Copy the labels on the board across the page: **A Adj Adj SN V Adv Adv**. Make sure you leave plenty of room for the words that you will write under the labels.

© SHURLEY INSTRUCTIONAL MATERIALS, INC.

CHAPTER 5 LESSON 1 CONTINUED

I will guide you through the process of writing a sentence using a given set of labels again. I will lead you each time we cover a new concept in Pattern 1. Writing a sentence using English labels is total sentence control. It is very easy if you know how, but it is also something very few people can do without training.

1. Go to the **SN** label for the subject noun. Think of a noun that you want to use as your subject. Write the noun you have chosen on the line *under* the **SN** label.

2. Go to the **V** label for the verb. Think of a verb that tells what your subject does. Make sure that your verb makes sense with the subject noun. Write the verb you have chosen on the line *under* the **V** label.

3. Go to the **Adv** label for the adverb. Go to the verb in your sentence and ask an adverb question. What are the adverb questions? (*How? When? Where?*) Choose one adverb question to ask and write your adverb answer *under* the first **Adv** label.

4. Go to the **Adv** label for another adverb. Go to the verb again and ask another adverb question. You can use the same adverb question, or you can use a different adverb question. Write another adverb *under* the second **Adv** label.

5. Go to the **Adj** label for the adjective. Go to the subject noun of your sentence and ask an adjective question. What are the adjective questions? (*What kind? Which one? How many?*) Choose one adjective question to ask and write your adjective answer *under* the **Adj** label next to the subject noun. Always check to make sure your answers are making sense in the sentence.

6. Go to the next **Adj** label for another adjective. Go to the subject noun again and ask another adjective question. You can use the same adjective question, or you can use a different adjective question. Write another adjective *under* the second **Adj** label.

7. Go to the **A** label for the article adjective. What are the three article adjectives? (*a*, *an*, and *the*) Choose the article adjective that makes the best sense in your sentence. Write the article adjective you have chosen *under* the **A** label.

8. Finally, check your Practice Sentence to make sure it has the necessary parts to be a complete sentence. What are the five parts of a complete sentence? (*subject, verb, complete sense, capital letter, and an end mark*) Does your Practice Sentence have the five parts of a complete sentence? (*Allow time for students to read over their sentences and to make any necessary corrections.*)

© SHURLEY INSTRUCTIONAL MATERIALS, INC.

CHAPTER 5 LESSON 1 CONTINUED

9. Under your Practice Sentence, write the title *Improved Sentence* on another line. To improve your Practice Sentence, you will make two synonym changes, one antonym change, and your choice of a complete word change or another synonym or antonym change.

Since it is harder to find words that can be changed to an antonym, it is usually wise to go through your sentence to find an antonym change first. Then, look through your sentence again to find words that can be improved with synonyms. Finally, make a decision about whether your last change will be a complete word change, another synonym change, or another antonym change.

I will give you time to write your Improved Sentence. *(Always encourage students to use a thesaurus, synonym-antonym book, or a dictionary to help them develop an interesting and improved writing vocabulary. After students have finished, check and discuss students' Practice and Improved Sentences.)*

 VOCABULARY TIME

Assign Chapter 5, Vocabulary Words **#1** on page 8 in the Reference Section for students to define in their Vocabulary notebooks. Tell students they are to use a dictionary or thesaurus to look up the meanings of the vocabulary words. After they write each word and its meaning, students are to write a sentence using the vocabulary word.

Chapter 5, Vocabulary Words #1
(watch, vigil, flabby, firm)

 ACTIVITY / ASSIGNMENT TIME

Make a list of five people in your family (and/or extended family/friends). Write each family member's name on an index card. On the back of each index card, write a descriptive sentence about the person listed on the front. Be sure to include as many adjectives and adverbs as possible. Finally, play a guessing game with different members of your family. Read aloud or hold up the side of the card with the description and let family members guess whose name is written on the other side. Discuss the family members that were the hardest and easiest to guess. Also, discuss which family members were the hardest and easiest to describe.

(End of lesson.)

© SHURLEY INSTRUCTIONAL MATERIALS, INC.

CHAPTER 5 LESSON 2
Objectives: Jingles, Grammar (Introductory Sentences, Preposition, Object of the Preposition, Prepositional Phrase, add Object of the Preposition to the Noun Check, Oral Skill Builder, add the Preposition to the parts of speech), Vocabulary #2.

 **JINGLE TIME**

Have students turn to the Jingle Section in their books. The teacher will lead the students in reciting the previously-taught jingles.

 GRAMMAR TIME

Put the introductory sentences from the box below on the board. Use these sentences as you go through each new concept covered in your teaching script. For the greatest benefit, students must participate orally with the teacher. (*You might put the introductory sentences on notebook paper if you are doing one-on-one instruction with your students.*)

Chapter 5, Introductory Sentences for Lesson 2
1. _____ An enormous branch fell from the top of the tree!
2. _____ The flickering fireflies soared gracefully through the night sky.
3. _____ The frightened birds flew hastily away from the barking dogs.

TEACHING SCRIPT FOR PREPOSITION, OBJECT OF THE PREPOSITION, AND PREPOSITIONAL PHRASE

We will now begin the really "fun stuff" in English. We are going to start with prepositions! The preposition jingles have already told you a lot about prepositions, but now we are going to learn even more. A **preposition** is a joining word. It joins a noun or a pronoun to the rest of the sentence. To know whether a word is a preposition, say the preposition word and ask *What* or *Whom*. If the answer is a noun or pronoun, then the word is a preposition. Prepositions are labeled with a *P*.

An **object of the preposition** is a noun or pronoun after the preposition in a sentence. An object of the preposition is labeled with an *OP*.

It is important for you to know the difference between prepositions and adverbs. Look at Reference 20 on page 20 as I explain how you can tell the difference between prepositions and adverbs.

A word can be a <u>preposition </u>or an <u>adverb</u>, depending on how it is used in a sentence. For example, the word *down* can be an adverb or a preposition. How do you decide if the word *down* is an adverb or a preposition? If *down* is used alone, with no noun after it, it is an adverb. If *down* has a noun after it that answers the question *what* or *whom*, then *down* is a preposition, and the noun after *down* is an object of the preposition. (*Have students follow along as you read and discuss the information in the reference box on the next page.*)

© SHURLEY INSTRUCTIONAL MATERIALS, INC.

CHAPTER 5 LESSON 2 CONTINUED

Reference 20: Knowing the Difference Between Prepositions and Adverbs

Adv
In the sample sentence, *Alexander fell **down***, the word ***down*** is an adverb because it does not have a noun after it.

P   noun (OP)
In the sample sentence, *Alexander fell **down the steps***, the word ***down*** is a preposition because it has the noun ***steps*** (the object of the preposition) after it. To find the preposition and object of the preposition in the Question and Answer Flow, say: **down – P**   (Say: *down – preposition*)
down what? steps – OP (Say: *down what? steps – object of the preposition*)

Now, we will learn about prepositional phrases. A **prepositional phrase** starts with the preposition and ends with the object of the preposition. It includes any modifiers between the preposition and the object of the preposition.

A prepositional phrase adds meaning to a sentence and can be located anywhere in the sentence. Prepositional phrases can modify like adjectives or adverbs. For example, the prepositional phrase (*down the steps*) tells where Alexander fell.

A single word that modifies a verb is called an adverb. A prepositional phrase that modifies a verb is called an adverb, or adverbial, phrase. Prepositional phrases can also modify like adjectives. (*Students are not required to identify adjectival and adverbial phrases in sentences until seventh grade.*)

Prepositional phrases are identified in the Question and Answer Flow after you say the word *Check*. Now, when you say *Check*, you are also looking for prepositional phrases in the sentence. If you find a prepositional phrase, you will read the whole prepositional phrase and put parentheses around it.

For example, after you classify the sentence, ***Sue ran behind the house***, you say, <u>**Subject Noun Verb Pattern 1 Check: (Behind the house) - Prepositional phrase**</u>. If there is more than one prepositional phrase in a sentence, read all prepositional phrases during this check time.

You will learn prepositional phrases very quickly simply by identifying and using them everyday. I will show you how quick and easy it is to identify prepositional phrases by using the Question and Answer Flow. Remember, the Question and Answer Flow will make learning prepositional phrases easy and fun. (*Classify Sentence 1 to demonstrate prepositional phrases in the Question and Answer Flow. You could also use the audio CD to introduce the Introductory Sentences.*)

© SHURLEY INSTRUCTIONAL MATERIALS, INC.

CHAPTER 5 LESSON 2 CONTINUED

Question and Answer Flow for Sentence 1: An enormous branch fell from the top of the tree!

1. What fell from the top of the tree? branch - SN
2. What is being said about branch? branch fell - V
3. From - P (Preposition)
4. From what? top - OP (Object of the Preposition)
5. The - A

Note: To test whether a word is a preposition, say your preposition and ask "what" or "whom." If your answer is a noun or pronoun, you will have a preposition. All prepositions will have a noun or pronoun object. (When the object of the preposition is a person use "whom" instead of "what.")

6. Of - P (Preposition)
7. Of what? tree - OP (Object of the Preposition)
8. The - A

9. What kind of branch? enormous - Adj
10. An - A
11. SN V P1 Check
12. (From the top) - Prepositional phrase

Note: Say "from the top - Prepositional phrase" as you put parentheses around the words. This also teaches your students how to read in complete phrases, so keep it smooth.

13. (Of the tree) - Prepositional phrase
14. Exclamation point, strong feeling, exclamatory sentence
15. Go back to the verb - divide the complete subject from the complete predicate.

Classified Sentence:

```
              A   Adj       SN     V    P   A  OP    P  A  OP
    SN  V     An enormous branch / fell (from the top) (of the tree)!  E
    ————
    P1
```

I will now classify Sentence 1 again, but this time you classify it with me. I will lead you as we say the questions and answers together. Remember, it is very important that you say the **questions** with me as well as the **answers**. *(Classify Sentence 1 again with your students.)*

We will classify Sentences 2 and 3 together to practice the new grammar concepts in the Question and Answer Flows. You must say the **questions and answers** with me. By asking and answering the questions orally, you will learn everything faster because you see it, hear it, say it, and then do it. Begin.

Question and Answer Flow for Sentence 2: The flickering fireflies soared gracefully through the night sky.

1. What soared gracefully through the night sky? fireflies - SN
2. What is being said about fireflies? fireflies soared - V
3. Soared how? gracefully - Adv
4. Through - P
5. Through what? sky - OP
6. What kind of sky? night - Adj
7. The - A

8. What kind of fireflies? flickering - Adj
9. The - A
10. SN V P1 Check
11. (Through the night sky) - Prepositional phrase
12. Period, statement, declarative sentence
13. Go back to the verb - divide the complete subject from the complete predicate.

Classified Sentence:

```
              A    Adj      SN      V     Adv        P   A  Adj OP
    SN  V     The flickering fireflies / soared gracefully (through the night sky).  D
    ————
    P1
```

© SHURLEY INSTRUCTIONAL MATERIALS, INC.

CHAPTER 5 LESSON 2 CONTINUED

Question and Answer Flow for Sentence 3: The frightened birds flew hastily away from the barking dogs.

1. What flew hastily away from the barking dogs? birds - SN
2. What is being said about birds? birds flew - V
3. Flew how? hastily - Adv
4. Flew where? away - Adv
5. From - P
6. From what? dogs - OP
7. What kind of dogs? barking - Adj
8. The - A

9. What kind of birds? frightened - Adj
10. The - A
11. SN V P1 Check
12. (From the barking dogs) - Prepositional phrase
13. Period, statement, declarative sentence
14. Go back to the verb - divide the complete subject from the complete predicate.

Classified Sentence:

			A	Adj	SN	V	Adv	Adv	P	A	Adj	OP

SN V
_____ The frightened birds / flew hastily away (from the barking dogs). **D**
P1

TEACHING SCRIPT FOR ADDING THE OBJECT OF THE PREPOSITION TO THE NOUN CHECK

We are going to use the sentences we have just classified to do an Oral Skill Builder Check. You have already learned how to do a Noun Check with the subject of the sentence. Today, we are going to add a new noun job, the object of the preposition, to the Noun Check. We will learn to identify nouns in the object of the preposition job. Therefore, to find nouns, you will go to the words marked SN and OP in the classified sentences.

Look at Sentences 1-3 that we have just classified on the board. Remember, we will go to the subject nouns **and** the objects of the prepositions to find nouns. We will circle each noun as we find it.

Look at Sentence 1. You will say, "Number 1: subject noun *branch, yes;* object of the preposition *top, yes;* object of the preposition *tree, yes.*" I will circle each noun as you identify it. *(Have students repeat number 1 with you as you circle each noun identified.)* We will find and circle the nouns in Sentences 2 and 3 the same way. *(Work through the rest of the sentences, identifying and circling the subject nouns and object-of-the-preposition nouns.)* *(Number 1:* subject noun *branch, yes;* object of the preposition *top, yes;* object of the preposition *tree, yes. Number 2:* subject noun *fireflies, yes;* object of the preposition *sky; yes. Number 3:* subject noun *birds, yes;* object of the preposition *dogs, yes.)*

Use the same Skill Builder procedures that were taught in previous chapters to have students identify each noun as singular or plural. Ask students to tell which nouns are common and which are proper. Check the vocabulary words used for each sentence. Select the words your students may not know and do a Vocabulary Check. For each word selected, make sure it is defined, used in a new sentence, and given a synonym and/or an antonym. You might also ask for synonyms and antonyms of several words just to check students' understanding of different words.

Now that you have finished the Noun Check, the Singular/Plural Check, the Common/Proper Check, and the Vocabulary Check, continue using Sentences 1-3 to do the rest of the Skill Builders from the checklist on the next page. This checklist will always be given to you every time you do an Oral Skill Builder Check.

© SHURLEY INSTRUCTIONAL MATERIALS, INC.

CHAPTER 5 LESSON 2 CONTINUED

Teacher's Note: You will be given directions for a Skill Builder Check only with the first set of sentences in a chapter. You could do Skill Builder Checks with every set of sentences, but it is usually not necessary. Your time allotment and the needs of your students will influence your decision.

Oral Skill Builder Check	
1. Noun check. (Say the job and then say the noun. Circle each noun.) **2. Identify the nouns as singular or plural.** (Write S or P above each noun.) **3. Identify the nouns as common or proper.** (Follow established procedure for oral identification.) **4. Do a vocabulary check.** (Follow established procedure for oral identification.)	**5. Identify the complete subject and the complete predicate.** (Underline the complete subject once and the complete predicate twice.) **6. Identify the simple subject and simple predicate.** (Underline the simple subject once and the simple predicate twice. Bold, or highlight, the lines to distinguish them from the complete subject and complete predicate.)

TEACHING SCRIPT FOR ADDING THE PREPOSITION TO THE PARTS OF SPEECH

Until now, we have had only four parts of speech. Do you remember the names of the four parts of speech we have already learned? *(noun, verb, adjective,* and *adverb)* Today, we have learned about prepositions. A preposition is also a part of speech; so, we will add it to our list. We do not add the object of the preposition because it is a noun, and nouns are already on our list. Now, you know five of the eight parts of speech. What are the five parts of speech we have studied? *(noun, verb, adjective, adverb,* and *preposition)* *(Recite the five parts of speech several times. Students will learn an Eight-Parts-of-Speech Jingle after the eight parts have been introduced)*

 VOCABULARY TIME

Assign Chapter 5, Vocabulary Words **#2** on page 8 in the Reference Section for students to define in their Vocabulary notebooks. Tell students they are to use a dictionary or thesaurus to look up the meanings of the vocabulary words. After they write each word and its meaning, students are to write a sentence using the vocabulary word.

Chapter 5, Vocabulary Words #2
(cheap, costly, lethal, deadly)

(End of lesson.)

© SHURLEY INSTRUCTIONAL MATERIALS, INC.

CHAPTER 5   LESSON 3

Objectives: Jingles, Grammar (Practice Sentences, Prepositional Phrase), Practice and Improved Sentence with a Prepositional Phrase, and Activity.

JINGLE TIME

Have students turn to the Jingle Section in their books and recite the previously-taught jingles.

GRAMMAR TIME

First-Year Option: Put the Practice Sentences from the box below on the board or on notebook paper. Use these sentences as you practice the concepts that have been taught. For the greatest benefit, students must participate orally with the teacher. **Second-Year Option:** Have students classify the Practice Sentences independently on paper. Check students' sentences with the answers provided below. (*If you have the CDs for Practice Sentences, have students check their sentences with the CD.*)

Chapter 5, Practice Sentences for Lesson 3
1. _____ A big, red fire engine roared down the street exceedingly fast!
2. _____ The new sailors waited patiently for the arrival of the ship.
3. _____ An ugly storm brewed off the coast of Mississippi.

TEACHING SCRIPT FOR PRACTICING PREPOSITIONAL PHRASES

We will classify three different sentences to practice using prepositional phrases in the Question and Answer Flows. We will classify the sentences together. Begin.

Question and Answer Flow for Sentence 1: A big, red fire engine roared down the street exceedingly fast!

1. What roared down the street exceedingly fast? engine - SN
2. What is being said about engine? engine roared - V
3. Down - P
4. Down what? street - OP
5. The - A
6. Roared how? fast - Adv
7. How fast? exceedingly - Adv
8. What kind of engine? fire - Adj
9. What kind of engine? red - Adj
10. What kind of engine? big - Adj
11. A - A
12. SN V P1 Check
13. (Down the street) - Prepositional phrase
14. Exclamation point, strong feeling, exclamatory sentence
15. Go back to the verb - divide the complete subject from the complete predicate.

Classified Sentence:

	A	Adj	Adj	Adj	SN	V	P	A	OP	Adv	Adv	
SN V	A	big,	red	fire	engine	/ roared	(down	the	street)	exceedingly	fast!	**E**
P1												

CHAPTER 5 LESSON 3 CONTINUED

Question and Answer Flow for Sentence 2: The new sailors waited patiently for the arrival of the ship.

1. Who waited patiently for the arrival of the ship?
   sailors - SN
2. What is being said about sailors? sailors waited - V
3. Waited how? patiently - Adv
4. For - P
5. For what? arrival - OP
6. The - A
7. Of - P
8. Of what? ship - OP
9. The - A

10. What kind of sailors? new - Adj
11. The - A
12. SN V P1 Check
13. (For the arrival) - Prepositional phrase
14. (Of the ship) - Prepositional phrase
15. Period, statement, declarative sentence
16. Go back to the verb - divide the complete subject from the complete predicate.

Classified Sentence:

<pre>
              A Adj SN   V   Adv   P A   OP   P A   OP
SN V   The new sailors / waited patiently (for the arrival) (of the ship). D
P1
</pre>

Question and Answer Flow for Sentence 3: An ugly storm brewed off the coast of Mississippi.

1. What brewed off the coast of Mississippi?
   storm - SN
2. What is being said about storm? storm brewed - V
3. Off - P
4. Off what? coast - OP
5. The - A
6. Of - P
7. Of what? Mississippi - OP

8. What kind of storm? ugly - Adj
9. An - A
10. SN V P1 Check
11. (Off the coast) - Prepositional phrase
12. (Of Mississippi) - Prepositional phrase
13. Period, statement, declarative sentence
14. Go back to the verb - divide the complete subject from the complete predicate.

Classified Sentence:

<pre>
              A Adj SN   V   P A   OP   P   OP
SN V   An ugly storm / brewed (off the coast) (of Mississippi). D
P1
</pre>

TEACHING SCRIPT FOR A PRACTICE SENTENCE WITH A PREPOSITIONAL PHRASE

Put these labels on the board: **A Adj Adj SN V Adv P A Adj OP**

Look at the new sentence labels on the board: **A Adj Adj SN V Adv P A Adj OP**. I will guide you again through the process of writing a sentence to practice all the parts that you have learned.

Get out a sheet of notebook paper. On the top line of your notebook paper, write the title *Practice Sentence*. Copy the sentence labels from the board onto your notebook paper. Be sure to leave plenty of writing space between each label. Now, I will guide you through the process you will use whenever you write a Practice Sentence with a prepositional phrase.

© SHURLEY INSTRUCTIONAL MATERIALS, INC.

CHAPTER 5 LESSON 3 CONTINUED

1. Go to the **SN** label for the subject noun. Think of a noun that you want to use as your subject. Write the noun you have chosen on the line *under* the **SN** label.

2. Go to the **V** label for the verb. Think of a verb that tells what your subject does. Make sure that your verb makes sense with the subject noun. Write the verb you have chosen on the line *under* the **V** label.

3. Go to the **Adv** label for the adverb. Immediately go to the verb in your sentence and ask an adverb question. What are the adverb questions? (*How? When? Where?*) Choose one adverb question to ask and write your adverb answer *under* the **Adv** label.

4. Go to the **P** label for the preposition. Think of a preposition word that tells something about your verb. You must be careful to choose a preposition word that makes sense with the noun you will choose for the object of the preposition in your next step. Write the word you have chosen for a preposition *under* the **P** label.

5. Go to the **OP** label for the object of the preposition. If you like the noun you thought of while thinking of a preposition, write it down under the **OP** label. If you prefer, think of another noun by asking **what** or **whom** after your preposition. Check to make sure the preposition and object of the preposition make sense together and also make sense with the rest of the sentence. Remember, the object of the preposition will always answer the question **what** or **whom** after the preposition. Write the word you have chosen for the object of the preposition *under* the **OP** label.

6. Go to the **Adj** label for the adjective. Go to the object of the preposition that you just wrote and ask an adjective question to describe the object of the preposition noun. What are the adjective questions? (*What kind? Which one? How many?*) Choose one adjective question to ask and write your adjective answer *under* the **Adj** label next to the object of the preposition. Always check to make sure your answers are making sense in the sentence.

7. Go to the **A** label for the article adjective that is part of your prepositional phrase. What are the three article adjectives? (*a, an,* and *the*) Choose the article adjective that makes the best sense in your sentence. Write the article adjective you have chosen *under* the **A** label.

8. Go to the **Adj** label for another adjective. Go to the subject noun of your sentence and ask an adjective question. What are the adjective questions again? (*What kind? Which one? How many?*) Choose one adjective question to ask and write your adjective answer *under* the **Adj** label next to the subject noun.

9. Go to the **Adj** label for the third adjective. Go to the subject noun again and ask another adjective question. You can use the same adjective question, or you can use a different adjective question. Write another adjective *under* the third **Adj** label.

10. Go to the **A** label for the article adjective in the subject area. What are the three article adjectives again? (*a, an,* and *the*) Choose the article adjective that makes the best sense in your sentence. Write the article adjective you have chosen *under* the **A** label.

© SHURLEY INSTRUCTIONAL MATERIALS, INC.

CHAPTER 5 LESSON 3 CONTINUED

11. Finally, check your Practice Sentence to make sure it has the necessary parts to be a complete sentence. What are the five parts of a complete sentence? *(subject, verb, complete sense, capital letter, and an end mark)* Does your Practice Sentence have the five parts of a complete sentence? *(Allow time for students to read over their sentences and to make any corrections they need to make.)*

TEACHING SCRIPT FOR THE IMPROVED SENTENCE

Under your Practice Sentence, write the title *Improved Sentence* on another line. To improve your Practice Sentence, you will make two synonym changes, one antonym change, and your choice of a complete word change or another synonym or antonym change.

Since it is harder to find words that can be changed to an antonym, it is usually wise to go through your sentence to find an antonym change first. Then, look through your sentence again to find words that can be improved with synonyms. Finally, make a decision about whether your last change will be a complete word change, another synonym change, or another antonym change.

I will give you time to write your Improved Sentence. *(Always encourage students to use a thesaurus, synonym-antonym book, or a dictionary to help them develop an interesting and improved writing vocabulary. After students have finished, check and discuss students' Practice and Improved Sentences.)*

 ACTIVITY / ASSIGNMENT TIME

Divide a white poster board into four parts. *(Draw one vertical line and one horizontal line through the center of the board. They do not have to be equal parts.)* Put one of the sentences below in each of the four sections. Each sentence will be the title of that section. Using the title sentence as the core, write as many prepositional phrases as possible that will fit that sentence. Use the Preposition Flow to help you think of prepositions. Illustrate and color each section. Discuss what you liked best about your project. Show your finished project to family members, friends, and relatives.

The monkeys ran...	**The children played...**	**My sister shopped...**	**Make up your own sentence.**
1. Under the tree.	1. In the park.	1. In the mall.	
2. Around the tree.	2. On the slide.	2. For shoes.	

(End of lesson.)

© SHURLEY INSTRUCTIONAL MATERIALS, INC.

CHAPTER 5   LESSON 4

Objectives: Jingles, Study, Test, Check, Activity, and Writing (journal).

JINGLE TIME

Have students turn to the Jingle Section in their books and recite the previously-taught jingles.

STUDY TIME

Have students study the vocabulary words in their vocabulary notebooks. Remind students that any vocabulary word in their notebooks could be on their test. Also, have students study any of the skills in the Practice Section that they need to review.

TEST TIME

Have students turn to page 100 in the Test Section of their book and find Chapter 5 Test. Go over the directions to make sure they understand what to do. (*Chapter 5 Test key is on the next page.*)

CHECK TIME

After students have finished, check and discuss their test papers. Make sure they understand why their answers are right or wrong. (*For total points, count each required answer as a point.*)

ACTIVITY / ASSIGNMENT TIME

(Have a recipe box and a package of lined index cards ready for your children to use for this activity.) Find a map of the United States. Draw or trace the state of Arizona on the blank side of an index card. On the lined side of the card, write the following questions and answers.

1. What is the state on the front of this card? **Arizona**
2. What is the capital of Arizona? **Phoenix**
3. What is the postal abbreviation of Arizona? **AZ**
4. What year was Arizona admitted to the Union? **1912**

Color this state. Look up an interesting fact about this state and write it on your card. Use the card to quiz family members, friends, and relatives. You may want to time the responses to your questions. Scatter your cards and see how long it takes you to put them in alphabetical order. For a higher level of difficulty, see if you can alphabetize your cards only by the picture of each state.

(End of lesson.)

© SHURLEY INSTRUCTIONAL MATERIALS, INC.

Chapter 5 Test
(Student Page 100)

Exercise 1: Classify each sentence.

                        SN   V   Adv   P   OP   P A Adj   OP   Adv
1. **SN V**   <u>Martha / sang beautifully (in front) (of a large audience) yesterday</u>. **D**
   P1

                        A Adj SN   V   Adv   P A   OP   P   A   OP
2. **SN V**   The lively ponies / ran gracefully (through the field) (toward the barn). **D**
   P1

                        A Adj SN   V   Adv   P A Adj   OP   P   A   Adj   OP
3. **SN V**   An old man / sat peacefully (on the park bench) (during the early morning). **D**
   P1

Exercise 2: Use Sentence 1 to underline the complete subject once and the complete predicate twice and to complete the table below.

List the Noun Used	List the Noun Job	Singular or Plural	Common or Proper	Simple Subject	Simple Predicate
1. **Martha**	2. **SN**	3. **S**	4. **P**	5. **Martha**	6. **sang**
7. **front**	8. **OP**	9. **S**	10. **C**		
11. **audience**	12. **OP**	13. **S**	14. **C**		

Exercise 3: Name the five parts of speech that you have studied. (*You may use abbreviations.*) **(The order may vary.)**

1. **Noun**	2. **Verb**	3. **Adjective**	4. **Adverb**	5. **Preposition**

Exercise 4: Identify each pair of words as synonyms or antonyms by putting parentheses ( ) around *syn* or *ant*.

1. attempt, try	**(syn)** ant	5. interest, curiosity	**(syn)** ant	9. amiable, friendly	**(syn)** ant
2. tasty, bland	syn **(ant)**	6. doubtful, certain	syn **(ant)**	10. pillar, column	**(syn)** ant
3. watch, vigil	**(syn)** ant	7. deadly, lethal	**(syn)** ant	11. flabby, firm	syn **(ant)**
4. sever, cut	**(syn)** ant	8. cheap, costly	syn **(ant)**	12. eager, indifferent	syn **(ant)**

Exercise 5: Match the definitions. Write the correct letter beside each numbered concept.

F	1. joins a noun or a pronoun to the rest of the sentence	A.	verb, adjective, or adverb
E	2. makes a statement	B.	object of the preposition
I	3. adjective modifies	C.	person, place, or thing
B	4. noun or pronoun after a preposition	D.	imperative sentence
H	5. subject questions	E.	declarative sentence
G	6. article adjectives can be called	F.	preposition
D	7. makes a request or gives a command	G.	noun markers
C	8. noun	H.	who or what
J	9. tells what the subject does	I.	noun or pronoun
A	10. adverb modifies	J.	verb

Exercise 6: On notebook paper, write as many prepositions as you can. **(Check prepositions with the Preposition Flow Jingle.)**

Exercise 7: In your journal, write a paragraph summarizing what you have learned this week.

© SHURLEY INSTRUCTIONAL MATERIALS, INC.

CHAPTER 5 LESSON 4 CONTINUED

TEACHER INSTRUCTIONS

Use the Question and Answer Flows below for the sentences on the Chapter 5 Test.

Question and Answer Flow for Sentence 1: Martha sang beautifully in front of a large audience yesterday.

1. Who sang beautifully in front of a large audience yesterday? Martha - SN
2. What is being said about Martha? Martha sang - V
3. Sang how? beautifully - Adv
4. In - P
5. In what? front - OP
6. Of - P
7. Of what? audience - OP
8. What kind of audience? large - Adj
9. A - A
10. Sang when? yesterday - Adv
11. SN V P1 Check
12. (In front) - Prepositional phrase
13. (Of a large audience) - Prepositional phrase
14. Period, statement, declarative sentence
15. Go back to the verb - divide the complete subject from the complete predicate.

Classified Sentence:

	SN	V	Adv	P	OP	P	A	Adj	OP	Adv
SN V	Martha / sang beautifully (in front) (of a large audience) yesterday. D
P1										

Question and Answer Flow for Sentence 2: The lively ponies ran gracefully through the field toward the barn.

1. What ran gracefully through the field toward the barn? ponies - SN
2. What is being said about ponies? ponies ran - V
3. Ran how? gracefully - Adv
4. Through - P
5. Through what? field - OP
6. The - A
7. Toward - P
8. Toward what? barn - OP
9. The - A
10. What kind of ponies? lively - Adj
11. The - A
12. SN V P1 Check
13. (Through the field) - Prepositional phrase
14. (Toward the barn) - Prepositional phrase
15. Period, statement, declarative sentence
16. Go back to the verb - divide the complete subject from the complete predicate.

Classified Sentence:

	A	Adj	SN	V	Adv	P	A	OP	P	A	OP
SN V	The lively ponies / ran gracefully (through the field) (toward the barn). D
P1											

Question and Answer Flow for Sentence 3: An old man sat peacefully on the park bench during the early morning.

1. Who sat peacefully on the park bench during the early morning? man - SN
2. What is being said about man? man sat - V
3. Sat how? peacefully - Adv
4. On - P
5. On what? bench - OP
6. What kind of bench? park - Adj
7. The - A
8. During - P
9. During what? morning - OP
10. What kind of morning? early - Adj
11. The - A
12. What kind of man? old - Adj
13. An - A
14. SN V P1 Check
15. (On the park bench) - Prepositional phrase
16. (During the early morning) - Prepositional phrase
17. Period, statement, declarative sentence
18. Go back to the verb - divide the complete subject from the complete predicate.

Classified Sentence:

	A	Adj	SN	V	Adv	P	A	Adj	OP	P	A	Adj	OP
SN V	An old man / sat peacefully (on the park bench) (during the early morning). D
P1													

© SHURLEY INSTRUCTIONAL MATERIALS, INC.

CHAPTER 5   LESSON 5

Objectives: Writing assignment #2, Bonus Option.

 WRITING TIME

TEACHING SCRIPT FOR USING THE WRITING PROCESS FOR WRITING ASSIGNMENTS

Give Writing Assignment #2 from the box below. As you begin this writing assignment, you will use the writing process again. First, you will think about your topic and gather any information you might need in order to do the writing. Second, you will write a rough draft. Remember, it is called a rough draft because it will be revised and edited. You do not have to worry about mistakes as you write your rough draft. After you write the first draft, you will make revisions, using the Revision Checklist in Reference 13. After you revise your writing, you will edit, using the Beginning Editing Checklist in Reference 13. Finally, after you are satisfied with your revising and editing, you will write a final paper, using the Final Paper Checklist in Reference 13. You will then give the finished writing assignment to me. (*Students should finish their writing during their free time if they do not finish during this lesson.*)

Writing Assignment Box

Writing Assignment #2: Two-Point Expository Paragraph

Writing topic choices: Why Trees Are Important or **My Favorite Adult** or **My Favorite Game**

Bonus Option: To solve the puzzle for Psalm 145:8, cross out every third letter to read the message.

**THXELFORUDIKSGSRAFCIEOUDSAWNDUF
UWLLMOFACOIMPWASKSIQONZSLLOWRT
OAANEGEKRAWNDMOFYGRWEAQTMMERZCYB**

Have students design their own puzzles and share them with other family members and friends.

TEACHER INSTRUCTIONS FOR CHECKING WRITING ASSIGNMENT #2

Read, check, and discuss Writing Assignment #2 after students have finished their final papers. Use the editing checklist (*Reference 13 on teacher's page 48*) as you check and discuss students' papers. Make sure students are using the editing checklist correctly. In the beginning, you must also check students' papers carefully for <u>form</u> mistakes. This will ensure that students are learning the two-point format correctly.

Bonus Option Answer: *The Lord is gracious, and full of compassion; slow to anger, and of great mercy.* **(King James Version)**

(End of lesson.)

© SHURLEY INSTRUCTIONAL MATERIALS, INC.

CHAPTER 6   LESSON 1

Objectives: Jingles, Grammar (Practice Sentences, Prepositional Phrase), Oral Skill Builder, Skill (Subject/Verb Agreement), Practice Exercise, and Vocabulary #1.

JINGLE TIME

Have students turn to the Jingle Section in their books and recite the previously-taught jingles.

GRAMMAR TIME

First-Year Option: Put the Practice Sentences from the box below on the board or on notebook paper. Use these sentences as you practice the concepts that have been taught. For the greatest benefit, students must participate orally with the teacher. **Second-Year Option:** Have students classify the Practice Sentences independently on paper. Check students' sentences with the answers provided below. (*If you have the CDs for Practice Sentences, have students check their sentences with the CDs.*)

Chapter 6, Practice Sentences for Lesson 1
1. _____ An enormous crowd gathered eagerly for the race of the century.
2. _____ Matthew left on an exciting cruise to several countries today.
3. _____ Mother searched diligently for a simple recipe.

TEACHING SCRIPT FOR PRACTICING PREPOSITIONAL PHRASES

We will classify three different sentences to practice using prepositional phrases in the Question and Answer Flows. We will classify the sentences together. Begin.

Question and Answer Flow for Sentence 1: An enormous crowd gathered eagerly for the race of the century.

1. Who gathered eagerly for the race of the century?
   crowd - SN
2. What is being said about crowd?
   crowd gathered - V
3. Gathered how? eagerly - Adv
4. For - P
5. For what? race - OP
6. The - A
7. Of - P
8. Of what? century - OP
9. The - A
10. What kind of crowd? enormous - Adj
11. An - A
12. SN V P1 Check
13. (For the race) - Prepositional phrase
14. (Of the century) - Prepositional phrase
15. Period, statement, declarative sentence
16. Go back to the verb - divide the complete subject from the complete predicate.

Classified Sentence:

```
                        A    Adj   SN      V      Adv    P  A  OP    P  A   OP
         SN  V      An enormous crowd / gathered eagerly (for the race) (of the century).  D
         ‾‾‾‾‾
          P1
```

CHAPTER 6 LESSON 1 CONTINUED

Question and Answer Flow for Sentence 2: Matthew left on an exciting cruise to several countries today.

1. Who left on an exciting cruise to several countries today?
   Matthew - SN
2. What is being said about Matthew? Matthew left - V
3. On - P
4. On what? cruise - OP
5. What kind of cruise? exciting - Adj
6. An - A
7. To - P
8. To what? countries - OP

9. How many countries? several - Adj
10. Left when? today - Adv
11. SN V P1 Check
12. (On an exciting cruise) - Prepositional phrase
13. (To several countries) - Prepositional phrase
14. Period, statement, declarative sentence
15. Go back to the verb - divide the complete subject from the complete predicate.

Classified Sentence:

                    SN   V   P A Adj   OP   P Adj   OP   Adv

    SN V   Matthew / left (on an exciting cruise) (to several countries) today. **D**
    —————
    P1

Question and Answer Flow for Sentence 3: Mother searched diligently for a simple recipe.

1. Who searched diligently for a simple recipe?
   Mother - SN
2. What is being said about Mother?
   Mother searched - V
3. Searched how? diligently - Adv
4. For - P
5. For what? recipe - OP

6. What kind of recipe? simple - Adj
7. A - A
8. SN V P1 Check
9. Period, statement, declarative sentence
10. Go back to the verb - divide the complete subject from the complete predicate.

Classified Sentence:

                    SN   V   Adv   P A Adj OP

    SN V   Mother / searched diligently (for a simple recipe). **D**
    —————
    P1

Use Sentences 1-3 that you just classified with your students to do an Oral Skill Builder Check. Use the guidelines below.

Oral Skill Builder Check

1. **Noun check.**
   (Say the job and then say the noun. Circle each noun.)
2. **Identify the nouns as singular or plural.**
   (Write S or P above each noun.)
3. **Identify the nouns as common or proper.**
   (Follow established procedure for oral identification.)
4. **Do a vocabulary check.**
   (Follow established procedure for oral identification.)

5. **Identify the complete subject and the complete predicate.** (Underline the complete subject once and the complete predicate twice.)
6. **Identify the simple subject and simple predicate.**
   (Underline the simple subject once and the simple predicate twice. Bold, or highlight, the lines to distinguish them from the complete subject and complete predicate.)

© SHURLEY INSTRUCTIONAL MATERIALS, INC.

CHAPTER 6 LESSON 1 CONTINUED

SKILL TIME

TEACHING SCRIPT FOR SUBJECT/VERB AGREEMENT

A sentence must have correct subject-verb agreement. The word **agreement** means to work together; therefore, subject-verb agreement means the special way in which the subject and verb work together to make the sentence correct.

We will use the following sentence to demonstrate the subject-verb agreement concept: **The young soldier marched in a straight line.** *(Put the demonstration sentence on the board.)* Whenever you work with subject-verb agreement, you must remember to work only with the subject and verb. Therefore, you must isolate the subject and verb before you begin. What are the subject and verb in the demonstration sentence? *(soldier marched)*

I will write the subject and verb *soldier marched* on a different section of the board so we can concentrate on what we need to do for subject-verb agreement. *(Write "soldier marched" on a clean area of the board so you will have room to work without other sentences distracting students.)*

You only worry about subject-verb agreement with present tense verbs. When a verb is past tense or ends with -ed, it doesn't matter if the subject is singular or plural; the verb remains the same: past tense.

Example: Soldier marched.   Soldiers marched.

The example clearly demonstrates that we must change a past tense verb to present tense in order to work with singular and plural forms. How do we change *marched* to present tense? *(Take off the -ed.)* Now that *march* is in present tense, we must check whether it agrees with its subject. If the subject is singular, we must use a singular verb form. If the subject is plural, we must use a plural verb form.

Is the subject *soldier* singular or plural? *(singular)* Since the subject *soldier* is singular, we must choose the singular form of the verb *march*. How do we make a verb singular? *(Add an **s** or **es** to the plain form to make the word **marches**.)*

Since we have checked to make sure the subject and verb are both singular, we know the subject agrees with the verb. Let's say both singular forms together so we can hear the singular combination as we say them. *(Have students say "soldier marches" several times to hear the subject-verb agreement forms.)*

Now, we will form the plural forms of the subject and verb. Since the subject *soldier* is singular, how do we make it plural? *(Add an **s** to make the word **soldiers**.)* We must also change the verb to a plural form. The plural form of a present tense verb is called the <u>plain form</u> because it does not end in *s* or *es*.

How would we write the plural form of the verb *marches*? *(march)* The verb *march* is plural because it does not end in *s* or *es*. Since we have changed both the subject and verb to plural forms, we know the subject agrees with the verb. Let's say both plural forms together so we can hear the plural combinations as we say them. *(Have students say "soldiers march" several times to hear the subject-verb agreement forms.)*

© SHURLEY INSTRUCTIONAL MATERIALS, INC.

CHAPTER 6 LESSON 1 CONTINUED

Sometimes, a word does not follow the regular rules because of spelling form. These are called exceptions. One such exception is the word *woman*. In the sentence, *Woman laughed*, what are the subject and verb? (*woman laughed*) What is the present tense of the verb *laughed*? (*laugh*) Is the subject *woman* singular or plural? (*singular*) Since the subject is singular, we must use the singular verb form. How do we make the verb *laugh* singular? (*Add an* **s** *or* **es** *to the plain form to make the word* **laughs**.)

Since our subject and verb are both singular, we know the subject agrees with the verb. Let's say both singular forms together so we can hear the singular combination as we say them. (*Have students say "woman laughs" several times to hear the subject-verb agreement forms.*)

Now, we will form the plural forms of the subject and verb. Since the subject *woman* is singular, how do we make it plural? This is one of the exceptions. Some words are made plural by changing the spelling form, not by adding an "s" or "es". To make *woman* plural, we must make a spelling change to make the plural word *women*. We must also change the verb to a plural form.

Remember, the plural form of a present tense verb is called the plain form because it does not end in *s* or *es*. What is the plural form of the verb *laughs*? (*laugh*) The verb *laugh* is plural because it does not end in *s* or *es*. Since we have changed both the subject and verb to plural forms, we know the subject agrees with the verb. Let's say both plural forms together so we can hear the plural combination as we say them. (*Have students say "women laugh" several times to hear the subject-verb agreement forms.*)

We will now discuss a set of rules that will also help you make the right subject-verb agreement choice with different kinds of verbs. Look at Reference 21 on page 20 in the Reference Section of your book. Rule 1 says that if you have a singular subject, you must use a singular verb form that ends in *s*: **is, was, has, does, or verbs ending with s or** *es*. Notice that singular verb forms end in *s*. The "s" stands for singular verb forms. Remember, a singular subject agrees with a singular verb form that ends in *s or es*.

Reference 21: Subject-Verb Agreement Rules			
Rule 1: A singular subject must use a singular verb form that ends in **s**: *is, was, has, does, or verbs ending with* **es**.			
Rule 2: A plural subject, a compound subject, or the subject **YOU** must use a plural verb form that has **no s** ending: *are, were, do, have, or verbs without* **s** *or* **es** *endings.* (A plural verb form is also called the *plain form*.)			
Examples: For each sentence, do these four things: (1) Write the subject. (2) Write S if the subject is singular or P if the subject is plural. (3) Write the rule number. (4) Underline the correct verb in the sentence.			
Subject	**S or P**	**Rule**	
clock	S	1	1. The cuckoo **clock** (**chimes**, chime) on the hour.
rosebush and lilacs	P	2	2. The **rosebush** and the **lilacs** (**were**, was) blooming beautifully.
You	P	2	3. **You** (waits, **wait**) until we have gone.

Rule 2 says that if you have a plural subject, a compound subject, or the subject *YOU*, you must use these verbs: **are, were, have, do, or verbs without** *s* **or** *es* **endings** because these verbs are plural verb forms. Any time the pronoun YOU is the subject of a sentence, you do not have to decide whether it is singular or plural. The subject pronoun YOU always uses a plural verb, and you MUST choose a plural verb form. Remember, a plural subject agrees with a plural verb form that does not end in *s or es*.

© SHURLEY INSTRUCTIONAL MATERIALS, INC.

CHAPTER 6 LESSON 1 CONTINUED

Look at the examples under the rules. The directions say you must write the subject, then write S if the subject is singular or write P if the subject is plural. You must also write the rule number (Rule 1 or 2) from the rule box and then underline the correct verb in the sentence. What is the subject in Sentence 1? (*clock*) Is the subject *clock* singular or plural? (*singular*)

Since the subject is singular, you will go to the rule box and find the rule that tells you which verb to choose if you have a singular subject. Which rule do we put in the blank? (*Rule 1*) Notice that a number 1 has been written in the blank for Rule 1. Using the list of singular verbs in Rule 1, which verb would we choose to agree with the singular subject *clock*? (*chimes, the verb with the s or es ending*) The verb *chimes* has been underlined as the correct verb choice.

What is the subject in Sentence 2? (rosebush and lilacs) Is the subject *rosebush* and *lilacs* singular or plural? (*Plural - because it is compound*) Since the subject is plural, you will go to the rule box and find the rule that tells you which verb to choose if you have a plural subject. Which rule do we put in the blank? (*Rule 2*) A number 2 has been written in the blank for Rule 2. Using the list of plural verbs in Rule 2, which verb would we choose to agree with the plural subject *rosebush* and *lilacs*? (*were*) The verb *were* has been underlined as the correct verb choice.

What is the subject in Sentence 3? (*You*) Is the subject *you* singular or plural? (*Plural*) Since the subject is plural, you will go to the rule box and find the rule that tells you which verb to choose if you have a plural subject. Which rule do we put in the blank? (*Rule 2*) A number 2 has been written in the blank for Rule 2. Using the list of plural verbs in Rule 2, which verb would we choose to agree with the plural subject *you*? (*wait*) The verb *wait* has been underlined as the correct verb choice.

Choosing verbs to agree with the subjects in the sentences on your test will be easy if you follow the rules you have just learned. Remember, first you must decide if the subject of the sentence is singular or plural. Next, you must look at the verb choices in parentheses in the sentence. Last, you must choose the verb that is listed under the singular or plural rule in the box. (*Discuss the subject I as an exception. The subject I takes a plural verb form. Examples: I have, I want, I walk, I talk, etc.*)

Teacher's Note: The singular subject I and the verb **be** present a special case of subject-verb agreement. Use the following examples to demonstrate the verb forms used with the pronoun I.
Examples: I am. I was. I have. I walk. I talk.

 **PRACTICE TIME**

Have students turn to page 67 in the Practice Section of their book and find Chapter 6, Lesson 1, Practice. Go over the directions to make sure they understand what to do. Check and discuss the Practice after students have finished. (*Chapter 6, Lesson 1, Practice key is given on the next page.*)

© SHURLEY INSTRUCTIONAL MATERIALS, INC.

CHAPTER 6 LESSON 1 CONTINUED

Chapter 6, Lesson 1, Practice: For each sentence, do these four things: (1) Write the subject. (2) Write S if the subject is singular or P if the subject is plural. (3) Write the rule number. (4) Underline the correct verb in the sentence.

Rule 1: A singular subject must use a singular verb form that ends in **s**: *is, was, has, does, or verbs ending with* **es.**

Rule 2: A plural subject, a compound subject, or the subject **YOU** must use a plural verb form that has **no s** ending: *are, were, do, have, or verbs without* **s** *or* **es** *endings.* (A plural verb form is also called the *plain form.*)

Subject	S or P	Rule	
peasants	P	2	1. The **peasants** (carries, <u>carry</u>) bags of coffee beans.
Katie and Julia	P	2	2. **Katie** and **Julia** (lives, <u>live</u>) in Peoria now.
ground	S	1	3. During the earthquake, the **ground** (<u>rumbles</u>, rumble).
She	S	1	4. **She** (believe, <u>believes</u>) in miracles.
You	P	2	5. **You** (needs, <u>need</u>) to ask for her permission.
turtles	P	2	6. Two **turtles** (<u>stick</u>, sticks) their heads out of the water.
He	S	1	7. **He** (<u>reads</u>, read) two books every night.
dogs	P	2	8. The **dogs** (chases, <u>chase</u>) the raccoons through the woods.
James and Lisa	P	2	9. **James** and **Lisa** (takes, <u>take</u>) turns on the playground.
Jacob	S	1	10. **Jacob** quickly (scribble, <u>scribbles</u>) notes onto scrap paper.
ducks	P	2	11. The **ducks** (<u>swim</u>, swims) to the other side of the pond.
children	P	2	12. Several **children** (<u>bounce</u>, bounces) happily on the trampoline.

VOCABULARY TIME

Assign Chapter 6, Vocabulary Words #1 on page 8 in the Reference Section for students to define in their Vocabulary notebooks. Tell students they are to use a dictionary or thesaurus to look up the meanings of the vocabulary words. After they write each word and its meaning, students are to write a sentence using the vocabulary word.

Chapter 6, Vocabulary Words #1
(explode, burst, present, absent)

(End of lesson.)

© SHURLEY INSTRUCTIONAL MATERIALS, INC.

CHAPTER 6   LESSON 2

Objectives: Jingles, Grammar (Practice Sentences, Prepositional Phrases, Practice and Improved Sentence with Prepositional Phrases), Practice Exercise, Activity, and Vocabulary #2.

 **JINGLE TIME**

Have students turn to the Jingle Section in their books and recite the previously-taught jingles.

 GRAMMAR TIME

First-Year Option: Put the Practice Sentences from the box below on the board or on notebook paper. Use these sentences as you practice the concepts that have been taught. For the greatest benefit, students must participate orally with the teacher. **Second-Year Option:** Have students classify the Practice Sentences independently on paper. Check students' sentences with the answers provided below. (*If you have the CDs for Practice Sentences, have students check their sentences with the CDs.*)

Chapter 6, Practice Sentences for Lesson 2
1. _____ The emperor of China spoke excitedly to the strangers from Europe.
2. _____ The children on shore waved at the marine biologist in the boat.
3. _____ The children ran eagerly to the bus in the parking lot.

TEACHING SCRIPT FOR PRACTICING PREPOSITIONAL PHRASES

We will classify three different sentences to practice using prepositional phrases in the Question and Answer Flows. We will classify the sentences together. Begin.

Question and Answer Flow for Sentence 1: The emperor of China spoke excitedly to the strangers from Europe.

1. Who spoke excitedly to the strangers from Europe? emperor - SN
2. What is being said about emperor? emperor spoke - V
3. Spoke how? excitedly - Adv
4. To - P
5. To whom? strangers - OP
6. The - A
7. From - P
8. From what? Europe - OP
9. Of - P
10. Of what? China - OP
11. The - A
12. SN V P1 Check
13. (Of China) - Prepositional phrase
14. (To the strangers) - Prepositional phrase
15. (From Europe) - Prepositional phrase
16. Period, statement, declarative sentence
17. Go back to the verb - divide the complete subject from the complete predicate.

Classified Sentence:

	A	SN	P	OP	V	Adv	P	A	OP	P	OP
SN V	The	emperor	(of	China) /	spoke	excitedly	(to	the	strangers)	(from	Europe). D
P1											

CHAPTER 6 LESSON 2 CONTINUED

Question and Answer Flow for Sentence 2: The children on shore waved at the marine biologist in the boat.

1. Who waved at the marine biologist in the boat?
   children - SN
2. What is being said about children? children waved - V
3. At - P
4. At whom? biologist - OP
5. What kind of biologist? marine - Adj
6. The - A
7. In - P
8. In what? boat - OP
9. The - A
10. On - P
11. On what? shore - OP
12. The - A
13. SN V P1 Check
14. (On shore) - Prepositional phrase
15. (At the marine biologist) - Prepositional phrase
16. (In the boat) - Prepositional phrase
17. Period, statement, declarative sentence
18. Go back to the verb - divide the complete subject from the complete predicate.

Classified Sentence:

	A	SN	P	OP	V	P	A	Adj	OP	P	A	OP
SN V P1	The children (on shore) / waved (at the marine biologist) (in the boat). **D**											

Question and Answer Flow for Sentence 3: The children ran eagerly to the bus in the parking lot.

1. Who ran eagerly to the bus in the parking lot?
   children - SN
2. What is being said about children? children ran - V
3. Ran how? eagerly - Adv
4. To - P
5. To what? bus - OP
6. The - A
7. In - P
8. In what? lot - OP
9. What kind of lot? parking - Adj
10. The - A
11. The - A
12. SN V P1 Check
13. (To the bus) - Prepositional phrase
14. (In the parking lot) - Prepositional phrase
15. Period, statement, declarative sentence
16. Go back to the verb - divide the complete subject from the complete predicate.

Classified Sentence:

	A	SN	V	Adv	P	A	OP	P	A	Adj	OP
SN V P1	The children / ran eagerly (to the bus) (in the parking lot). **D**										

TEACHING SCRIPT FOR A PRACTICE SENTENCE WITH PREPOSITIONAL PHRASES

Put these labels on the board: **A Adj Adj SN V Adv P A Adj OP**

Look at the new sentence labels on the board: **A Adj Adj SN V Adv P A Adj OP**. I will guide you again through the process of writing a sentence to practice all the parts that you have learned.

Get out a sheet of notebook paper. On the top line of your notebook paper, write the title *Practice Sentence*. Copy the sentence labels from the board onto your notebook paper. Be sure to leave plenty of writing space between each label. Now, I will guide you through the process you will use whenever you write a Practice Sentence with a prepositional phrase.

1. Go to the **SN** label for the subject noun. Think of a noun that you want to use as your subject. Write the noun you have chosen on the line *under* the **SN** label.

© SHURLEY INSTRUCTIONAL MATERIALS, INC.

CHAPTER 6 LESSON 2 CONTINUED

2. Go to the **V** label for the verb. Think of a verb that tells what your subject does. Make sure that your verb makes sense with the subject noun. Write the verb you have chosen on the line *under* the **V** label.

3. Go to the **Adv** label for the adverb. Immediately go to the verb in your sentence and ask an adverb question. What are the adverb questions? (*How? When? Where?*) Choose one adverb question to ask and write your adverb answer *under* the **Adv** label.

4. Go to the **P** label for the preposition. Think of a preposition word that tells something about your verb. You must be careful to choose a preposition word that makes sense with the noun you will choose for the object of the preposition in your next step. Write the word you have chosen for a preposition *under* the **P** label.

5. Go to the **OP** label for the object of the preposition. If you like the noun you thought of while thinking of a preposition, write it down under the **OP** label. If you prefer, think of another noun by asking **what** or **whom** after your preposition. Check to make sure the preposition and object of the preposition make sense together and also make sense with the rest of the sentence. Remember, the object of the preposition will always answer the question **what** or **whom** after the preposition. Write the word you have chosen for the object of the preposition *under* the **OP** label.

6. Go to the **Adj** label for the adjective. Go to the object of the preposition that you just wrote and ask an adjective question to describe the object of the preposition noun. What are the adjective questions? (*What kind? Which one? How many?*) Choose one adjective question to ask and write your adjective answer *under* the **Adj** label next to the object of the preposition. Always check to make sure your answers are making sense in the sentence.

7. Go to the **A** label for the article adjective that is part of your prepositional phrase. What are the three article adjectives? (*a, an,* and *the*) Choose the article adjective that makes the best sense in your sentence. Write the article adjective you have chosen *under* the **A** label.

8. Go to the **Adj** label for another adjective. Go to the subject noun of your sentence and ask an adjective question. What are the adjective questions again? (*What kind? Which one? How many?*) Choose one adjective question to ask and write your adjective answer *under* the **Adj** label next to the subject noun.

9. Go to the **Adj** label for the third adjective. Go to the subject noun again and ask another adjective question. You can use the same adjective question, or you can use a different adjective question. Write another adjective *under* the third **Adj** label.

10. Go to the **A** label for the article adjective in the subject area. What are the three article adjectives again? (*a, an,* and *the*) Choose the article adjective that makes the best sense in your sentence. Write the article adjective you have chosen *under* the **A** label.

11. Finally, check your Practice Sentence to make sure it has the necessary parts to be a complete sentence. What are the five parts of a complete sentence? (*subject, verb, complete sense, capital letter, and an end mark*) Does your Practice Sentence have the five parts of a complete sentence? (*Allow time for students to read over their sentences and to make any corrections they need to make.*)

© SHURLEY INSTRUCTIONAL MATERIALS, INC.

CHAPTER 6 LESSON 2 CONTINUED

TEACHING SCRIPT FOR THE IMPROVED SENTENCE

Under your Practice Sentence, write the title *Improved Sentence* on another line. To improve your Practice Sentence, you will make two synonym changes, one antonym change, and your choice of a complete word change or another synonym or antonym change.

Since it is harder to find words that can be changed to an antonym, it is usually wise to go through your sentence to find an antonym change first. Then, look through your sentence again to find words that can be improved with synonyms. Finally, make a decision about whether your last change will be a complete word change, another synonym change, or another antonym change.

I will give you time to write your Improved Sentence. (*Always encourage students to use a thesaurus, synonym-antonym book, or a dictionary to help them develop an interesting and improved writing vocabulary. After students have finished, check and discuss students' Practice and Improved Sentences.*)

 PRACTICE TIME

Have students turn to page 68 in the Practice Section of their book and find Chapter 6, Lesson 2, Practice. Go over the directions to make sure they understand what to do. Check and discuss the Practice after students have finished. (*Chapter 6, Lesson 2, Practice key is given below.*)

Chapter 6, Lesson 2, Practice: For each sentence, do these four things: (1) Write the subject. (2) Write S if the subject is singular or P if the subject is plural. (3) Write the rule number. (4) Underline the correct verb in the sentence.

Rule 1: A singular subject must use a singular verb form that ends in **s**: *is, was, has, does, or verbs ending with* **es**.

Rule 2: A plural subject, a compound subject, or the subject **YOU** must use a plural verb form that has **no s** ending: *are, were, do, have, or verbs without* **s** *or* **es** *endings.* (A plural verb form is also called the *plain form*.)

Subject	S or P	Rule	
gnats	P	2	1. The **gnats** (swarms, <u>swarm</u>) our picnic table.
Brian and Chris	P	2	2. **Brian** and **Chris** (hikes, <u>hike</u>) up the mountainside.
rainbow	S	1	3. The **rainbow** (<u>arches</u>, arch) over the treetops.
sister	S	1	4. My **sister** (fold, <u>folds</u>) the laundry.
You	P	2	5. **You** (watches, <u>watch</u>) your baby sister.
They	P	2	6. **They** (takes, <u>take</u>) pictures at the Christmas party.
car	S	1	7. The new sports **car** (race, <u>races</u>) quickly down the highway.
boxes	P	2	8. The **boxes** (collapses, <u>collapse</u>) under the heavy weight.
He	S	1	9. **He** (<u>passes</u>, pass) the football down the field.
Jenny	S	1	10. **Jenny** (<u>begs</u>, beg) her father for permission.

© SHURLEY INSTRUCTIONAL MATERIALS, INC.

CHAPTER 6 LESSON 2 CONTINUED

VOCABULARY TIME

Assign Chapter 6, Vocabulary Words **#2** on page 8 in the Reference Section for students to define in their Vocabulary notebooks. Tell students they are to use a dictionary or thesaurus to look up the meanings of the vocabulary words. After they write each word and its meaning, students are to write a sentence using the vocabulary word.

Chapter 6, Vocabulary Words #2
(send, receive, fowl, chicken)

ACTIVITY / ASSIGNMENT TIME

Make a list of seven different animals. Write the name of each animal on an index card. On the back of each index card, write descriptive sentences about the animal listed on the front. Be sure to include as many adjectives and adverbs as possible. Finally, play a guessing game with different members of your family. Read aloud or hold up the side of the card with the description and let family members guess which animal's name is written on the other side. Discuss which animals were the hardest and easiest to guess. Also, discuss which animals were the hardest and easiest to describe.

(End of lesson.)

© SHURLEY INSTRUCTIONAL MATERIALS, INC.

CHAPTER 6   LESSON 3
Objectives: Jingles, Grammar (Practice Sentences, Prepositional Phrases), Practice Exercise, and Activity.

 **JINGLE TIME**

Have students turn to the Jingle Section in their books and recite the previously-taught jingles.

 GRAMMAR TIME

First-Year Option: Put the Practice Sentences from the box below on the board or on notebook paper. Use these sentences as you practice the concepts that have been taught. For the greatest benefit, students must participate orally with the teacher. **Second-Year Option:** Have students classify the Practice Sentences independently on paper. Check students' sentences with the answers provided below. *(If you have the CDs for Practice Sentences, have students check their sentences with the CDs.)*

Chapter 6, Practice Sentences for Lesson 3
1. _____ The wealthy man spoke passionately yesterday about the new library.
2. _____ The little red fox hid shyly behind the bushes.
3. _____ The teacher looked longingly at the new computer in the store.

TEACHING SCRIPT FOR PRACTICING PREPOSITIONAL PHRASES

We will classify three different sentences to practice using prepositional phrases in the Question and Answer Flows. We will classify the sentences together. Begin.

Question and Answer Flow for Sentence 1: The wealthy man spoke passionately yesterday about the new library.	
1. Who spoke passionately yesterday about the new library? man - SN	8. The - A
	9. What kind of man? wealthy - Adj
2. What is being said about man? man spoke - V	10. The - A
	11. SN V P1 Check
3. Spoke how? passionately - Adv	12. (About the new library) - Prepositional phrase
4. Spoke when? yesterday - Adv	13. Period, statement, declarative sentence
5. About - P	14. Go back to the verb - divide the complete subject
6. About what? library - OP	from the complete predicate.
7. What kind of library? new - Adj	

Classified Sentence:

                              A   Adj   SN   V   Adv   Adv   P   A   Adj OP

            SN V   The wealthy man / spoke passionately yesterday (about the new library). **D**
            ‾‾‾‾‾
              P1

© SHURLEY INSTRUCTIONAL MATERIALS, INC.

CHAPTER 6 LESSON 3 CONTINUED

Question and Answer Flow for Sentence 2: The little red fox hid shyly behind the bushes.

1. What hid shyly behind the bushes? fox - SN
2. What is being said about fox? fox hid - V
3. Hid how? shyly - Adv
4. Behind - P
5. Behind what? bushes - OP
6. The - A
7. What kind of fox? red - Adj

8. What kind of fox? little - Adj
9. The - A
10. SN V P1 Check
11. (Behind the bushes) - Prepositional phrase
12. Period, statement, declarative sentence
13. Go back to the verb - divide the complete subject from the complete predicate.

Classified Sentence:

	A	Adj	Adj	SN	V	Adv	P	A	OP
SN V	The	little	red	fox /	hid	shyly	(behind	the	bushes). D
P1									

Question and Answer Flow for Sentence 3: The teacher looked longingly at the new computer in the store.

1. Who looked longingly at the new computer in the store? teacher - SN
2. What is being said about teacher? teacher looked - V
3. Looked how? longingly - Adv
4. At - P
5. At what? computer - OP
6. What kind of computer? new - Adj
7. The - A
8. In - P

9. In what? store - OP
10. The - A
11. The - A
12. SN V P1 Check
13. (At the new computer) - Prepositional phrase
14. (In the store) - Prepositional phrase
15. Period, statement, declarative sentence
16. Go back to the verb - divide the complete subject from the complete predicate.

Classified Sentence:

	A	SN	V	Adv	P	A	Adj	OP	P	A	OP
SN V	The	teacher /	looked	longingly	(at	the	new	computer)	(in	the	store). D
P1											

PRACTICE TIME

Have students turn to page 68 in the Practice Section of their book and find Chapter 6, Lesson 3, Practice. Go over the directions to make sure they understand what to do. Check and discuss the Practice after students have finished. (*Chapter 6, Lesson 3, Practice key is given on the next page.*)

© SHURLEY INSTRUCTIONAL MATERIALS, INC.

CHAPTER 6 LESSON 3 CONTINUED

Chapter 6, Lesson 3, Practice: For each sentence, do these four things: (1) Write the subject. (2) Write S if the subject is singular or P if the subject is plural. (3) Write the rule number. (4) Underline the correct verb in the sentence.

Rule 1: A singular subject must use a singular verb form that ends in **s**: *is, was, has, does, or verbs ending with* **es**.

Rule 2: A plural subject, a compound subject, or the subject **YOU** must use a plural verb form that has **no s** ending: *are, were, do, have, or verbs without* **s** *or* **es** *endings.* (A plural verb form is also called the *plain form*.)

Subject	S or P	Rule	
sprinklers	P	2	1. The **sprinklers** (turns, <u>turn</u>) on automatically in the summer.
Butterflies	P	2	2. **Butterflies** (enjoys, <u>enjoy</u>) our flower garden.
address	S	1	3. Her **address** (<u>changes</u>, change) every six months.
sun	S	1	4. The summer **sun** (destroy, <u>destroys</u>) the cabbage crops.
You	P	2	5. **You** (helps, <u>help</u>) me with my chores.
fingers	P	2	6. My **fingers** (is, <u>are</u>) blistered.
chef	S	1	7. The new **chef** (<u>prepares</u>, prepare) seafood salads.
artists	P	2	8. The young **artists** (paints, <u>paint</u>) a beautiful mural.
snowflakes	P	2	9. The **snowflakes** (lands, <u>land</u>) on my tongue.

ACTIVITY / ASSIGNMENT TIME

Part 1:
The first part of this activity will strengthen your understanding of subject-verb agreement. I will give you a list of subjects. Write these words on a sheet of paper. (*Have the subject words below on the board for students to copy.*) Then, you will write a present tense verb beside each subject word. A present tense verb does not end in *ed*. Be sure to check for subject-verb agreement as you write your sentences.

Subject Words
1. Birds
2. Boat
3. Flowers
4. Kite

Part 2:
The next portion of your activity is a little more challenging. After you have finished writing your subject-verb sentences, you will follow the four steps below. You are allowed to change some of the verbs in your sentences if you wish.

1. Choose one sentence to expand by adding adjectives, adverbs, and prepositional phrases.
2. Choose one sentence to illustrate.
3. Choose one sentence to change a singular subject and verb to a plural subject and verb.
4. Choose one sentence to remain the same.

(End of lesson.)

© SHURLEY INSTRUCTIONAL MATERIALS, INC.

CHAPTER 6   LESSON 4
Objectives: Jingles, Study, Test, Check, Activity, and Writing (journal).

 JINGLE TIME

Have students turn to the Jingle Section in their books and recite the previously-taught jingles.

 STUDY TIME

Have students study the vocabulary words in their vocabulary notebooks. Remind students that any vocabulary word in their notebooks could be on their test. Also, have students study any of the skills in the Practice Section that they need to review.

 TEST TIME

Have students turn to page 101 in the Test Section of their book and find Chapter 6 Test. Go over the directions to make sure they understand what to do. (*Chapter 6 Test key is on the next page.*)

 CHECK TIME

After students have finished, check and discuss their test papers. Make sure they understand why their answers are right or wrong. (*For total points, count each required answer as a point.*)

 ACTIVITY / ASSIGNMENT TIME

(Have a recipe box and a package of lined index cards ready for your children to use for this activity.) Find a map of the United States. Draw or trace the state of Arkansas on the blank side of an index card. On the lined side of the card, write the following questions and answers.

1. What is the state on the front of this card? **Arkansas**
2. What is the capital of Arkansas? **Little Rock**
3. What is the postal abbreviation of Arkansas? **AR**
4. What year was Arkansas admitted to the Union? **1836**

Color this state. Look up an interesting fact about this state and write it on your card. Use the card to quiz family members, friends, and relatives. You may want to time the responses to your questions. Scatter your cards and see how long it takes you to put them in alphabetical order. For a higher level of difficulty, see if you can alphabetize your cards only by the picture of each state.

(End of lesson.)

© SHURLEY INSTRUCTIONAL MATERIALS, INC.

Chapter 6 Test
(Student Page 101)

Exercise 1: Classify each sentence.

```
          A   Adj   Adj      SN    V   P   OP   P    OP
1. SN V   The young pioneer children / rode (to school) (on horseback).  D
   P1
```

```
          Adj   Adj      SN     V   P  A   OP    P  A  OP
2. SN V   Many strange creatures / live (in the depths) (of the sea).  D
   P1
```

```
          A    Adv     Adj SN    V   Adv   P  A   OP     P  A  OP
3. SN V   The extremely light arrow / flew straight (for the center) (of the target)!  E
   P1
```

Exercise 2: Use Sentence 3 to underline the complete subject once and the complete predicate twice and to complete the table below.

List the Noun Used	List the Noun Job	Singular or Plural	Common or Proper	Simple Subject	Simple Predicate
1. arrow	2. SN	3. S	4. C	5. arrow	6. flew
7. center	8. OP	9. S	10. C		
11. target	12. OP	13. S	14. C		

Exercise 3: Name the five parts of speech that you have studied. (*You may use abbreviations.*) **(The order may vary.)**

1. **Noun**   2. **Verb**   3. **Adjective**   4. **Adverb**   5. **Preposition**

Exercise 4: Identify each pair of words as synonyms or antonyms by putting parentheses ( ) around *syn* or *ant*.

1. weary, tired	**(syn)** ant	5. soiled, clean	syn **(ant)**	9. lethal, deadly	**(syn)** ant
2. present, absent	syn **(ant)**	6. firm, flabby	syn **(ant)**	10. burst, explode	**(syn)** ant
3. friendly, amiable	**(syn)** ant	7. chicken, fowl	**(syn)** ant	11. cheap, costly	syn **(ant)**
4. vigil, watch	**(syn)** ant	8. receive, send	syn **(ant)**	12. kind, irreverent	syn **(ant)**

Exercise 5: For each sentence, do these four things: (1) Write the subject. (2) Write S if the subject is singular or P if the subject is plural. (3) Write the rule number. (4) Underline the correct verb in the sentence.

Rule 1: A singular subject must use a singular verb form that ends in **s**: *is, was, has, does,* or *verbs ending with* **es**.

Rule 2: A plural subject, a compound subject, or the subject **YOU** must use a plural verb form that has **no s** ending: *are, were, do, have, or verbs without* **s** *or* **es** *endings.* (A plural verb form is also called the *plain form*.)

Subject	S or P	Rule	
worms	P	2	1. Those **worms** (builds, <u>build</u>) tunnels in the ground.
They	P	2	2. **They** (is, <u>are</u>) fishing near the dam.
doorbell	S	1	3. The **doorbell** (<u>startles</u>, startle) the baby.
herd	S	1	4. The elephant **herd** (make, <u>makes</u>) its way through the jungle.
You	P	2	5. **You** (plays, <u>play</u>) the drums in our band.
pictures	P	2	6. The **pictures** (falls, <u>fall</u>) out of the album.
astronomer	S	1	7. The **astronomer** (<u>looks</u>, look) through his telescope.

Exercise 6: In your journal, write a paragraph summarizing what you have learned this week.

© SHURLEY INSTRUCTIONAL MATERIALS, INC.

CHAPTER 6 LESSON 4 CONTINUED

TEACHER INSTRUCTIONS

Use the Question and Answer Flows below for the sentences on the Chapter 6 Test.

Question and Answer Flow for Sentence 1: The young pioneer children rode to school on horseback.

1. Who rode to school on horseback? children - SN
2. What is being said about children?
   children rode - V
3. To - P
4. To what? school - OP
5. On - P
6. On what? horseback - OP
7. What kind of children? pioneer - Adj
8. What kind of children? young - Adj
9. The - A
10. SN V P1 Check
11. (To school) - Prepositional phrase
12. (On horseback) - Prepositional phrase
13. Period, statement, declarative sentence
14. Go back to the verb - divide the complete subject from the complete predicate.

Classified Sentence:

	A	Adj	Adj	SN	V	P	OP	P	OP

SN V   The young pioneer children / rode (to school) (on horseback). **D**
P1

Question and Answer Flow for Sentence 2: Many strange creatures live in the depths of the sea.

1. What live in the depths of the sea? creatures - SN
2. What is being said about creatures? creatures live - V
3. In - P
4. In what? depths - OP
5. The - A
6. Of - P
7. Of what? sea - OP
8. The - A
9. What kind of creatures? strange - Adj
10. How many creatures? many - Adj
11. SN V P1 Check
12. (In the depths) - Prepositional phrase
13. (Of the sea) - Prepositional phrase
14. Period, statement, declarative sentence
15. Go back to the verb - divide the complete subject from the complete predicate.

Classified Sentence:

	Adj	Adj	SN	V	P	A	OP	P	A	OP

SN V   Many strange creatures / live (in the depths) (of the sea). **D**
P1

Question and Answer Flow for Sentence 3: The extremely light arrow flew straight for the center of the target!

1. What flew straight for the center of the target? arrow - SN
2. What is being said about arrow? arrow flew - V
3. Flew how? straight - Adv
4. For - P
5. For what? center - OP
6. The - A
7. Of - P
8. Of what? target - OP
9. The - A
10. What kind of arrow? light - Adj
11. How light? extremely - Adv
12. The - A
13. SN V P1 Check
14. (For the center) - Prepositional phrase
15. (Of the target) - Prepositional phrase
16. Exclamation point, strong feeling, exclamatory sentence
17. Go back to the verb - divide the complete subject from the complete predicate.

Classified Sentence:

	A	Adv	Adj	SN	V	Adv	P	A	OP	P	A	OP

SN V   The extremely light arrow / flew straight (for the center) (of the target)! **E**
P1

© SHURLEY INSTRUCTIONAL MATERIALS, INC.

CHAPTER 6   LESSON 5

Objectives: Writing assignment #3, Bonus Option.

 **WRITING TIME**

TEACHING SCRIPT FOR USING THE WRITING PROCESS FOR A WRITING ASSIGNMENT

Give Writing Assignment #3 from the box below. As you begin this writing assignment, you will use the writing process again. First, you will think about your topic and gather any information you might need in order to do the writing. Second, you will write a rough draft. Remember, it is called a rough draft because it will be revised and edited. You do not have to worry about mistakes as you write your rough draft. After you write the first draft, you will make revisions, using the Revision Checklist in Reference 13. After you revise your writing, you will edit, using the Beginning Editing Checklist in Reference 13. Finally, after you are satisfied with your revising and editing, you will write a final paper, using the Final Paper Checklist in Reference 13. You will then give the finished writing assignment to me. (*Students should finish their writing during their free time if they do not finish during this lesson.*)

Writing Assignment Box

Writing Assignment #3: Two-Point Expository Paragraph

Writing topic choices:　　**Things I Like About Christmas**　or　**My Favorite Season**　or　**Why My Room Is Important to Me**

Bonus Option: To solve the puzzle for Proverbs 22:1, cross out every third letter to read the message.

**AGQOOHDNYAMREIBSRIATZHEERTMOBO
ECXHONSEPNTLHAENGNREIATZRIPCHWESBANXDLNOVQINB
GFOAVBORQRAPTHCERKTHQANPSINLVZERMANYDGCOLBD.**

Have students design their own puzzles and share them with other family members and friends.

TEACHER INSTRUCTIONS FOR CHECKING WRITING ASSIGNMENT #3

Read, check, and discuss Writing Assignment #3 after students have finished their final papers. Use the editing checklist (*Reference 13 on teacher's page 48*) as you check and discuss students' papers. Make sure students are using the editing checklist correctly. In the beginning, you must also check students' papers carefully for <u>form</u> mistakes. This will ensure that students are learning the two-point format correctly.

Bonus Option Answer: *A good name is rather to be chosen than great riches, and loving favor rather than silver and gold.* (King James Version)

(End of lesson.)

© SHURLEY INSTRUCTIONAL MATERIALS, INC.

CHAPTER 7 LESSON 1 CONTINUED

TEACHING SCRIPT FOR UNDERSTOOD SUBJECT PRONOUN

The second kind of pronoun we will study is the <u>understood subject pronoun</u>. Look at Reference 23 on page 21 as I explain the four things you should know about the understood subject pronoun.

Reference 23: Understood Subject Pronoun
1. A sentence has an **understood subject** when someone gives a command or makes a request and leaves the subject unwritten or unspoken. It is understood that the unspoken subject will always be the pronoun *you*.
2. An imperative sentence gives a command or makes a request. It ends with a period or an exclamation point and always has the word *you* understood, but not expressed, as the subject.
3. The understood subject pronoun *you* is always written in parentheses at the beginning of the sentence with the label *SP* beside or above it: **(You) SP**.
4. Call the abbreviation **(You) SP** an understood subject pronoun.

As you can see, an understood subject is not spoken or written. Whenever a sentence gives a command or makes a request and leaves the subject unwritten and unspoken, the subject is always called an UNDERSTOOD SUBJECT. This understood subject will always be the pronoun YOU.

In this example, *Drive the car,* who is being commanded to drive the car? It is understood that someone is being commanded to drive the car even though the person's name is not mentioned. The person receiving the command is always the understood subject pronoun YOU.

Let's classify Sentence 2 for identification of the understood subject pronoun *you*.

Question and Answer Flow for Sentence 2: Look at the beautiful sunrise.	
1. Who look at the beautiful sunrise? you - SP (understood subject pronoun) **Note:** Say, "you - understood subject pronoun." Demonstrate how to write (You) - SP above the pattern to the left of the sentence. 2. What is being said about you? you look - V 3. At - P 4. At what? sunrise - OP 5. What kind of sunrise? beautiful - Adj 6. The - A	7. SN V P1 Check 8. (At the beautiful sunrise) - Prepositional phrase 9. Period, command, imperative sentence **Note:** Emphasize that when they have an understood subject pronoun, they will usually have an imperative sentence. 10. Go back to the verb - divide the complete subject from the complete predicate.

Classified Sentence: (You) SP   V   P A   Adj   OP
                                    SN V _____ / Look (at the beautiful sunrise). **Imp**
                                    P1	

© SHURLEY INSTRUCTIONAL MATERIALS, INC.

CHAPTER 7 LESSON 1 CONTINUED

At this point, it is wise to note an exception because you will have to make decisions based on this knowledge. When a sentence has an understood subject pronoun, it will <u>usually</u> be an imperative sentence. The only time an imperative sentence is not classified as imperative is when it is a command that shows very strong feeling or excitement and has (or should have) an exclamation point. Then, it is classified as an exclamatory sentence. (*Examples: Call the police! Go get help!*)

Teacher's Note: Question and Answer Flow Disclaimer.

For consistency, the Question and Answer Flow will use the verb form that is written in each sentence to complete the subject question, regardless of whether the verb is singular or plural.
    Example: They <u>are</u> laughing. Q & A: Who <u>are</u> laughing?
If you prefer using the singular verb form, just make the necessary change whenever it occurs.

Question and Answer Flow for Sentence 3: He lives in the United States during the summer months.

1. Who lives in the United States during the summer months? he - SP (subject pronoun)
2. What is being said about he? he lives - V
3. In - P
4. In what? United States - OP
5. The - A
6. During - P
7. During what? months - OP
8. What kind of months? summer - Adj
9. The - A
10. SN V P1 Check
11. (In the United States) - Prepositional phrase
12. (During the summer months) - Prepositional phrase
13. Period, statement, declarative sentence
14. Go back to the verb - divide the complete subject from the complete predicate.

Classified Sentence:

	SP	V	P	A	OP	P	A	Adj	OP
<u>SN V</u> P1	He / lives	(in the United States)				(during the summer months).			**D**

TEACHING SCRIPT FOR A NOUN CHECK WHEN PRONOUNS ARE IN THE SENTENCES

A Noun Check is a check for nouns. Since nouns are located in noun jobs, it is essential to know the noun jobs so that you know where to go to find nouns. You have had two noun jobs so far: the subject noun job and the object of the preposition noun job.

Since we are looking for nouns, we will say the noun job, say the noun or pronoun, and then say *yes* if it is a noun or *no* if it is a pronoun. Let's start with number one and go through the Noun Check for Sentences 1-3, identifying nouns by using the procedure below.

Sentence 1: Subject pronoun *she, no.* Object of the preposition *corner, yes.* (*Circle **corner** because it is a noun.*) Object of the preposition *building, yes.* (*Circle **building** because it is a noun.*)

Sentence 2: Understood subject pronoun *you, no.* Object of the preposition *sunrise, yes.* (*Circle **sunrise** because it is a noun.*)

Sentence 3: Subject pronoun *he, no.* Object of the preposition *United States, yes.* (*Circle **United States** because it is a noun.*) Object of the preposition *months, yes.* (*Circle **months** because it is a noun.*)

© SHURLEY INSTRUCTIONAL MATERIALS, INC.

CHAPTER 7 LESSON 1 CONTINUED

Use Sentences 1-3 that you just classified with your students to do an Oral Skill Builder Check. Use the guidelines below.

Oral Skill Builder Check	
1. Noun check. (Say the job and then say the noun. Circle each noun.) **2. Identify the nouns as singular or plural.** (Write S or P above each noun.) **3. Identify the nouns as common or proper.** (Follow established procedure for oral identification.) **4. Do a vocabulary check.** (Follow established procedure for oral identification.)	**5. Identify the complete subject and the complete predicate.** (Underline the complete subject once and the complete predicate twice.) **6. Identify the simple subject and simple predicate.** (Underline the simple subject once and the simple predicate twice. Bold, or highlight, the lines to distinguish them from the complete subject and complete predicate.)

TEACHING SCRIPT FOR ADDING THE PRONOUN TO THE PARTS OF SPEECH

Do you remember that all words in the English language have been put into one of eight groups called the **Parts of Speech**? We learned that how a word is used in a sentence determines its part of speech. Do you remember the names of the five parts of speech we have already studied? *(noun, verb, adjective, adverb,* and *preposition)*

Today, we have learned about pronouns. A pronoun is also a part of speech; so, we will add it to our list. Now, we know six of the eight parts of speech. What are the six parts of speech that we have covered? *(noun, verb, adjective, adverb, preposition,* and *pronoun)* *(Chant the six parts of speech that the students have learned several times for immediate reinforcement. Students will learn an Eight-Parts-of-Speech Jingle after all eight parts have been introduced.)*

 VOCABULARY TIME

Assign Chapter 7, Vocabulary Words **#1** on page 8 in the Reference Section for students to define in their Vocabulary notebooks. Tell students they are to use a dictionary or thesaurus to look up the meanings of the vocabulary words. After they write each word and its meaning, students are to write a sentence using the vocabulary word.

Chapter 7, Vocabulary Words #1
(truthful, honest, congeal, melt)

(End of lesson.)

© SHURLEY INSTRUCTIONAL MATERIALS, INC.

CHAPTER 7   LESSON 2
Objectives: Jingles (Possessive Pronoun), Grammar (Introductory Sentences, Possessive Pronouns), Practice and Improved Sentences with Pronouns, and Vocabulary #2.

 JINGLE TIME

Have students turn to the Jingle Section in their books and recite the previously-taught jingles. Then, lead students in reciting the new jingle (*Possessive Pronoun*) below. Practice the new jingle several times until students can recite it smoothly. Emphasize reciting with a rhythm. Students and teacher should be together! (*Do not try to explain the jingles at this time. Just have fun reciting them. Remember, add motions for more fun and laughter.*)

Jingle 12: Possessive Pronoun Jingle	
There are seven possessive pronouns	
That are easy as can be:	
My and our,	(clap 2 times)
His and her,	(clap 2 times)
Its and their and your.	(clap 3 times)

 GRAMMAR TIME

Put the introductory sentences from the box below on the board. Use these sentences as you go through each new concept covered in your teaching script. For the greatest benefit, students must participate orally with the teacher. (*You might put the introductory sentences on notebook paper if you are doing one-on-one instruction with your students.*)

Chapter 7, Introductory Sentences for Lesson 2
1. _____ Our new car rides smoothly over bumpy roads.
2. _____ My expensive digital camera fell in the mud yesterday!
3. _____ Chip screamed at the top of his lungs!

TEACHING SCRIPT FOR POSSESSIVE PRONOUNS

The third kind of pronoun we will study is the possessive pronoun. Look at Reference 24 on page 21 in the Reference Section of your book. Follow along as I explain the six things you should know about the possessive pronoun. (*Read and discuss the information about possessive pronouns in the reference box on the next page.*)

© SHURLEY INSTRUCTIONAL MATERIALS, INC.

Reference 24: Possessive Pronouns

1. A possessive pronoun takes the place of a possessive noun.

2. A possessive pronoun's spelling form makes it possessive. These are the most common possessive pronouns: *my, our, his, her, its, their,* and *your.* Use the Possessive Pronoun Jingle to remember the most common possessive pronouns.

3. A possessive pronoun has two jobs: to show ownership or possession and to modify like an adjective.

4. When classifying a possessive pronoun, both jobs will be recognized by labeling the pronoun as a possessive pronoun adjective. Use the abbreviation **PPA** (possessive pronoun adjective).

5. Include possessive pronouns when you are asked to identify pronouns, possessives, or adjectives.

6. To find a possessive pronoun, begin with the question *whose.* (*Whose medicine? His - PPA*)

You will use this information as you classify Sentence 1 with me to find the possessive pronoun. Remember, you use the question *whose* to find the possessive pronoun. Begin.

Question and Answer Flow for Sentence 1: Our new car rides smoothly over bumpy roads.

1. What rides smoothly over bumpy roads? car - SN
2. What is being said about car? car rides - V
3. Rides how? smoothly - Adv
4. Over - P
5. Over what? roads - OP
6. What kind of roads? bumpy - Adj
7. What kind of car? new - Adj

8. Whose car? our - PPA (Possessive pronoun adjective)
9. SN V P1 Check
10. (Over bumpy roads) - Prepositional phrase
11. Period, statement, declarative sentence
12. Go back to the verb - divide the complete subject from the complete predicate.

Classified Sentence:

```
                        PPA  Adj  SN    V     Adv      P    Adj    OP
          SN  V         Our  new  car / rides smoothly (over bumpy roads).  D
          P1
```

Question and Answer Flow for Sentence 2: My expensive digital camera fell in the mud yesterday!

1. What fell in the mud yesterday? camera - SN
2. What is being said about camera? camera fell - V
3. In - P
4. In what? mud - OP
5. The - A
6. Fell when? yesterday - Adv
7. What kind of camera? digital - Adj

8. What kind of camera? expensive - Adj
9. Whose camera? my - PPA
10. SN V P1 Check
11. (In the mud) - Prepositional phrase
12. Exclamation point, strong feeling, exclamatory sentence
13. Go back to the verb - divide the complete subject from the complete predicate.

Classified Sentence:

```
                        PPA  Adj       Adj     SN     V  P A  OP   Adv
          SN  V         My expensive digital camera / fell (in the mud) yesterday!  E
          P1
```

CHAPTER 7 LESSON 2 CONTINUED

Question and Answer Flow for Sentence 3: Chip screamed at the top of his lungs!	
1. Who screamed at the top of his lungs? Chip - SN	8. Whose lungs? his - PPA
2. What is being said about Chip? Chip screamed - V	9. SN V P1 Check
3. At - P	10. (At the top) - Prepositional phrase
4. At what? top - OP	11. (Of his lungs) - Prepositional phrase
5. The - A	12. Exclamation point, strong feeling, exclamatory sentence
6. Of - P	13. Go back to the verb - divide the complete subject
7. Of what? lungs - OP	from the complete predicate.

Classified Sentence

```
                          SN        V      P   A   OP  P PPA  OP
              SN V    Chip / screamed (at the top) (of his lungs)! E
              P1
```

TEACHING SCRIPT FOR A PRACTICE SENTENCE WITH PRONOUNS

Put these labels on the board: **SP V Adv P PPA Adj OP**

Look at the new sentence labels on the board: **SP V Adv P PPA Adj OP**. I will guide you through the process of writing a sentence to practice the new parts that you have learned.

Get out a sheet of notebook paper. On the top line of your notebook paper, write the title *Practice Sentence*. Copy the sentence labels from the board onto your notebook paper. Be sure to leave plenty of writing space between each label. I will guide you through the process you will use whenever you write a Practice Sentence with pronouns.

1. Go to the **SP** label for the subject pronoun. Repeat the Subject Pronoun Jingle to help you think of a pronoun that you want to use as your subject. Write the pronoun you have chosen on the line *under* the **SP** label.

2. Go to the **V** label for the verb. Think of a verb that tells what your subject does. Make sure that your verb makes sense with the subject pronoun. Write the verb you have chosen on the line *under* the **V** label.

3. Go to the **Adv** label for the adverb. Immediately go to the verb in your sentence and ask an adverb question. What are the adverb questions? (*How? When? Where?*) Choose one adverb question to ask and write your adverb answer *under* the **Adv** label.

4. Go to the **P** label for the preposition. Think of a preposition word that tells something about your verb. You must be careful to choose a preposition word that makes sense with the noun you will choose for the object of the preposition in your next step. Write the word you have chosen for a preposition *under* the **P** label.

© SHURLEY INSTRUCTIONAL MATERIALS, INC.

CHAPTER 7 LESSON 2 CONTINUED

5. Now, go to the **OP** label for the object of the preposition. If you like the noun you thought of while thinking of a preposition, write it down under the **OP** label. If you prefer, think of another noun by asking **what** or **whom** after your preposition. Check to make sure the preposition and object of the preposition make sense together and also make sense with the rest of the sentence. Remember, the object of the preposition will always answer the question **what** or **whom** after the preposition. Write the word you have chosen for the object of the preposition *under* the **OP** label.

6. Go to the **Adj** label for the adjective. Go to the object of the preposition that you just wrote and ask an adjective question to describe the object of the preposition noun. What are the adjective questions? (*What kind? Which one? How many?*) Choose one adjective question to ask and write your adjective answer *under* the **Adj** label next to the object of the preposition. Always check to make sure your answers are making sense in the sentence.

7. Go to the **PPA** label for the possessive pronoun adjective that is part of your prepositional phrase. Repeat the Possessive Pronoun Jingle to help you think of a pronoun that you want to use as your possessive pronoun adjective.   You will choose one of the possessive pronouns that makes the best sense in your sentence. Write the possessive pronoun you have chosen *under* the **PPA** label.

8. Finally, check your Practice Sentence to make sure it has the necessary parts to be a complete sentence. What are the five parts of a complete sentence? (*subject, verb, complete sense, capital letter, and an end mark*) Does your Practice Sentence have the five parts of a complete sentence? (*Allow time for students to read over their sentences and to make any corrections they need to make.*)

TEACHING SCRIPT FOR AN IMPROVED SENTENCE

Under your Practice Sentence, write the title *Improved Sentence* on another line. To improve your Practice Sentence, you will make two synonym changes, one antonym change, and your choice of a complete word change or another synonym or antonym change.

Since it is harder to find words that can be changed to an antonym, it is usually wise to go through your sentence to find an antonym change first. Look through your sentence again to find words that can be improved with synonyms. Finally, make a decision about whether your last change will be a complete word change, another synonym change, or another antonym change.

I will give you time to write your Improved Sentence. (*Always encourage students to use a thesaurus, synonym-antonym book, or a dictionary to help them develop an interesting and improved writing vocabulary. After students have finished, check and discuss students' Practice and Improved Sentences.*)

 VOCABULARY TIME

Assign Chapter 7, Vocabulary Words **#2** on page 8 in the Reference Section for students to define in their Vocabulary notebooks. Students may use a dictionary or thesaurus to look up the meanings of the vocabulary words and to help them write a sentence using the vocabulary words.

Chapter 7, Vocabulary Words #2
(foe, friend, pain, discomfort)

(End of lesson.)

© SHURLEY INSTRUCTIONAL MATERIALS, INC.

CHAPTER 7   LESSON 3

Objectives: Jingles (Object Pronoun Jingle), Grammar (Practice Sentences, Object Pronoun), Practice Exercise, Activity, and Writing (journal).

 **JINGLE TIME**

Have students turn to the Jingle Section in their books and recite the previously-taught jingles. Then, lead students in reciting the new jingle (*Object Pronoun*) below. Practice the new jingle several times until students can recite it smoothly. Emphasize reciting with a rhythm. Students and teacher should be together! (*Do not try to explain the jingles at this time. Just have fun reciting them. Remember, add motions for more fun and laughter.*)

Teacher's Note: Again, do not spend a large amount of time practicing the new jingles. Students learn the jingles best by spending a small amount of time consistently, **every** day.

Jingle 13: Object Pronoun Jingle	
There are seven object pronouns	
That are easy as can be:	
Me and us,	(clap 2 times)
Him and her,	(clap 2 times)
It and them and you.	(clap 3 times)

 GRAMMAR TIME

First-Year Option: Put the Practice Sentences from the box below on the board or on notebook paper. Use these sentences as you practice the concepts that have been taught. For the greatest benefit, students must participate orally with the teacher. **Second-Year Option:** Have students classify the Practice Sentences independently on paper. Check students' sentences with the answers provided below. (*If you have the CDs for Practice Sentences, have students check their sentences with the CDs.*)

Chapter 7, Practice Sentences for Lesson 3
1. _____ We went to the zoo with her today.
2. _____ Mom waited patiently for me at the airport for two hours.
3. _____ He jumped vigorously on the trampoline with them for an hour.

TEACHING SCRIPT FOR PRACTICING PATTERN 1 SENTENCES

We will classify three different sentences to practice the grammar concepts in the Question and Answer Flows. We will classify the sentences together. Begin.

© SHURLEY INSTRUCTIONAL MATERIALS, INC.

CHAPTER 7 LESSON 3 CONTINUED

Question and Answer Flow for Sentence 1: We went to the zoo with her today.

1. Who went to the zoo with her today? we - SP
2. What is being said about we? we went - V
3. To - P
4. To what? zoo - OP
5. The - A
6. With - P
7. With whom? her - OP

8. Went when? today - Adv
9. SN V P1 Check
10. (To the zoo) - Prepositional phrase
11. (With her) - Prepositional phrase
12. Period, statement, declarative sentence
13. Go back to the verb - divide the complete subject from the complete predicate.

Classified Sentence:

	SP	V	P A OP	P OP	Adv
SN V	We /	went	(to the zoo)	(with her)	today. D
P1					

Question and Answer Flow for Sentence 2: Mom waited patiently for me at the airport for two hours.

1. Who waited patiently for me at the airport for two hours? Mom - SN
2. What is being said about Mom? Mom waited - V
3. Waited how? patiently - Adv
4. For - P
5. For whom? me - OP
6. At - P
7. At what? airport - OP
8. The - A
9. For - P

10. For what? hours - OP
11. How many hours? two - Adj
12. SN V P1 Check
13. (For me) - Prepositional phrase
14. (At the airport) - Prepositional phrase
15. (For two hours) - Prepositional phrase
16. Period, statement, declarative sentence
17. Go back to the verb - divide the complete subject from the complete predicate.

Classified Sentence:

	SN	V	Adv	P OP	P A OP	P Adj OP
SN V	Mom /	waited	patiently	(for me)	(at the airport)	(for two hours). D
P1						

Question and Answer Flow for Sentence 3: He jumped vigorously on the trampoline with them for an hour.

1. Who jumped vigorously on the trampoline with them for an hour? he - SP
2. What is being said about he? he jumped - V
3. Jumped how? vigorously - Adv
4. On - P
5. On what? trampoline - OP
6. The - A
7. With - P
8. With whom? them - OP
9. For - P

10. For what? hour - OP
11. An - A
12. SN V P1 Check
13. (On the trampoline) - Prepositional phrase
14. (With them) - Prepositional phrase
15. (For an hour) - Prepositional phrase
16. Period, statement, declarative sentence
17. Go back to the verb - divide the complete subject from the complete predicate.

Classified Sentence:

	SP	V	Adv	P A OP	P OP	P A OP
SN V	He /	jumped	vigorously	(on the trampoline)	(with them)	(for an hour). D
P1						

© SHURLEY INSTRUCTIONAL MATERIALS, INC.

CHAPTER 7 LESSON 3 CONTINUED

TEACHING SCRIPT FOR OBJECT PRONOUN

We are now ready to learn a new type of pronoun. But, first, let's review the two jingles that tell us about two other types of pronouns: the Subject Pronoun Jingle and the Possessive Pronoun Jingle. (*Recite the two jingles*.) Now, we are going to recite the Object Pronoun Jingle that you learned at the beginning of this lesson. (*Have students turn to page 5 in the Jingle section of their books and recite the Object Pronoun Jingle with you.*)

Look at Reference 25 on page 22 in your Reference Section. Follow along as I explain three things you need to know about object pronouns. (*You may want to write the examples on the board as a visual aid for your students.*)

Reference 25: Object Pronoun

1. If a pronoun does any job that has the word *object* in it, that pronoun is an object pronoun. Object pronouns can be used as objects of the prepositions, direct objects, or indirect objects.

2. The object pronouns are listed in your Object Pronoun Jingle: *me, us, him, her, it, them,* and *you.*

3. An object pronoun does not have a special label. An object pronoun keeps the OP, DO, or IO label that tells its job.

	OP	DO	IO
Examples:	My dad played with *us.*	The boss called *him.*	Send *her* a message.

Did you notice that these jobs all have the word *object* in them? Listen to the list again. *Object* pronouns are used as *objects* of the prepositions, direct *objects*, and indirect *objects*.

As you can see, an object pronoun can perform many jobs. Remember, the object pronoun will not be labeled object pronoun. It will take the name of the pronoun job that you use when you classify the sentence. For example, the object pronoun is labeled *OP* for object of the preposition (*not object pronoun*). It may also be labeled *DO* for direct object or *IO* for indirect object. You will learn about the other object pronoun jobs in later grades. For now, we will concentrate on using the object pronoun as an object of the preposition.

Look at Sentence 1, which we have just classified. It has two prepositional phrases. In the first prepositional phrase, the object of the preposition is a noun. In the second prepositional phrase, the object of the preposition is a pronoun. Notice that we classify both objects of the prepositions as "OP."

(*Put this sample sentence on the board: A bike was given **to me** yesterday. Read and discuss the sample sentence.*) Can we substitute other object pronouns for the object pronoun that is used here? (*yes*) What are some of the object pronouns that we could substitute? (**her, him, them, us**) How would you label the object pronouns that we could substitute? (*Keep the same OP label for the object of the preposition.*)

© SHURLEY INSTRUCTIONAL MATERIALS, INC.

CHAPTER 7 LESSON 3 CONTINUED

The main reason you should learn about the different kinds of pronouns is to use them correctly in speaking. You would not say, **"Emily is going to the concert with Margaret and I."** You should know to select an object pronoun to use in this sentence because the pronoun is an object of the preposition. You would say, **"Emily is going to the concert with Margaret and me."** You also would not say, **"Margaret and me are going to the concert with Emily."** You should know to select a subject pronoun to use in this sentence because the pronoun is a subject. You would say, **"Margaret and I are going to the concert with Emily."**

 PRACTICE TIME

Have students turn to page 69 in the Practice Section of their book and find the skills under Chapter 7, Lesson 3, Practice *(1-2)*. Go over the directions to make sure they understand what to do. Check and discuss the Practices after students have finished. (*The practices are listed below.*)

Chapter 7, Lesson 3, Practice 1: On a sheet of paper, write seven subject pronouns, seven possessive pronouns, and seven object pronouns. **(Use the pronoun jingles to check students' papers.)**

Chapter 7, Lesson 3, Practice 2: Video tape or tape record all the jingles you have learned.

 ACTIVITY / ASSIGNMENT TIME

For the rest of the day, try not to say any pronouns. Down the left side of a sheet of paper, make a list of all the pronouns that are used in the pronoun jingles. Keep the list with you at all times. Every time you say a pronoun, place a tally mark beside that pronoun. At the end of the day, total up the number of times you used pronouns. Discuss the pronouns that were used the most.

Extension: Try this experiment again with family members or friends. Have a contest. Set up the rules and time frame for the pronoun contest. See if anyone can go several hours without saying any pronouns. Discuss the importance of pronouns in our communications.

 WRITING TIME

Have students make an entry in their journals.

(End of lesson.)

© SHURLEY INSTRUCTIONAL MATERIALS, INC.

CHAPTER 7   LESSON 4

Objectives: Jingles, Study, Test, Check, Activity, and Writing (journal).

 **JINGLE TIME**

Have students turn to the Jingle Section in their books and recite the previously-taught jingles.

 STUDY TIME

Have students study the vocabulary words in their vocabulary notebooks. Remind students that any vocabulary word in their notebooks could be on their test. Also, have students study any of the skills in the Practice Section that they need to review.

 TEST TIME

Have students turn to page 102 in the Test Section of their book and find Chapter 7 Test. Go over the directions to make sure they understand what to do. (*Chapter 7 Test key is on the next page.*)

 CHECK TIME

After students have finished, check and discuss their test papers. Make sure they understand why their answers are right or wrong. (*For total points, count each required answer as a point.*)

 ACTIVITY / ASSIGNMENT TIME

(*Beginning with Chapter 7, two states will be introduced. If more time is needed, continue working in the next lesson.*)
Students will continue to draw or trace the states and write the following questions and answers.

California	Colorado
1. What is the state on the front of this card? **California**	1. What is the state on the front of this card? **Colorado**
2. What is the capital of California? **Sacramento**	2. What is the capital of Colorado? **Denver**
3. What is the postal abbreviation of California? **CA**	3. What is the postal abbreviation of Colorado? **CO**
4. What year was California admitted to the Union? **1850**	4. What year was Colorado admitted to the Union? **1876**

Color these states and look up an interesting fact about each state to write on the cards. Use the cards to quiz family members, friends, and relatives. You may want to time the responses to your questions. Also, along with previous suggestions, think of other ways to have fun with your United States card file.

(End of lesson.)

Level 3 Homeschool Teacher's Manual
© SHURLEY INSTRUCTIONAL MATERIALS, INC.

Chapter 7 Test
(Student Page 102)

Exercise 1: Classify each sentence.

```
             SP    V    P A  OP  P A   OP
1.  SN V     They / cried (at the end) (of the movie).  D
    P1
    (You) SP    V   P   OP    P  A   Adj  OP    P  A   OP    P  A    OP
2.  SN V        /Sit (with them) (at the round table) (in the corner) (of the restaurant)
    P1          P    Adj     OP
                (for excellent service).  Imp

              SN     V    P  PPA  OP    P  A  Adj  OP
3.  SN V      Jenny / talked (on her phone) (for a long time).  D
    P1
```

Exercise 2: Use Sentence 1 to underline the complete subject once and the complete predicate twice and to complete the table below.

List the Noun Used	List the Noun Job	Singular or Plural	Common or Proper	Simple Subject	Simple Predicate
1. **end**	2. **OP**	3. **S**	4. **C**	5. **they**	6. **cried**
7. **movie**	8. **OP**	9. **S**	10. **C**		

Exercise 3: Name the six parts of speech that you have studied. (*You may use abbreviations.*) **(The order may vary.)**

1. **noun**   2. **verb**   3. **adjective**   4. **adverb**   5. **preposition**   6. **pronoun**

Exercise 4: Identify each pair of words as synonyms or antonyms by putting parentheses ( ) around *syn* or *ant*.

1. melt, congeal	syn **(ant)**	4. honest, truthful	**(syn)** ant	7. pain, discomfort	**(syn)** ant
2. present, absent	syn **(ant)**	5. burst, explode	**(syn)** ant	8. eager, indifferent	syn **(ant)**
3. try, attempt	**(syn)** ant	6. friend, foe	syn **(ant)**	9. kind, irreverent	syn **(ant)**

Exercise 5: For each sentence, write the subject, then write S if the subject is singular or P if the subject is plural, write the rule number, and underline the correct verb in the sentence.

Rule 1: A singular subject must use a singular verb form that ends in **s**: *is, was, has, does,* or verbs ending with **s** or **es**.
Rule 2: A plural subject, a compound subject, or the subject **YOU** must use a plural verb form that has **no s** ending: *are, were, do, have,* or verbs without **s** or **es** endings. (A plural verb form is also called the *plain form*.)

Subject	S or P	Rule
water	S	1
Thomas and Angie	P	2
brothers	P	2
sculpture	S	1
dolphins	P	2
hoses	P	2
highway	S	1
you	P	2
waitress	S	1

1. The **water** (<u>rushes</u>, rush) quickly down the brook.
2. **Thomas** and **Angie** (is, <u>are</u>) leaving for vacation.
3. My **brothers** (rides, <u>ride</u>) motorcycles.
4. That **sculpture** (are, <u>is</u>) new to the museum.
5. The **dolphins** (glides, <u>glide</u>) through the ocean water.
6. The **hoses** (was, <u>were</u>) tangled in a knot.
7. The new **highway** (curve, <u>curves</u>) through the hills.
8. (<u>Do</u>, Does) **you** know where Tammy lives?
9. The **waitress** (ask, <u>asks</u>) for our order.

Exercise 6: On notebook paper, write as many prepositions as you can.

Exercise 7: On notebook paper, write seven subject pronouns, seven possessive pronouns, and seven object pronouns. **(Use the pronoun jingles to check students' papers.)**

Exercise 8: In your journal, write a paragraph summarizing what you have learned this week.

© SHURLEY INSTRUCTIONAL MATERIALS, INC.

CHAPTER 7 LESSON 4 CONTINUED

TEACHER INSTRUCTIONS

Use the Question and Answer Flows below for the sentences on the Chapter 7 Test.

Question and Answer Flow for Sentence 1: They cried at the end of the movie.

1. Who cried at the end of the movie? they - SP
2. What is being said about they? they cried - V
3. At - P
4. At what? end - OP
5. The - A
6. Of - P
7. Of what? movie - OP
8. The - A
9. SN V P1 Check
10. (At the end) - Prepositional phrase
11. (Of the movie) - Prepositional phrase
12. Period, statement, declarative sentence
13. Go back to the verb - divide the complete subject from the complete predicate.

Classified Sentence:

	SP	V	P	A	OP	P	A	OP

SN V / P1   They / cried (at the end) (of the movie). **D**

Question and Answer Flow for Sentence 2: Sit with them at the round table in the corner of the restaurant for excellent service.

1. Who sit with them at the round table in the corner of the restaurant for excellent service? you - SP (understood subject pronoun)
2. What is being said about you? you sit - V
3. With - P
4. With whom? them - OP
5. At - P
6. At what? table - OP
7. What kind of table? round - Adj
8. The - A
9. In - P
10. In what? corner - OP
11. The - A
12. Of - P
13. Of what? restaurant - OP
14. The - A
15. For - P
16. For what? service - OP
17. What kind of service? excellent - Adj
18. SN V P1 Check
19. (With them) - Prepositional phrase
20. (At the round table) - Prepositional phrase
21. (In the corner) - Prepositional phrase
22. (Of the restaurant) - Prepositional phrase
23. (For excellent service) - Prepositional phrase
24. Period, command, imperative sentence
25. Go back to the verb - divide the complete subject from the complete predicate.

Classified Sentence:

(YOU) SP	V	P	OP	P	A	Adj	OP	P	A	OP	P	A	OP	P	Adj	OP

SN V / P1   / Sit (with them) (at the round table) (in the corner) (of the restaurant) (for excellent service). **Imp**

Question and Answer Flow for Sentence 3: Jenny talked on her phone for a long time.

1. Who talked on her phone for a long time? Jenny - SN
2. What is being said about Jenny? Jenny talked - V
3. On - P
4. On what? phone - OP
5. Whose phone? her - PPA
6. For - P
7. For what? time - OP
8. What kind of time? long - Adj
9. A - A
10. SN V P1 Check
11. (On her phone) - Prepositional phrase
12. (For a long time) - Prepositional phrase
13. Period, statement, declarative sentence
14. Go back to the verb - divide the complete subject from the complete predicate.

Classified Sentence:

	SN	V	P	PPA	OP	P	A	Adj	OP

SN V / P1   Jenny / talked (on her phone) (for a long time). **D**

© SHURLEY INSTRUCTIONAL MATERIALS, INC.

CHAPTER 7   LESSON 5

Objectives: Writing (changing plural categories to singular points), Writing Assignment #4, and Bonus Option.

 **WRITING TIME**

TEACHING SCRIPT FOR CHANGING PLURAL CATEGORIES TO SINGULAR POINTS

When you have a topic such as *My favorite fruits*, you will usually name your favorite fruits by categories, or groups, like peaches and pineapples. When this happens, you need to know how to change plural points to singular points. I will demonstrate how this is done in a paragraph. Look at Reference 26 on page 22 as I read the paragraph to you. Then, I will show you how to change each of the two points in the paragraph. *(Read the paragraph to your students from beginning to end. Then, go through the teaching script given for each sentence in the paragraph.)*

Reference 26: Singular and Plural Points

Two-Point Expository Paragraph

Topic: My favorite fruits
2-points: 1. peaches   2. pineapples
     I have two favorite fruits. These fruits are peaches and pineapples. My first favorite fruit is a peach. I like peaches because they are so refreshing and sweet. My second favorite fruit is a pineapple. I love the tropical flavor of ice-cold pineapples. I enjoy eating all kinds of fruits, but my favorites will always be peaches and pineapples.

Notice that the topic is written first because it is the subject of the paragraph. Having the topic written first will help us focus on what the paragraph is about. Next, the two points that we will discuss are listed. Again, having the two points written down before we start will help us focus on what we will say in the paragraph.

We are now ready to begin our paragraph because we are clear about our topic and about the points we will cover as we write. We start with a topic sentence because it tells the reader what the paragraph is about: *I have two favorite fruits.* Knowing what the paragraph is about helps the reader focus on the main points as the reader progresses through the paragraph.

Our next sentence is the two-point sentence: *These fruits are peaches and pineapples.* The two-point sentence lists the two main points that will be discussed in the paragraph, so in this paragraph we know the two main points are *peaches* and *pineapples*. Now, I want you to notice that each of the two points listed is plural (*peaches* and *pineapples*). These main points are actually categories, or groups, of fruits, and that is why they are listed in plural form.

© SHURLEY INSTRUCTIONAL MATERIALS, INC.

CHAPTER 7 LESSON 5 CONTINUED

Let's look at the sentence written for the first point. The sentence for the first point starts out like this: *My first favorite fruit is*. Since this phrase is singular, we could change the plural listing to a singular listing to agree with the type of sentence that is written. To do this, we will change *peaches* from plural to singular: *My first favorite fruit is a peach*. Usually, an article adjective is needed to make the sentence sound better.

Just remember: If your two points are plural, you usually make them singular as you name them for your first point and second point. Use an article adjective with your singular form to make it sound better. Notice that the second main point follows this same format. Look at the form as I read them to you. (*2nd point: My second favorite fruit is a pineapple.*)

After each main point, there is a supporting sentence. Supporting sentences make each point clearer by telling extra information about each main point. Remember, we have stated in the main points that peaches and pineapples are two of our favorite fruits. Each supporting sentence should state some kind of information that proves each of the main points. (*1st Supporting sentence: I like peaches because they are so refreshing and sweet.* *2nd Supporting sentence: I love the tropical flavor of ice-cold pineapples.*) Notice that we also used the plural forms in the supporting sentences.

Our last sentence is a concluding sentence. It summarizes our three points by restating some of the words in the topic sentence and by adding an extra thought that finalizes the paragraph. (*Concluding sentence: I enjoy eating all kinds of fruits, but my favorites will always be peaches and pineapples.*)

TEACHING SCRIPT FOR USING THE WRITING PROCESS FOR WRITING ASSIGNMENT #4

For writing Assignment #4, you will write a two-point paragraph that will demonstrate the use of singular and plural points. As you begin this writing assignment, you will again go through the writing process.

First, you will think about your topic and gather any information you might need in order to do the writing. Second, you will write a rough draft. Remember, it is called a rough draft because it will be revised and edited. You do not have to worry about mistakes as you write your rough draft. After you write the first draft, you will make revisions, using the Revision Checklist in Reference 13. After you revise your writing, you will edit, using the Beginning Editing Checklist in Reference 13.

Finally, after you are satisfied with your revising and editing, you will write a final paper, using the Final Paper Checklist in Reference 13. You will then give the finished writing assignment to me. (*Use the Writing Assignment box on the next page for students' writing assignment.*)

© SHURLEY INSTRUCTIONAL MATERIALS, INC.

CHAPTER 7 LESSON 5 CONTINUED

Writing Assignment Box

Writing Assignment #4: Two-Point Expository Paragraph, demonstrating singular/plural points

Writing topics: **My Favorite Cartoon** or **Things That Make Me Happy** or **My Best Friend**

<u>Bonus Option:</u> To solve the puzzle for Proverbs 24:5, Write the letter missing from each set of letters on notebook paper. (1. A) The two ** indicate the end of a word. (2. W) There are 12 words.

1. YZBC**	7. ZBCD	13. QSTU	19. XYZB**	25. EGHI**	31. DFGH	37. ABDE	43. SUVW	49. MOPQ
2. UVXY	8. KLMO**	14. MNPQ	20. ZBCD**	26. IJLM	32. CEFG	38. PQST	44. GIJK**	50. EFHI
3. GHJK	9. GHJK	15. MOPQ	21. KLNO	27. MOPQ	33. FHIJ	39. DFGH	45. RTUV	51. RSUV
4. RTUV	10. RTUV**	16. EFHI**	22. ZBCD	28. MNPQ	34. DFGH**	40. ZBCD	46. QRSU	52. GIJK**
5. DFGH**	11. RTUV	17. XZAB	23. MOPQ**	29. UVXY	35. HJKL	41. RTUV	47. PQST	
6. KLNO	12. RSUV	18. DFGH	24. MNPQ	30. KMNO	36. MOPQ	42. DFGH	48. DFGH	

TEACHER INSTRUCTIONS FOR CHECKING WRITING ASSIGNMENT #4

Read, check, and discuss Writing Assignments #4 after students have finished their final papers. Use the editing checklist (*Reference 13 on teacher's page 48*) as you check and discuss students' papers. Make sure students are using the editing checklist correctly. In the beginning, you must also check students' papers carefully for <u>form</u> mistakes.

Bonus Option Answer: *A wise man is strong; yea, a man of knowledge increaseth strength.* (King James Version)

(End of lesson.)

CHAPTER 8   LESSON 1

Objectives: Jingles, Grammar (Introductory Sentences, Possessive Noun, Noun Check with Possessive Nouns), Oral Skill Builder Check, Practice Exercise, and Vocabulary #1.

 **JINGLE TIME**

Have students turn to the Jingle Section in their books and recite the previously-taught jingles.

 GRAMMAR TIME

Put the introductory sentences from the box below on the board. Use these sentences as you go through each new concept covered in your teaching script. For the greatest benefit, students must participate orally with the teacher. (*You might put the introductory sentences on notebook paper if you are doing one-on-one instruction with your students.*)

Chapter 8, Introductory Sentences for Lesson 1

1. _____ Jane's swollen ankle ached during her performance.
2. _____ My little dog barked excitedly at his shadow.
3. _____ The queen's army camped on the hillside.

TEACHING SCRIPT FOR POSSESSIVE NOUN

Today, we will learn about a very special noun: the possessive noun. Since there is not a jingle for a possessive noun, information about the possessive noun is listed in the Reference Section on page 22. Look at Reference 27. Follow along as I explain the six things you should know about the possessive noun. (*Read and discuss the information about possessive nouns in the reference box below.*)

Reference 27: Possessive Nouns

1. A possessive noun is the name of a person, place, or thing that owns something.

2. A possessive noun will always have an apostrophe after it. It will be either an *apostrophe s* (*'s*) or an *s apostrophe* (*s'*). The apostrophe makes a noun show ownership. (*Linda's car*)

3. A possessive noun has two jobs: to show ownership or possession and to modify like an adjective.

4. When classifying a possessive noun, both jobs will be recognized by labeling it as a possessive noun adjective. Use the abbreviation **PNA** (possessive noun adjective).

5. Include possessive nouns when you are asked to identify possessive nouns or adjectives. Do not include possessive nouns when you are asked to identify regular nouns.

6. To find a possessive noun, begin with the question *whose*. (*Whose car? Linda's - PNA*)

© SHURLEY INSTRUCTIONAL MATERIALS, INC.

CHAPTER 8 LESSON 1 CONTINUED

Since you use the *whose* question to find a possessive noun and a possessive pronoun, you must remember one important fact about each one in order to tell them apart. Remember, all possessive nouns have an apostrophe, and the seven possessive pronouns do not. They are used in the Possessive Pronoun Jingle you have already learned. *(You may want your students to recite the Possessive Pronoun Jingle again to reinforce what you have just said.)* You will use this information as you classify Sentences 1-3 with me. Begin.

Question and Answer Flow for Sentence 1: Jane's swollen ankle ached during her performance.

1. What ached during her performance? ankle - SN
2. What is being said about ankle? ankle ached - V
3. During - P
4. During what? performance - OP
5. Whose performance? her - PPA
6. What kind of ankle? swollen - Adj
7. Whose ankle? Jane's - PNA (Possessive Noun Adjective)

8. SN V P1 Check
9. (During her performance) - Prepositional phrase
10. Period, statement, declarative sentence
11. Go back to the verb - divide the complete subject from the complete predicate.

Classified Sentence:

<pre>
            PNA   Adj   SN   V   P   PPA   OP
SN V ___   Jane's swollen ankle / ached (during her performance). D
     P1
</pre>

Question and Answer Flow for Sentence 2: My little dog barked excitedly at his shadow.

1. What barked excitedly at his shadow? dog - SN
2. What is being said about dog? dog barked - V
3. Barked how? excitedly - Adv
4. At - P
5. At what? shadow - OP
6. Whose shadow? his - PPA
7. What kind of dog? little - Adj

8. Whose dog? my - PPA
9. SN V P1 Check
10. (At his shadow) - Prepositional phrase
11. Period, statement, declarative sentence
12. Go back to the verb - divide the complete subject from the complete predicate.

Classified Sentence:

<pre>
            PPA Adj SN   V   Adv   P PPA   OP
SN V ___   My little dog / barked excitedly (at his shadow). D
     P1
</pre>

Question and Answer Flow for Sentence 3: The queen's army camped on the hillside.

1. Who camped on the hillside? army - SN
2. What is being said about army? army camped - V
3. On - P
4. On what? hillside - OP
5. The - A
6. Whose army? queen's - PNA (Possessive Noun Adjective)

7. The - A
8. SN V P1 Check
9. (On the hillside) - Prepositional phrase
10. Period, statement, declarative sentence
11. Go back to the verb - divide the complete subject from the complete predicate.

Classified Sentence:

<pre>
            A   PNA   SN   V   P   A   OP
SN V ___   The queen's army / camped (on the hillside). D
     P1
</pre>

© SHURLEY INSTRUCTIONAL MATERIALS, INC.

CHAPTER 8 LESSON 1 CONTINUED

TEACHING SCRIPT FOR A NOUN CHECK WHEN POSSESSIVE NOUNS ARE IN THE SENTENCES

We will only do a Noun Check today to show you how to deal with possessive nouns when you are identifying nouns. A possessive noun's part of speech is an adjective. Remember, a Noun Check is a check for nouns. If there is a possessive noun, we will not classify it as a noun because we are looking only for noun jobs that give us regular nouns, not special nouns that function as possessives and adjectives. Let's start with number one and go through the Noun Check for Sentences 1-3, looking for nouns. (*Recite the information below with your students.*)

Sentence 1: Subject noun *ankle*, yes. (*Circle **ankle** because it is a noun.*) Object of the preposition *performance*, yes. (*Circle **performance** because it is a noun.*)

Sentence 2: Subject noun, *dog*, yes. (*Circle **dog** because it is a noun.*) Object of the preposition *shadow*, yes. (*Circle **shadow** because it is a noun.*)

Sentence 3: Subject noun *army*, yes. (*Circle army because it is a noun.*) Object of the preposition *hillside*, yes. (*Circle **hillside** because it is a noun.*)

Use Sentences 1-3 that you just classified with your students to do an Oral Skill Builder Check. Use the guidelines below.

Oral Skill Builder Check	
1. Noun check. (Say the job and then say the noun. Circle each noun.) **2. Identify the nouns as singular or plural.** (Write S or P above each noun.) **3. Identify the nouns as common or proper.** (Follow established procedure for oral identification.) **4. Do a vocabulary check.** (Follow established procedure for oral identification.)	**5. Identify the complete subject and the complete predicate.** (Underline the complete subject once and the complete predicate twice.) **6. Identify the simple subject and simple predicate.** (Underline the simple subject once and the simple predicate twice. Bold, or highlight, the lines to distinguish them from the complete subject and complete predicate.)

 **PRACTICE TIME**

Have students turn to pages 69 and 70 in the Practice Section of their book and find the skills under Chapter 8, Lesson 1, Practice *(1-3)*. Go over the directions to make sure they understand what to do. Check and discuss the Practices after students have finished. (*Chapter 8, Lesson 1, Practice keys are given below and on the next page.*)

Chapter 8, Lesson 1, Practice 1: On a sheet of paper, write seven subject pronouns, seven possessive pronouns, and seven object pronouns. **(Use the pronoun jingles to check students' papers.)**

© SHURLEY INSTRUCTIONAL MATERIALS, INC.

CHAPTER 8 LESSON 1 CONTINUED

Chapter 8, Lesson 1, Practice 2: For each sentence, do these four things: (1) Write the subject. (2) Write S if the subject is singular or P if the subject is plural. (3) Write the rule number. (4) Underline the correct verb in the sentence.

Rule 1: A singular subject must use a singular verb form that ends in **s**: *is, was, has, does, or verbs ending with* **es**.

Rule 2: A plural subject, a compound subject, or the subject **YOU** must use a plural verb form that has **no s** ending: *are, were, do, have, or verbs without* **s** *or* **es** *endings.* (A plural verb form is also called the *plain form*.)

Subject	S or P	Rule		
children	P	2	1.	The **children** (plays, <u>play</u>) in the sand.
wind	S	1	2.	The **wind** (<u>blows</u>, blow) the trash into the street.
librarian	S	1	3.	The **librarian** (ask, <u>asks</u>) my sister to speak softly.
Vines	P	2	4.	**Vines** (covers, <u>cover</u>) the willow tree.
You	P	2	5.	**You** (goes, <u>go</u>) to the amusement park with my family.
Sam and Sarah	P	2	6.	**Sam** and **Sarah** (walks, <u>walk</u>) through the mall.
She	S	1	7.	**She** (<u>sleds</u>, sled) down the big hill behind our house.
chickens	P	2	8.	The **chickens** (pecks, <u>peck</u>) at the ground.
Bill and Joe	P	2	9.	**Bill** and **Joe** (chases, <u>chase</u>) the girls around the yard.
money	S	1	10.	(<u>Was</u>, Were) your **money** in your pocket?
brother	S	1	11.	My **brother** (<u>slides</u>, slide) into home base.
pilots	P	2	12.	(<u>Do</u>, Does) the **pilots** fly every day?

Chapter 8, Lesson 1, Practice 3: Match the definitions. Write the correct letter beside each numbered concept.

G	1. subject of an imperative sentence	A.	noun markers
F	2. joins a noun or a pronoun to the rest of the sentence	B.	object of the preposition
E	3. takes the place of a noun	C.	person, place, or thing
I	4. adjective modifies	D.	possessive noun
B	5. noun or pronoun after a preposition	E.	pronoun
H	6. subject question	F.	preposition
A	7. article adjectives can be called	G.	you
D	8. noun that shows ownership and modifies like an adjective	H.	who or what
C	9. noun	I.	noun or pronoun
K	10. tells what the subject does	J.	verb, adjective, or adverb
J	11. adverb modifies	K.	verb

VOCABULARY TIME

Assign Chapter 8, Vocabulary Words **#1** on page 8 in the Reference Section for students to define in their Vocabulary notebooks. Tell students they are to use a dictionary or thesaurus to look up the meanings of the vocabulary words. After they write each word and its meaning, students are to write a sentence using the vocabulary word.

Chapter 8, Vocabulary Words #1
(safe, endangered, unity, accord)

(End of lesson.)

© SHURLEY INSTRUCTIONAL MATERIALS, INC.

CHAPTER 8   LESSON 2

Objectives: Jingles, Grammar (Practice Sentences), Skill (making Nouns Possessive), Practice Exercise, and Vocabulary #2.

 **JINGLE TIME**

Have students turn to the Jingle Section in their books and recite the previously-taught jingles.

 GRAMMAR TIME

First-Year Option: Put the Practice Sentences from the box below on the board or on notebook paper. Use these sentences as you practice the concepts that have been taught. For the greatest benefit, students must participate orally with the teacher. **Second-Year Option:** Have students classify the Practice Sentences independently on paper. Check students' sentences with the answers provided below. *(If you have the CDs for Practice Sentences, have students check their sentences with the CDs.)*

Chapter 8, Practice Sentences for Lesson 2

1. _____ The plane's engines roared during takeoff.
2. _____ Fred's sister moved into her new home recently.
3. _____ My aunt's black cat disappeared yesterday.

TEACHING SCRIPT FOR PRACTICING PRONOUNS AND POSSESSIVE NOUNS

We will classify three different sentences to practice the new skills in the Question and Answer Flows. We will classify the sentences together. Begin. *(You might have your students write the labels above the sentences at this time.)*

Question and Answer Flow for Sentence 1: The plane's engines roared during takeoff.

1. What roared during takeoff? engines - SN
2. What is being said about engines? engines roared - V
3. During - P
4. During what? takeoff - OP
5. Whose engines? plane's - PNA
6. The - A

7. SN V P1 Check
8. (During takeoff) - Prepositional phrase
9. Period, statement, declarative sentence
10. Go back to the verb - divide the complete subject from the complete predicate.

Classified Sentence:

            A   PNA   SN   V   P   OP
___SN V___ The plane's engines / roared (during takeoff). **D**
   P1

© SHURLEY INSTRUCTIONAL MATERIALS, INC.

CHAPTER 8 LESSON 2 CONTINUED

Question and Answer Flow for Sentence 2: Fred's sister moved into her new home recently.

1. Who moved into her new home recently? sister - SN
2. What is being said about sister? sister moved - V
3. Into - P
4. Into what? home - OP
5. What kind of home? new - Adj
6. Whose home? her - PPA

7. Moved when? recently - Adv
8. Whose sister? Fred's - PNA
9. SN V P1 Check
10. (Into her new home) - Prepositional phrase
11. Period, statement, declarative sentence
12. Go back to the verb - divide the complete subject from the complete predicate.

Classified Sentence:

	PNA	SN	V	P	PPA	Adj	OP	Adv
SN V P1	Fred's	sister	/ moved	(into	her	new	home)	recently. D

Question and Answer Flow for Sentence 3: My aunt's black cat disappeared yesterday.

1. What disappeared yesterday? cat - SN
2. What is being said about cat? cat disappeared - V
3. Disappeared when? yesterday - Adv
4. What kind of cat? black - Adj
5. Whose cat? aunt's - PNA
6. Whose aunt? my - PPA

7. SN V P1 Check
8. No prepositional phrases.
9. Period, statement, declarative sentence
10. Go back to the verb - divide the complete subject from the complete predicate.

Classified Sentence:

	PPA	PNA	Adj	SN	V	Adv
SN V P1	My	aunt's	black	cat	/ disappeared	yesterday. D

SKILL TIME

TEACHING SCRIPT FOR MAKING NOUNS POSSESSIVE

Learning how to make nouns possessive is the next skill you will learn. This skill is really simple, but, again, students and adults alike have a lot of trouble with it when they write. The more practice you have in making nouns possessive, the more likely you will use possessive nouns correctly in your writing.

In order to form possessive nouns that show ownership, you must first decide if the noun is singular or plural before you add the apostrophe. After you know whether a noun is singular or plural, you can then use three rules to tell you how to make the noun possessive.

Look at Reference 28 on page 23 in the Reference Section of your book and follow along as we go through the three rules and practice examples. (_The information and practice examples are reproduced for you on the next page._) Remember, we always read the directions first. Listen carefully because you have several things to do. (_Read the directions for Part A and Part B on the next page._)

© SHURLEY INSTRUCTIONAL MATERIALS, INC.

CHAPTER 8 LESSON 2 CONTINUED

Reference 28: Making Nouns Possessive		
1. For a singular noun - add (**'s**) **Rule 1: girl's**	2. For a plural noun that ends in **s** - add (**'**) **Rule 2: girls'**	3. For a plural noun that does not end in **s** - add (**'s**) **Rule 3: women's**

Part A: Underline each noun to be made possessive and write singular or plural (S-P), the rule number, and the possessive form. Part B: Write each noun as singular possessive and then as plural possessive.

Part A	S-P	Rule	Possessive Form	Part B	Singular Poss	Plural Poss
1. <u>carpenter</u> saw	S	1	carpenter's saw	5. knife	knife's	knives'
2. <u>lawyers</u> clients	P	2	lawyers' clients	6. plane	plane's	planes'
3. <u>Frank</u> address	S	1	Frank's address	7. scientist	scientist's	scientists'
4. <u>animal</u> dens	S	1	animal's dens	8. boy	boy's	boys'

TEACHING SCRIPT FOR MAKING NOUNS POSSESSIVE, PART A

For Part A, let's review the four things that the directions tell us to do. First, we decide which noun is to be made possessive and underline it. Second, we are going to identify the noun as singular or plural. Third, we are going to write the number of the rule to be followed from the rule box. Last, we are going to write the correct possessive form in the blank.

Look at number 1. The first thing we must do is underline the noun that will be made possessive. An easy way to test for the correct possessive noun is to do the "of" test. We would say "the saw **of** the carpenter, not the carpenter **of** the saw!" Now, we know the noun we want to make possessive. The word *carpenter* is underlined, as shown in the reference.

Next, we must decide whether our underlined noun is singular or plural before we can make it possessive. Is *carpenter* singular or plural? (*Singular*) The letter *S* is written in the blank under the column marked *S-P*.

Now, we will look at the rule box for making nouns possessive. Which rule do we use since *carpenter* is singular? (*Rule 1*) A number 1 is written in the blank under the column marked *Rule*. What does Rule 1 tell us to do? (*For a singular noun, add an apostrophe and s.*) The singular possessive noun *carpenter's* is written under the column marked *Possessive Form*. (*Work through the rest of Part A in the same way to make sure your students understand how to use the rule box for making nouns possessive.*)

TEACHING SCRIPT FOR MAKING NOUNS POSSESSIVE, PART B

Look at Part B. Every noun listed is singular. The directions tell us to do two things. First, we are going to write the singular possessive form of the noun. Next, we are going to change the singular noun to plural and then write the plural possessive form of the noun. <u>That means you may need to check a dictionary for the correct plural spelling of the noun. Dictionaries should always be available for looking up words.</u>

© SHURLEY INSTRUCTIONAL MATERIALS, INC.

CHAPTER 8 LESSON 2 CONTINUED

Look at number 5 under Part B. It says *knife*. Since we know that *knife* is singular, we go to Rule 1 so it will tell us how to make the word *knife* possessive. What does Rule 1 tell us to do? (*For a singular noun, add an apostrophe and* **s**.) The word *knife's* is written under the column marked *Singular Possessive*.

We must change *knife* to its plural form before we can make it plural possessive. How do we make *knife* plural? (*By changing the* **f** *to* **v** *and adding* **es**: *knives*.) We still need to make the plural word *knives* possessive. Since the plural form of *knives* ends in an **s**, which rule do we need to follow? (*Rule 2*) What does Rule 2 say to add to *knives* to make it possessive? (*An apostrophe*.) The word *knives'* is written with an apostrophe in the *Plural Possessive* column. (*Work through the rest of Part B in the same way. After the singular possessive form has been demonstrated and discussed, make sure your students understand how the plural form of the noun is written before making it possessive with the apostrophe by following Rule 2 or Rule 3. Always encourage your students to use the dictionary to check plural spellings.*)

 PRACTICE TIME

Have students turn to page 70 in the Practice Section of their book and find Chapter 8, Lesson 2, Practice. Go over the directions to make sure they understand what to do. Guide students closely as they do the practice exercises for the first time. Check and discuss the Practice after students have finished. (*Chapter 8, Lesson 2, Practice key is given below.*)

Chapter 8, Lesson 2, Practice: Part A: Underline each noun to be made possessive and write singular or plural (S-P), the rule number, and the possessive form. Part B: Write each noun as singular possessive and then as plural possessive.

1. For a singular noun - add (**'s**)				2. For a plural noun that ends in **s** - add (**'**)		3. For a plural noun that does not end in **s** - add (**'s**)		
Rule 1: boy's				**Rule 2: boys'**		**Rule 3: men's**		
Part A	**S-P**	**Rule**	**Possessive Form**			**Part B**	**Singular Poss**	**Plural Poss**
1. <u>sister</u> key	S	1	**sister's key**			5. bush	**bush's**	**bushes'**
2. <u>elephants</u> peanuts	P	2	**elephants' peanuts**			6. fox	**fox's**	**foxes'**
3. <u>women</u> dresses	P	3	**women's dresses**			7. boss	**boss's**	**bosses'**
4. <u>doctor</u> coat	S	1	**doctor's coat**			8. fireman	**fireman's**	**firemen's**

 VOCABULARY TIME

Assign Chapter 8, Vocabulary Words #2 on page 8 in the Reference Section for students to define in their Vocabulary notebooks. Tell students they are to use a dictionary or thesaurus to look up the meanings of the vocabulary words. After they write each word and its meaning, students are to write a sentence using the vocabulary word.

Chapter 8, Vocabulary Words #2
(tempt, lure, savage, tame)

(End of lesson.)

CHAPTER 8   LESSON 3

Objectives: Jingles, Grammar (Practice Sentences, Practice and Improved Sentence), and Practice Exercise.

 **JINGLE TIME**

Have students turn to the Jingle Section in their books and recite the previously-taught jingles.

 GRAMMAR TIME

First-Year Option: Put the Practice Sentences from the box below on the board or on notebook paper. Use these sentences as you practice the concepts that have been taught. For the greatest benefit, students must participate orally with the teacher. **Second-Year Option:** Have students classify the Practice Sentences independently on paper. Check students' sentences with the answers provided below. (*If you have the CDs for Practice Sentences, have students check their sentences with the CDs.*)

Chapter 8, Practice Sentences for Lesson 3

1. _____ The coach's whistle blew loudly during the practice game today.
2. _____ Richard's mom works at the city hospital.
3. _____ My friend's experiment worked perfectly during the science fair.

TEACHING SCRIPT FOR PRACTICING PATTERN 1 SENTENCES

We will classify three different sentences to practice using pronouns and possessive nouns in the Question and Answer Flows. We will classify the sentences together. Begin. (*You might have your students write the labels above the sentences at this time.*)

Question and Answer Flow for Sentence 1: The coach's whistle blew loudly during the practice game today.

1. What blew loudly during the practice game? whistle - SN
2. What is being said about whistle? whistle blew - V
3. Blew how? loudly - Adv
4. During - P
5. During what? game - OP
6. What kind of game? practice - Adj
7. The - A
8. Blew when? today - Adv
9. Whose whistle? coach's - PNA
10. The - A
11. SN V P1 Check
12. (During the practice game) - Prepositional phrase
13. Period, statement, declarative sentence
14. Go back to the verb - divide the complete subject from the complete predicate.

Classified Sentence:

<pre>
            A   PNA   SN   V   Adv   P   A   Adj   OP   Adv
  SN V   The coach's whistle / blew loudly (during the practice game) today. D
  P1
</pre>

© SHURLEY INSTRUCTIONAL MATERIALS, INC.

CHAPTER 8 LESSON 3 CONTINUED

Question and Answer Flow for Sentence 2: Richard's mom works at the city hospital.

1. Who works at the city hospital? mom - SN
2. What is being said about mom? mom works - V
3. At - P
4. At what? hospital - OP
5. What kind of hospital? city - Adj
6. The - A

7. Whose mom? Richard's - PNA
8. SN V P1 Check
9. (At the city hospital) - Prepositional phrase
10. Period, statement, declarative sentence
11. Go back to the verb - divide the complete subject from the complete predicate.

Classified Sentence:

                          PNA   SN   V   P A Adj OP

      __SN V__   Richard's mom / works (at the city hospital). D

        P1

Question and Answer Flow for Sentence 3: My friend's experiment worked perfectly during the science fair.

1. What worked perfectly during the science fair?
   experiment - SN
2. What is being said about experiment?
   experiment worked - V
3. Worked how? perfectly - Adv
4. During - P
5. During what? fair - OP
6. What kind of fair? science - Adj
7. The - A

8. Whose experiment? friend's - PNA
9. Whose friend? my - PPA
10. SN V P1 Check
11. (During the science fair) - Prepositional phrase
12. Period, statement, declarative sentence
13. Go back to the verb - divide the complete subject from the complete predicate.

Classified Sentence:

                          PPA PNA   SN   V   Adv   P   A   Adj   OP

      __SN V__   My friend's experiment / worked perfectly (during the science fair). D

        P1

TEACHING SCRIPT FOR THE PRACTICE SENTENCE

Put these labels on the board: **SP V Adv P PPA PNA Adj OP**

Look at the new sentence labels on the board: **SP V Adv P PPA PNA Adj OP**. I will guide you again through the process of writing a sentence to practice the different parts that you have learned.

Get out a sheet of notebook paper. On the top line of your notebook paper, write the title *Practice Sentence*. Copy the sentence labels from the board onto your notebook paper. Be sure to leave plenty of writing space between each label. I will guide you through the process you will use whenever you write a Practice Sentence with pronouns and possessive nouns.

© SHURLEY INSTRUCTIONAL MATERIALS, INC.

CHAPTER 8 LESSON 3 CONTINUED

1. Go to the **SP** label for the subject pronoun. Repeat the Subject Pronoun Jingle to help you think of a pronoun that you want to use as your subject. Write the pronoun you have chosen on the line *under* the **SP** label.

2. Go to the **V** label for the verb. Think of a verb that tells what your subject does. Make sure that your verb makes sense with the subject pronoun. Write the verb you have chosen on the line *under* the **V** label.

3. Go to the **Adv** label for the adverb. Immediately go to the verb in your sentence and ask an adverb question. What are the adverb questions? (*How, When, Where?*) Choose one adverb question to ask and write your adverb answer *under* the **Adv** label.

4. Go to the **P** label for the preposition. Think of a preposition word that tells something about your verb. You must be careful to choose a preposition word that makes sense with the noun you will choose for the object of the preposition in your next step. Write the word you have chosen for a preposition *under* the **P** label.

5. Go to the **OP** label for the object of the preposition. If you like the noun you thought of while thinking of a preposition, write it down under the **OP** label. If you prefer, think of another noun by asking **what** or **whom** after your preposition. Check to make sure the preposition and object of the preposition make sense together and also make sense with the rest of the sentence. Remember, the object of the preposition will always answer the question **what** or **whom** after the preposition. Write the word you have chosen for the object of the preposition *under* the **OP** label.

6. Go to the **Adj** label for the adjective. Go to the object of the preposition that you just wrote and ask an adjective question to describe the object of the preposition noun. What are the adjective questions? (*What kind, Which one, How many?*) Choose one adjective question to ask and write your adjective answer *under* the **Adj** label next to the object of the preposition. Always check to make sure your answers are making sense in the sentence.

7. Go to the **PNA** label for the possessive noun adjective that is part of your prepositional phrase. Think of a possessive noun that answers "whose" when you refer to the object of the preposition noun. Make sure the possessive noun makes sense in your sentence. Also, make sure you write the apostrophe correctly as you write the possessive noun you have chosen *under* the **PNA** label.

8. Go to the **PPA** label for the possessive pronoun adjective that is part of your prepositional phrase. Repeat the Possessive Pronoun Jingle to help you think of a pronoun that you want to use as your possessive pronoun adjective. Now, you will choose one of the possessive pronouns that makes the best sense in your sentence. Write the possessive pronoun you have chosen *under* the **PPA** label.

9. Finally, check your Practice Sentence to make sure it has the necessary parts to be a complete sentence. What are the five parts of a complete sentence? (*subject, verb, complete sense, capital letter, and an end mark*) Does your Practice Sentence have the five parts of a complete sentence? (*Allow time for students to read over their sentences and to make any corrections they need to make.*)

© SHURLEY INSTRUCTIONAL MATERIALS, INC.

CHAPTER 8 LESSON 3 CONTINUED

TEACHING SCRIPT FOR THE IMPROVED SENTENCE

Under your Practice Sentence, write the title *Improved Sentence* on another line. To improve your Practice Sentence, you will make two synonym changes, one antonym change, and your choice of a complete word change or another synonym or antonym change.

Since it is harder to find words that can be changed to an antonym, it is usually wise to go through your sentence to find an antonym change first. Then, look through your sentence again to find words that can be improved with synonyms. Finally, make a decision about whether your last change will be a complete word change, another synonym change, or another antonym change.

I will give you time to write your Improved Sentence. *(Always encourage students to use a thesaurus, synonym-antonym book, or a dictionary to help them develop an interesting and improved writing vocabulary. After students have finished, check and discuss students' Practice and Improved Sentences.)*

 PRACTICE TIME

Now, have students turn to page 71 in the Practice Section of their book and find Chapter 8, Lesson 3, Practice *(1-2)*. Go over the directions to make sure they understand what to do. Check and discuss the Practices after students have finished. Discuss strong areas as well as weak areas. *(Chapter 8, Lesson 3, Practice keys are given below.)*

Chapter 8, Lesson 3, Practice 1: Number 1-11 on a sheet of paper. Write the answers to the questions listed below.
1. What are the three article adjectives? **an, an, the**
2. Name the understood subject pronoun. **you**
3. What is an imperative sentence? **a command or request**
4. What is a declarative sentence? **a statement**
5. What is an interrogative sentence? **a question**
6. What punctuation mark does a possessive noun always have? **an apostrophe** *or (')*
7. What part of speech is a possessive noun classified as, and what is the abbreviation used? **adjective, PNA**
8. What is the definition of a pronoun?
   A pronoun takes the place of a noun.
9. Name the seven object pronouns.
   me, us, him, her, it, them, you
10. Name the seven subject pronouns.
    I, we, he, she, it, they, you
11. Name the seven possessive pronouns.
    my, our, his, her, its, their, your

Chapter 8, Lesson 3, Practice 2: Part A: Underline each noun to be made possessive and write singular or plural (S-P), the rule number, and the possessive form. Part B: Write each noun as singular possessive and then as plural possessive.

1. For a singular noun - add (**'s**)			2. For a plural noun that ends in *s* - add (**'**)		3. For a plural noun that does not end in *s* - add (**'s**)		
Rule 1: boy's			**Rule 2: boys'**		**Rule 3: men's**		
Part A	**S-P**	**Rule**	**Possessive Form**	**Part B**	**Singular Poss**	**Plural Poss**
1. <u>dress</u> hem	S	1	**dress's hem**	5. brother	**brother's**	**brothers'**
2. <u>kittens</u> paws	P	2	**kittens' paws**	6. woman	**woman's**	**women's**
3. <u>leaves</u> colors	P	2	**leaves' colors**	7. puppy	**puppy's**	**puppies'**
4. <u>children</u> candy	P	3	**children's candy**	8. ship	**ship's**	**ships'**

(End of lesson.)

CHAPTER 8   LESSON 4

Objectives: Jingles, Study, Test, Check, Activity, and Writing (journal).

JINGLE TIME

Have students turn to the Jingle Section in their books and recite the previously-taught jingles.

STUDY TIME

Have students study the vocabulary words in their vocabulary notebooks. Remind students that any vocabulary word in their notebooks could be on their test. Also, have students study any of the skills in the Practice Section that they need to review.

TEST TIME

Have students turn to page 103 in the Test Section of their book and find Chapter 8 Test. Go over the directions to make sure they understand what to do. (*Chapter 8 Test key is on the next page.*)

CHECK TIME

After students have finished, check and discuss their test papers. Make sure they understand why their answers are right or wrong. (*For total points, count each required answer as a point.*)

ACTIVITY / ASSIGNMENT TIME

Students will continue to draw or trace the states and write the following questions and answers.

Connecticut	Delaware
1. What is the state on the front of this card? **Connecticut**	1. What is the state on the front of this card? **Delaware**
2. What is the capital of Connecticut? **Hartford**	2. What is the capital of Delaware? **Dover**
3. What is the postal abbreviation of Connecticut? **CT**	3. What is the postal abbreviation of Delaware? **DE**
4. What year was Connecticut admitted to the Union? **1788**	4. What year was Delaware admitted to the Union? **1787**

Color these states and look up an interesting fact about each state to write on the cards. Use the cards to quiz family members, friends, and relatives. You may want to time the responses to your questions. Also, along with previous suggestions, think of other ways to have fun with your United States card file.

(End of lesson.)

Level 3 Homeschool Teacher's Manual

© SHURLEY INSTRUCTIONAL MATERIALS, INC.

Chapter 8 Test
(Student Page 103)

Exercise 1: Classify each sentence.

        A   PNA SN   V   Adv   P A   OP   Adv

1. <u>SN V</u>   <u>The man's car</u> / <u>broke down (on the freeway)</u> yesterday. **D**
   P1

        PPA PNA   Adj   SN   V   Adv   Adv   P   A   OP

2. <u>SN V</u>   Our church's softball team / played exceptionally well (during the tournament). **D**
   P1

   (You) SP   V Adv Adv   P A   OP   P A OP

3. <u>SN V</u>   / Think very carefully (about the questions) (on the test). **Imp**
   P1

Exercise 2: Use Sentence 1 to underline the complete subject once and the complete predicate twice and to complete the table below.

List the Noun Used	List the Noun Job	Singular or Plural	Common or Proper	Simple Subject	Simple Predicate
1. **car**	2. **SN**	3. **S**	4. **C**	5. **car**	6. **broke**
7. **freeway**	8. **OP**	9. **S**	10. **C**		

Exercise 3: Name the six parts of speech that you have studied. (*You may use abbreviations.*) **(The order may vary.)**

1. **noun**   2. **verb**   3. **adjective**   4. **adverb**   5. **preposition**   6. **pronoun**

Exercise 4: Identify each pair of words as synonyms or antonyms by putting parentheses ( ) around *syn* or *ant*.

1. fowl, chicken	**(syn)** ant	4. tame, savage	syn **(ant)**	7. accord, unity	**(syn)** ant
2. receive, send	syn **(ant)**	5. bland, tasty	syn **(ant)**	8. endangered, safe	syn **(ant)**
3. tempt, lure	**(syn)** ant	6. honest, truthful	**(syn)** ant	9. watch, vigil	**(syn)** ant

Exercise 5: Part A: Underline each noun to be made possessive and write singular or plural (S-P), the rule number, and the possessive form. Part B: Write each noun as singular possessive and then as plural possessive.

1. For a singular noun - add (**'s**)		2. For a plural noun that ends in **s** - add (**'**)		3. For a plural noun that does not end in **s** - add (**'s**)	
Rule 1: girl's		**Rule 2: girls'**		**Rule 3: women's**	

Part A	S-P	Rule	Possessive Form	Part B	Singular Poss	Plural Poss
1. <u>pot</u> handle	S	1	**pot's handle**	10. leaf	**leaf's**	**leaves'**
2. <u>authors</u> ideas	P	2	**authors' ideas**	11. bucket	**bucket's**	**buckets'**
3. <u>cows</u> tails	P	2	**cows' tails**	12. pony	**pony's**	**ponies'**
4. <u>orange</u> peel	S	1	**orange's peel**	13. snake	**snake's**	**snakes'**
5. <u>women</u> slacks	P	3	**women's slacks**	14. yard	**yard's**	**yards'**
6. <u>Jason</u> camera	S	1	**Jason's camera**	15. driver	**driver's**	**drivers'**
7. <u>flowers</u> petals	P	2	**flowers' petals**	16. child	**child's**	**children's**
8. <u>men</u> suits	P	3	**men's suits**	17. mouse	**mouse's**	**mice's**
9. <u>children</u> toys	P	3	**children's toys**	18. video	**video's**	**videos'**

Exercise 6: On notebook paper, write seven subject pronouns, seven possessive pronouns, and seven object pronouns.

Exercise 7: In your journal, write a paragraph summarizing what you have learned this week.

© SHURLEY INSTRUCTIONAL MATERIALS, INC.

CHAPTER 8 LESSON 4 CONTINUED

TEACHER INSTRUCTIONS

Use the Question and Answer Flows below for the sentences on the Chapter 8 Test.

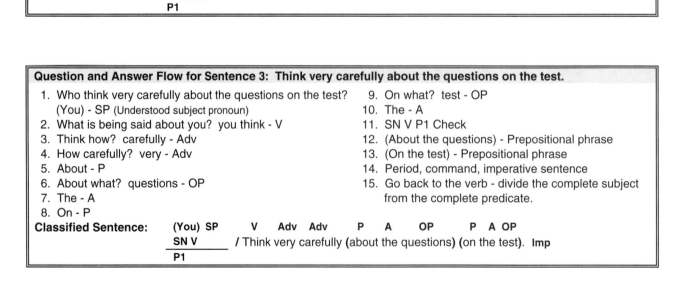

Question and Answer Flow for Sentence 1: The man's car broke down on the freeway yesterday.

1. What broke down on the freeway yesterday? car - SN
2. What is being said about car? car broke - V
3. Broke how? down - Adv
4. On - P
5. On what? freeway - OP
6. The - A
7. Broke when? yesterday - Adv
8. Whose car? man's - PNA
9. The - A
10. SN V P1 Check
11. (On the freeway) - Prepositional phrase
12. Period, statement, declarative sentence
13. Go back to the verb - divide the complete subject from the complete predicate.

Classified Sentence:

                           A   PNA   SN   V   Adv   P A   OP   Adv

         SN V   The man's car / broke down (on the freeway) yesterday. **D**
           P1

Question and Answer Flow for Sentence 2: Our church's softball team played exceptionally well during the tournament.

1. What played exceptionally well during the tournament? team - SN
2. What is being said about team? team played - V
3. Played how? well - Adv
4. How well? exceptionally - Adv
5. During - P
6. During what? tournament - OP
7. The - A
8. What kind of team? softball - Adj
9. Whose team? church's - PNA
10. Whose church? our - PPA
11. SN V P1 Check
12. (During the tournament) - Prepositional phrase
13. Period, statement, declarative sentence
14. Go back to the verb - divide the complete subject from the complete predicate.

Classified Sentence:

                          PPA PNA   Adj   SN   V   Adv   Adv   P   A   OP

        SN V   Our church's softball team / played exceptionally well (during the tournament). **D**
          P1

Question and Answer Flow for Sentence 3: Think very carefully about the questions on the test.

1. Who think very carefully about the questions on the test? (You) - SP (Understood subject pronoun)
2. What is being said about you? you think - V
3. Think how? carefully - Adv
4. How carefully? very - Adv
5. About - P
6. About what? questions - OP
7. The - A
8. On - P
9. On what? test - OP
10. The - A
11. SN V P1 Check
12. (About the questions) - Prepositional phrase
13. (On the test) - Prepositional phrase
14. Period, command, imperative sentence
15. Go back to the verb - divide the complete subject from the complete predicate.

Classified Sentence:

                    (You) SP   V   Adv   Adv   P   A   OP   P   A OP

        SN V   / Think very carefully (about the questions) (on the test). **Imp**
         P1

© SHURLEY INSTRUCTIONAL MATERIALS, INC.

CHAPTER 8   LESSON 5

Objectives: Writing (3-point Expository Paragraph) and Writing Assignment #5, Bonus Option.

WRITING TIME

TEACHING SCRIPT FOR INTRODUCING THE THREE-POINT EXPOSITORY PARAGRAPH

In this writing lesson, you will learn to write a three-point expository paragraph. Remember, **expository paragraphs** give facts or directions, explain ideas, or define words. Any time you write an expository paragraph, you should focus on making your meaning clear and understandable. The three-point paragraph is basically like the two-point paragraph except that there are three points instead of two. This means that a three-point paragraph will have two more sentences: a third-point sentence and a supporting sentence for that point. These two new sentences will come right before the concluding sentence.

Now we will make a comparison between the two-point expository paragraph and the three-point expository paragraph. Look at Reference 29 on page 23. (*Read and discuss the two guidelines, showing students the similarities and differences.*)

Reference 29: Two- and Three-Point Expository Paragraph Guidelines	
2-Point Expository Paragraph Guidelines	3-Point Expository Paragraph Guidelines
Paragraph (7 sentences) A. Topic sentence B. A two-point sentence C. A **first-point sentence** D. A **supporting** sentence for the first point E. A **second-point sentence** F. A **supporting** sentence for the second point G. A concluding sentence	Paragraph (9 sentences) A. Topic sentence B. A three-point sentence C. A **first-point sentence** D. A **supporting** sentence for the first point E. A **second-point sentence** F. A **supporting** sentence for the second point G. A **third-point sentence** H. A **supporting** sentence for the third point I. A concluding sentence

Now look at Reference 30 on page 24. You follow the three-point expository paragraph guideline and example paragraph at the bottom of Reference 30 as I go over the steps in writing a three-point expository paragraph. (*Read the steps and examples provided on the next page as students follow the guidelines for a three-point expository paragraph in Reference 30.*)

© SHURLEY INSTRUCTIONAL MATERIALS, INC.

CHAPTER 8 LESSON 5 CONTINUED

Reference 30: Three-Point Expository Paragraph Example

Topic: **My favorite colors**
Three main points: 1. **green**   2. **yellow**   3. **red**

Sentence #1 – <u>Topic Sentence</u> (*Use words in the topic and tell how many points will be used.*)
I have three favorite colors.

Sentence #2 – <u>3-Point Sentence</u> (*List the 3 points in the order you will present them.*)
These colors are green, yellow, and red.

Sentence #3 – <u>First Point</u>
My first favorite color is green.

Sentence #4 – <u>Supporting Sentence</u> for the first point.
I like green because I love budding leaves after a long winter.

Sentence #5 – <u>Second Point</u>
My second favorite color is yellow.

Sentence #6 – <u>Supporting Sentence</u> for the second point.
Yellow reminds me of warm sunshine and summer days.

Sentence #7 – <u>Third Point</u>
My third favorite color is red.

Sentence #8 – <u>Supporting Sentence</u> for the third point.
Red is a wonderful, rich color for celebrating winter holidays.

Sentence #9 – <u>Concluding (final) Sentence</u>. (*Restate the topic sentence and add an extra thought.*)
My three favorite colors remind me of special seasons throughout the year.

SAMPLE PARAGRAPH

My Favorite Colors

    I have three favorite colors. These colors are green, yellow, and red. My first favorite color is green. I like green because I love budding leaves after a long winter. My second favorite color is yellow. Yellow reminds me of warm sunshine and summer days. My third favorite color is red. Red is a wonderful, rich color for celebrating winter holidays. My three favorite colors remind me of special seasons throughout the year.

General Checklist: Check the Finished Paragraph	The Three-Point Expository Paragraph Outline
(1) Have you followed the pattern for a 3-point paragraph? (*Indent, topic sentence, 3-point sentence, 3 main points, 3 supporting sentences, and a concluding sentence.*)	Topic 3 points about the topic Sentence #1: **Topic** sentence Sentence #2: A **three-point** sentence
(2) Do you have complete sentences?	Sentence #3: A **first-point sentence**
(3) Have you capitalized the first word and put an end mark at the end of every sentence?	Sentence #4: A **supporting** sentence for the 1st point
(4) Have you checked your sentences for capitalization and punctuation mistakes?	Sentence #5: A **second-point sentence** Sentence #6: A **supporting** sentence for the 2nd point
(5) Have you checked your verb tenses?	Sentence #7: A **third-point sentence** Sentence #8: A **supporting** sentence for the 3rd point
(6) Have you varied your sentence structure?	Sentence #9: A **concluding** sentence

© SHURLEY INSTRUCTIONAL MATERIALS, INC.

CHAPTER 8 LESSON 5 CONTINUED

TEACHER INSTRUCTIONS FOR WRITING ASSIGNMENT

Give Writing Assignment #5 from the box below. Remind students to follow the Writing Guidelines as they prepare their writings.

Writing Assignment Box

Writing Assignment #5: Three-Point Expository Paragraph

Writing topic choices: **My Best Birthday Present** or **My Favorite Foods** or **My Favorite Movie**

Bonus Option: Write the following questions in your Journal along with today's date. Leave space in your Journal to record the answers.
(1) What is the name of the character in the Bible who killed a giant with a sling?
(2) Where does this story begin in the Bible?
(3) What did he take from the brook?
(4) Write the story in your own words.
(5) Draw the character with his weapon.

TEACHING SCRIPT FOR USING THE WRITING PROCESS FOR THIS WRITING ASSIGNMENT

As you begin this writing assignment, you will use the writing process again. First, you will think about your topic and gather any information you might need in order to do the writing. Second, you will write a rough draft. Remember, it is called a rough draft because it will be revised and edited. You do not have to worry about mistakes as you write your rough draft. After you write the first draft, you will make revisions, using the Revision Checklist in Reference 13. After you revise your writing, you will edit, using the Beginning Editing Checklist in Reference 13. Finally, after you are satisfied with your revising and editing, you will write a final paper, using the Final Paper Checklist in Reference 13. You will then give the finished writing assignment to me. (*Students should finish their writing during their free time if they do not finish during this lesson.*)

TEACHER INSTRUCTIONS FOR CHECKING WRITING ASSIGNMENT #5

Read, check, and discuss Writing Assignment #5 after students have finished their final papers. Use the editing checklist (*Reference 13 on teacher's page 48*) as you check and discuss students' papers. Make sure students are using the editing checklist correctly. In the beginning, you must also check students' papers carefully for <u>form</u> mistakes. This will ensure that students are learning the three-point format correctly.

Bonus Option Answers:
(1) **David**
(2) **I Samuel 17**
(3) **5 smooth stones**
(4) **Stories will vary.**
(5) **David with sling (Pictures will vary.)**

(End of lesson.)

CHAPTER 9   LESSON 1

Objectives: Jingles (The 23 Helping Verbs of the Mean, Lean Verb machine), Grammar (Introductory Sentences, Helping Verb, **not** Adverb, Question Verb), Oral Skill Builder Check, Writing (journal) and Vocabulary #1.

 **JINGLE TIME**

Have students turn to the Jingle Section in their books and recite the previously-taught jingles. Then, lead students in reciting the new jingle (*The 23 Helping Verbs of the Mean, Lean Verb Machine*) below. Practice the new jingle several times until students can recite it smoothly. Emphasize reciting with a rhythm. Students and teacher should be together! (*Do not try to explain the jingle at this time. Just have fun reciting it. Remember, add motions for more fun and laughter.*)

Teacher's Note: Again, do not spend a large amount of time practicing the new jingles. Students learn the jingles best by spending a small amount of time consistently, **every** day.

Jingle 14:   The 23 Helping Verbs of the Mean, Lean Verb Machine Jingle

These 23 helping verbs will be on my test.
I gotta remember them so I can do my best.
I'll start out with 8 and finish with 15;
Just call me the mean, lean verb machine.

There are 8 **be** verbs that are easy as can be:
   am, is, are – was and were,
   am, is, are – was and were,
   am, is, are – was and were,
   be, being, and been.
All together now, the 8 **be** verbs:
am, is, are – was and were – be, being, and been,
am, is, are – was and were – be, being, and been.

There're 23 helping verbs, and I've recited only 8.
That leaves fifteen more that I must relate:
   has, have, and had – do, does, and did,
   has, have, and had – do, does, and did,
   might, must, may – might, must, may.

Knowing these verbs will save my grade:
   can and could – would and should,
   can and could – would and should,
   shall and will,
   shall and will.
In record time, I did this drill.
I'm the mean, lean verb machine – STILL!

 GRAMMAR TIME

Put the introductory sentences from the box below on the board. Use these sentences as you go through each new concept covered in your teaching script. For the greatest benefit, students must participate orally with the teacher. (*You might put the introductory sentences on notebook paper if you are doing one-on-one instruction with your students.*)

Chapter 9, Introductory Sentences for Lesson 1

1. _____ My grandmother has worked hard for many years.
2. _____ The workers in the warehouse are not working during the summer months.
3. _____ Are the automobiles built in your factories?

Level 3 Homeschool Teacher's Manual

© SHURLEY INSTRUCTIONAL MATERIALS, INC.

CHAPTER 9 LESSON 1 CONTINUED

TEACHING SCRIPT FOR THE HELPING VERB

Today, we will learn about helping verbs. When there are two or more verbs used together in a sentence, the verbs in front are known as the **helping verbs**, and the last verb is the main verb. Helping verbs are also called **auxiliary verbs**. Helping verbs are labeled with *HV*. The main verb and helping verbs together are called a **verb phrase**.

When directions are given to underline the verb, the helping verb and the main verb should be underlined because they are both part of the verb phrase. We will use this sentence for an example: **My daughter is singing in the choir.** *Is singing* is the verb phrase and both verbs would be underlined. If you are labeling *is singing*, you would label the helping verb *is* with the letters *HV* and the main verb *singing* with the letter *V*.

You will use this information as you classify Sentence 1 with me to find the helping verb. Remember, you use the same subject question, *who* or *what*, to start classifying all sentences. Begin.

Question and Answer Flow for Sentence 1: My grandmother has worked hard for many years.

1. Who has worked hard for many years? grandmother - SN
2. What is being said about grandmother?
   grandmother has worked - V

Note: There are 2 verbs. W*orked* is the main verb and will be labeled with a V. *Has* is the helping verb in front of *worked* and will be labeled with HV.

3. Has - HV (helping verb) (Write HV above *has*.)
4. Has worked how? hard - Adv
5. For - P

6. For what? years - OP
7. How many years? many - Adj
8. Whose grandmother? my - PPA
9. SN V P1 Check
10. (For many years) - Prepositional phrase
11. Period, statement, declarative sentence
12. Go back to the verb - divide the complete subject from the complete predicate. (You will divide in front of the helping verb.)

Classified Sentence:

		PPA	SN	HV	V	Adv	P	Adj	OP

<u>SN V</u> My grandmother / has worked hard (for many years). **D**
P1

---

*TEACHING SCRIPT FOR THE **NOT** ADVERB*

Even though the word *NOT* is not a verb, we will study it now because it is so often confused as part of a verb phrase. The helping verb can be split from the main verb by the adverb *NOT*. The word *NOT* is usually an adverb telling *how*. Many negative words are adverbs telling *how* or *to what extent*. (*For example: Jeffery is **not** playing in the game tonight*.) We will now classify Sentence 2 to find the "*NOT*" adverb. Begin.

CHAPTER 9 LESSON 1 CONTINUED

Question and Answer Flow for Sentence 2: The workers in the warehouse are not working during the summer months.

1. Who are not working during the summer months? workers - SN
2. What is being said about workers? workers are working - V
3. Are - HV
4. Are working how? not - Adv
5. During - P
6. During what? months - OP
7. What kind of months? summer - Adj
8. The - A
9. In - P
10. In what? warehouse - OP
11. The - A
12. The - A
13. SN V P1 Check
14. (In the warehouse) - Prepositional phrase
15. (During the summer months) - Prepositional phrase
16. Period, statement, declarative sentence
17. Go back to the verb - divide the complete subject from the complete predicate.

Classified Sentence:

```
                          A   SN    P A   OP        HV Adv  V    P    A  Adj   OP
          SN  V    The workers (in the warehouse) / are not working (during the summer months).  D
          P1
```

TEACHING SCRIPT FOR THE QUESTION VERB

Earlier, we studied interrogative sentences. Now, we are going to review the interrogative sentence that starts with a helping verb. When the helping verb is placed before the subject, the sentence is usually a question. The subject will come between the helping verb and the main verb. You can check the parts of a question by making a statement: (For example: **Are** we **running** in the marathon? We **are running** in the marathon.)

Let's classify Sentence 3 for identification of the question verb. Begin.

Question and Answer Flow for Sentence 3: Are the automobiles built in your factories?

1. What are built in your factories? automobiles - SN
2. What is being said about automobiles? automobiles are built - V
3. Are - HV
4. In - P
5. In what? factories - OP
6. Whose factories? your - PPA
7. The - A
8. SN V P1 Check
9. (In your factories) - Prepositional phrase
10. Question mark, question, interrogative sentence
11. Go back to the verb - divide the complete subject from the complete predicate.

Classified Sentence:

```
                     HV A    SN          V    P PPA  OP
          SN  V    Are the automobiles / built (in your factories)?  Int
          P1
```

© SHURLEY INSTRUCTIONAL MATERIALS, INC.

CHAPTER 9 LESSON 1 CONTINUED

TEACHER INSTRUCTIONS

Use Sentences 1-3 that you just classified with your students to do an Oral Skill Builder Check. Use the guidelines below.

Oral Skill Builder Check	
1. Noun check. (Say the job and then say the noun. Circle each noun.) **2. Identify the nouns as singular or plural.** (Write S or P above each noun.) **3. Identify the nouns as common or proper.** (Follow established procedure for oral identification.) **4. Do a vocabulary check.** (Follow established procedure for oral identification.)	**5. Identify the complete subject and the complete predicate.** (Underline the complete subject once and the complete predicate twice.) **6. Identify the simple subject and simple predicate.** (Underline the simple subject once and the simple predicate twice. Bold, or highlight, the lines to distinguish them from the complete subject and complete predicate.)

 WRITING TIME

Have students make an entry in their journals.

 VOCABULARY TIME

Assign Chapter 9, Vocabulary Words **#1** on page 8 in the Reference Section for students to define in their Vocabulary notebooks. Tell students they are to use a dictionary or thesaurus to look up the meanings of the vocabulary words. After they write each word and its meaning, students are to write a sentence using the vocabulary word.

Chapter 9, Vocabulary Words #1
(timid, bold, hurry, rush)

(End of lesson.)

© SHURLEY INSTRUCTIONAL MATERIALS, INC.

CHAPTER 9   LESSON 2

Objectives: Jingles, Grammar (Practice Sentences), Practice and Improved Sentence, Practice Exercise, and Vocabulary #2.

 JINGLE TIME

Have students turn to the Jingle Section in their books and recite the previously-taught jingles.

 GRAMMAR TIME

First-Year Option: Put the Practice Sentences from the box below on the board or on notebook paper. Use these sentences as you practice the concepts that have been taught. For the greatest benefit, students must participate orally with the teacher. **Second-Year Option:** Have students classify the Practice Sentences independently on paper. Check students' sentences with the answers provided below. (*If you have the CDs for Practice Sentences, have students check their sentences with the CDs.*)

Chapter 9, Practice Sentences for Lesson 2

_____1. Seven people will not fit into my small car!
_____2. Can you go with us to the water park today?
_____3. I am not running for office again.

---

*TEACHING SCRIPT FOR PRACTICING WITH HELPING VERBS AND THE **NOT** ADVERB*

We will classify three different sentences to practice using our new skills in the Question and Answer Flows. We will classify the sentences together. Begin. (*You might have your child write the labels above the sentences at this time.*)

Question and Answer Flow for Sentence 1: Seven people will not fit into my small car!

1. Who will not fit into my small car? people - SN
2. What is being said about people? people will fit - V
3. Will - HV
4. Will fit how? not - Adv
5. Into - P
6. Into what? car - OP
7. What kind of car? small - Adj
8. Whose car? my - PPA
9. How many people? seven - Adj
10. SN V P1 Check
11. (Into my small car) - Prepositional phrase
12. Exclamation point, strong feeling, exclamatory sentence
13. Go back to the verb - divide the complete subject from the complete predicate.

Classified Sentence:

		Adj	SN	HV	Adv	V	P	PPA	Adj	OP
SN V		Seven	people /	will	not	fit	(into	my	small	car)! E
P1

© SHURLEY INSTRUCTIONAL MATERIALS, INC.

CHAPTER 9 LESSON 2 CONTINUED

Question and Answer Flow for Sentence 2: Can you go with us to the water park today?

1. Who can go with us to the water park today? you - SP
2. What is being said about you?   you can go - V
3. Can - HV
4. With - P
5. With whom? us - OP
6. To - P
7. To what? park - OP
8. What kind of park? water - Adj

9. The - A
10. Can go when? today - Adv
11. SN V P1 Check
12. (With us) - Prepositional phrase
13. (To the water park) - Prepositional phrase
14. Question mark, question, interrogative sentence
15. Go back to the verb - divide the complete subject from the complete predicate.

Classified Sentence:

<pre>
                       HV SP V   P   OP   P A   Adj OP   Adv
          SN V   Can you / go (with us) (to the water park) today? Int
          P1
</pre>

Question and Answer Flow for Sentence 3: I am not running for office again.

1. Who am not running for office again? I - SP
2. What is being said about I? I am running - V
3. Am - HV
4. Am running how? not - Adv
5. For - P
6. For what? office - OP
7. Am running when? again - Adv

8. SN V P1 Check
9. (For office) - Prepositional phrase
10. Period, statement, declarative sentence
11. Go back to the verb - divide the complete subject from the complete predicate.

Classified Sentence:

<pre>
                       SP HV Adv   V   P   OP   Adv
          SN V   I / am not running (for office) again. D
          P1
</pre>

TEACHING SCRIPT FOR THE PRACTICE SENTENCE

Put these labels on the board: **HV A Adj SN V P PPA OP**

Look at the new sentence labels on the board: **HV A Adj SN V P PPA OP**. I will guide you through the process of writing a sentence to practice the new parts that you have learned.

Get out a sheet of notebook paper. On the top line of your notebook paper, write the title *Practice Sentence*. Copy the sentence labels from the board onto your notebook paper. Be sure to leave plenty of writing space between each label. I will guide you through the process you will use whenever you write a Practice Sentence with helping verbs.

© SHURLEY INSTRUCTIONAL MATERIALS, INC.

CHAPTER 9 LESSON 2 CONTINUED

1. Go to the **SN** label for the subject noun. Think of a noun that you want to use as your subject. Write the noun you have chosen on the line *under* the **SN** label.

2. Go to the **V** label for the verb. Think of a verb that tells what your subject does. Make sure that your verb makes sense with the subject noun. Write the verb you have chosen on the line *under* the **V** label.

3. Go to the **P** label for the preposition. Think of a preposition word that tells something about your verb. You must be careful to choose a preposition word that makes sense with the noun you will choose for the object of the preposition in your next step. Write the word you have chosen for a preposition *under* the **P** label.

4. Go to the **OP** label for the object of the preposition. If you like the noun you thought of while thinking of a preposition, write it down under the **OP** label. If you prefer, think of another noun by asking **what** or **whom** after your preposition. Check to make sure the preposition and object of the preposition make sense together and also make sense with the rest of the sentence. Remember, the object of the preposition will always answer the question **what** or **whom** after the preposition. Write the word you have chosen for the object of the preposition *under* the **OP** label.

5. Go to the **PPA** label for the possessive pronoun adjective that is part of your prepositional phrase. Recite the Possessive Pronoun Jingle to help you think of a pronoun that you want to use as your possessive pronoun adjective. Choose the possessive pronoun that makes the best sense in your sentence. Write the possessive pronoun you have chosen *under* the **PPA** label.

6. Go to the **Adj** label for the adjective. Go to the subject noun of your sentence and ask an adjective question. What are the adjective questions again? (*What kind? Which one? How many?*) Choose one adjective question to ask and write your adjective answer *under* the **Adj** label next to the subject noun.

7. Go to the **A** label for the article adjective in the subject area. What are the three article adjectives again? (*a, an, the*) Choose the article adjective that makes the best sense in your sentence. Write the article adjective you have chosen *under* the **A** label.

8. Go to the **HV** label for the helping verb. Choose a helping verb that asks a question and that makes sense in your sentence. Write the helping verb you have chosen *under* the **HV** label.

9. Finally, check your Practice Sentence to make sure it has the necessary parts to be a complete sentence. What are the five parts of a complete sentence? (*subject, verb, complete sense, capital letter, and an end mark*) Does your Practice Sentence have the five parts of a complete sentence? (*Allow time for students to read over their sentences and to make any corrections they need to make.*)

© SHURLEY INSTRUCTIONAL MATERIALS, INC.

CHAPTER 9 LESSON 2 CONTINUED

TEACHING SCRIPT FOR THE IMPROVED SENTENCE

Under your Practice Sentence, write the title *Improved Sentence* on another line. To improve your Practice Sentence, you will make two synonym changes, one antonym change, and your choice of a complete word change or another synonym or antonym change.

Since it is harder to find words that can be changed to an antonym, it is usually wise to go through your sentence to find an antonym change first. Look through your sentence again to find words that can be improved with synonyms. Finally, make a decision about whether your last change will be a complete word change, another synonym change, or another antonym change.

I will give you time to write your Improved Sentence. *(Always encourage students to use a thesaurus, synonym-antonym book, or a dictionary to help them develop an interesting and improved writing vocabulary. After students have finished, check and discuss students' Practice and Improved Sentences.)*

 PRACTICE TIME

Have students write the three sentences that they classified at the beginning of the lesson on a sheet of paper. *(See page 156.)* Have them tape-record the Question and Answer Flows for all three sentences. Students should write labels above the sentences as they classify them. They especially need the second practice if this is their first year in the program. *(After students have finished, check the tape and sentence labels. Make sure students understand any mistakes they have made.)*

 VOCABULARY TIME

Assign Chapter 9, Vocabulary Words **#2** on page 8 in the Reference Section for students to define in their Vocabulary notebooks. Tell students they are to use a dictionary or thesaurus to look up the meanings of the vocabulary words. After they write each word and its meaning, students are to write a sentence using the vocabulary word.

Chapter 9, Vocabulary Words #2
(fragrance, aroma, join, withdraw)

(End of lesson.)

© SHURLEY INSTRUCTIONAL MATERIALS, INC.

CHAPTER 9   LESSON 3

Objectives: Jingles, Grammar (Practice Sentences), Oral Skill Builder Check, Add Irregular Verb Chart to the Skill Builder Check, Practice Exercise, and Activity.

JINGLE TIME

Have students turn to the Jingle Section in their books and recite the previously-taught jingles.

GRAMMAR TIME

First-Year Option: Put the Practice Sentences from the box below on the board or on notebook paper. Use these sentences as you practice the concepts that have been taught. For the greatest benefit, students must participate orally with the teacher. **Second-Year Option:** Have students classify the Practice Sentences independently on paper. Check students' sentences with the answers provided below. *(If you have the CDs for Practice Sentences, have students check their sentences with the CDs.)*

Chapter 9, Practice Sentences for Lesson 3
_____1. The football players are not practicing on the field today.
_____2. Are we going to the theatre tonight?
_____3. The funny clowns waved enthusiastically to the children after their absolutely incredible performance.

---

*TEACHING SCRIPT FOR PRACTICING HELPING VERBS AND THE **NOT** ADVERB*

We will practice classifying the new concepts in the Question and Answer Flows. We will classify the sentences together. Begin. *(You might have your students write the labels above the sentences at this time.)*

Question and Answer Flow for Sentence 1: The football players are not practicing on the field today.

1. Who are not practicing on the field today? players - SN
2. What is being said about players? players are practicing - V
3. Are - HV
4. Are practicing how? not - Adv
5. On - P
6. On what? field - OP
7. The - A
8. Are practicing when? today - Adv
9. What kind of players? football - Adj
10. The - A
11. SN V P1 Check
12. (On the field) - Prepositional phrase
13. Period, statement, declarative sentence
14. Go back to the verb - divide the complete subject from the complete predicate.

Classified Sentence:

<pre>
                        A   Adj   SN   HV Adv   V   P   A   OP   Adv
          SN V   The football players / are not practicing (on the field) today. D
          P1
</pre>

© SHURLEY INSTRUCTIONAL MATERIALS, INC.

Question and Answer Flow for Sentence 2: Are we going to the theatre tonight?

1. Who are going to the theatre tonight? we - SP
2. What is being said about we? we are going - V
3. Are - HV
4. To - P
5. To what? theatre - OP
6. The - A

7. Are going when? tonight - Adv
8. SN V P1 Check
9. (To the theatre) - Prepositional phrase
10. Question mark, question, interrogative sentence
11. Go back to the verb - divide the complete subject from the complete predicate.

Classified Sentence:

		HV	SP	V	P	A	OP	Adv
SN	V	Are	We /	going	(to the	theatre)	tonight.	**Int**
P1								

Question and Answer Flow for Sentence 3: The funny clowns waved enthusiastically to the children after their absolutely incredible performance?

1. Who waved enthusiastically to the children after their absolutely incredible performance? clowns - SN
2. What is being said about clowns? clowns waved - V
3. Waved how? enthusiastically - Adv
4. To - P
5. To whom? children - OP
6. The - A
7. After - P
8. After what? performance - OP
9. What kind of performance? incredible - Adj

10. How incredible? absolutely - Adv
11. Whose performance? their - PPA
12. What kind of clowns? funny - Adj
13. The - A
14. SN V P1 Check
15. (To the children) - Prepositional phrase
16. (After their absolutely incredible performance) - Prepositional phrase
17. Period, statement, declarative sentence
18. Go back to the verb - divide the complete subject from the complete predicate.

Classified Sentence:

SN V A Adj SN V Adv P A OP P PPA Adv Adj

P1   The funny clowns / waved enthusiastically (to the children) (after their absolutely incredible

OP

performance). **D**

TEACHER INSTRUCTIONS

Use Sentences 1-3 that you just classified with your students to do an Oral Skill Builder Check. Use the guidelines below.

Oral Skill Builder Check

1. **Noun check.**
   (Say the job and then say the noun. Circle each noun.)

2. **Identify the nouns as singular or plural.**
   (Write S or P above each noun.)

3. **Identify the nouns as common or proper.**
   (Follow established procedure for oral identification.)

4. **Do a vocabulary check.**
   (Follow established procedure for oral identification.)

5. **Identify the complete subject and the complete predicate.** (Underline the complete subject once and the complete predicate twice.)

6. **Identify the simple subject and simple predicate.**
   (Underline the simple subject once and the simple predicate twice. Bold, or highlight, the lines.)

7. **Recite the irregular verb chart.**
   (This new skill is explained on the next page.)

© SHURLEY INSTRUCTIONAL MATERIALS, INC.

CHAPTER 9 LESSON 3 CONTINUED

TEACHING SCRIPT FOR ADDING AN IRREGULAR VERB CHART TO THE SKILL BUILDER CHECK

We will now add an Irregular Verb Chart to the Skill Builder Check. Look at the Irregular Verb Chart that is located in Reference 31 on page 25 in your book. (*The irregular verb chart is reproduced for you on the next page.*) We will recite the Irregular Verb Chart during the Skill Builder Checks to help you learn the different principal parts of some irregular verbs.

Even though this is only a partial listing of irregular verbs, it will expose you to the correct forms on a consistent basis. We can add more irregular verbs as we think of them. (*You do not need to chant all of the verb chart for every Skill Builder Check. Pick only a few verbs to chant if your child does not have a problem with irregular verb usage.*)

If you use an irregular verb incorrectly, either spoken or written, I will say, "I need a correction for the verb ____," and you will be expected to recite the verb correctly two ways. You will recite the two corrections several times in short sentences. If you cannot remember how to use the two corrections in short sentences, you should use the chart to help you. (*Explain the example below.*)

Example: He **seen** the movie.   Verb used incorrectly: **seen**

1. Correction with the past tense form: He **saw** the movie; He **saw** the movie; He **saw** the movie; He **saw** the movie.

2. Correction with a helping verb: He **had seen** the movie; He **had seen** the movie; He **had seen** the movie; He **had seen** the movie.

© SHURLEY INSTRUCTIONAL MATERIALS, INC.

CHAPTER 9 LESSON 3 CONTINUED

Reference 31: Irregular Verb Chart			
PRESENT	PAST	PAST PARTICIPLE	PRESENT PARTICIPLE
become	became	(has) become	(is) becoming
blow	blew	(has) blown	(is) blowing
break	broke	(has) broken	(is) breaking
bring	brought	(has) brought	(is) bringing
burst	burst	(has) burst	(is) bursting
buy	bought	(has) bought	(is) buying
choose	chose	(has) chosen	(is) choosing
come	came	(has) come	(is) coming
drink	drank	(has) drunk	(is) drinking
drive	drove	(has) driven	(is) driving
eat	ate	(has) eaten	(is) eating
fall	fell	(has) fallen	(is) falling
fly	flew	(has) flown	(is) flying
freeze	froze	(has) frozen	(is) freezing
get	got	(has) gotten	(is) getting
give	gave	(has) given	(is) giving
grow	grew	(has) grown	(is) growing
know	knew	(has) known	(is) knowing
lie	lay	(has) lain	(is) lying
lay	laid	(has) laid	(is) laying
make	made	(has) made	(is) making
ride	rode	(has) ridden	(is) riding
ring	rang	(has) rung	(is) ringing
rise	rose	(has) risen	(is) rising
sell	sold	(has) sold	(is) selling
sing	sang	(has) sung	(is) singing
sink	sank	(has) sunk	(is) sinking
set	set	(has) set	(is) setting
sit	sat	(has) sat	(is) sitting
shoot	shot	(has) shot	(is) shooting
swim	swam	(has) swum	(is) swimming
take	took	(has) taken	(is) taking
tell	told	(has) told	(is) telling
throw	threw	(has) thrown	(is) throwing
wear	wore	(has) worn	(is) wearing
write	wrote	(has) written	(is) writing

© SHURLEY INSTRUCTIONAL MATERIALS, INC.

CHAPTER 9 LESSON 3 CONTINUED

PRACTICE TIME

Now, have students turn to page 72 in the Practice Section of their book and find Chapter 9, Lesson 3, Practice *(1-2)*. Go over the directions to make sure they understand what to do. Check and discuss the Practices after students have finished. Discuss strong areas as well as weak areas. *(Chapter 9, Lesson 3, Practice keys are given below.)*

Chapter 9, Lesson 3, Practice 1: Number 1-11 on a sheet of paper. Write the answers to the questions listed below.

1. What part of speech is the word NOT? **adverb**
2. Name the understood subject pronoun. **you**
3. What is an imperative sentence? **a command**
4. What is a declarative sentence? **a statement**
5. What is an interrogative sentence? **a question**
6. What punctuation mark does a possessive noun always have? **an apostrophe or (')**
7. What part of speech is a possessive noun classified as, and what is the abbreviation used? **adjective, PNA**

8. List the 8 *be* verbs.
   am, is, are, was, were, be, being, been
9. What are the parts of a verb phrase?
   helping verb and main verb
10. Name the seven subject pronouns.
    I, we, he, she, it, they, you
11. Name the seven possessive pronouns.
    my, our, his, her, its, their, your

Chapter 9, Lesson 3, Practice 2: Part A: Underline each noun to be made possessive and write singular or plural (S-P), the rule number, and the possessive form. Part B: Write each noun as singular possessive and as plural possessive.

1. For a singular noun - add (**'s**)			2. For a plural noun that ends in *s* - add (')			3. For a plural noun that does not end in *s* - add (**'s**)		
Rule 1: boy's			**Rule 2: boys'**			**Rule 3: men's**		
Part A	**S-P**	**Rule**	**Possessive Form**		**Part B**	**Singular Poss**	**Plural Poss**	
1. <u>tree</u> height	S	1	tree's height		5. light	light's	lights'	
2. <u>rabbits</u> ears	P	2	rabbits' ears		6. baby	baby's	babies'	
3. <u>quilts</u> threads	P	2	quilts' threads		7. dolphin	dolphin's	dolphins'	
4. <u>men</u> hair	P	3	men's hair		8. child	child's	children's	

ACTIVITY / ASSIGNMENT TIME

Write the letters of each of your family member's names vertically, including your own name. Beside each letter, write an adjective or short phrase that starts with that letter to describe each family member. Have students research the word **acrostic**. Discuss this type of poem. *(Write the example below on the board for your students.)*

Example:

J – jubilant
A – active
M – mischievous
E – energetic
S – smart

(End of lesson.)

© SHURLEY INSTRUCTIONAL MATERIALS, INC.

CHAPTER 9   LESSON 4

Objectives: Jingles, Study, Test, Check, Activity, and Writing (journal).

 JINGLE TIME

Have students turn to the Jingle Section in their books and recite the previously-taught jingles.

 STUDY TIME

Have students study the vocabulary words in their vocabulary notebooks. Remind students that any vocabulary word in their notebooks could be on their test. Also, have students study any of the skills in the Practice Section that they need to review.

 TEST TIME

Have students turn to page 104 in the Test Section of their book and find Chapter 9 Test. Go over the directions to make sure they understand what to do. (*Chapter 9 Test key is on the next page.*)

 CHECK TIME

After students have finished, check and discuss their test papers. Make sure they understand why their answers are right or wrong. (*For total points, count each required answer as a point.*)

 ACTIVITY / ASSIGNMENT TIME

Students will continue to draw or trace the states and write the following questions and answers.

Florida	Georgia
1. What is the state on the front of this card? **Florida**	1. What is the state on the front of this card? **Georgia**
2. What is the capital of Florida? **Tallahassee**	2. What is the capital of Georgia? **Atlanta**
3. What is the postal abbreviation of Florida? **FL**	3. What is the postal abbreviation of Georgia? **GA**
4. What year was Florida admitted to the Union? **1845**	4. What year was Georgia admitted to the Union? **1788**

Color these states and look up an interesting fact about each state to write on the cards. Use the cards to quiz family members, friends, and relatives. You may want to time the responses to your questions. Also, along with previous suggestions, think of other ways to have fun with your United States card file.

(End of lesson.)

© SHURLEY INSTRUCTIONAL MATERIALS, INC.

Chapter 9 Test
(Student Page 104)

Exercise 1: Classify each sentence.

```
              PPA  SN    HV Adv V  P    OP        P    A    OP
1. SN  V      My family / did not go (on vacation) (during the summer).  D
   ‾‾‾‾
   P1

              HV  A  SN    V     P    A  Adj  Adj   OP
2. SN  V      Did the pond / freeze (during the cold winter storm)?  Int
   ‾‾‾‾
   P1

              SP  HV  V     P  A  OP    P  A   OP
3. SN  V      We /are riding (on a bus) (to the party).  D
   ‾‾‾‾
   P1
```

Exercise 2: Use Sentence 3 to underline the complete subject once and the complete predicate twice and to complete the table below.

List the Noun Used	List the Noun Job	Singular or Plural	Common or Proper	Simple Subject	Simple Predicate
1. **bus**	2. **OP**	3. **S**	4. **C**	5. **We**	6. **are riding**
7. **party**	8. **OP**	9. **S**	10. **C**		

Exercise 3: Name the six parts of speech that you have studied. (*You may use abbreviations.*) **(The order may vary.)**

1. **noun**   2. **verb**   3. **adjective**   4. **adverb**   5. **preposition**   6. **pronoun**

Exercise 4: Identify each pair of words as synonyms or antonyms by putting parentheses ( ) around *syn* or *ant*.

1. accord, unity	**(syn)** ant	5. explode, burst	**(syn)** ant	9. fragrance, aroma	**(syn)** ant
2. rush, hurry	**(syn)** ant	6. timid, bold	syn **(ant)**	10. pain, discomfort	**(syn)** ant
3. cheap, costly	syn **(ant)**	7. tempt, lure	**(syn)** ant	11. endangered, safe	syn **(ant)**
4. friend, foe	syn **(ant)**	8. congeal, melt	syn **(ant)**	12. withdraw, join	syn **(ant)**

Exercise 5: For each sentence, write the subject, then write S if the subject is singular or P if the subject is plural, write the rule number (Rule 1 for singular and Rule 2 for plural), and underline the correct verb in the sentence.

Subject	S or P	Rule		
game	S	1	1.	The **game** (<u>is</u>, are) played on the grass.
windows	P	2	2.	Our **windows** (was, <u>were</u>) left open last night.
Angela and Joseph	P	2	3.	**Angela** and **Joseph** (writes, <u>write</u>) silly stories together.
audience	S	1	4.	The **audience** (<u>claps</u>, clap) at the marvelous act.
chips	P	2	5.	My **chips** (is, <u>are</u>) stale.
flowers	P	2	6.	The **flowers** (was, <u>were</u>) sent in a vase.

Exercise 6: Part A: Underline each noun to be made possessive and write singular or plural (S-P), the rule number, and the possessive form. Part B: Write each noun as singular possessive and then as plural possessive.

1. For a singular noun - add (**'s**)			2. For a plural noun that ends in **s** - add (**'**)		3. For a plural noun that does not end in **s** - add (**'s**)		
Rule 1: girl's			**Rule 2: girls'**		**Rule 3: women's**		
Part A	**S-P**	**Rule**	**Possessive Form**	**Part B**	**Singular Poss**	**Plural Poss**	
1. <u>teacher</u> desk	S	1	**teacher's desk**	4. wife	**wife's**	**wives'**	
2. <u>vine</u> branch	S	1	**vine's branch**	5. cake	**cake's**	**cakes'**	
3. <u>men</u> jobs	P	3	**men's jobs**	6. puppy	**puppy's**	**puppies'**	

Exercise 7: In your journal, write a paragraph summarizing what you have learned this week.

© SHURLEY INSTRUCTIONAL MATERIALS, INC.

CHAPTER 9 LESSON 4 CONTINUED

TEACHER INSTRUCTIONS

Use the Question and Answer Flows below for the sentences on the Chapter 9 Test.

Question and Answer Flow for Sentence 1: My family did not go on vacation during the summer.

1. Who did not go on vacation during the summer? family - SN
2. What is being said about family? family did go - V
3. Did - HV
4. Did go how? not - Adv
5. On - P
6. On what? vacation - OP
7. During - P
8. During what? summer - OP
9. The - A
10. Whose family? my - PPA
11. SN V P1 Check
12. (On vacation) - Prepositional phrase
13. (During the summer) - Prepositional phrase
14. Period, statement, declarative sentence
15. Go back to the verb - divide the complete subject from the complete predicate.

Classified Sentence:

| | PPA | SN | HV | Adv | V | P | OP | P | A | OP |
| SN V | My | family / | did | not | go | (on | vacation) | (during | the | summer). | **D** |
| P1 |

Question and Answer Flow for Sentence 2: Did the pond freeze during the cold winter storm?

1. What did freeze during the cold winter storm? pond - SN
2. What is being said about pond? pond did freeze - V
3. Did - HV
4. During - P
5. During what? storm - OP
6. What kind of storm? winter - Adj
7. What kind of storm? cold - Adj
8. The - A
9. The - A
10. SN V P1 Check
11. (During the cold winter storm) - Prepositional phrase
12. Question mark, question, interrogative sentence
13. Go back to the verb - divide the complete subject from the complete predicate.

Classified Sentence:

| | HV | A | SN | V | P | A | Adj | Adj | OP |
| SN V | Did | the | pond / | freeze | (during | the | cold | winter | storm)? | **Int** |
| P1 |

Question and Answer Flow for Sentence 3: We are riding on a bus to the party.

1. Who are riding on a bus to the party? we - SP
2. What is being said about we? we are riding - V
3. Are - HV
4. On - P
5. On what? bus - OP
6. A - A
7. To - P
8. To what? party - OP
9. The - A
10. SN V P1 Check
11. (On a bus) - Prepositional phrase
12. (To the party) - Prepositional phrase
13. Period, statement, declarative sentence
14. Go back to the verb - divide the complete subject from the complete predicate.

Classified Sentence:

| | SP | HV | V | P | A | OP | P | A | OP |
| SN V | We / | are | riding | (on | a | bus) | (to | the | party). | **D** |
| P1 |

© SHURLEY INSTRUCTIONAL MATERIALS, INC.

CHAPTER 9   LESSON 5

Objectives: Writing (standard and time-order forms) and Writing Assignment #6, Bonus Option.

 WRITING TIME

TEACHING SCRIPT FOR STANDARD AND TIME-ORDER FORMS

When you learned to write a three-point paragraph, you learned to state your points by beginning each sentence that stated a point with an article adjective or a possessive pronoun. (**My** first favorite, **My** second favorite, **My** third favorite, or **The** first thing, **The** second thing, **The** third thing.) We will call what you have been doing the **standard form** because it is used often and is a good, reliable three-point form. But now you are ready to learn another way to state each point in a three-point paragraph. This will give you some variety in your writing. We will call the new way to state each point the **time-order form**.

In the time-order form, you should begin each sentence that states a point with words that suggest a definite time or number order, such as *first, second, third*, etc. or *first, next, last*, or *finally*, etc. <u>When you begin your sentence with time order words, you leave out the article adjectives and possessive pronouns.</u> For example, instead of saying "**My first** favorite" you would say "**First**, I like." You must remember this word of caution: Whichever form you choose, you must use that same form throughout your paragraph to introduce each of your points. You cannot mix forms in the same paragraph.

I will demonstrate how to use the time-order form to write a paragraph. Turn to page 26 and look at Reference 32 as I read the paragraph to you. Then, I will go through each of the three points in the paragraph and show you how it was written in time-order form. *(Read the paragraph to your students from beginning to end. Then, go through the teaching script given for each sentence in the paragraph.)*

Reference 32: Paragraphs Using Different Writing Forms

Topic: My favorite collectibles **3-points:** 1. stuffed animals   2. sea shells   3. rocks

Example 1: Three-point paragraph using time-order points

    I have three favorite collectibles. They are stuffed animals, sea shells, and rocks. **<u>First</u>**, I like to collect stuffed animals. Stuffed animals are so cuddly and adorable. **<u>Second</u>**, I like to collect sea shells. It is fun collecting seashells while I walk along the beach and wade in the water. **<u>Third</u>**, I like to collect rocks. (*or* **Finally**, *I like to collect rocks.*) Since rocks can be found in so many different sizes, shapes, and colors, I use them to make a memory garden. I enjoy collecting many things, but collecting stuffed animals, sea shells, and rocks holds a special fascination for me.

Notice that the topic is written first because it is the subject of the paragraph. Having the topic written first will help us focus on what the paragraph is about. Next, the three points that we will discuss are listed. Again, having the three points written down before we start will help us focus on what we will say in the paragraph.

We are now ready to begin our paragraph because we are clear about our topic and about the points we will cover as we write. We start with a topic sentence because it tells the reader what the paragraph is about. Our topic sentence is, *"I have three favorite collectibles."* Knowing what the paragraph is about helps the reader focus on the main points as the reader progresses through the paragraph.

© SHURLEY INSTRUCTIONAL MATERIALS, INC.

CHAPTER 9 LESSON 5 CONTINUED

Our next sentence is the three-point sentence: *They are stuffed animals, sea shells, and rocks.* The three-point sentence lists the three main points that will be discussed in the paragraph; so, in this paragraph, we know the three main points are *stuffed animals, seashells, and rocks.*

Let's look at the sentence written for the first point. The sentence for the first point starts out like this: *First, I like to collect stuffed animals.* As you can see, we do not use the possessive pronoun *my* or the article *the* in front of the word *first*, and a comma is placed after the order word because it is an introductory word.

Notice that the second and third main points have been written in the same format selected for the first point. Look at their form as I read them to you. (**2nd point:** *Second, I like to collect sea shells.* **3rd point:** *Third, I like to collect rocks.*) You could also use *finally* instead of *third* to introduce your last point.

After each main point, there is a supporting sentence. The supporting sentences make each point clearer by telling extra information about each main point. Remember, we have stated in the main points that <u>stuffed animals</u>, <u>sea shells</u>, and <u>rocks</u> are three of our favorite collectibles. Each supporting sentence should state some kind of information that proves each of the main points. (**1st Supporting sentence:** ***Stuffed animals*** *are so cuddly and adorable.* **2nd Supporting sentence:** *It is fun collecting* **seashells** *while I walk along the beach and wade in the water.* **3rd Supporting sentence:** *Since* **rocks** *can be found in so many different sizes, shapes, and colors, I use them to make a memory garden.*)

Our last sentence is a concluding sentence. It summarizes our three points by restating some of the words in the topic sentence and by adding an extra thought that finalizes the paragraph. (**Concluding sentence:** *I enjoy collecting many things, but collecting stuffed animals, sea shells, and rocks holds a special fascination for me.*)

I will read the same paragraph to you again, but this time I will use different order words to introduce each point. In the first example, the order words were *first, second,* and *third*. In the second example, the order words are *first, next,* and *last*. It is a minor change, but it definitely adds variety to the paragraph. (*As you read the following paragraph, emphasize the different words that introduce each point sentence.*)

Reference 32: Paragraphs Using Different Writing Forms (continued)

<u>**Example 2: Three-point paragraph using a standard topic sentence with different time-order points**</u>

    I have three favorite collectibles. They are stuffed animals, sea shells, and rocks. <u>**First**</u>, I like to collect stuffed animals. Stuffed animals are so cuddly and adorable. <u>**Next**</u>, I like to collect sea shells. It is fun collecting seashells while I walk along the beach and wade in the water. <u>**Last**</u>, I like to collect rocks. (*or* <u>**Finally**</u>, *I like to collect rocks.*) Since rocks can be found in so many different sizes, shapes, and colors, I use them to make a memory garden. I enjoy collecting many things, but collecting stuffed animals, sea shells, and rocks holds a special fascination for me.

As a review, I will go over the four things you need to know whenever you are using the time-order form to write a three-point paragraph. Listen carefully because I will ask you a few questions after I have finished the review. (*Go over the four items listed below. Then, discuss the questions on the next page.*)

Using the Time-Order Form

1. Use time-order words at the beginning of each of the main point sentences. (*first, second, third*, etc.) or (*first, next, last, finally*, etc.)
2. Do not use a possessive pronoun or article in front of the time-order word.
3. Put a comma after the introductory time-order word.
4. For consistency, use the same style to introduce each point in your paragraph.

© SHURLEY INSTRUCTIONAL MATERIALS, INC.

CHAPTER 9 LESSON 5 CONTINUED

1. The words you use in the time-order form usually come in sets. We have discussed two sets. What are they? (*first, second, third*, etc.) and (*first, next, last, finally*, etc.)

2. What two kinds of words are generally not used in the time-order form? (*possessive pronouns and articles*)

3. When you use time-order words to introduce the point sentences, they are introductory words. What punctuation is required after the time-order words when they are used as introductory words? (*comma*)

TEACHER INSTRUCTIONS FOR WRITING ASSIGNMENT

For Writing Assignment #6, students are to write a three-point paragraph, using the time-order form. They are to <u>underline all time-order words</u> used at the beginning of each sentence that states a point. Also, tell students to look up any words they cannot spell as they check over their writing. A spelling check is being added to the general editing list for the students. (*See "More Editing Skills" in Reference 13 on student page 16.*)

Writing Assignment Box

Writing Assignment #6: Three-Point Expository Paragraph (Time-Order Form)

Writing topics: Things That Make Me Laugh or **My Favorite Way of Traveling** or **Ways to Enjoy a Saturday**

Bonus Option: Visit the nursing home or an elderly relative or neighbor. Find out their favorite Bible verses and discuss them. Have them select a story from the Bible and read it to them. Write about your experiences in your Journal.

TEACHING SCRIPT FOR USING THE WRITING PROCESS FOR THIS WRITING ASSIGNMENT

As you begin this writing assignment, you will start through the writing process. First, you will think about your topic and gather any information you might need in order to do the writing. Second, you will write a rough draft. Remember, it is called a rough draft because it will be revised and edited. You do not have to worry about mistakes as you write your rough draft. After you write the first draft, you will make revisions, using the Revision Checklist in Reference 13. After you revise your writing, you will edit, using the Beginning Editing Checklist in Reference 13. Finally, you will write a final paper, using the Final Paper Checklist in Reference 13. You will then give the finished writing assignment to me.

TEACHER INSTRUCTIONS FOR CHECKING WRITING ASSIGNMENT

Read, check, and discuss Writing Assignment #6 after students have finished their final paper. Use the editing checklist (*Reference 13 on teacher's page 48*) as you check and discuss students' papers. Make sure students are using the editing checklist correctly.

(End of lesson.)

© SHURLEY INSTRUCTIONAL MATERIALS, INC.

CHAPTER 10   LESSON 1

Objectives: Jingles (The Eight Parts of Speech), Grammar (Introductory Sentences, Conjunctions, Compound Parts, Interjection, Eight Parts of Speech), Oral Skill Builder Check, Vocabulary #1 and Activity.

JINGLE TIME

Have students turn to the Jingle Section in their books and recite the previously-taught jingles. Then, lead students in reciting the new jingle (*The Eight Parts of Speech*) below. Practice the new jingle several times until students can recite it smoothly. Emphasize reciting with a rhythm. Students and teacher should be together! (*Do not try to explain the jingle at this time. Just have fun reciting it. Remember, add motions for more fun and laughter.*)

Teacher's Note: Again, do not spend a large amount of time practicing the new jingles. Students learn the jingles best by spending a small amount of time consistently, **every** day.

Jingle 15: Eight Parts of Speech Jingle
Want to know how to write?   Use the eight parts of speech - They're dynamite!   **N**ouns, **V**erbs, and **P**ronouns - They rule!   They're called the **NVP's**, and they're really cool!   The **Double A's** are on the move;   **A**djectives and **A**dverbs help you groove!   Next come the **PIC's**, and then we're done!   The **PIC's** are **P**reposition, **I**nterjection, and **C**onjunction!   All together now, the eight parts of speech, abbreviations please: NVP, AA, PIC   NVP, AA, PIC!

GRAMMAR TIME

Put the introductory sentences from the box below on the board. Use these sentences as you go through each new concept covered in your teaching script. For the greatest benefit, students must participate orally with the teacher. (*You might put the introductory sentences on notebook paper if you are doing one-on-one instruction with your students.*)

Chapter 10, Introductory Sentences for Lesson 1
1. _____ My mom and dad are leaving early in the morning.   2. _____ We screamed and cheered loudly for our favorite team.   3. _____ Yikes! The lightning flashed and struck close to my house!

© SHURLEY INSTRUCTIONAL MATERIALS, INC.

CHAPTER 10 LESSON 1 CONTINUED

TEACHING SCRIPT FOR CONJUNCTIONS AND COMPOUND PARTS

Today, we will learn about conjunctions and compound parts. A **conjunction** is a word that joins words or groups of words together. The three most common conjunctions are *and, or,* and *but.* The conjunctions *and, or,* and *but* are used so often that they should be memorized. Since conjunctions are memorized, there are no questions to ask to find a conjunction. Conjunctions are labeled with a *C.* Let's chant the three most common conjunctions together several times. (*Have students chant the three most common conjunctions with you several times. Try "**and** (stand up), **or** (sit down), **but** (arms up in a V)" as you recite them. Other motions will also work well.*)

When words or groups of words in a sentence are joined by a conjunction, the parts that are joined are called **compound parts**. The label *C* is written in front of the regular labels for the compound parts. Example: **CSN** for each compound subject noun or **CV** for each compound verb.

You will use what you have just learned as you classify Sentences 1-2 with me to find the conjunction and compound parts. We will classify the sentences together, and I will show you how to say the new part as we say the Question and Answer Flow. Begin.

Question and Answer Flow for Sentence 1: My mom and dad are leaving early in the morning.

1. Who are leaving early in the morning?
   mom and dad - CSN, CSN (compound subject noun, compound subject noun)
2. What is being said about mom and dad?
   mom and dad are leaving - V
3. Are - HV
4. Are leaving when? early - Adv
5. In - P
6. In what? morning - OP
7. The - A

8. And - C
   Note: Say: and - conjunction. Label "and" with a "C."
9. Whose mom and dad? my - PPA
10. SN V P1 Check
11. (In the morning) - Prepositional phrase
12. Period, statement, declarative sentence
13. Go back to the verb - divide the complete subject from the complete predicate.

Classified Sentence:

	PPA	CSN	C	CSN	HV	V	Adv	P	A	OP
SN V	My	mom	and	dad /	are	leaving	early	(in	the	morning). **D**
P1										

Question and Answer Flow for Sentence 2: We screamed and cheered loudly for our favorite team.

1. Who screamed and cheered loudly for our favorite team? we - SP
2. What is being said about we?
   we screamed and cheered - CV, CV (compound verb, compound verb)
3. Screamed and cheered how? loudly - Adv
4. For - P
5. For what? team - OP
6. What kind of team? favorite - Adj

7. Whose team? our - PPA
8. And - C
9. SN V P1 Check
10. (For our favorite team) - Prepositional phrase
11. Period, statement, declarative sentence
12. Go back to the verb - divide the complete subject from the complete predicate.

Classified Sentence:

	SP	CV	C	CV	Adv	P	PPA	Adj	OP
SN V	We /	screamed	and	cheered	loudly	(for	our	favorite	team). **D**
P1									

© SHURLEY INSTRUCTIONAL MATERIALS, INC.

CHAPTER 10 LESSON 1 CONTINUED

TEACHING SCRIPT FOR INTERJECTION

We will now learn about interjections. An **interjection** is one or more words used to express mild or strong emotion. Interjections are usually located at the beginning of a sentence and are separated from the rest of the sentence with a punctuation mark. Mild interjections are followed by a comma or period; strong interjections are followed by an exclamation point. Example: **Oh!   Well,   Wow!   Yes,   Hey!**

Interjections are not to be considered when you are deciding whether a sentence is declarative, interrogative, exclamatory, or imperative. There are no questions to find interjections. Interjections are named and then labeled with the abbreviation *I* above them.

You will use what you have just learned about interjections as you classify Sentence 3 with me. We will classify the sentence together, and I will show you how to say the new part as we say the Question and Answer Flow. Begin.

Question and Answer Flow for Sentence 3: Yikes! The lightning flashed and struck close to my house!	
1. What flashed and struck close to my house? lightning - SN	9. Yikes - I
2. What is being said about lightning? lightning flashed and struck - CV, CV	**Note:** Say: Yikes - interjection. Label "Yikes" with an " I ".
3. Flashed and struck where? close - Adv	10. SN V P1 Check
4. To - P	11. (To my house) - Prepositional phrase
5. To what? house - OP	12. Exclamation point, strong feeling, exclamatory sentence
6. Whose house? my - PPA	13. Go back to the verb - divide the complete subject from the complete predicate.
7. And - C	
8. The - A	

Classified Sentence:

                                             I   A   SN   CV   C   CV   Adv   P PPA OP

      <u>SN V</u>   Yikes! The lightning / flashed and struck close (to my house)! **E**

        P1

TEACHER INSTRUCTIONS

Use Sentences 1-3 that you just classified with your students to do an Oral Skill Builder Check. Use the guidelines below.

Oral Skill Builder Check	
1. **Noun check.** (Say the job and then say the noun. Circle each noun.)	5. **Identify the complete subject and the complete predicate.** (Underline the complete subject once and the complete predicate twice.)
2. **Identify the nouns as singular or plural.** (Write S or P above each noun.)	
3. **Identify the nouns as common or proper.** (Follow established procedure for oral identification.)	6. **Identify the simple subject and simple predicate.** (Underline the simple subject once and the simple predicate twice. Bold, or highlight, the lines.)
4. **Do a vocabulary check.** (Follow established procedure for oral identification.)	7. **Recite the irregular verb chart.** (Located on student page 25 and teacher page 163.)

CHAPTER 10 LESSON 1 CONTINUED

TEACHING SCRIPT FOR ALL EIGHT PARTS OF SPEECH

We can add the final two parts of speech, conjunctions and interjections, to our eight parts of speech list. Remember, all words in the English language have been put into one of eight groups called the **Parts of Speech**. How a word is used in a sentence determines its part of speech.

It is very important to know the eight parts of speech because they are the vocabulary for writing. We will now celebrate learning the eight parts of speech by reciting the Eight Parts of Speech Jingle. This jingle will help you remember the eight parts of speech quickly and easily. Turn to page 5 in the Jingle Section of your books and recite Jingle 15, the Eight Parts of Speech jingle. (*The Eight Parts of Speech jingle is located on page 171.*)

 VOCABULARY TIME

Assign Chapter 10, Vocabulary Words #1 on page 8 in the Reference Section for students to define in their Vocabulary notebooks. Tell students they are to use a dictionary or thesaurus to look up the meanings of the vocabulary words. After they write each word and its meaning, students are to write a sentence using the vocabulary word.

Chapter 10, Vocabulary Words #1
(abundant, scarce, wilt, droop)

 ACTIVITY / ASSIGNMENT TIME

You will create a noun puzzle by using the following directions:

Across	Down
1. The type of noun that shows ownership	1. A noun is an object to what part of speech
3. A noun meaning more than one, usually ending in s or es	2. A noun that tells what the sentence is about
5. A noun that names ANY person, place, or thing	3. A noun that means a particular person, place, or thing
6. A noun meaning one in number	4. What all proper nouns begin with

①P	O	②S	S	E	S	S	I	V	E							
R		U														
E		B														
P		J				③P	L	U	R	A	L		④C			
O		E				R							A			
S		⑤C	O	M	M	O	N					P			
I		T				P						I			
T						E						T			
I						R						A			
O							⑥S	I	N	G	U	L	A	R	
N												S			

(End of lesson.)

© SHURLEY INSTRUCTIONAL MATERIALS, INC.

CHAPTER 10   LESSON 2
Objectives: Jingles, Grammar (Practice Sentences), Skill (Homonyms), Practice Exercise, Vocabulary #2, and Activity.

 **JINGLE TIME**

Have students turn to the Jingle Section in their books and recite the previously-taught jingles.

 GRAMMAR TIME

First-Year Option: Put the Practice Sentences from the box below on the board or on notebook paper. Use these sentences as you practice the concepts that have been taught. For the greatest benefit, students must participate orally with the teacher. **Second-Year Option:** Have students classify the Practice Sentences independently on paper. Check students' sentences with the answers provided below. *(If you have the CDs for Practice Sentences, have students check their sentences with the CDs.)*

Chapter 10, Practice Sentences for Lesson 2
1. _____ Wow! Mom's yellow rosebush is blooming brilliantly in the front yard!
2. _____ Bob and Annie traveled to Mexico on a mission trip.
3. _____ Oh, no! Grandfather's old fishing boat stalled in the middle of the lake!

TEACHING SCRIPT FOR PRACTICING PATTERN 1 SENTENCES WITH THE 8 PARTS OF SPEECH

We will classify three different sentences to practice using the eight parts of speech in the Question and Answer Flows. We will classify the sentences together. Begin. *(You might have your students write the labels above the sentences at this time.)*

Question and Answer Flow for Sentence 1: Wow! Mom's yellow rosebush is blooming brilliantly in the front yard!	
1. What is blooming brilliantly in the front yard? rosebush – SN	9. What kind of rosebush? yellow - Adj
2. What is being said about rosebush? rosebush is blooming - V	10. Whose rosebush? Mom's - PNA
3. Is – HV	11. Wow - I
4. Is blooming how? brilliantly - Adv	12. SN V P1 Check
5. In – P	13. (In the front yard) - Prepositional phrase
6. In what? yard – OP	14. Exclamation point, strong feeling, exclamatory sentence
7. What kind of yard? front - Adj	15. Go back to the verb - divide the complete subject from the complete predicate.
8. The – A	

Classified   I   PNA   Adj   SN   HV   V   Adv   P A Adj OP
Sentence: SN V   Wow! Mom's yellow rosebush / is blooming brilliantly (in the front yard)! E
                  P1

CHAPTER 10 LESSON 2 CONTINUED

Question and Answer Flow for Sentence 2: Bob and Annie traveled to Mexico on a mission trip.

1. Who traveled to Mexico on a mission trip?
   Bob and Annie - CSN, CSN
2. What is being said about Bob and Annie?
   Bob and Annie traveled - V
3. To – P
4. To what? Mexico – OP
5. On – P
6. On what? trip – OP
7. What kind of trip? mission - Adj

8. A - A
9. And - C
10. SN V P1 Check
11. (To Mexico) - Prepositional phrase
12. (On a mission trip) - Prepositional phrase
13. Period, statement, declarative sentence
14. Go back to the verb - divide the complete subject from the complete predicate.

Classified Sentence:

<pre>
                    CSN C CSN   V   P   OP   P A Adj OP
       SN V   Bob and Annie / traveled (to Mexico) (on a mission trip). D
       P1
</pre>

Question and Answer Flow for Sentence 3: Oh, no! Grandfather's old fishing boat stalled in the middle of the lake!

1. What stalled in the middle of the lake?
   boat – SN
2. What is being said about boat? boat stalled - V
3. In - P
4. In what? middle – OP
5. The – A
6. Of - P
7. Of what? lake – OP
8. The - A
9. What kind of boat? fishing - Adj

10. What kind of boat? old - Adj
11. Whose boat? Grandfather's - PNA
12. Oh, no - I
13. SN V P1 Check
14. (In the middle) - Prepositional phrase
15. (Of the lake) - Prepositional phrase
16. Exclamation point, strong feeling, exclamatory sentence
17. Go back to the verb - divide the complete subject from the complete predicate.

Classified Sentence:

<pre>
                      I   PNA   Adj Adj SN   V   P A   OP   P A OP
       SN V   Oh, no! Grandfather's old fishing boat / stalled (in the middle) (of the lake)! E
       P1
</pre>

SKILL TIME

TEACHING SCRIPT FOR HOMONYMS

Today, we will learn about homonyms. Look at Reference 33 on page 26 in the Reference section of your book. The definition says that homonyms are words that sound the same but have different meanings and different spellings. You should study the Homonym Chart until you are familiar enough with each homonym that you can choose the correct form easily. Since this is only a partial listing, you must look up homonyms that you do not know and that are not listed on the chart. (*The homonym chart is located on the next page.*)

© SHURLEY INSTRUCTIONAL MATERIALS, INC.

CHAPTER 10 LESSON 2 CONTINUED

Look at the examples for choosing the right homonyms at the bottom of the reference box. The directions say to underline the correct homonym. Read number 1. Look at the homonyms *week* and *weak*. Go to the Homonym Chart and read the definition for each spelling. How do we spell the homonym that means *seven days*? (*w-e-e-k*) How do we spell the homonym that means *not strong*? (*w-e-a-k*)

Which homonym would you choose to complete the first sentence correctly? (*week*) How did you decide? It makes sense for Sally not to call for *seven days*. The word *week* means the same thing as *seven days*.

Now, look at number 2. Which homonym would you choose to complete the second sentence correctly? (*weak*) How did you decide? It makes sense for James *not to feel strong* after his knee surgery. The word *weak* means the same thing as *not strong*. Always check the Homonym Chart or use a dictionary if you have a question about which homonym to use.

Reference 33: Homonym Chart		
Homonyms are words that sound the same but have different meanings and different spellings.		
1. **capital** - upper part, main	15. **lead** – metal	29. **their** - belonging to them
2. **capitol** - statehouse	16. **led** – guided	30. **there** - in that place
3. **coarse** - rough	17. **no -** not so	31. **they're** - they are
4. **course** - route	18. **know** - to understand	32. **threw** - did throw
5. **council** - assembly	19. **right** – correct	33. **through** -from end to end
6. **counsel** - advice	20. **write** - to form letters	34. **to** - toward, preposition
7. **forth** - forward	21. **principle** - a truth/rule/law	35. **too** - denoting excess
8. **fourth** - ordinal number	22. **principal** - chief/head person	36. **two** - a couple
9. **its** - possessive pronoun	23. **stationary** – motionless	37. **your** - belonging to you
10. **it's** - it is	24. **stationery** – paper	38. **you're** - you are
11. **hear** - to listen	25. **peace** – quiet	39. **weak** - not strong
12. **here** - in this place	26. **piece** - a part	40. **week** - seven days
13. **knew** - understood	27. **sent** - caused to go	41. **days** - more than one day
14. **new** - not old	28. **scent** – odor	42. **daze** - a confused state
Directions: Underline the correct homonym.		
1. One (weak, **week**) has passed, and Sally hasn't called.		
2. James felt (**weak**, week) after his knee surgery.		

 PRACTICE TIME

Now, have students turn to page 72 in the Practice Section of their book and find Chapter 10, Lesson 2, Practice. Go over the directions to make sure they understand what to do. Check and discuss the Practice after students have finished. Discuss strong areas as well as weak areas. (*Chapter 10, Lesson 2, Practice key is given below.*)

Chapter 10, Lesson 2, Practice: Underline the correct homonym in each sentence.

1. She looked at (<u>their</u>, there) vacation pictures.
2. Joseph (<u>knew</u>, new) about the surprise.
3. He (<u>threw</u>, through) the towel into the basket.
4. The puppy ran (threw, <u>through</u>) the mud.
5. Our team (<u>won</u>, one) the championship game.
6. The (knew, <u>new</u>) stamps were blue and red.
7. We have only (won, <u>one</u>) dollar left.
8. Andrea left the books over (their, <u>there</u>).
9. I wanted another (<u>piece</u>, peace) of pie.
10. Timothy ran (<u>by</u>, buy) the bleachers.
11. She wanted to (by, <u>buy</u>) a new dress.
12. The country prayed for (piece, <u>peace</u>).

© SHURLEY INSTRUCTIONAL MATERIALS, INC.

CHAPTER 10 LESSON 2 CONTINUED

 VOCABULARY TIME

Assign Chapter 10, Vocabulary Words **#2** on page 8 in the Reference Section for students to define in their Vocabulary notebooks. Tell students they are to use a dictionary or thesaurus to look up the meanings of the vocabulary words. After they write each word and its meaning, students are to write a sentence using the vocabulary word.

Chapter 10, Vocabulary Words #2
(tepid, warm, frivolous, serious)

 ACTIVITY / ASSIGNMENT TIME

Part 1: Put the paragraph below on the board without underlining the homonyms. Have students copy the paragraph onto notebook paper. There are 14 homonyms in the paragraph. See if students can find all the homonyms by underlining them. Then, they should check the homonyms to see if the spellings are correct. Students are to put a second line under the homonyms that are not used correctly. They should have 9 homonyms underlined two times and 5 homonyms underlined one time.

The last time Aunt Barbara **scent** me a letter, it got lost in the **male**. **I** don't **know** what the problem was, and the postal authorities didn't **no** either. Besides the letter, Aunt Barbara enclosed a check **too** me for my graduation. Now that **eye** know the letter was lost, **I** need to **right** her back and tell her **knot** to worry. **I** was more interested in her being **their** to **sea** me in my cap and gown than **I** was in getting her check.

Part 2: Have students rewrite the first paragraph and correct the homonyms. Then students are to identify the homonyms by underlining them. Compare the homonyms in the two paragraphs. Then compare and discuss each paragraph. Make sure students understand how the meanings of the homonyms affect how they are used.

The last time Aunt Barbara **sent** me a letter, it got lost in the **mail**. **I** don't **know** what the problem was, and the postal authorities didn't **know** either. Besides the letter, Aunt Barbara enclosed a check **to** me for my graduation. Now that **I** know the letter was lost, **I** need to **write** her back and tell her **not** to worry. **I** was more interested in her being **there** to **see** me in my cap and gown than **I** was in getting her check.

(End of lesson.)

© SHURLEY INSTRUCTIONAL MATERIALS, INC.

CHAPTER 10   LESSON 3

Objectives: Jingles, Grammar (Practice Sentences), Practice and Improved Sentence, Practice Exercise and Activity.

 **JINGLE TIME**

Have students turn to the Jingle Section in their books and recite the previously-taught jingles.

 GRAMMAR TIME

First-Year Option: Put the Practice Sentences from the box below on the board or on notebook paper. Use these sentences as you practice the concepts that have been taught. For the greatest benefit, students must participate orally with the teacher. **Second-Year Option:** Have students classify the Practice Sentences independently on paper. Check students' sentences with the answers provided below. (*If you have the CDs for Practice Sentences, have students check their sentences with the CDs.*)

Chapter 10, Practice Sentences for Lesson 3
1. _____ The dogs and cats in the neighborhood stay in Sue's backyard.
2. _____ We do not eat or drink in the new car.
3. _____ Yea! Our parents are returning today from their week-long vacation!

TEACHING SCRIPT FOR PRACTICING PATTERN 1 SENTENCES WITH THE 8 PARTS OF SPEECH

We will classify three different sentences to practice using the eight parts of speech in the Question and Answer Flows. We will classify the sentences together. Begin. (*You might have your students write the labels above the sentences at this time.*)

Question and Answer Flow for Sentence 1: The dogs and cats in the neighborhood stay in Sue's backyard.

1. What stay in Sue's backyard?
   dogs and cats - CSN, CSN
2. What is being said about dogs and cats?
   dogs and cats stay - V
3. In - P
4. In what? backyard - OP
5. Whose backyard? Sue's - PNA
6. In - P
7. In what? neighborhood - OP

8. The - A
9. And - C
10. The - A
11. SN V P1 Check
12. (In the neighborhood) - Prepositional phrase
13. (In Sue's backyard) - Prepositional phrase
14. Period, statement, declarative sentence
15. Go back to the verb - divide the complete subject
    from the complete predicate.

Classified Sentence:

<u>SN   V</u>
P1

A CSN C CSN P A   OP   V   P PNA   OP
The dogs and cats (in the neighborhood) / stay (in Sue's backyard). **D**

CHAPTER 10 LESSON 3 CONTINUED

Question and Answer Flow for Sentence 2: We do not eat or drink in the new car.

1. Who do not eat or drink in the new car? we - SP
2. What is being said about we? we do eat or drink - CV, CV
3. Do - HV
4. We do eat or drink how? not - Adv
5. Or - C
6. In - P
7. In what? car - OP

8. What kind of car? new - Adj
9. The - A
10. SN V P1 Check
11. (In the new car) - Prepositional phrase
12. Period, statement, declarative sentence
13. Go back to the verb - divide the complete subject from the complete predicate.

		SP	HV	Adv	CV	C	CV	P	A	Adj	OP	
Classified Sentence:	SN V	We	/ do	not	eat	or	drink	(in	the	new	car).	D
	P1											

Question and Answer Flow for Sentence 3: Yea! Our parents are returning today from their week-long vacation!

1. Who are returning today from their week-long vacation? parents - SN
2. What is being said about parents? parents are returning - V
3. Are - HV
4. Are returning when? today - Adv
5. From - P
6. From what? vacation - OP
7. What kind of vacation? week-long - Adj

8. Whose vacation? their - PPA
9. Whose parents? Our - PPA
10. Yea - I
11. SN V P1 Check
12. (From their week-long vacation) - Prepositional phrase
13. Exclamation point, strong feeling, exclamatory sentence
14. Go back to the verb - divide the complete subject from the complete predicate.

		I	PPA	SN	HV	V	Adv	P	PPA	Adj	OP	
Classified Sentence:	SN V	Yea!	Our	parents	/ are	returning	today	(from	their	week-long	vacation)!	E
	P1											

TEACHING SCRIPT FOR THE PRACTICE SENTENCE

Put these labels on the board: **I CSN C CSN HV V P PPA OP**

Look at the new sentence labels on the board: **I CSN C CSN HV V P PPA OP**. I will guide you again through the process of writing a sentence to practice the different parts that you have learned.

Get out a sheet of notebook paper. On the top line of your notebook paper, write the title *Practice Sentence*. Copy the sentence labels from the board onto your notebook paper. Be sure to leave plenty of writing space between each label. I will guide you through the process you will use whenever you write a Practice Sentence with pronouns and possessive nouns.

1. Go to the two **CSN** labels for the compound subject nouns. Think of two nouns that you want to use as your compound subject. Remember, these two nouns must make sense together and with the verb that you choose. Write the two nouns you have chosen on the line *under* the two **CSN** labels.

© SHURLEY INSTRUCTIONAL MATERIALS, INC.

CHAPTER 10 LESSON 3 CONTINUED

2. Go to the **HV** and the **V** labels for the helping verb and the main verb. Think of a helping verb and a main verb that tell what your subjects do. Make sure that your verb makes sense with the two subject nouns. Also, check to make sure you have proper subject-verb agreement. Write the two verbs you have chosen on the line *under* the **HV** and the **V** labels.

3. Go to the **P** label for the preposition. Think of a preposition word that tells something about your verb. You must be careful to choose a preposition word that makes sense with the noun you will choose for the object of the preposition in your next step. Write the word you have chosen for a preposition *under* the **P** label.

4. Go to the **OP** label for the object of the preposition. If you like the noun you thought of while thinking of a preposition, write it down under the **OP** label. If you prefer, think of another noun by asking **what** or **whom** after your preposition. Check to make sure the preposition and object of the preposition make sense together and also make sense with the rest of the sentence. Remember, the object of the preposition will always answer the question **what** or **whom** after the preposition. Write the word you have chosen for the object of the preposition *under* the **OP** label.

5. Go to the **PPA** label for the possessive pronoun adjective that is part of your prepositional phrase. Repeat the possessive pronoun jingle to help you think of a pronoun that you want to use as your possessive pronoun adjective. Choose the possessive pronoun that makes the best sense in your sentence. Write the possessive pronoun you have chosen *under* the **PPA** label.

6. Go to the **C** label for the conjunction in your sentence and choose a conjunction that makes sense. What are the three main conjunctions again? (*and, but, or*) Write the conjunction you have chosen *under* the **C** label.

7. Go to the **I** label for the interjection at the beginning of the sentence. Choose an interjection that makes the best sense in your sentence. Write the interjection you have chosen *under* the **I** label.

8. Finally, check your Practice Sentence to make sure it has the necessary parts to be a complete sentence. What are the five parts of a complete sentence? (*subject, verb, complete sense, capital letter, and an end mark*) Does your Practice Sentence have the five parts of a complete sentence? (*Allow time for students to read over their sentences and to make any corrections they need to make.*)

TEACHING SCRIPT FOR THE IMPROVED SENTENCE

Under your Practice Sentence, write the title *Improved Sentence* on another line. To improve your Practice Sentence, you will make two synonym changes, one antonym change, and your choice of a complete word change or another synonym or antonym change.

Since it is harder to find words that can be changed to an antonym, it is usually wise to go through your sentence to find an antonym change first. Look through your sentence again to find words that can be improved with synonyms. Finally, make a decision about whether your last change will be a complete word change, another synonym change, or another antonym change.

I will give you time to write your Improved Sentence. (*Always encourage students to use a thesaurus, synonym-antonym book, or a dictionary to help them develop an interesting and improved writing vocabulary.*) (*After students have finished, check and discuss students' Practice and Improved Sentences.*)

© SHURLEY INSTRUCTIONAL MATERIALS, INC.

CHAPTER 10 LESSON 3 CONTINUED

PRACTICE TIME

Now, have students turn to page 73 in the Practice Section of their book and find Chapter 10, Lesson 3, Practice. Go over the directions to make sure they understand what to do. Check and discuss the Practice after students have finished. Discuss strong areas as well as weak areas. (*Chapter 10, Lesson 3, Practice key is given below.*)

Chapter 10, Lesson 3, Practice: Underline the correct homonym in each sentence.

1. We went (<u>through</u>, threw) the lesson together.
2. My brother and I had to (weight, <u>wait</u>) too long.
3. Yesterday, I went (<u>to</u>, two, too) the mall.
4. She couldn't (here, <u>hear</u>) the speaker.
5. Do I (<u>know</u>, no) what you are talking about?
6. There is (know, <u>no</u>) way I am going!
7. The sandpaper was very (<u>coarse</u>, course).
8. My legs felt (week, <u>weak</u>) after the race.
9. The band was on tour for a (<u>week</u>, weak).
10. The golf (<u>course</u>, coarse) was well kept.

Have students write the three sentences that they classified at the beginning of the lesson on a sheet of paper (see page 179). Have them tape-record the Question and Answer Flows for all three sentences. Students should write labels above the sentences as they classify them. They especially need the second practice if this is their first year in the program. (*After the students have finished, check the tape and sentence labels. Make sure students understand any mistakes they have made.*)

ACTIVITY / ASSIGNMENT TIME

Create a word search puzzle and/or a crossword puzzle for the eight parts of speech (*noun, verb, adjective, adverb, preposition, pronoun, conjunction, and interjection*). Make a "key" for each puzzle. Check the puzzles to make sure they work with the puzzle keys. (*This project may take several days.*) Give your finished project to family members and friends and have them complete your puzzles.

After you have finished, write an evaluation of this project in your Journal. Tell what you enjoyed most about the project. Tell what you would do differently next time. Share the most interesting and inspiring part of the project. Share the most frustrating part of the project. How long did it take you to finish your project? Did you share your project and get feedback from friends and family members? Did you create more puzzles? Compare your creative efforts with other projects that you have done. Are you happy with the finished product? What grade would you give this project? Explain why.

(End of lesson.)

© SHURLEY INSTRUCTIONAL MATERIALS, INC.

CHAPTER 10   LESSON 4

Objectives: Jingles, Study, Test, Check, Activity and Writing (journal)

 JINGLE TIME

Have students turn to the Jingle Section in their books and recite the previously-taught jingles.

 STUDY TIME

Have students study the vocabulary words in their vocabulary notebooks. Remind students that any vocabulary word in their notebooks could be on their test. Also, have students study any of the skills in the Practice Section that they need to review.

 TEST TIME

Have students turn to page 105 in the Test Section of their book and find Chapter 10 Test. Go over the directions to make sure they understand what to do. (*Chapter 10 Test key is on the next page.*)

 CHECK TIME

After students have finished, check and discuss their test papers. Make sure they understand why their answers are right or wrong. (*For total points, count each required answer as a point.*)

 ACTIVITY / ASSIGNMENT TIME

Students will continue to draw or trace the states and write the following questions and answers.

Hawaii	Idaho
1. What is the state on the front of this card? **Hawaii**	1. What is the state on the front of this card? **Idaho**
2. What is the capital of Hawaii? **Honolulu**	2. What is the capital of Idaho? **Boise**
3. What is the postal abbreviation of Hawaii? **HI**	3. What is the postal abbreviation of Idaho? **ID**
4. What year was Hawaii admitted to the Union? **1959**	4. What year was Idaho admitted to the Union? **1890**

Color these states and look up an interesting fact about each state to write on the cards. Use the cards to quiz family members, friends, and relatives. You may want to time the responses to your questions. Also, along with previous suggestions, think of other ways to have fun with your United States card file.

(End of lesson.)

Chapter 10 Test
(Student Page 105)

Exercise 1: Classify each sentence.

```
                    CSN    C   CSN      CV   C   CV    P  A  Adj   OP
1. SN V             Thomas and Andrew / sang and danced (at the talent show). D
   P1

   (You) SP     V     P  A   Adj   COP    C  COP   P  A   Adj    OP
2. SN V         / Look (at the colorful plants and fish) (in the large aquarium). Imp
   P1

                I      A  Adj  SN      V     P   A  PNA  Adj    OP
3. SN V         Oops!  The red juice / spilled (on the boy's white shirt). D
   P1
```

Exercise 2: Use Sentence 2 to underline the complete subject once and the complete predicate twice and to complete the table below.

List the Noun Used	List the Noun Job	Singular or Plural	Common or Proper	Simple Subject	Simple Predicate
1. plants	2. COP	3. P	4. C	5. You	6. look
7. fish	8. COP	9. P	10. C		
11. aquarium	12. OP	13. S	14. C		

Exercise 3: Name the eight parts of speech that you have studied. (*You may use abbreviations.*) **(The order may vary.)**

1. noun 2. verb 3. adjective 4. adverb 5. preposition 6. pronoun 7. conjunction 8. interjection

Exercise 4: Answer each question below.

1. List the 8 *be* verbs. am, is, are, was, were, be, being, been

2. What are the parts of a verb phrase? helping verb and main verb

3. Name the seven subject pronouns. I, we, he, she, it, they, you

4. Name the seven possessive pronouns. my, our, his, her, its, their, your

5. Name the seven object pronouns. me, us, him, her, it, them, you

6. What part of speech is the word NOT? adverb

Exercise 5: Identify each pair of words as synonyms or antonyms by putting parentheses ( ) around *syn* or *ant*.

1. tepid, warm	**(syn)** ant	4. honest, truthful	**(syn)** ant	7. fragrance, aroma	**(syn)** ant
2. savage, tame	syn **(ant)**	5. serious, frivolous	syn **(ant)**	8. flabby, firm	syn **(ant)**
3. deadly, lethal	**(syn)** ant	6. wilt, droop	**(syn)** ant	9. scarce, abundant	syn **(ant)**

Exercise 6: Underline the correct homonym in each sentence.

1. He wants to (<u>buy</u>, by) my stamp collection.
2. I can't (weight, <u>wait</u>) for our summer break.
3. My sister ran (<u>through</u>, threw) the sprinkler.
4. My brothers (<u>know</u>, no) the owner of the restaurant.
5. My family left for a (weak, <u>week</u>) of vacation.
6. James gave money (<u>to</u>, too, two) the church.
7. She finally (one, <u>won</u>) the radio contest.
8. The university offered a summer (<u>course</u>, coarse).

Exercise 7: In your journal, write a paragraph summarizing what you have learned this week.

© SHURLEY INSTRUCTIONAL MATERIALS, INC.

CHAPTER 10 LESSON 4 CONTINUED

TEACHER INSTRUCTIONS

Use the Question and Answer Flows below for the sentences on the Chapter 10 Test.

Question and Answer Flow for Sentence 1: Thomas and Andrew sang and danced at the talent show.

1. Who sang and danced at the talent show?
   Thomas and Andrew - CSN, CSN
2. What is being said about Thomas and Andrew?
   Thomas and Andrew sang and danced - CV, CV
3. At - P
4. At what? show - OP
5. What kind of show? talent - Adj
6. The - A

7. And - C
8. And - C
9. SN V P1 Check
10. (At talent show) - Prepositional phrase
11. Period, statement, declarative sentence
12. Go back to the verb - divide the complete subject from the complete predicate.

Classified Sentence:

| | | CSN | C | CSN | CV | C | CV | P | A | Adj | OP |
| SN V | Thomas and Andrew / sang and danced (at the talent show). D |
| P1 |

Question and Answer Flow for Sentence 2: Look at the colorful plants and fish in the large aquarium.

1. Who look at the colorful plants and fish in the large
   aquarium? you - SP (understood subject pronoun)
2. What is being said about you? you look - V
3. At - P
4. At what? plants and fish - COP, COP (compound object
   of the preposition, compound object of the preposition)
5. And - C
6. What kind of plants and fish? colorful - Adj
7. The - A
8. In - P
9. In what? aquarium - OP

10. What kind of aquarium? large - Adj
11. The - A
12. SN V P1 Check
13. (At the colorful plants and fish) - Prepositional
    phrase
14. (In the large aquarium) - Prepositional phrase
15. Period, command, imperative sentence
16. Go back to the verb - divide the complete subject
    from the complete predicate.

Classified Sentence:

| (You) SP | | V | P | A | Adj | COP | C | COP | P | A | Adj | OP |
| SN V | / Look (at the colorful plants and fish) (in the large aquarium). Imp |
| P1 |

Question and Answer Flow for Sentence 3: Oops! The red juice spilled on the boy's white shirt.

1. What spilled on the boy's white shirt? juice - SN
2. What is being said about juice? juice spilled - V
3. On - P
4. On what? shirt - OP
5. What kind of shirt? white - Adj
6. Whose shirt? boy's - PNA
7. The - A
8. What kind of juice? red - Adj

9. The - A
10. Oops - I
11. SN V P1 Check
12. (On the boy's white shirt) - Prepositional phrase
13. Period, statement, declarative sentence
14. Go back to the verb - divide the complete subject
    from the complete predicate.

Classified Sentence:

| | | I | A | Adj | SN | V | P | A | PNA | Adj | OP |
| SN V | Oops! The red juice / spilled (on the boy's white shirt). D |
| P1 |

© SHURLEY INSTRUCTIONAL MATERIALS, INC.

CHAPTER 10   LESSON 5

Objectives: Writing (topic sentences) and Writing Assignment #7.

 WRITING TIME

TEACHING SCRIPT FOR REVIEWING THE TOPIC SENTENCE

When we learned how to write a topic sentence, we listed three things we needed to know about a topic sentence in order to recognize it and to write one correctly. I will go over those three things again.

1. A topic sentence should tell the main idea of a paragraph. The topic sentence will give you a general overview of what the paragraph is about. Notice that I said a **general** overview, not a detailed overview. A topic sentence does not give details because its job is to inform the reader very quickly what the reader can expect to find in the paragraph.

2. Most of the time, the topic sentence is the first sentence in the paragraph because most writers prefer to tell their readers at the very beginning what they can expect from the paragraph. Placing the topic sentence first also helps the writer stay focused on the topic of the paragraph. Occasionally, writers will place the topic sentence last or in the middle of a paragraph, but we will concentrate on what happens the majority of the time.

3. A topic sentence usually tells the number of points that will be discussed in the paragraph. This helps narrow the topic and keeps the writer on target.

TEACHER INSTRUCTIONS FOR WRITING ASSIGNMENT

Give Writing Assignment #7 from the box on the next page. For Writing Assignment #7, students are to write a three-point expository paragraph. They will choose the writing form (standard or time order). They are to underline all time-order words used at the beginning of each point sentence. Have them follow the Writing Guidelines as they prepare their writing.

© SHURLEY INSTRUCTIONAL MATERIALS, INC.

CHAPTER 10 LESSON 5 CONTINUED

Writing Assignment Box

Writing Assignment #7: Three-Point Expository Paragraph (You choose the writing form.)

Writing topics: Things I Like to Do With My Family or **Things to Do During A Home Fire Drill**
or **Ways to Help My Parents**

TEACHING SCRIPT FOR USING THE WRITING PROCESS FOR THIS WRITING ASSIGNMENT

As you begin this writing assignment, you will start through the writing process. First, you will think about your topic and gather any information you might need in order to do the writing. Second, you will write a rough draft. Remember, it is called a rough draft because it will be revised and edited. You do not have to worry about mistakes as you write your rough draft. After you write the first draft, you will make revisions, using the Revision Checklist in Reference 13. After you revise your writing, you will edit, using the Beginning Editing Checklist in Reference 13.

Finally, after you are satisfied with your revising and editing, you will write a final paper, using the Final Paper Checklist in Reference 13. You will then give the finished writing assignment to me.

TEACHER INSTRUCTIONS FOR CHECKING WRITING ASSIGNMENT

Read, check, and discuss Writing Assignment #7 after students have finished their final paper. Use the editing checklist (*Reference 13 on teacher's page 48*) as you check and discuss students' papers. Make sure students are using the editing checklist correctly.

(End of lesson.)

CHAPTER 11 LESSON 1

Objectives: Jingles, Grammar (Practice Sentences), Oral Skill Builder Check, Skill (capitalization), Activity, and Vocabulary #1.

 JINGLE TIME

Have students turn to the Jingle Section in their books and recite the previously-taught jingles.

 GRAMMAR TIME

First-Year Option: Put the Practice Sentences from the box below on the board or on notebook paper. Use these sentences as you practice the concepts that have been taught. For the greatest benefit, students must participate orally with the teacher. **Second-Year Option:** Have students classify the Practice Sentences independently on paper. Check students' sentences with the answers provided below. *(If you have the CDs for Practice Sentences, have students check their sentences with the CDs.)*

Chapter 11, Practice Sentences for Lesson 1
1. _____ Whoa! This old mule will not step over that small branch.
2. _____ Wait for me at the front entrance of the mall.

TEACHING SCRIPT FOR PRACTICING PATTERN 1 SENTENCES

We will practice classifying Pattern 1 Sentences. We will classify the sentences together. Begin. *(You might have your students write the labels above the sentences at this time.)*

Question and Answer Flow for Sentence 1: Whoa! This old mule will not step over that small branch.
1. What will not step over that small branch? mule - SN
2. What is being said about mule? mule will step - V
3. Will - HV
4. Will step how? not - Adv
5. Over - P
6. Over what? branch - OP
7. What kind of branch? small - Adj
8. Which branch? that - Adj
9. What kind of mule? old - Adj
10. Which mule? this - Adj
11. Whoa - I
12. SN V P1 Check
13. (Over that small branch) - Prepositional phrase
14. Period, statement, declarative sentence
15. Go back to the verb - divide the complete subject from the complete predicate.

Classified Sentence:

```
            I   Adj Adj SN   HV Adv V    P  Adj Adj    OP
  SN V      Whoa! This old mule / will not step (over that small branch).  D
  P1
```

© SHURLEY INSTRUCTIONAL MATERIALS, INC.

CHAPTER 11 LESSON 1 CONTINUED

Question and Answer Flow for Sentence 2: Wait for me at the front entrance of the mall.

1. Who wait for me at the front entrance of the mall?
   (You) - SP (Understood subject pronoun)
2. What is being said about you? you wait - V
3. For - P
4. For whom? me - OP
5. At - P
6. At what? entrance - OP
7. What kind of entrance? front - Adj
8. The - A
9. Of - P

10. Of what? mall - OP
11. The - A
12. SN V P1 Check
13. (For me) - Prepositional phrase
14. (At the front entrance) - Prepositional phrase
15. (Of the mall) - Prepositional phrase
16. Period, command, imperative sentence
17. Go back to the verb - divide the complete subject from the complete predicate.

Classified Sentence:

(You) SP		V	P	OP	P	A	Adj	OP	P	A	OP
SN V		/ Wait (for me) (at the front entrance) (of the mall). **Imp**									
P1											

Use Sentences 1-2 that you just classified with your students to do an Oral Skill Builder Check. Use the guidelines below.

Oral Skill Builder Check

1. **Noun check.**
   (Say the job and then say the noun. Circle each noun.)

2. **Identify the nouns as singular or plural.**
   (Write S or P above each noun.)

3. **Identify the nouns as common or proper.**
   (Follow established procedure for oral identification.)

4. **Do a vocabulary check.**
   (Follow established procedure for oral identification.)

5. **Identify the complete subject and the complete predicate.** (Underline the complete subject once and the complete predicate twice.)

6. **Identify the simple subject and simple predicate.** (Underline the simple subject once and the simple predicate twice. Bold, or highlight, the lines.)

7. **Recite the irregular verb chart.**
   (Located on student page 25 and teacher page 163.)

SKILL TIME

TEACHING SCRIPT FOR INTRODUCING THE CAPITALIZATION RULES

Turn to page 27 in the Reference Section and look at Reference 34 in your student book. These are the rules for capitalization. The capitalization rules are organized into sections of similar rules. (*Read and discuss each section and the rules contained in each section.*) Your knowledge of capitalization rules will help you as you write and edit your writing. You will find that readers appreciate writers who use capitalization rules well. (*The capitalization rules are reproduced for you on page 191.*)

© SHURLEY INSTRUCTIONAL MATERIALS, INC.

CHAPTER 11 LESSON 1 CONTINUED

 ACTIVITY / ASSIGNMENT TIME

Students will make and then play a Capitalization Memory game. Have students follow the directions below to play Capitalization Memory.

1. Gather 24 index cards. Write one capitalization rule on the back of each card. On the front of each card, write an example that demonstrates that rule.

2. Play with a partner if possible (family member, friend, etc.).

3. Shuffle the 24 cards and spread them out in your hand. Have a player point to a card. Hold the card so the player can read the example. See if the player can recite the capitalization rule that applies to the example.

4. Variation: Have a player point to a card. Hold the card so the player can read the capitalization rule. See if the player can recite 3 examples that apply to the capitalization rule.

5. Assign points to the different capitalization rules. Harder rules could be worth more points. Total up the points for each player.

6. Discuss the rules that players do and do not know. Think of new capitalization games to play.

 VOCABULARY TIME

Assign Chapter 11, Vocabulary Words **#1** on page 8 in the Reference Section for students to define in their Vocabulary notebooks. Tell students they are to use a dictionary or thesaurus to look up the meanings of the vocabulary words. After they write each word and its meaning, students are to write a sentence using the vocabulary word.

Chapter 11, Vocabulary Words #1
(intentional, unintended, annoy, aggravate)

© SHURLEY INSTRUCTIONAL MATERIALS, INC.

CHAPTER 11 LESSON 1 CONTINUED

Reference 34: Capitalization Rules

SECTION 1: CAPITALIZE THE FIRST WORD

1. The first word of a sentence. (*He likes to take a nap.*)
2. The first word in the greeting and closing of letters. (*Dear, Yours truly*)
3. The first and last word and important words in titles of literary works.
(*books, songs, short stories, poems, articles, movie titles, magazines*)
(*Note: Conjunctions, articles, and prepositions with fewer than five letters are not capitalized unless they are the first or last word.*)
4. The first word of a direct quotation. (*Dad said, "We are going home."*)
5. The first word in each line of a topic outline.

SECTION 2: CAPITALIZE NAMES, INITIALS, AND TITLES OF PEOPLE

6. The pronoun I. (*May I go with you?*)
7. The names and nicknames of people. (*Sam, Joe, Jones, Slim, Shorty*)
8. Family names when used in place of or with the person's name.
(*Grandmother, Auntie, Uncle Joe, Mother – Do NOT capitalize my mother.*)
9. Titles used with, or in place of, people's names.
(*Mr., Ms., Miss, Dr. Smith, Doctor, Captain, President, Sir*)
10. People's initials. (*J. D., C. Smith*)

SECTION 3: CAPITALIZE WORDS OF TIME

11. The days of the week and months of the year. (*Monday, July*)
12. The names of holidays. (*Christmas, Thanksgiving, Easter*)
13. The names of historical events, periods, laws, documents, conflicts, and distinguished awards. (*Civil War, Middle Ages, Medal of Honor*)

SECTION 4: CAPITALIZE NAMES OF PLACES

14. The names and abbreviations of cities, towns, counties, states, countries, and nations.
(*Dallas, Texas, Fulton County, Africa, America, USA, AR, TX*)
15. The names of avenues, streets, roads, highways, routes, and post office boxes.
(*Main Street, Jones Road, Highway 89, Rt. 1, Box 2, P.O. Box 45*)
16. The names of lakes, rivers, oceans, mountain ranges, deserts, parks, stars, planets, and constellations.
(*Beaver Lake, Rocky Mountains, Venus*)
17. The names of schools and titles of school courses that are numbered or are languages.
(*Walker Elementary School, Mathematics II*)
18. North, south, east, and west when they refer to sections of the country.
(*up North, live in the East, out West*)

SECTION 5: CAPITALIZE NAMES OF OTHER NOUNS AND PROPER ADJECTIVES

19. The names of pets. (*Spot, Tweety Bird, etc.*)
20. The names of products. (*Campbell's soup, Kelly's chili, Ford cars, etc.*)
21. The names of companies, buildings, ships, planes, space ships.
(*Empire State Building, Titanic, IBM, The Big Tire Co.*)
22. Proper adjectives. (*the English language, Italian restaurant, French test*)
23. The names of clubs, organizations, or groups. (*Lion's Club, Jaycees, Beatles*)
24. The names of political parties, religious preferences, nationalities, and races.
(*Democratic party, Republican, Jewish synagogue, American*)

(End of lesson.)

© SHURLEY INSTRUCTIONAL MATERIALS, INC.

CHAPTER 11   LESSON 2

Objectives: Jingles, Grammar (Practice Sentences), Pattern 1 Practice and Improved Sentence, Skill (punctuation), Activity, and Vocabulary #2.

JINGLE TIME

Have students turn to the Jingle Section in their books and recite the previously-taught jingles.

GRAMMAR TIME

First-Year Option: Put the Practice Sentences from the box below on the board or on notebook paper. Use these sentences as you practice the concepts that have been taught. For the greatest benefit, students must participate orally with the teacher. **Second-Year Option:** Have students classify the Practice Sentences independently on paper. Check students' sentences with the answers provided below. (*If you have the CDs for Practice Sentences, have students check their sentences with the CDs.*)

Chapter 11, Practice Sentences for Lesson 2
1. _____ I talked and laughed on the phone with my friends.
2. _____ Sue and Pete walked on the beach by the ocean.

TEACHING SCRIPT FOR PRACTICING PATTERN 1 SENTENCES

Today, we will practice classifying Pattern 1 Sentences. We will classify the sentences together. Begin. (*You might have your students write the labels above the sentences at this time.*)

Question and Answer Flow for Sentence 1: I talked and laughed on the phone with my friends.	
1. Who talked and laughed on the phone with my friends? I - SP	7. With whom? friends - OP
2. What is being said about I? I talked and laughed - CV, CV	8. Whose friends? my - PPA
3. On - P	9. And - C
4. On what? phone - OP	10. SN V P1 Check
5. The - A	11. (On the phone) - Prepositional phrase
6. With - P	12. (With my friends) - Prepositional phrase
	13. Period, statement, declarative sentence
	14. Go back to the verb - divide the complete subject from the complete predicate.

Classified Sentence:

```
              SP CV   C    CV    P A  OP    P PPA OP
   SN  V      I / talked and laughed (on the phone) (with my friends).  D
      P1
```

Level 3 Homeschool Teacher's Manual

© SHURLEY INSTRUCTIONAL MATERIALS, INC.

CHAPTER 11 LESSON 2 CONTINUED

Question and Answer Flow for Sentence 2: Sue and Pete walked on the beach by the ocean.

1. Who walked on the beach by the ocean?
   Sue and Pete - CSN, CSN
2. What is being said about Sue and Pete?
   Sue and Pete walked - V
3. On - P
4. On what? beach - OP
5. The - A
6. By - P
7. By what? ocean - OP

8. The - A
9. And - C
10. SN V P1 Check
11. (On the beach) - Prepositional phrase
12. (By the ocean) - Prepositional phrase
13. Period, statement, declarative sentence
14. Go back to the verb - divide the complete subject
    from the complete predicate.

Classified Sentence:

		CSN	C	CSN	V		P	A	OP	P	A	OP	
SN V		Sue	and	Pete	/ walked	(on	the	beach)	(by	the	ocean).	D
P1													

TEACHING SCRIPT FOR INTRODUCING A PATTERN 1 PRACTICE SENTENCE

Put these words on the board: **Pattern 1 Practice Sentence**

Get out a sheet of notebook paper. On the top line of your notebook paper, write the title _Pattern 1 Practice Sentence_. Look at the new words on the board: **Pattern 1 Practice Sentence**. I will guide you again through the process as we learn to write a Pattern 1 sentence.

You have already learned how to write a Practice Sentence according to labels that have been provided for you. Today, you will learn how to write a Practice Sentence in which you select the parts of the sentence and the order they appear in your sentence. You will use only sentence parts of a Pattern 1 sentence.

Name the parts of a Pattern 1 sentence that YOU MUST USE. (_All Pattern 1 sentences must have a subject and a verb._) Now, name the parts of a sentence that YOU CAN CHOOSE to add to your sentence. (_adjectives, adverbs, article adjectives, prepositional phrases, subject pronouns, possessive nouns, possessive pronouns, helping verbs, conjunctions, and interjections._)

Let's write the labels for a Pattern 1 sentence on a sheet of notebook paper. First, write the _SN_ and _V_ labels that a Pattern 1 sentence must have, on your paper. Be sure to place them in the middle of your paper. (_Demonstrate by writing the SN and V labels on the board._) Now, using what you know about writing Practice Sentences, we will decide what other parts we want to add to our Pattern 1 sentence. But first, we will look at a Reference box that will list all the parts that we can use. Turn to page 28 and look at Reference 35 (_Read and discuss the information in Reference 35 with your students. Reference 35 is reproduced for you on the next page._)

CHAPTER 11 LESSON 2 CONTINUED

Reference 35: Sentence Parts That Can Be Used for a Pattern 1 Sentence

1. Nouns
Use <u>only</u> subject nouns or object of the preposition nouns.

2. Adverbs
Tell how, when, or where.
Can be placed before or after verbs, at the beginning or end of a sentence, and in front of adjectives or other adverbs.

3. Adjectives
Tell what kind, which one, or how many.
Can be placed in front of nouns. Sometimes, two or three adjectives can modify the same noun.
Articles
Adjectives that are used in front of nouns (a, an, the).

4. Verbs *(Can include helping verbs.)*

5. Prepositional Phrases
Can be placed before or after nouns, after verbs, adverbs, or other prepositional phrases, and at the beginning or end of a sentence.

6. Pronouns
(subjective, possessive, or objective)

7. Conjunctions
Connecting words for compound parts: and, or, but.

8. Interjections
Usually found at the beginning of a sentence. Can show strong or mild emotion.

Teacher's Note: You may want to make a poster of the information in the box above to show students that they are actually using the eight parts of speech from which to choose the different sentence parts that can be used for a Pattern 1 Sentence.

TEACHER INSTRUCTIONS

Use the information in the box above to help your students choose other parts to add to a Pattern 1 sentence. Help students select sentence labels and place them in the order in which they have decided. As students choose the sentence parts they want in their sentence, you should write the labels in the designated order on the board. Students should write the labels on their papers when they are ready to write a Pattern 1 Sentence. (*Students will have the same sentence labels in the same order this first time.*)

After your students have finished writing the <u>Teacher-guided</u> Pattern 1 Practice Sentence on their papers, each student should then write his or her own Pattern 1 sentence, choosing their own labels. Tell students they can use any sentence part listed in Reference 35 every time they write an independent Pattern 1 Sentence. Some students may add only adjectives, adverbs, and one or two prepositional phrases the first time. Other students may have the confidence to use a variety of sentence parts: pronouns, possessives, inverted order, adverb exceptions, etc.

TEACHING SCRIPT FOR THE IMPROVED SENTENCE

Under your Practice Sentence, write the title *Improved Sentence* on another line. To improve your Practice Sentence, you will make two synonym changes, one antonym change, and your choice of a complete word change or another synonym or antonym change. I will give you time to write your Improved Sentence. (*Always encourage students to use a thesaurus, synonym-antonym book, or a dictionary to help them develop an interesting and improved writing vocabulary.*) (*After students have finished, check and discuss students' Practice and Improved Sentences.*)

© SHURLEY INSTRUCTIONAL MATERIALS, INC.

CHAPTER 11 LESSON 2 CONTINUED

SKILL TIME

<u>*TEACHING SCRIPT FOR INTRODUCING THE PUNCTUATION RULES*</u>

Turn to pages 29 and 30 in the Reference Section and look at References 36A and 36B in your student book. These are the rules for punctuation. The punctuation rules are organized into sections of similar rules. *(Read and discuss each section and the rules under each section.)* Your knowledge of punctuation rules will help you as you write and as you edit your writing. You will find that readers also appreciate writers who use punctuation rules well. Correct use of punctuation keeps writing clear and easy to understand. *(The punctuation rules are reproduced for you on the next two pages.)*

ACTIVITY / ASSIGNMENT TIME

Directions: Rewrite the following story. Use the symbol key below to help punctuate it.

honk susan shouted yelp beep honk can you believe it hiccup honk can you even imagine hiccup honk a brand new sports car at no cost giggle beep honk susan was dancing around with excitement groan

Symbol Key

1. capitalization – honk
2. question mark – hiccup
3. exclamation point – giggle
4. comma – yelp
5. period – groan
6. quotation marks – beep

Directions: Rewrite the sentence below. Put in the symbols from the symbol key above to show how to punctuate the sentence. Give your sentence to several people and have them read it and then punctuate it by following the symbols.

on **s**aturday, **l**arry and **r**onnie ran happily down **m**ain **s**treet to play with **a**aron and **j**ason.

VOCABULARY TIME

Assign Chapter 11, Vocabulary Words **#2** on page 8 in the Reference Section for students to define in their Vocabulary notebooks. Tell students they are to use a dictionary or thesaurus to look up the meanings of the vocabulary words. After they write each word and its meaning, students are to write a sentence using the vocabulary word.

Chapter 11, Vocabulary Words #2
(evade, avoid, oppose, support)

© SHURLEY INSTRUCTIONAL MATERIALS, INC.

CHAPTER 11 LESSON 2 CONTINUED

Reference 36A: Punctuation Rules

SECTION 1: END MARK PUNCTUATION

1. Use a (.) for the end punctuation of a sentence that makes a statement.
   (*Mom baked us a cake.*)

2. Use a (?) for the end punctuation of a sentence that asks a question.
   (*Are you going to town?*)

3. Use an (!) for the end punctuation of a sentence that expresses strong feeling.
   (*That bee stung me!*)

4. Use a (.) for the end punctuation of a sentence that gives a command or makes a request.
   (*Close the door.*)

SECTION 2: COMMAS TO SEPARATE TIME WORDS

5. Use a comma between the day of the week and the month. (*Friday, July 23*)
   Use a comma between the day and year. (*July 23, 2009*)

6. Use a comma to separate the year from the rest of the sentence when the year follows the month or the month and the day.
   (*We spent May, 2001, with Mom. We spent July 23, 2001, with Dad.*)

SECTION 3: COMMAS TO SEPARATE PLACE WORDS

7. Use a comma to separate the city from the state or country.
   (*I will go to Dallas, Texas. He is from Paris, France.*)

8. Use a comma to separate the state or country from the rest of the sentence when the name of the state or country follows the name of a city.
   (*We flew to Dallas, Texas, in June. We flew to Paris, France, in July.*)

SECTION 4: COMMAS TO MAKE MEANINGS CLEAR

9. Use a comma to separate words or phrases in a series.
   (*We had soup, crackers, and milk.*)

10. Use commas to separate introductory words such as *Yes, Well, Oh,* and *No* from the rest of a sentence.
    (*Oh, I didn't know that.*)

11. Use commas to set off most appositives. An appositive is a word, phrase, title, or degree used directly after another word or name to rename it.
    (*Sue, the girl next door, likes to draw.*)
    One-word appositives can be written two different ways: (1) *My brother, Tim, is riding in the horse show.* (2) *My brother Tim is riding in the horse show.* Your assignments will require one-word appositives to be set off with commas.

12. Use commas to separate a noun of direct address (the name of a person directly spoken to) from the rest of the sentence.
    (*Mom, do I really have to go?*)

SECTION 5: PUNCTUATION IN GREETINGS AND CLOSINGS OF LETTERS

13. Use a comma (,) after the salutation (greeting) of a friendly letter. (*Dear Sam,*)

14. Use a comma (,) after the closing of any letter. (*Yours truly,*)

15. Use a colon (:) after the salutation (greeting) of a business letter. (*Dear Madam:*)

© SHURLEY INSTRUCTIONAL MATERIALS, INC.

CHAPTER 11 LESSON 2 CONTINUED

Reference 36B: Punctuation Rules

SECTION 6: PERIODS

16. Use a period after most abbreviations or titles that are accepted in formal writing. *(Mr., Ms., Dr., Capt., St., Ave., St. Louis) (Note: These abbreviations cannot be used by themselves. They must always be used with a proper noun.)*

    In the abbreviations of many well-known organizations or words, periods are not required. *(USA, GM, TWA, GTE, AT&T, TV, AM, FM, GI, etc.)* Use only one period after an abbreviation at the end of a statement. Do not put an extra period for the end mark punctuation.

17. Use a period after initials.
    (C. Smith, D.J. Brewton, Thomas A. Jones)

18. Place a period after Roman numerals, Arabic numbers, and letters of the alphabet in an outline.
    (II., IV., 5., 25., A., B.)

SECTION 7: APOSTROPHES

19. Form a contraction by using an apostrophe in place of a letter or letters that have been left out.
    (I'll, he's, isn't, wasn't, can't)

20. Form the possessive of singular and plural nouns by using an apostrophe.
    (boy's baseball, boys' baseball, children's baseball)

21. Form the plurals of letters, symbols, numbers, and signs with the apostrophe plus *s* *('s)*. *(9's, B's, b's)*

SECTION 8: UNDERLINING

22. Use underlining or italics for titles of books, magazines, works of art, ships, newspapers, motion pictures, etc. *(A famous movie is <u>Gone With the Wind</u>. Our newspaper is the <u>Cabot Star Herald</u>.) (<u>Titanic</u>, <u>Charlotte's Web</u>, etc.)*

SECTION 9: QUOTATION MARKS

23. Use quotation marks to set off the titles of songs, short stories, short poems, articles, essays, short plays, and book chapters.
    (Do you like to sing the song "America" in music class?)

24. Quotation marks are used at the beginning and end of the person's words to separate what the person actually said from the rest of the sentence. Since the quotation tells what is being said, it will always have quotation marks around it.

25. The words that tell who is speaking are the explanatory words. Do not set explanatory words off with quotation marks. *(Fred said, "I'm here.")* (**Fred said** *are explanatory words and should not be set off with quotations.)*

26. A new paragraph is used to indicate a change of speaker.

27. When a speaker's speech is longer than one paragraph, quotation marks are used at the beginning of each paragraph and at the end of the last paragraph of that speaker's speech.

28. Use single quotation marks to enclose a quotation within a quotation.
    "My teddy bear says 'I love you' four different ways," said little Amy.

29. Use a period at the end of explanatory words that come at the end of a sentence.

30. Use a comma to separate a direct quotation from the explanatory words.

(End of lesson.)

© SHURLEY INSTRUCTIONAL MATERIALS, INC.

CHAPTER 11   LESSON 3

Objectives: Jingles, Grammar (Practice Sentences), Skills (capitalization and punctuation), Practice Exercise, Activity.

 **JINGLE TIME**

Have students turn to the Jingle Section in their books and recite the previously-taught jingles.

 GRAMMAR TIME

First-Year Option: Put the Practice Sentences from the box below on the board or on notebook paper. Use these sentences as you practice the concepts that have been taught. For the greatest benefit, students must participate orally with the teacher. **Second-Year Option:** Have students classify the Practice Sentences independently on paper. Check students' sentences with the answers provided below. *(If you have the CDs for Practice Sentences, have students check their sentences with the CDs.)*

Chapter 11, Practice Sentences for Lesson 3
1. _____ Yikes! I stepped on a cactus plant without my shoes!
2. _____ Did you go to the opening of the new play?

TEACHING SCRIPT FOR PRACTICING PATTERN 1 SENTENCES

Today, we will practice classifying Pattern 1 Sentences. We will classify the sentences together. Begin. *(You might have your students write the labels above the sentences at this time.)*

Question and Answer Flow for Sentence 1: Yikes! I stepped on a cactus plant without my shoes!

1. Who stepped on a cactus plant without my shoes? I - SP
2. What is being said about I? I stepped - V
3. On - P
4. On what? plant - OP
5. What kind of plant? cactus - Adj
6. A - A
7. Without - P
8. Without what? shoes - OP
9. Whose shoes? my - PPA
10. Yikes - I
11. SN V P1 Check
12. (On a cactus plant) - Prepositional phrase
13. (Without my shoes) - Prepositional phrase
14. Exclamation point, strong feeling, exclamatory sentence
15. Go back to the verb - divide the complete subject from the complete predicate.

Classified Sentence:

<pre>
                              I   SP   V   P A Adj   OP   P PPA OP
        SN V   Yikes! I / stepped (on a cactus plant) (without my shoes)! E
        P1
</pre>

© SHURLEY INSTRUCTIONAL MATERIALS, INC.

CHAPTER 11 LESSON 3 CONTINUED

Question and Answer Flow for Sentence 2: Did you go to the opening of the new play?

1. Who did go to the opening of the new play? you - SP
2. What is being said about you? you did go - V
3. Did - HV
4. To - P
5. To what? opening - OP
6. The - A
7. Of - P
8. Of what? play - OP

9. What kind of play? new - Adj
10. The - A
11. SN V P1 Check
12. (To the opening) - Prepositional phrase
13. (Of the new play) - Prepositional phrase
14. Question mark, question, interrogative sentence
15. Go back to the verb - divide the complete subject from the complete predicate.

Classified Sentence:

		HV	SP	V	P	A	OP	P	A	Adj	OP
SN	V	Did you / go (to the opening) (of the new play)? Int
P1

SKILL TIME

TEACHING SCRIPT FOR CAPITALIZATION AND PUNCTUATION

You are ready to learn how to use the rules for capitalization and punctuation to edit sentences, paragraphs, and letters. It is important for you to know how to capitalize and punctuate any type of writing correctly. Expertise comes with years of practice and being able to apply all capitalization and punctuation rules automatically to edit your writing.

Teacher's Note: You will find a copy of the capitalization rules at the end of Lesson 1 and the punctuation rules at the end of Lesson 2 in this chapter. Refer to them as needed.

Look at References 34, 36A, and 36B for the capitalization and punctuation rules on pages 27, 29, and 30 in the Reference Section of your book. You should know most of these rules by now, but I want you to know how the rules pages are set up with similar rules grouped in a given section. Let's read over the titles of all the sections on the rules pages. If you can find the right section, you'll be able to find the specific rule number.

TEACHER INSTRUCTIONS

Go over the different sections and one or two specific rules in each section of all three rules pages at this time. Reading over every capitalization and punctuation rule is not necessary. Students will get plenty of practice finding and applying these rules as they correct errors in the different exercises. They will learn the rules by using them over and over again while they are correcting the errors.

© SHURLEY INSTRUCTIONAL MATERIALS, INC.

CHAPTER 11 LESSON 3 CONTINUED

You may have your students color-code the different sections. To make sure the color of their marker does not cover the rules or rule numbers, have students draw a box around each section instead of coloring each section.

Teacher's Note: Make sure students understand the concept of proper adjectives during the discussion of the capitalization rules. Ask for examples of proper adjectives.

I'm going to show you how to use capitalization and punctuation rules to correct capitalization and punctuation errors. You will correct all capitalization errors first so you don't have to work with more than one page of rules at a time. For capitalization corrections, you will use only Reference 34, the capitalization rules page. You will correct all punctuation errors, using only References 36A and 36B, the punctuation rules pages. Using this method will prevent you from flipping back and forth from page to page for every correction.

Look at the *Capitalization and Punctuation Examples* on References 37 on page 28 in the Reference Section. Look at number 1. All capitalization errors have been corrected and bolded so we can clearly see them. Our job in this format is to supply only the correct rule numbers above the corrections that were made.

Look at the editing guide that is located under Sentence 1. The number beside CAPITALS in the editing guide tells how many total capitalization errors are in that sentence. There is a number 6 after the word CAPITALS. This means that there are 6 capitalization errors to correct. You are to write the rule number above each of the six corrections. Let's look at one bolded correction at a time and find the rule number listed on the rules page that matches the correction. (*Have students look up each capitalization rule number to see how it relates to each bolded correction.*)

Reference 37: Capitalization and Punctuation Examples

   1 6   9   7   3   3

1. **No, I** did not see the article **Mr. Melbourne** wrote for the popular magazine called <u>**Popular Science**</u>.

   10   16   22   1

Editing Guide for Sample 1 Sentence: Capitals: 6   Periods: 1   Commas: 1   Underlining: 1   End Marks: 1

   Y   D   A

2. **y**es, **d**onald, my brother's boss, is **a**ustralian.

Editing Guide for Sample 2 Sentence: Capitals: 3   Commas: 3   Apostrophes: 1   End Marks: 1

We will check the editing guide for the specific punctuation errors. If you see a number beside the word PERIODS, it is for the periods used after abbreviations and initials within the sentence. A period at the end of a sentence is listed beside the words END MARKS in the editing guide. (*Have students look up each punctuation rule number to see how it relates to each bolded correction.*)

Look at Sentence 2. For this sentence, we will make corrections only. We do not have to put the rule numbers. Look at how you are to correct capitalization mistakes. Do you see how a capital letter is put above each small letter that needs to be capitalized?

© SHURLEY INSTRUCTIONAL MATERIALS, INC.

CHAPTER 11 LESSON 3 CONTINUED

Now, look at the punctuation examples. Do you see how you are to write each punctuation correction? Since punctuation is sometimes hard to see, you are to bold your punctuation answers by making them a little bigger and darker than normal. (*Lead students in a discussion of the corrections and why they were made.*)

 PRACTICE TIME

Have students turn to page 73 in the Practice Section of their book and find Chapter 11, Lesson 3, Practice. Go over the directions to make sure they understand what to do. Check and discuss the Practice after students have finished. (*Chapter 11, Lesson 3, Practice key is given below.*)

Chapter 11, Lesson 3, Practice: Use the Editing Guide below each sentence to know how many capitalization and punctuation errors to correct. For Sentence 1, write the capitalization and punctuation rule numbers for each correction in bold. For Sentence 2, write the capitalization and punctuation corrections. Use the capitalization and punctuation rule pages to help you.

```
   9  7                          12              11      11
1. Mr. Lewis, will you come to our Christmas pageant on Friday, December 21?
   16   12                                            5              2
```

Editing Guide: Capitals: 5   Commas: 2   Periods: 1   End Marks: 1

```
   M        J B T                          W   V
2. my uncle, j. b. thornton, owns a trucking company in west virginia.
```

Editing Guide: Capitals: 6   Commas: 2   Periods: 2   End Marks: 1

Teacher's Note: Remind students to look at the Editing Guide several times for the total number of capitalization and punctuation mistakes.

 ACTIVITY / ASSIGNMENT TIME

Directions: Write a sentence or short story. Put in the symbols from the symbol key below to show how to punctuate it. Give your sentence or story to several people and have them read it and then punctuate it by following the symbols. You may also make up your own symbols.

Symbol Key

1. capitalization – honk
2. question mark – hiccup
3. exclamation point – giggle
4. comma – yelp
5. period – groan
6. quotation marks – beep

(End of lesson.)

© SHURLEY INSTRUCTIONAL MATERIALS, INC.

CHAPTER 11   LESSON 4

Objectives: Jingles, Study, Test, Check, Activity, and Writing (journal).

JINGLE TIME

Have students turn to the Jingle Section in their books and recite the previously-taught jingles.

STUDY TIME

Have students study the vocabulary words in their vocabulary notebooks. Remind students that any vocabulary word in their notebooks could be on their test. Also, have students study any of the skills in the Practice Section that they need to review.

TEST TIME

Have students turn to page 106 in the Test Section of their book and find Chapter 11 Test. Students should use the capitalization and punctuation rules in their Reference Section if needed. Go over the directions to make sure they understand what to do. (*Chapter 11 Test key is on the next page.*)

CHECK TIME

After students have finished, check and discuss their test papers. Make sure they understand why their answers are right or wrong. (*For total points, count each required answer as a point.*)

ACTIVITY / ASSIGNMENT TIME

Students will continue to draw or trace the states and write the following questions and answers.

Illinois	Indiana
1. What Is the state on the front of this card? **Illinois**	1. What is the state on the front of this card? **Indiana**
2. What is the capital of Illinois? **Springfield**	2. What is the capital of Indiana? **Indianapolis**
3. What is the postal abbreviation of Illinois? **IL**	3. What is the postal abbreviation of Indiana? **IN**
4. What year was Illinois admitted to the Union? **1818**	4. What year was Indiana admitted to the Union? **1816**

Color these states and look up an interesting fact about each state to write on the cards. Use the cards to quiz family members, friends, and relatives. You may want to time the responses to your questions. Also, along with previous suggestions, think of other ways to have fun with your United States card file.

(End of lesson.)

Level 3 Homeschool Teacher's Manual

© SHURLEY INSTRUCTIONAL MATERIALS, INC.

Chapter 11 Test
(Student Page 106)

Exercise 1: Classify each sentence.

| | I | A | SN | P | PPA | OP | | V | P | A | OP | Adv |
1. **SN V**
P1   Yea! The present (from my grandparents) / arrived (in the mail) today! **E**

     PPA   SN   V   P   A   Adj   OP   P A   OP
2. **SN V**   My brother / fell (down the steep stairs) (to the basement)! **E**
P1

     CSN   C   PPA CSN   V   P A   OP   P OP   P A   OP
3. **SN V**   Helen and her sister / waited (in the car) (in front) (of the store). **D**
P1

Exercise 2: Use Sentence 2 to underline the complete subject once and the complete predicate twice and to complete the table below.

List the Noun Used	List the Noun Job	Singular or Plural	Common or Proper	Simple Subject	Simple Predicate
1. **brother**	2. **SN**	3. **S**	4. **C**	5. **brother**	6. **fell**
7. **stairs**	8. **OP**	9. **P**	10. **C**		
11. **basement**	12. **OP**	13. **S**	14. **C**		

Exercise 3: Name the eight parts of speech that you have studied. (*You may use abbreviations.*) **(The order may vary.)**

1. **noun**   2. **verb**   3. **adjective**   4. **adverb**   5. **preposition**   6. **pronoun**   7. **conjunction**   8. **interjection**

Exercise 4: Identify each pair of words as synonyms or antonyms by putting parentheses ( ) around *syn* or *ant*.

1. rush, hurry	**(syn)** ant	4. evade, avoid	**(syn)** ant	7. annoy, aggravate	**(syn)** ant
2. support, oppose	syn **(ant)**	5. bold, timid	syn **(ant)**	8. abundant, scarce	syn **(ant)**
3. droop, wilt	**(syn)** ant	6. tepid, warm	**(syn)** ant	9. intentional, unintended	syn **(ant)**

Exercise 5: Underline the correct homonym in each sentence.
1. Her made-up story was one big (tail, tale).
2. I drove her (knew, new) car today.
3. Those (too, two, to) girls stayed in the car.
4. We knew he was (to, too, two) friendly.
5. The dog yelped when I stepped on his (tail, tale).
6. We did not (here, hear) our mother's warning.
7. The boys found the arrowhead (here, hear).
8. The road that leads (to, two, too) town is steep.

Exercise 6: Use the Editing Guide below each sentence to know how many capitalization and punctuation errors to correct. For Sentence 1, write the capitalization and punctuation rule numbers for each correction in bold. For Sentence 2, make the capitalization and punctuation corrections. Use the capitalization and punctuation rule pages to help you.

> 1 or 9 7   7   7   11   23   23   23
> 1. **B**ro. **S**mith, **S**arah, and **S**imon were in charge of the **A**ugust report of the **N**ational **C**ouncil of **C**hurches.
>   16   9   9   1
>
> Editing Guide: Capitals: 8   Commas: 2   Periods: 1   End Marks: 1

>   J   S   S   F
> 2. julie's brother, stephen, won first place at the science fair in san francisco.
>
> Editing Guide: Capitals: 4   Commas: 2   Apostrophes: 1   End Marks: 1

Exercise 7: In your journal, write a paragraph summarizing what you have learned this week.

© SHURLEY INSTRUCTIONAL MATERIALS, INC.

CHAPTER 11 LESSON 4 CONTINUED

TEACHER INSTRUCTIONS

Use the Question and Answer Flows below for the sentences on the Chapter 11 Test.

Question and Answer Flow for Sentence 1: Yea! The present from my grandparents arrived in the mail today!

1. What arrived in the mail today? present - SN
2. What is being said about present? present arrived - V
3. In - P
4. In what? mail - OP
5. The - A
6. Arrived when? today - Adv
7. From - P
8. From whom? grandparents - OP
9. Whose grandparents? my - PPA
10. The - A
11. Yea - I
12. SN V P1 Check
13. (From my grandparents) - Prepositional phrase
14. (In the mail) - Prepositional phrase
15. Exclamation point, strong feeling, exclamatory sentence
16. Go back to the verb - divide the complete subject from the complete predicate.

Classified Sentence:

         I   A   SN   P   PPA   OP   V   P A   OP   Adv
  SN V   Yea! The present (from my grandparents) / arrived (in the mail) today! **E**
  P1

Question and Answer Flow for Sentence 2: My brother fell down the steep stairs to the basement!

1. Who fell down the steep stairs to the basement? brother - SN
2. What is being said about brother? brother fell - V
3. Down - P
4. Down what? stairs - OP
5. What kind of stairs? steep - Adj
6. The - A
7. To - P
8. To what? basement - OP
9. The - A
10. Whose brother? my - PPA
11. SN V P1 Check
12. (Down the steep stairs) - Prepositional phrase
13. (To the basement) - Prepositional phrase
14. Exclamation point, strong feeling, exclamatory sentence
15. Go back to the verb - divide the complete subject from the complete predicate.

Classified Sentence:

         PPA SN   V   P   A   Adj   OP   P   A   OP
  SN V   My brother / fell (down the steep stairs) (to the basement)! **E**
  P1

Question and Answer Flow for Sentence 3: Helen and her sister waited in the car in front of the store.

1. Who waited in the car in front of the store? Helen and sister - CSN, CSN
2. What is being said about Helen and sister? Helen and sister waited - V
3. In - P
4. In what? car - OP
5. The - A
6. In - P
7. In what? front - OP
8. Of - P
9. Of what? store - OP
10. The - A
11. Whose sister? her - PPA
12. And - C
13. SN V P1 Check
14. (In the car) - Prepositional phrase
15. (In front) - Prepositional phrase
16. (Of the store) - Prepositional phrase
17. Period, statement, declarative sentence
18. Go back to the verb - divide the complete subject from the complete predicate.

Classified Sentence:

         CSN   C PPA CSN   V   P A   OP   P   OP   P   A   OP
  SN V   Helen and her sister / waited (in the car) (in front) (of the store). **D**
  P1

© SHURLEY INSTRUCTIONAL MATERIALS, INC.

CHAPTER 11   LESSON 5

Objectives: Writing (Essay, 3-paragraph Essay), Writing Assignment #8, and Bonus Option.

 **WRITING TIME**

TEACHING SCRIPT FOR INTRODUCING AN ESSAY

You have been writing expository paragraphs in a three-point paragraph format. Remember, writing in a three-point paragraph format is a way to organize your paragraph by defining your topic, listing each of your points, supporting each of your points, and ending with a conclusion. Now, in this writing section, you will learn to expand your basic three-point format into several paragraphs. When you write several paragraphs about a certain topic, it is called an essay.

The essay is an easy and fun form of writing. The **essay** is a written discussion of one idea and is made up of several paragraphs. It might be interesting to know that the word *essay* comes from the French word *essai*, meaning "a trial" or "a try." Many students consider essay writing a real "trial." However, with Shurley English, you will find essay writing quite easy and even pleasant. In fact, anyone who reads your essays will be very impressed with your ability to organize and discuss any writing topic.

In this writing section, you will write expository essays. **Expository essays** give facts or directions, explain ideas, or define words, just like the expository paragraphs. Expository writing is often used for writing assignments in different subject areas. Any time you do an expository writing, whether it is an essay or a paragraph, you should focus on making your meaning clear and understandable. The three-point format you use will help your reader understand exactly what you mean. You will now learn to expand a three-point paragraph into an expository essay.

TEACHING SCRIPT FOR INTRODUCING HOW TO WRITE A 3-PARAGRAPH ESSAY

To make essay writing easier, you will first learn how to develop a three-paragraph essay using the three-point format. Remember, the three-point format is a way of organizing your essay that will help make your meaning clear and understandable.

A three-paragraph essay has three parts: **1. Introduction 2. Body 3. Conclusion**. These parts should be written in this order. Although a title will be the first item appearing at the top of your essay, you will not write the title until you have finished the essay. In a three-paragraph essay, there will be three paragraphs, no more and no fewer. The introduction forms the first paragraph, the body forms the second paragraph, and the conclusion forms the third paragraph of the essay.

As you are learning to write a three-paragraph essay, it will help to remember the outline for the three-point paragraph that you have already learned. Look at the two outlines in Reference 38 on page 31 in your book. Let's compare and discuss the differences in the paragraph and essay. Notice that there are more sentences in the introduction and conclusion for the essay. Of course, the second paragraph contains all the points and their supporting sentences. (*Reference 38 is on the next page.*)

© SHURLEY INSTRUCTIONAL MATERIALS, INC.

CHAPTER 11 LESSON 5 CONTINUED

Reference 38: Three-Point Paragraph and Three-Paragraph Essay	
Outline of a Three-Point Paragraph	**Outline of a Three-Paragraph Essay**

I. Title
II. Paragraph (9 sentences)
  A. Topic sentence
  B. A three-point sentence
  C. A **first-point** sentence
  D. A **supporting** sentence for the 1st point
  E. A **second-point** sentence
  F. A **supporting** sentence for the 2nd point
  G. A **third-point** sentence
  H. A **supporting** sentence for the 3rd point
  I. A concluding sentence
	I. Title
	II. Paragraph 1 - Introduction (3 sentences)
	  A. Topic and general number sentence
	  B. Extra information about the topic sentence
	  C. Three-point sentence
	III. Paragraph 2 - Body (6-9 sentences)
	  A. **First-point** sentence
	  B. One or two **supporting** sentences for the 1st point
	  C. **Second-point** sentence
	  D. One or two **supporting** sentences for the 2nd point
	  E. **Third-point** sentence
	  F. One or two **supporting** sentences for the 3rd point
	IV. Paragraph 3 - Conclusion (2 sentences)
	  A. Concluding general statement
	  B. Concluding summary sentence

You will learn how to write each sentence and paragraph in the three-paragraph expository essay by following the steps in Reference 39 on pages 31, 32 and 33 in your book. (*Read and discuss Reference 39 with your students.*)

Reference 39: Steps in Writing a Three-Paragraph Expository Essay

WRITING TOPIC: State Parks

LIST THE POINTS FOR THE TOPIC

♦ Select three points to list about the topic.
    1. exploration
    2. education
    3. relaxation

WRITING THE INTRODUCTION AND TITLE

1. Sentence #1 – Topic Sentence
   Write the topic sentence by using the words in your topic and adding a general number word, such as *several, many, some,* or *numerous,* instead of the exact number of points you will discuss.
   (I have discovered that state parks are beneficial in many ways.)

2. Sentence #2 – Extra Information about the topic sentence
   This sentence can clarify, explain, define, or just be an extra interesting comment about the topic sentence. If you need another sentence to complete your information, write an extra sentence here. If you write an extra sentence, your introductory paragraph will have four sentences in it instead of three.
   (Although many people believe entertainment is found only through technology and its advances, I think nature can be just as entertaining.)

3. Sentence #3 – Three-point sentence
   This sentence will list the three points to be discussed in the order that you will present them in the body of your paper. You can list the points with or without the specific number in front.
   (State parks provide opportunities for exploration, education, and relaxation for everyone.) or **(The three reasons why I enjoy state parks are that they provide opportunities for exploration, education, and relaxation for everyone.)**

© SHURLEY INSTRUCTIONAL MATERIALS, INC.

CHAPTER 11 LESSON 5 CONTINUED

Reference 39: Steps in Writing a Three-Paragraph Expository Essay (continued)

♦ <u>The Title</u> – Since there are many possibilities for titles, look at the topic and the three points listed about the topic. Use some of the words in the topic and write a phrase to tell what your paragraph is about. Your title can be short or long. Capitalize the first, last, and important words in your title. **(The Benefits of State Parks)**

WRITING THE BODY

4. <u>Sentence #4 – First Point</u> – Write a sentence stating your first point.
   (One of the reasons I enjoy state parks is that they allow for endless exploration of nature.)

5. <u>Sentence #5 – Supporting Sentence(s)</u> – Write one or two sentences that give more information about your first point. **(Each park offers various landscapes and a variety of wildlife for one to seek out and explore.)**

6. <u>Sentence #6 – Second Point</u> – Write a sentence stating your second point.
   (Another reason I enjoy state parks is that they offer a wonderful opportunity for education.)

7. <u>Sentence #7 – Supporting Sentence(s)</u> – Write one or two sentences that give more information about your second point. **(Upon arrival, each park becomes an outdoor classroom filled with sights, sounds, smells, and hands-on experience.)**

8. <u>Sentence #8 – Third Point</u> – Write a sentence stating your third point.
   (I also enjoy state parks because they are the perfect place for a relaxing vacation.)

9. <u>Sentence #9 – Supporting Sentence(s)</u> – Write one or two sentences that give more information about your third point. **(Whether you spend a weekend on the lake or a week camping in the mountains, there is no better place to relax than at a state park.)**

WRITING THE CONCLUSION

10. <u>Sentence #10 – Concluding General Statement</u> – Read the topic sentence again and then rewrite it, using some of the same words to say the same thing in a different way.
    (Clearly, state parks have many advantages.)

11. <u>Sentence #11 – Concluding Summary (Final) Sentence</u> – Read the three-point sentence again and then rewrite it using some of the same words to say the same thing in a different way.
    (For those who enjoy the beauty of nature, state parks can be very exhilarating.)

SAMPLE THREE-PARAGRAPH ESSAY

The Benefits of State Parks

I have discovered that state parks are beneficial in many ways. Although many people believe entertainment is found only through technology and its advances, I think nature can be just as entertaining. State parks provide opportunities for exploration, education, and relaxation for everyone.

One of the reasons I enjoy state parks is that they allow for endless exploration of nature. Each park offers various landscapes and a variety of wildlife for one to seek out and explore. Another reason I enjoy state parks is that they offer a wonderful opportunity for education. Upon arrival, each park becomes an outdoor classroom filled with sights, sounds, smells, and hands-on experience. I also enjoy state parks because they are the perfect place for a relaxing vacation. Whether you spend a weekend on the lake or a week camping in the mountains, there is no better place to relax than at a state park.

Clearly, state parks have many advantages. For those who enjoy the beauty of nature, state parks can be very exhilarating.

© SHURLEY INSTRUCTIONAL MATERIALS, INC.

CHAPTER 11 LESSON 5 CONTINUED

TEACHER INSTRUCTIONS FOR WRITING ASSIGNMENTS

Give Writing Assignment #8 from the box below. For Writing Assignment #8, students are to write a **three-paragraph expository essay**. Remind students to follow the Writing Guidelines as they prepare their writings. Have students use the three-paragraph essay steps and the essay outline to do the writing assignment below. After students have finished writing their essay, have them circle the capital letter and end mark at the beginning and end of each sentence.

Writing Assignment Box

Writing Assignment #8: Three-Paragraph Expository Essay
Remind students that the 3-paragraph essay has three parts: 1. Introduction 2. Body 3. Conclusion.

Writing topics: My Least Favorite Vegetable or **Chores I Must Do** or **Qualities I Look For In A Friend**

Bonus Option: To solve the puzzle for Psalms 145:17, write the letter missing from each set of letters on notebook paper. (1. T   2. H) The two ** indicate the end of a word. There are 14 words.

1. RSUV	7. BCEF**	13. EFGI	19. HJKL	25. HJKL	31. ZBCD	37. WXZA**	43. GIJK	49. JLMN
2. FGIJ	8. GHJK	14. RSUV	20. LMOP**	26. RTUV**	32. KLMO	38. GHJK	44. GHJK	50. RTUV**
3. DFGH**	9. RTUV**	15. DFGH	21. ZBCD	27. TUVX	33. CEFG**	39. MOPQ**	45. RTUV**	
4. KMNO	10. QSTU	16. MNPQ	22. KMNO	28. YZBC	34. EFGI	40. ZBCD	46. UVXY	
5. LMNP	11. FGHJ	17. STVW	23. JKMN**	29. XZAB	35. MNPQ	41. JKMN	47. MNPQ	
6. QSTU	12. FHIJ	18. RTUV**	24. GIJK	30. QRTU**	36. JKMN	42. KMNO**	48. QSTU	

TEACHING SCRIPT FOR USING THE WRITING PROCESS FOR THIS WRITING ASSIGNMENT

As you begin this writing assignment, you will start through the writing process. First, you will think about your topic and gather any information you might need in order to do the writing. Second, you will write a rough draft. Remember, it is called a rough draft because it will be revised and edited. You do not have to worry about mistakes as you write your rough draft. After you write the first draft, you will make revisions, using the Revision Checklist in Reference 13. After you revise your writing, you will edit, using the Beginning Editing Checklist in Reference 13. Finally, after you are satisfied with your revising and editing, you will write a final paper, using the Final Paper Checklist in Reference 13. You will then give the finished writing assignment to me.

TEACHER INSTRUCTIONS FOR CHECKING WRITING ASSIGNMENTS

Read, check, and discuss Writing Assignment #8 after students have finished their final papers. Use the editing checklist (*Reference 13 on teacher's page 48*) as you check and discuss students' papers. Make sure students are using the editing checklist correctly. In the beginning, you must also check students' papers carefully for <u>form</u> mistakes. This will ensure that students are learning the three-point essay format correctly.

Bonus Option Answer: *The Lord is righteous in all his ways, and holy in all his works.* (King James Version)

(End of lesson.)

Level 3 Homeschool Teacher's Manual
© SHURLEY INSTRUCTIONAL MATERIALS, INC.

CHAPTER 12   LESSON 1

Objectives: Jingles, Grammar (Practice Sentences), Oral Skill Builder Check, Skills (capitalization and punctuation of a friendly letter using rule numbers), Practice Exercise, and Vocabulary #1.

JINGLE TIME

Have students turn to the Jingle Section in their books and recite the previously-taught jingles.

GRAMMAR TIME

First-Year Option: Put the Practice Sentences from the box below on the board or on notebook paper. Use these sentences as you practice the concepts that have been taught. For the greatest benefit, students must participate orally with the teacher. **Second-Year Option:** Have students classify the Practice Sentences independently on paper. Check students' sentences with the answers provided below. *(If you have the CDs for Practice Sentences, have students check their sentences with the CDs.)*

Chapter 12, Practice Sentences for Lesson 1
1. _____   A magical adventure began on the first page of the book.
2. _____   Wow! That basketball player can jump high in the air!

TEACHING SCRIPT FOR PRACTICING PATTERN 1 SENTENCES

We will practice classifying Pattern 1 Sentences. We will classify the sentences together. Begin. (*You might have your students write the labels above the sentences at this time.*)

Question and Answer Flow for Sentence 1: A magical adventure began on the first page of the book.

1. What began on the first page of the book?
   adventure - SN
2. What is being said about adventure?
   adventure began - V
3. On - P
4. On what? page - OP
5. Which page? first - Adj
6. The - A
7. Of - P
8. Of what? book - OP

9. The - A
10. What kind of adventure? magical - Adj
11. A - A
12. SN V P1 Check
13. (On the first page) - Prepositional phrase
14. (Of the book) - Prepositional phrase
15. Period, statement, declarative sentence
16. Go back to the verb - divide the complete subject from the complete predicate.

Classified Sentence:

<pre>
                        A   Adj   SN   V   P A Adj OP   P A OP
    SN V   A magical adventure / began (on the first page) (of the book). D
    ─────
      P1
</pre>

© SHURLEY INSTRUCTIONAL MATERIALS, INC.

CHAPTER 12 LESSON 1 CONTINUED

Question and Answer Flow for Sentence 2: Wow! That basketball player can jump high in the air!

1. Who can jump high in the air? player - SN
2. What is being said about player? player can jump - V
3. Can - HV
4. Can jump how? high - Adv
5. In - P
6. In what? air - OP
7. The - A
8. What kind of player? basketball - Adj

9. Which player? that - Adj
10. Wow - I
11. SN V P1 Check
12. (In the air) - Prepositional phrase
13. Exclamation point, strong feeling, exclamatory sentence
14. Go back to the verb - divide the complete subject from the complete predicate.

Classified Sentence:

                              I   Adj   Adj   SN   HV   V   Adv   P   A   OP

      <u>SN V</u>   Wow! That basketball player **/** can jump high (in the air)! **E**

      P1

Use Sentences 1-2 that you just classified with your students to do an Oral Skill Builder Check. Use the guidelines below.

Oral Skill Builder Check

1. **Noun check.**
   (Say the job and then say the noun. Circle each noun.)
2. **Identify the nouns as singular or plural.**
   (Write S or P above each noun.)
3. **Identify the nouns as common or proper.**
   (Follow established procedure for oral identification.)
4. **Do a vocabulary check.**
   (Follow established procedure for oral identification.)

5. **Identify the complete subject and the complete predicate.** (Underline the complete subject once and the complete predicate twice.)
6. **Identify the simple subject and simple predicate.**
   (Underline the simple subject once and the simple predicate twice. Bold, or highlight, the lines.)
7. **Recite the irregular verb chart.**
   (Located on student page 25 and teacher page 163.)

SKILL TIME

TEACHING SCRIPT FOR CAPITALIZATION AND PUNCTUATION OF A FRIENDLY LETTER, USING RULE NUMBERS ONLY

Today, you will learn how to apply the capitalization and punctuation rules to a friendly letter. A friendly letter is a letter written to talk to a friend or relative. The capitalization and punctuation rules apply to friendly letters in the same way they apply to any other type of writing. The only difference is that there are more address-related punctuation rules and a few new terms that you will learn as you punctuate letters. You do not have to learn the friendly-letter form at this time because it has already been set up for you.

The first friendly letter you will use in Practice Time has already been corrected. The corrections are identified in bold type. You need only to put the rule number above each correction in bold type that justifies each capitalization or mark of punctuation. I must also remind you to look at the editing guide to find the total number of errors you need to correct in each section. Remember that the end-mark total tells you how many sentences need end mark punctuation. For instance, if you have the number *seven* beside the words END MARKS in your editing guide, it means there are seven sentences in your letter. Also, make sure you pay attention to the greeting and closing of a friendly letter.

© SHURLEY INSTRUCTIONAL MATERIALS, INC.

CHAPTER 12 LESSON 1 CONTINUED

PRACTICE TIME

Have students turn to page 73 in the Practice Section of their books and find the skill under Chapter 12, Lesson 1, Practice. Go over the directions to make sure they understand what to do. Students must use the Reference Section in their books to find the capitalization and punctuation rule numbers to edit the friendly letter. They will write a rule number for each correction in bold type. Check and discuss the Practice after students have finished. (*Chapter 12, Lesson 1, Practice key is given below.*)

Chapter 12, Lesson 1, Practice: Write the capitalization and punctuation rule number for each correction in bold.

                                     15   15
           2616 **J**enson **D**rive

             14   14
     Alpino**,** **A**rizona 75643
                     7
       11
     August 2**,** 20—
                  5

2   8   7
Dear **A**unt **L**inda**,**
          13
  1   1 or 6   1
  You are so thoughtful**!** **I** appreciate your saving stamps for me for so long. **M**y album is now
             3   1
     1 or 6   1
complete. **I** have been asked to display it at the local library next month. **T**his is a big honor for me.
     1   1   1
1 or 6   19
I thought you might like to see it while it**'**s on display**.**
                            1

                                     2
                                 Your devoted nephew**,**
                                          14
                                 7
                                 Tyler

Editing Guide: Capitals: 16   Commas: 4   Apostrophes: 1   End Marks: 6

VOCABULARY TIME

Assign Chapter 12, Vocabulary Words **#1** on page 9 in the Reference Section for students to define in their Vocabulary notebooks. After they write each word and its meaning, students are to write a sentence using the vocabulary word.

Chapter 12, Vocabulary Words #1
(stay, depart, victor, winner)

(End of lesson.)

© SHURLEY INSTRUCTIONAL MATERIALS, INC.

CHAPTER 12   LESSON 2

Objectives: Jingles, Grammar (Practice Sentences), Independent Pattern 1 Practice Sentence, Skills (capitalization and punctuation of a friendly letter using corrections only), Practice Exercise, and Vocabulary #2.

 JINGLE TIME

Have students turn to the Jingle Section in their books and recite the previously-taught jingles.

 GRAMMAR TIME

First-Year Option: Put the Practice Sentences from the box below on the board or on notebook paper. Use these sentences as you practice the concepts that have been taught. For the greatest benefit, students must participate orally with the teacher. **Second-Year Option:** Have students classify the Practice Sentences independently on paper. Check students' sentences with the answers provided below. *(If you have the CDs for Practice Sentences, have students check their sentences with the CDs.)*

Chapter 12, Practice Sentences for Lesson 2

1. _____ Yikes! The crazy motorcyclist fell off his bike during the sharp turn!
2. _____ Mom and I worked in the yard during the hot afternoon.

TEACHING SCRIPT FOR PRACTICING PATTERN 1 SENTENCES

We will practice classifying Pattern 1 Sentences. We will classify the sentences together. Begin. (*You might have your students write the labels above the sentences at this time.*)

Question and Answer Flow for Sentence 1: Yikes! The crazy motorcyclist fell off his bike during the sharp turn!

1. Who fell off his bike during the sharp turn?
   motorcyclist - SN
2. What is being said about motorcyclist?
   motorcyclist fell - V
3. Off - P
4. Off what? bike - OP
5. Whose bike? his - PPA
6. During - P
7. During what? turn - OP
8. What kind of turn? sharp - Adj
9. The - A

10. What kind of motorcyclist? crazy - Adj
11. The - A
12. Yikes - I
13. SN V P1 Check
14. (Off his bike) - Prepositional phrase
15. (During the sharp turn) - Prepositional phrase
16. Exclamation point, strong feeling, exclamatory sentence
17. Go back to the verb - divide the complete subject from the complete predicate.

Classified Sentence:

	I	A	Adj	SN	V	P	PPA	OP	P	A	Adj	OP	
SN V	Yikes!	The	crazy	motorcyclist /	fell	(off	his	bike)	(during	the	sharp	turn)!	**E**
P1													

© SHURLEY INSTRUCTIONAL MATERIALS, INC.

CHAPTER 12 LESSON 2 CONTINUED

Question and Answer Flow for Sentence 2: Mom and I worked in the yard during the hot afternoon.

1. Who worked in the yard during the hot afternoon?
   Mom and I - CSN, CSP
2. What is being said about Mom and I?
   Mom and I worked - V
3. In - P
4. In what? yard - OP
5. The - A
6. During - P
7. During what? afternoon - OP
8. What kind of afternoon? hot - Adj
9. The - A
10. And - C
11. SN V P1 Check
12. (In the yard) - Prepositional phrase
13. (During the hot afternoon) - Prepositional phrase
14. Period, statement, declarative sentence
15. Go back to the verb - divide the complete subject from the complete predicate.

Classified Sentence:

	CSN	C	CSP	V	P	A	OP	P	A	Adj	OP	
SN V	Mom	and	I /	worked	(in	the	yard)	(during	the	hot	afternoon).	D
P1												

TEACHER INSTRUCTIONS FOR A PATTERN 1 SENTENCE

Tell students that their sentence writing assignment today is to write a Pattern 1 sentence. They are to follow the same procedure used in the previous lessons. They should decide on their labels, arrange them in a selected order, write their sentences, and edit their sentences for improved word choices. (*Students do not have to write an Improved Sentence at this point unless you feel they need more one-on-one word choice writing practice.*) Make sure students check Reference 35 on page 28 in the Reference Section for the sentence parts that can be used in a Pattern 1 sentence. Check and discuss the Pattern 1 sentence after students have finished. (*Independent sentence assignments will be given in an assignment box like the one below.*)

Sentence Writing Assignment Box

Independent Pattern 1 Sentence

(In order to write a Pattern 1 sentence, students should decide on their labels, arrange them in a selected order, write their sentences, and edit their sentences for improved word choices.)

 SKILL TIME

TEACHING SCRIPT FOR CAPITALIZATION AND PUNCTUATION OF A FRIENDLY LETTER, USING CORRECTIONS ONLY

Your second friendly letter has not been punctuated. You are to write capitalization corrections above the capitalization mistakes and write the punctuation corrections where they belong in the letter. I must remind you again to look at the editing guide to find the total number of errors you need to correct in each section. Remember that the end mark total tells you how many sentences need end mark punctuation. You may also use your capitalization and punctuation rules as a reference if you need them.

© SHURLEY INSTRUCTIONAL MATERIALS, INC.

CHAPTER 12 LESSON 2 CONTINUED

 PRACTICE TIME

Have students turn to page 74 in the Practice Section of their book and find the skill under Chapter 12, Lesson 2, Practice. Go over the directions to make sure they understand what to do. Remind students to look at the editing guide to find the total number of errors they need to correct in each section. Students may also use their capitalization and punctuation rules as a reference if they need them. Check and discuss the Practice after students have finished. (*Chapter 12, Lesson 2, Practice key is given below.*)

Chapter 12, Lesson 2, Practice: Write the capitalization and punctuation corrections only.

            M   L
201 mustang lane
K   F   K
kettle field, kentucky 24431
M
may 19, 20—

D   J
dear jennifer,

    W
we have decided to have some kind of theme at the family reunion this year.   we decided to elect a

               T
committee to get things going.   this group of family members would be in charge of organizing and

         A   P   U   P
planning the food, music, and games for august 4.   please contact your uncle phil if you are interested in

serving on this special committee.

       A
affectionately yours,
A   S
aunt susan

Editing Guide: Capitals: 18   Commas: 6   End Marks: 4

 VOCABULARY TIME

Assign Chapter 12, Vocabulary Words **#2** on page 9 in the Reference Section for students to define in their Vocabulary notebooks. Tell students they are to use a dictionary or thesaurus to look up the meanings of the vocabulary words. After they write each word and its meaning, students are to write a sentence using the vocabulary word.

Chapter 12, Vocabulary Words #2
(fixed, repaired, gorgeous, unsightly)

(End of lesson.)

© SHURLEY INSTRUCTIONAL MATERIALS, INC.

CHAPTER 12   LESSON 3

Objectives: Jingles, Grammar (Practice Sentences), Study, Test A, Check, and Activity.

 JINGLE TIME

Have students turn to the Jingle Section in their books and recite the previously-taught jingles.

 GRAMMAR TIME

First-Year Option: Put the Practice Sentences from the box below on the board or on notebook paper. Use these sentences as you practice the concepts that have been taught. For the greatest benefit, students must participate orally with the teacher. **Second-Year Option:** Have students classify the Practice Sentences independently on paper. Check students' sentences with the answers provided below. (*If you have the CDs for Practice Sentences, have students check their sentences with the CDs.*)

Chapter 12, Practice Sentences for Lesson 3

1. _____The chocolate candies fell out of the bag onto the floor.
2. _____Can you see out of the foggy window?

TEACHING SCRIPT FOR PRACTICING PATTERN 1 SENTENCES

We will practice classifying Pattern 1 Sentences. We will classify the sentences together. Begin. (*You might have your students write the labels above the sentences at this time.*)

Question and Answer Flow for Sentence 1: The chocolate candies fell out of the bag onto the floor.

1. What fell out of the bag onto the floor? candies - SN
2. What is being said about candies? candies fell - V
3. Fell where? out - Adv
4. Of - P
5. Of what? bag - OP
6. The - A
7. Onto - P
8. Onto what? floor - OP
9. The - A

10. What kind of candies? chocolate - Adj
11. The - A
12. SN V P1 Check
13. (Of the bag) - Prepositional phrase
14. (Onto the floor) - Prepositional phrase
15. Period, statement, declarative sentence
16. Go back to the verb - divide the complete subject from the complete predicate.

```
                          A     Adj    SN    V Adv P A  OP    P   A  OP
Classified Sentence:   SN  V      The chocolate candies / fell out (of the bag) (onto the floor).  D
                       P1
```

© SHURLEY INSTRUCTIONAL MATERIALS, INC.

CHAPTER 12 LESSON 3 CONTINUED

Question and Answer Flow for Sentence 2: Can you see out of the foggy window?

1. Who can see out of the foggy window? you - SP
2. What is being said about you? you can see - V
3. Can - HV
4. Can see where? out - Adv
5. Of - P
6. Of what? window - OP
7. What kind of window? foggy - Adj

8. The - A
9. SN V P1 Check
10. (Of the foggy window) - Prepositional phrase
11. Question mark, question, interrogative sentence
12. Go back to the verb - divide the complete subject
     from the complete predicate.

		HV	SP	V	Adv	P	A	Adj	OP
Classified Sentence:	SN V	Can	you	/ see	out	(of	the	foggy	window)?	Int
	P1									

STUDY TIME

Have students study any of the skills in the Practice Section that they need to review.   Students should also study their homonym chart.

TEST TIME

Have students turn to page 107 in the Test Section of their book and find Chapter 12 Test A. Students should use the Reference Section in their books to find the capitalization and punctuation rule numbers to edit the sentence and friendly letter. Go over the directions to make sure they understand what to do. (*Chapter 12 Test A key is on the next page.*)

CHECK TIME

After students have finished, check and discuss their test papers. Make sure they understand why their answers are right or wrong. (*For total points, count each required answer as a point.*)

ACTIVITY / ASSIGNMENT TIME

Write the descriptive words in the box below on the board or on notebook paper. Allow time for students to study the words. Give students each word one at a time. Then, have them name five nouns for each descriptive word. Use the sample below as a guide.

Descriptive Word: **Soft** - cotton balls, stuffed animals, pillow, kitten, feather bed.

Descriptive Words	
1. Tall	6. Round
2. Slippery	7. Hot
3. Yellow	8. Sharp
4. Sweet	9. Hard
5. Noisy	10. Green

(End of lesson.)

Level 3 Homeschool Teacher's Manual

© SHURLEY INSTRUCTIONAL MATERIALS, INC.

Chapter 12 Test A
(Student Page 107)

Exercise 1: <u>Sentence</u>: Write the capitalization and punctuation rule numbers for each correction in bold.

```
    1              9  10 10  7                    16      16      14      14
1.  Our neighbor, Mr. L. D. Coffee, was born across the Atlantic Ocean in Paris, France.
         11 16 17 17      11                                          7      1
```

Editing Guide:	Capitals: 9	Commas: 3	Periods: 3	End Marks: 1

Exercise 2: <u>Friendly Letter</u>: Write the capitalization and punctuation corrections only.

```
                                    C     D
                                    113 calico drive
                                    C         T
                                    chateau, tennessee 22006
                                    J
                                    june 6, 20—
  D   J
  dear jonathan,
    I                                                       I
    i heard that your science class was researching different kinds of animals.  i am able to obtain many
                     I         T         G         F    C            I
  helpful resources because i work with the tennessee game and fish commission.  i would be more than

  happy to send some of our booklets if you think they would be helpful in your research.
                                    A
                                    affectionately yours,
                                    U    J
                                    uncle james
```

Editing Guide:	Capitals: 18	Commas: 4	End Marks: 3

Exercise 3: Name the eight parts of speech that you have studied. (*You may use abbreviations.*) **(The order may vary.)**

1. **noun**   2. **verb**   3. **adjective**   4. **adverb**   5. **preposition**   6. **pronoun**   7. **conjunction**   8. **interjection**

Exercise 4: Identify each pair of words as synonyms or antonyms by putting parentheses ( ) around *syn* or *ant*.

1. winner, victor	**(syn)** ant	4. tempt, lure	**(syn)** ant	7. annoy, aggravate	**(syn)** ant
2. depart, stay	syn **(ant)**	5. fragrance, aroma	**(syn)** ant	8. withdraw, join	syn **(ant)**
3. repaired, fixed	**(syn)** ant	6. evade, avoid	**(syn)** ant	9. unsightly, gorgeous	syn **(ant)**

Exercise 5: Underline the correct homonym in each sentence.

1. He prints with his (write, <u>right</u>) hand.
2. He (<u>knew</u>, new) this phone number.
3. The student (<u>council</u>, counsel) meets on Monday.
4. The skunk has a bad (<u>scent</u>, cent).
5. The quarterback (through, <u>threw</u>) a pass.
6. There are seven (daze, <u>days</u>) in a week.
7. Austin is the (capitol, <u>capital</u>) of Texas.
8. I think you (no, <u>know</u>) the correct answer.

© SHURLEY INSTRUCTIONAL MATERIALS, INC.

CHAPTER 12   LESSON 4

Objectives: Study, Test B, Check, Activity, and Writing (journal).

STUDY TIME

Have students study any of the skills in the Practice Section that they need to review.

TEST TIME

Have students turn to page 108 in the Test Section of their book and find Chapter 12 Test B. Students should use the Reference Section in their books to find the capitalization and punctuation rule numbers to edit the sentence and friendly letter. Go over the directions to make sure they understand what to do. (*Chapter 12 Test B key is on the next page.*)

CHECK TIME

After students have finished, check and discuss their test papers. Make sure they understand why their answers are right or wrong. (*For total points, count each required answer as a point.*)

ACTIVITY / ASSIGNMENT TIME

Students will continue to draw or trace the states and write the following questions and answers.

Iowa	Kansas
1. What is the state on the front of this card? **Iowa**	1. What is the state on the front of this card? **Kansas**
2. What is the capital of Iowa? **Des Moines**	2. What is the capital of Kansas? **Topeka**
3. What is the postal abbreviation of Iowa? **IA**	3. What is the postal abbreviation of Kansas? **KS**
4. What year was Iowa admitted to the Union? **1846**	4. What year was Kansas admitted to the Union? **1861**

Color these states and look up an interesting fact about each state to write on the cards. Use the cards to quiz family members, friends, and relatives. You may want to time the responses to your questions. Also, along with previous suggestions, think of other ways to have fun with your United States card file.

(End of lesson.)

© SHURLEY INSTRUCTIONAL MATERIALS, INC.

Chapter 12 Test B
(Student Page 108)

Exercise 1: Classify each sentence.

          CSN C CSN   V   P A   OP   P OP   P A   Adj   OP

1. **SN V**   Tina and Eric / sat (on the blanket) (in front) (of the television set). **D**
   P1

          A   Adj   Adj   SN   V   Adv   P   A OP   P A OP

2. **SN V**   The sweet maple syrup / dripped slowly (down the side) (of the bottle). **D**
   P1

          PPA Adj   SN   V   P   A   OP   P A   OP

3. **SN V**   My youngest brother / visited (with the manager) (of the store). **D**
   P1

Exercise 2: <u>Sentence</u>: Write the capitalization and punctuation corrections only.

   T   J   C   M   N   S   H   T   A

1.   thomas, jenny, and calvin visited the museum of natural science and history in tuscon, arizona.

Editing Guide: Capitals: 9   Commas: 3   End Marks: 1

Exercise 3: <u>Friendly Letter</u>: Write the capitalization and punctuation rule numbers for each correction in bold.

          15   15   15
         233 **E**ast **S**alem **A**ve.
                     16
       14   14   14
       Mulvert **P**ass, **M**innesota 77009
                      7
       11
       January 10, 20—
                 5

 2   7
Dear **M**ichelle,
     13

  1   1
  We woke up to the most beautiful winter wonderland this morning. **T**he snow that covered the ground
                                    1
              1   1 or 7   6
was at least three feet deep. **A**ll classes were cancelled. **J**ennifer and **I** played out in the snow
           1   1
   1   1
all morning. **W**e spent the afternoon sipping hot cocoa and watching our favorite cartoons. **I**t really was
   1   1

a wonderful day!
   3   2
                               Your cousin,
                                   14
                             7
                           Julia

Editing Guide: Capitals: 18   Commas: 4   Periods: 1   End Marks: 6

Exercise 4: In your journal, write a paragraph summarizing what you have learned this week.

© SHURLEY INSTRUCTIONAL MATERIALS, INC.

CHAPTER 12 LESSON 4 CONTINUED

TEACHER INSTRUCTIONS

Use the Question and Answer Flows below for the sentences on Chapter 12 Test B.

Question and Answer Flow for Sentence 1: Tina and Eric sat on the blanket in front of the television set.

1. Who sat on the blanket in front of the television set? Tina and Eric - CSN, CSN
2. What is being said about Tina and Eric? Tina and Eric sat - V
3. On - P
4. On what? blanket - OP
5. The - A
6. In - P
7. In what? front - OP
8. Of - P
9. Of what? set - OP
10. What kind of set? television - Adj
11. The - A
12. And - C
13. SN V P1 Check
14. (On the blanket) - Prepositional phrase
15. (In front) - Prepositional phrase
16. (Of the television set) - Prepositional phrase
17. Period, statement, declarative sentence
18. Go back to the verb - divide the complete subject from the complete predicate.

Classified Sentence:

	CSN	C	CSN	V	P	A	OP	P	OP	P	A	Adj	OP
SN V	Tina	and	Eric /	sat	(on	the	blanket)	(in	front)	(of	the	television	set). **D**

P1

Question and Answer Flow for Sentence 2: The sweet maple syrup dripped slowly down the side of the bottle.

1. What dripped slowly down the side of the bottle? syrup - SN
2. What is being said about syrup? syrup dripped - V
3. Dripped how? slowly - Adv
4. Down - P
5. Down what? side - OP
6. The - A
7. Of - P
8. Of what? bottle - OP
9. The - A
10. What kind of syrup? maple - Adj
11. What kind of syrup? sweet - Adj
12. The - A
13. SN V P1 Check
14. (Down the side) - Prepositional phrase
15. (Of the bottle) - Prepositional phrase
16. Period, statement, declarative sentence
17. Go back to the verb - divide the complete subject from the complete predicate.

Classified Sentence:

	A	Adj	Adj	SN	V	Adv	P	A	OP	P	A	OP
SN V	The	sweet	maple	syrup /	dripped	slowly	(down	the	side)	(of	the	bottle). **D**

P1

Question and Answer Flow for Sentence 3: My youngest brother visited with the manager of the store.

1. Who visited with the manager of the store? brother - SN
2. What is being said about brother? brother visited - V
3. With - P
4. With whom? manager - OP
5. The - A
6. Of - P
7. Of what? store - OP
8. The - A
9. Which brother? youngest - Adj
10. Whose brother? my - PPA
11. SN V P1 Check
12. (With the manager) - Prepositional phrase
13. (Of the store) - Prepositional phrase
14. Period, statement, declarative sentence
15. Go back to the verb - divide the complete subject from the complete predicate.

Classified Sentence:

	PPA	Adj	SN	V	P	A	OP	P	A	OP
SN V	My	youngest	brother /	visited	(with	the	manager)	(of	the	store). **D**

P1

© SHURLEY INSTRUCTIONAL MATERIALS, INC.

CHAPTER 12   LESSON 5
Objectives: Writing (persuasive essay) and Writing Assignment #9.

 WRITING TIME

TEACHING SCRIPT FOR A PERSUASIVE ESSAY

Persuasion means getting other people to see things your way. When you write a persuasive essay, your topic is something you want to "persuade" people to do or believe. A persuasive essay expresses an opinion and tries to convince the reader that this opinion is correct. Persuading someone to agree with you requires careful thinking and planning. As a writer, you must make the issue clear and present facts and reasons that give strong support to your opinion. You are encouraging your audience to take a certain action or to feel the same way you do.

In attempting to persuade anyone to your way of thinking, it is VERY important to consider just who the reader is that you are trying to persuade. Your reader is your audience. When you know who your reader is, you must use persuasive reasoning that will appeal to that reader. Know your reader well enough to use arguments that will appeal to him/her. You would not use the same kind of argument to persuade your five-year-old sister to tell you where she hid your pack of gum that you would use to persuade your parents to allow you to have a second helping of dessert.

The three-point writing format is one of the best ways to present your persuasive argument because it gives you an organized way of stating your opinion and supporting it. The persuasive writing format is the same as your earlier expository writing format. They both use the three-point organization. The differences between persuasive and expository writing are your purpose for writing, the content of your paper, and the wording of your sentences.

You will find that the main difference is that the topic sentence is an opinion statement. In addition, all the points and supporting sentences are persuasive in nature and are intended to back up the opinion statement. Remember, persuasive writing states your opinion with supporting facts that try to convince your reader to think or act in a certain way, and expository writing attempts to give an explanation or information to your reader.

We will go through the steps for writing a persuasive essay by reading and discussing the guidelines for a three-paragraph persuasive essay in Reference 40 on page 34 in your book. You actually have two guidelines in your reference box. Let's go through the persuasive essay first so you will know all the parts. (*Read and discuss the parts of a persuasive essay below. Reference 40 is on page 223 in your TM.*)

Your first paragraph is an introductory paragraph and will have three sentences. Sentence #1 is the Topic Sentence. You will state your opinion in the topic sentence: **Everyone should learn how to cook.**

Sentence #2 is the Reason Sentence. You will give a general reason why you think the topic sentence is true: **Although cooking is an essential part of our survival, it can also be very rewarding.**

Sentence #3 is the General Number Sentence. You will use a general number word and restate the main idea in the topic sentence: **There are numerous reasons why learning to cook is beneficial.**

© SHURLEY INSTRUCTIONAL MATERIALS, INC.

CHAPTER 12 LESSON 5 CONTINUED

The second paragraph is the body of the essay and will have 6 sentences. Sentence #4 is the <u>First-Point Persuasive Sentence.</u> You will give your first reason to support your opinion: **The first benefit of learning to cook is that cooking is an enjoyable and easy form of education.** Sentence #5 is the <u>First-Point Supporting Sentence.</u> You will give an example that supports and explains your first point: **Without realizing it, you can easily learn different forms of measurements, time, temperature, and even fractions.**

Sentence #6 is the <u>Second-Point Persuasive Sentence.</u> You will give your second reason to support your opinion: **The second benefit of learning to cook is the variety that this hobby offers.** Sentence #7 is the <u>Second-Point Supporting Sentence.</u> You will give an example that supports and explains your second point: **Thousands of recipes are available to amateurs and professionals alike.**

Sentence #8 is the <u>Third-Point Persuasive Sentence.</u> You will give your third reason to support your opinion: **The third benefit of learning to cook is self-satisfaction.** Sentence #9 is the <u>Third-Point Supporting Sentence.</u> You will give an example that supports and explains your third point: **Not only do you feel a sense of value in what you have accomplished, but you can share your bounty with others.**

The third paragraph is the conclusion of the essay and will have two concluding sentences. The first concluding sentence is simply a restatement sentence that forcefully restates your original opinion in the topic sentence and usually starts with IN CONCLUSION. Sentence #10 is the <u>In Conclusion Sentence:</u> **In conclusion, everyone should learn to cook, not only out of necessity, but also for the pleasure and pride in a job well done.**

The second concluding sentence is a summary sentence. This sentence summarizes one or more of the reasons stated. Sentence #11 is the <u>Final Summary Sentence:</u> **Without a doubt, cooking is a great mixture of education and fun.**

Sometimes, you will only want to write a persuasive paragraph, not an essay. We will now go through the persuasive paragraph so you will know all the parts and will be familiar with the patterns for persuasive paragraphs and essays. Look at the persuasive paragraph guidelines in Reference 40. (*Read and discuss the guidelines for a persuasive paragraph and a persuasive essay in the reference box on the next page with your students. Make sure you use the sample essay to point out how each sentence is made.*)

© SHURLEY INSTRUCTIONAL MATERIALS, INC.

CHAPTER 12 LESSON 5 CONTINUED

Reference 40: Persuasive Paragraph and Essay Guidelines	
Guidelines for a Persuasive Paragraph	Guidelines for a 3-Paragraph Persuasive Essay

Paragraph   (10-13 sentences)
A. **Topic** sentence (opinion statement)
B. **General number** sentence
C. **First-point** persuasive sentence
D. 1 or 2 **supporting** sentences for the 1st point
E. **Second-point** persuasive sentence
F. 1 or 2 **supporting** sentences for the 2nd point
G. **Third-point** persuasive sentence
H. 1 or 2 **supporting** sentences for the 3rd point
I. **In conclusion** sentence (Repeat topic idea)
J. **Final summary** sentence (Summarize reasons)
	I. Paragraph 1 – Introduction (3 sentences)
	    A. **Topic** sentence (opinion statement)
	    B. **Reason** sentence
	    C. **General number** sentence
	II. Paragraph 2 – Body (6-9 sentences)
	    A. **First-point** persuasive sentence
	    B. 1 or 2 **supporting** sentences for the 1st point
	    C. **Second-point** persuasive sentence
	    D. 1 or 2 **supporting** sentences for the 2nd point
	    E. **Third-point** persuasive sentence
	    F. 1 or 2 **supporting** sentences for the 3rd point
	III. Paragraph 3 - Conclusion (2 sentences)
	    A. **In conclusion** sentence (Repeat topic idea)
	    B. **Final summary** sentence (Summarize reasons)

Cooking

   Everyone should learn how to cook. Although cooking is an essential part of our survival, it can also be very rewarding. There are numerous reasons why learning to cook is beneficial.

   The first benefit of learning to cook is that cooking is an enjoyable and easy form of education. Without realizing it, you can easily learn different forms of measurements, time, temperature, and even fractions. The second benefit of learning to cook is the variety that this hobby offers. Thousands of recipes are available to amateurs and professionals alike. The third benefit of learning to cook is self-satisfaction. Not only do you feel a sense of value in what you have accomplished, but also you can share your bounty with others.

   In conclusion, everyone should learn to cook, not only out of necessity, but also for the pleasure and pride in a job well done. Without a doubt, cooking is a great mixture of education and fun.

Now, you will write, revise, and edit a persuasive essay. As you edit, make sure you use all the checklists in Reference 13. Remember to read through the whole essay, starting with the title. After you are satisfied with your revising and editing, you will write a final paper, using the Final Paper Checklist in Reference 13. You will then give the finished writing assignment to me.

Writing Assignment Box
Writing Assignment #9: Three-Paragraph Persuasive Essay
Writing topics: Why Education Is Important   or   Why I Need an Allowance   or   Why Honesty Is Important

Read, check, and discuss the final paper for Writing Assignment #9 after students have finished writing, revising, and editing their writing assignment. Use the checklists in Reference 13 as you check and discuss students' papers.

(End of lesson.)

© SHURLEY INSTRUCTIONAL MATERIALS, INC.

CHAPTER 13   LESSON 1
Objectives: Jingles (Direct Object), Grammar (Introductory sentences, direct objects, transitive verbs, add direct objects to the Noun Check), Oral Skill Builder Check, and Vocabulary #1.

 **JINGLE TIME**

Have students turn to the Jingle Section in their books and recite the previously-taught jingles. Then, lead students in reciting the new jingle (*Direct Object*) below. Practice the new jingle several times until students can recite it smoothly. Emphasize reciting with a rhythm. Students and teacher should be together! (*Do not try to explain the jingle at this time. Just have fun reciting it.*)

Teacher's Note: Again, do not spend a large amount of time practicing the new jingles. Students learn the jingles best by spending a small amount of time consistently, **every** day.

Jingle 16: Direct Object Jingle
1. A direct object is a noun or pronoun.
2. A direct object completes the meaning of the sentence.
3. A direct object is located after the verb-transitive.
4. To find the direct object, ask WHAT or WHOM after your verb.

 GRAMMAR TIME

Put the introductory sentences from the box below on the board. Use these sentences as you go through each new concept covered in your teaching script. For the greatest benefit, students must participate orally with the teacher. (*You might put the introductory sentences on notebook paper if you are doing one-on-one instruction with your students.*)

Chapter 13, Introductory Sentences for Lesson 1
1. _____ Bill bought a new pen with his allowance.
2. _____ My grandmother baked a cake for my birthday party.
3. _____ The brilliant writer explained her poem to the audience.

TEACHING SCRIPT FOR DIRECT OBJECTS AND TRANSITIVE VERBS

We have been studying Pattern 1, which has the (subject) noun and verb as its main parts (N V). Now, we will learn a new sentence pattern. This new sentence pattern is called Pattern 2, and it will have some new parts that you will learn today. Pattern 2 is different from Pattern 1 because its main parts are noun, verb, noun (N V N). The second noun is called a direct object. There are five things you need to know about a direct object. For this information, look at Reference 41 on page 35 in the Reference Section of your book and follow along as I read this information to you.

© SHURLEY INSTRUCTIONAL MATERIALS, INC.

CHAPTER 13 LESSON 1 CONTINUED

I want you to notice that these five things are very similar to the Direct Object jingle. You will read the example with me so you will know what to say when you classify Pattern 2 sentences. (*Read the information about direct objects to your students. Then, have students read and classify the sample sentence with you.*)

Reference 41: Direct Object, Verb-transitive, and Pattern 2

1. A **direct object** is a noun or pronoun after the verb that completes the meaning of the sentence.
2. A **direct object** is labeled as DO.
3. To find the **direct object**, ask WHAT or WHOM after the verb.
4. A **direct object** must be verified to mean someone or something different from the subject noun.
5. A **verb-transitive** is an action verb with a direct object after it and is labeled V-t. (Whatever receives the action of a transitive verb is the direct object.)

Sample Sentence for the exact words to say to find the direct object and transitive verb.

1. The children built a snowman.
2. Who built a snowman? children - SN
3. What is being said about children? children built - V
4. Children built what? snowman - verify the noun
5. Does snowman mean the same thing as children? No.
6. Snowman - DO (*Say: Snowman - direct object.*)
7. Built - V-t (*Say: Built - verb-transitive.*)
8. A - A
9. The - A
10. SN V-t DO P2 Check
(*Say: Subject Noun, Verb-transitive, Direct Object, Pattern 2, Check. This first check is to make sure the "t" is added to the verb.*)
11. Verb-transitive - check again.
(*"Check again" means to check for prepositional phrases and then go through the rest of the Question and Answer Flow.*)
12. No prepositional phrases.
13. Period, statement, declarative sentence
14. Go back to the verb - divide the complete subject from the complete predicate.

Earlier you learned that nouns can have different jobs, or functions, in a sentence. You have studied two of these jobs already: A noun can be a subject, or a noun can be an object of a preposition. You must remember, however, that a noun used as a subject is a <u>core part of a sentence pattern</u> (like **SN V**). But a noun that is used as an object of a preposition is not part of the core pattern of a sentence. Nouns used as objects of prepositions can be used with every sentence pattern since they are not part of the core pattern.

You will now study how nouns function in different sentence patterns. The first pattern, **Pattern 1**, has a **Noun Verb** for the core sentence pattern and is written **N V**. However, notice that when you write Pattern 1, you write **SN V** because you name the job of each core part as well, which is *Subject Noun / Verb.* You will also add the pattern number to each pattern to make it easier to identify. Therefore, the **first pattern** is *subject noun / verb / Pattern 1,* and it is written as **SN V P1**.

In the new sentence pattern, **Pattern 2**, there are two nouns in the core sentence pattern: **N V N.** The first noun is a subject noun and is still written as **SN**. The second noun will always come after the verb (*as its position in the pattern indicates*) and is required to complete the meaning of the sentence. This second noun is called a direct object and is written with the abbreviation **DO**. Any time there is a direct object in a sentence pattern, the verb is transitive and is written as **V-t** to indicate that it is an action verb used with a direct object noun. The **second pattern** is *subject noun / verb-transitive / direct object / Pattern 2,* and it is written as **SN V-t DO P2**.

CHAPTER 13 LESSON 1 CONTINUED

What is Pattern 2? *(SN V-t DO)* What are the core parts of a Pattern 2 sentence? *(SN V-t DO)* What parts of speech are used in a Pattern 2 sentence? *(N V N)* You will use what you have just learned as you classify Sentences 1-3 with me to find the direct object and verb-transitive. As we classify the sentences together, I will show you how to say the new part as we say the Question and Answer Flow. Begin.

Question and Answer Flow for Sentence 1: Bill bought a new pen with his allowance.

1. Who bought a new pen with his allowance? Bill - SN
2. What is being said about Bill? Bill bought - V
3. Bill bought what? pen - verify the noun

Note: "Verify the noun" is a check to make sure the second noun does not mean the same thing as the subject noun. If it does not, then the second noun is a direct object.

4. Does pen mean the same thing as Bill? No.
5. Pen - DO (Direct Object)
6. Bought - V-t (Verb-transitive)

Note: Always ask the WHAT question immediately after finding the SN and V to get the DO. Mark the verb with a V until the DO has been identified. After you verify that the noun is a direct object, mark your verb as transitive by adding the "t" to the main verb.

The verb is changed to a V-t when a direct object has been identified. Always get the core, SN V-t DO, before you classify the rest of the sentence.

7. What kind of pen? new - Adj
8. A - A
9. With - P
10. With what? allowance - OP
11. Whose allowance? his - PPA
12. SN V-t DO P2 Check

   (Subject noun, Verb-transitive, Direct object, Pattern 2 Check. Write *SN V-t DO P2* in the blank beside the sentence.)

Note: Check for the "t" on the verb by saying, verb transitive. Check for prepositional phrases by saying, "check again".

13. Verb-transitive - Check again.
14. (With his allowance) - Prepositional phrase
15. Period, statement, declarative sentence
16. Go back to the verb - divide the complete subject from the complete predicate.

Classified Sentence:

| | SN | V-t | A | Adj | DO | P | PPA | OP |

SN V-t   Bill / bought a new pen (with his allowance). **D**
DO P2

Teacher's Note: A verb-transitive check has been added in Chapter 13 because students tend to forget to add the "t" to the verb, even after they say verb-transitive while classifying the direct object. If they leave the "t" off, it is wrong. This is the reason the verb-transitive check is so important for them to remember.

Question and Answer Flow for Sentence 2: My grandmother baked a cake for my birthday party.

1. Who baked a cake for my birthday party? grandmother - SN
2. What is being said about grandmother? grandmother baked - V
3. Grandmother baked what? cake - verify the noun
4. Does cake mean the same thing as grandmother? No.
5. Cake - DO
6. Baked - V-t
7. A - A
8. For - P

9. For what? party - OP
10. What kind of party? birthday - Adj
11. Whose party? my - PPA
12. Whose grandmother? my - PPA
13. SN V-t DO P2 Check
14. Verb-transitive - Check again.
15. (For my birthday party) - Prepositional phrase
16. Period, statement, declarative sentence
17. Go back to the verb - divide the complete subject from the complete predicate.

Classified Sentence:

| | PPA | SN | | V-t | A | DO | P | PPA | Adj | OP |

SN V-t   My grandmother / baked a cake (for my birthday party). **D**
DO P2

© SHURLEY INSTRUCTIONAL MATERIALS, INC.

CHAPTER 13 LESSON 1 CONTINUED

Question and Answer Flow for Sentence 3: The brilliant writer explained her poem to the audience.

1. Who explained her poem to the audience? writer - SN
2. What is being said about writer? writer explained - V
3. Writer explained what? poem - verify the noun
4. Does poem mean the same thing as writer? No.
5. Poem - DO
6. Explained - V-t
7. Whose poem? her - PPA
8. To - P
9. To whom? audience - OP

10. The - A
11. What kind of writer? brilliant - Adj
12. The - A
13. SN V-t DO P2 Check
14. Verb-transitive - Check again.
15. (To the audience) - Prepositional phrase
16. Period, statement, declarative sentence
17. Go back to the verb - divide the complete subject from the complete predicate.

Classified Sentence:

		A	Adj	SN	V-t	PPA DO	P A	OP

SN V-t
DO P2   The brilliant writer / explained her poem (to the audience). D

Teacher's Note: Question and Answer Flow Notice.

For consistency, the Question and Answer Flow will verify the direct object by using the verb **Do** if the direct object is plural and **Does** if the direct object is singular. On the other hand, you may prefer to use the singular form because you are actually saying, "Does the **word** *eggs* mean the same thing as Sara?" Therefore, if you choose to use the singular verb form, just make the necessary change whenever it occurs.

Example: Sara dyed the eggs. Q & A: <u>Do eggs</u> mean the same thing as Sara?

Example: Sara dyed the eggs. Q & A: <u>Does eggs</u> mean the same thing as Sara?

TEACHING SCRIPT FOR ADDING THE DIRECT OBJECTS TO THE NOUN CHECK

Name the noun jobs we have had before today. (*SN and OP*) Today, we have added another noun job. What is the new noun job that we have just added? (*direct object - DO*) So, if I want to find nouns in a sentence, where would I go? (*To the SN, OP, and DO jobs*) After I go to the subject noun, object of the preposition, and direct object jobs, what do I do next? (*As you do a Noun Check, look at each job to see if the word is a noun or a pronoun. If it is a pronoun, leave it alone and go to the next job. If it is a noun, circle it to indicate that it is a noun.*) (*Continue the Oral Skill Builder Check, using the guidelines below.*)

Oral Skill Builder Check

1. **Noun check.**
   (Say the job and then say the noun. Circle each noun.)

2. **Identify the nouns as singular or plural.**
   (Write S or P above each noun.)

3. **Identify the nouns as common or proper.**
   (Follow established procedure for oral identification.)

4. **Do a vocabulary check.**
   (Follow established procedure for oral identification.)

5. **Identify the complete subject and the complete predicate.** (Underline the complete subject once and the complete predicate twice.)

6. **Identify the simple subject and simple predicate.**
   (Underline the simple subject once and the simple predicate twice. Bold, or highlight, the lines.)

7. **Recite the irregular verb chart**.
   (Located on student page 25 and teacher page 163.)

 VOCABULARY TIME

Assign Chapter 13, Vocabulary Words **#1** on page 9 in the Section for students to define in their Vocabulary notebooks.

Chapter 13, Vocabulary Words #1
(cover, wrap, courage, fear)

(End of lesson.)

© SHURLEY INSTRUCTIONAL MATERIALS, INC.

CHAPTER 13   LESSON 2

Objectives: Jingles, Grammar (Practice Sentences), Independent Pattern 2 Practice Sentence, Vocabulary #2, and Activity.

 **JINGLE TIME**

Have students turn to the Jingle Section in their books and recite the previously-taught jingles.

 GRAMMAR TIME

First-Year Option: Put the Practice Sentences from the box below on the board or on notebook paper. Use these sentences as you practice the concepts that have been taught. For the greatest benefit, students must participate orally with the teacher. **Second-Year Option:** Have students classify the Practice Sentences independently on paper. Check students' sentences with the answers provided below. *(If you have the CDs for Practice Sentences, have students check their sentences with the CDs.)*

Chapter 13, Practice Sentences for Lesson 2

1. _____ The precious baby closed her sleepy eyes.
2. _____ Thomas Edison invented the electric light.
3. _____ Oh, no! I missed two easy words on the spelling test today!

TEACHING SCRIPT FOR PRACTICING PATTERN 2 SENTENCES

We will classify three different sentences to practice Pattern 2 sentences. We will classify the sentences together. Begin. (*You might have your students write the labels above the sentences at this time.*)

Question and Answer Flow for Sentence 1: The precious baby closed her sleepy eyes.

1. Who closed her sleepy eyes? baby - SN
2. What is being said about baby? baby closed - V
3. Baby closed what? eyes - verify the noun
4. Do eyes mean the same thing as baby? No.
5. Eyes - DO
6. Closed - V-t
7. What kind of eyes? sleepy - Adj
8. Whose eyes? her - PPA

9. What kind of baby? precious - Adj
10. The - A
11. SN V-t DO P2 Check
12. Verb-transitive - Check again.
13. No prepositional phrases.
14. Period, statement, declarative sentence
15. Go back to the verb - divide the complete subject from the complete predicate.

Classified Sentence:

                          A   Adj   SN   V-t PPA Adj   DO
    <u>SN V-t</u>   The precious baby **/** closed her sleepy eyes. **D**
    DO P2

© SHURLEY INSTRUCTIONAL MATERIALS, INC.

CHAPTER 13 LESSON 2 CONTINUED

Question and Answer Flow for Sentence 2: Thomas Edison invented the electric light.

1. Who invented the electric light? Thomas Edison - SN
2. What is being said about Thomas Edison?
   Thomas Edison invented - V
3. Thomas Edison invented what? light - verify the noun
4. Does light mean the same thing as Thomas Edison? No.
5. Light - DO
6. Invented - V-t
7. What kind of light? electric - Adj

8. The - A
9. SN V-t DO P2 Check
10. Verb-transitive - Check again.
11. No prepositional phrases.
12. Period, statement, declarative sentence
13. Go back to the verb - divide the complete subject from the complete predicate.

Classified Sentence:

                        SN   V-t   A   Adj   DO

    __SN V-t__   Thomas Edison / invented the electric light. **D**
      DO P2

Question and Answer Flow for Sentence 3: Oh, no! I missed two easy words on the spelling test today!

1. Who missed two easy words on the spelling test today?
   I - SP
2. What is being said about I? I missed - V
3. I missed what? words - verify the noun
4. Do words mean the same thing as I? No.
5. Words - DO
6. Missed - V-t
7. What kind of words? easy - Adj
8. How many words? two - Adj
9. On - P
10. On what? test - OP

11. What kind of test? spelling - Adj
12. The - A
13. Missed when? today - Adv
14. Oh, no - I
15. SN V-t DO P2 Check
16. Verb-transitive - Check again.
17. (On the spelling test) - Prepositional phrase
18. Exclamation point, strong feeling, exclamatory sentence
19. Go back to the verb - divide the complete subject from the complete predicate.

Classified Sentence:

                I   SP   V-t Adj Adj DO   P A   Adj OP Adv

    __SN V-t__ Oh, no! I / missed two easy words (on the spelling test) today! **E**
      DO P2

TEACHING SCRIPT FOR INTRODUCING A PATTERN 2 PRACTICE SENTENCE

Put these words on the board: **Pattern 2 Practice Sentence**

Get out a sheet of notebook paper. On the top line of your notebook paper, write the title *Pattern 2 Practice Sentence*. Look at the new words on the board: **Pattern 2 Practice Sentence**. I will guide you again through the process as we learn to write a Pattern 2 sentence.

You have already learned how to write an independent Pattern 1 sentence according to labels you select. You will now learn how to write an independent Pattern 2 sentence the same way. First, you start out with the core labels for a Pattern 2 sentence. This means that you <u>must always have a subject, a verb-transitive, and a direct object before you add any extra parts</u>. (*SN V-t DO*)

CHAPTER 13 LESSON 2 CONTINUED

Next, you build the rest of your Pattern 2 sentence from the regular sentence parts learned in Pattern 1. I will ask you a few questions to make sure you understand. What are the parts of a Pattern 2 sentence that YOU MUST USE? (*All Pattern 2 sentences must have a subject, a verb-transitive, and a direct object.*) I want you to name the extra sentence parts that YOU CAN USE with your sentence. There are ten parts. (*adjectives, adverbs, articles, prepositional phrases, subject pronouns, possessive nouns, possessive pronouns, helping verbs, conjunctions, and interjections*) Remember, you will use the core parts of a Pattern 2 sentence and then add the extra parts that you want your sentence to have.

Let's write the labels for a Pattern 2 sentence on a sheet of notebook paper. First, on your paper, write the *SN, V-t,* and *DO* labels that a Pattern 2 sentence must have. Be sure to place them in the middle of your paper. (*Demonstrate by writing the SN V-t DO labels on the board.*) Using what you know about writing Practice Sentences, decide which other parts you want to add to your Pattern 2 Practice Sentence. (*Have students finish writing a Pattern 2 sentence and turn it in to you. Students do not have to write an Improved Sentence at this point unless you feel they need the practice. If your students cannot handle this much independence so soon, give them the labels you want them to follow for a Pattern 2 sentence. (Example: A Adj SN V-t DO P A OP P OP) Check and discuss students' sentences after they have finished.*)

 VOCABULARY TIME

Assign Chapter 13, Vocabulary Words #2 on page 9 in the Reference Section for students to define in their Vocabulary notebooks. After they write each word and its meaning, students are to write a sentence using the vocabulary word.

Chapter 13, Vocabulary Words #2
(famous, obscure, pleasure, joy)

 ACTIVITY / ASSIGNMENT TIME

Have students write the three sentences that they classified at the beginning of the lesson on a sheet of paper. (See page 228.) Have them tape-record the Question and Answer Flows for all three sentences. Students should write labels above the sentences as they classify them. They especially need the second practice if this is their first year in the program. (*After the students have finished, check the tape and sentence labels. Make sure students understand any mistakes they have made.*)

(End of lesson.)

© SHURLEY INSTRUCTIONAL MATERIALS, INC.

CHAPTER 13   LESSON 3

Objectives: Jingles, Grammar (Practice Sentences), Skill (Editing Checklist), and Practice Exercise.

 **JINGLE TIME**

Have students turn to the Jingle Section in their books and recite the previously-taught jingles.

 GRAMMAR TIME

First-Year Option: Put the Practice Sentences from the box below on the board or on notebook paper. Use these sentences as you practice the concepts that have been taught. For the greatest benefit, students must participate orally with the teacher. **Second-Year Option:** Have students classify the Practice Sentences independently on paper. Check students' sentences with the answers provided below. (*If you have the CDs for Practice Sentences, have students check their sentences with the CDs.*)

Chapter 13, Practice Sentences for Lesson 3
1. _____ Clay and Ben explore their new neighborhood daily.
2. _____ The excited children received an animal balloon from the circus clown.
3. _____ We cleaned the outside of the dirty windows on our house.

TEACHING SCRIPT FOR PRACTICING PATTERN 2 SENTENCES

We will classify three different sentences to practice Pattern 2 sentences. We will classify the sentences together. Begin. (*You might have your students write the labels above the sentences at this time.*)

Question and Answer Flow for Sentence 1: Clay and Ben explore their new neighborhood daily.

1. Who explore their new neighborhood daily?
   Clay and Ben - CSN, CSN
2. What is being said about Clay and Ben?
   Clay and Ben explore - V
3. Explore what? neighborhood - verify the noun
4. Does neighborhood mean the same thing as Clay and Ben? No.
5. Neighborhood - DO
6. Explore - V-t
7. What kind of neighborhood? new - Adj

8. Whose neighborhood? their - PPA
9. Explore when? daily - Adv
10. And - C
11. SN V-t DO P2 Check
12. Verb-transitive - Check again.
13. No prepositional phrases.
14. Period, statement, declarative sentence
15. Go back to the verb - divide the complete
    subject from the complete predicate.

Classified Sentence:

                            CSN C CSN   V-t   PPA Adj   DO   Adv

           <u>SN V-t</u>   Clay and Ben / explore their new neighborhood daily. **D**

           DO P2

CHAPTER 13 LESSON 3 CONTINUED

Question and Answer Flow for Sentence 2: The excited children received an animal balloon from the circus clown.

1. Who received an animal balloon from the circus clown? children - SN
2. What is being said about children? children received - V
3. Children received what? balloon - verify the noun
4. Does balloon mean the same thing as children? No.
5. Balloon - DO
6. Received - V-t
7. What kind of balloon? animal - Adj
8. An - A
9. From - P
10. From whom? clown - OP
11. What kind of clown? circus - Adj
12. The - A
13. What kind of children? excited - Adj
14. The - A
15. SN V-t DO P2 Check
16. Verb-transitive - Check again.
17. (From the circus clown) - Prepositional phrase
18. Period, statement, declarative sentence
19. Go back to the verb - divide the complete subject from the complete predicate.

Classified Sentence:

A   Adj   SN   V-t   A   Adj   DO   P   A   Adj   OP

<u>SN V-t</u> The excited children / received an animal balloon (from the circus clown). **D**
DO P2

Question and Answer Flow for Sentence 3: We cleaned the outside of the dirty windows on our house.

1. Who cleaned the outside of the dirty windows on our house? we - SP
2. What is being said about we? we cleaned - V
3. We cleaned what? outside - verify the noun
4. Does outside mean the same thing as we? No.
5. Outside - DO
6. Cleaned - V-t
7. The - A
8. Of - P
9. Of what? windows - OP
10. What kind of windows? dirty - Adj
11. The - A
12. On - P
13. On what? house - OP
14. Whose house? our - PPA
15. SN V-t DO P2 Check
16. Verb-transitive - Check again.
17. (Of the dirty windows) - Prepositional phrase
18. (On our house) - Prepositional phrase
19. Period, statement, declarative sentence
20. Go back to the verb - divide the complete subject from the complete predicate.

Classified Sentence:

SP   V-t   A   DO   P   A   Adj   OP   P   PPA   OP

<u>SN V-t</u> We / cleaned the outside (of the dirty windows) (on our house). **D**
DO P2

SKILL TIME

TEACHING SCRIPT FOR INTRODUCING A REGULAR EDITING CHECKLIST

The process of finding and correcting errors in writing is called editing. Remember, the writing that you edit is called a rough draft. Before we begin detailed editing, I want you to know that total editing is a slow, meticulous (careful) process. You do not get in a hurry when you edit. It is like being a detective. You have all the clues, but you must study the clues carefully in order to solve the editing mystery.

After a while, the editing process will become automatic, but you must remember that editing is never a fast process. As you mature in your writing ability, editing will become more and more important because, without it, you just cannot have a top-quality piece of writing. Editing is like icing on a cake: It puts the finishing touches on a paper.

© SHURLEY INSTRUCTIONAL MATERIALS, INC.

CHAPTER 13 LESSON 3 CONTINUED

To make regular editing easier, you must have a system. If you have a system when you edit, you will get the maximum benefit of editing. The Shurley English editing system is simple: Use a checklist. All high-tech businesses use checklists to keep track of everything that's important and productive. They are simple but very effective when used correctly. Editing should become an automatic process that enables you to produce a top-quality writing product every time you write.

You have been using the Beginning Editing Checklist. That is a good checklist, but now you are ready to use the regular editing checklist. It is more detailed and establishes an editing routine that will be easy for you to follow. We will now go over the regular editing checklist, and then I will show you how to use it to edit a rough draft. Look at Reference 42 on page 36 in your Reference Section. *(The Editing Checklist below includes a few skills that students have not had. Add these skills as they are introduced during Skill Time.)*

Reference 42: Regular Editing Checklist

Read each sentence and go through the Sentence Checkpoints below.

_____ E1. Sentence sense check. (Check for words left out or words repeated.)

_____ E2. First word, capital letter check. End mark check. Any other capitalization check. Any other punctuation check.

_____ E3. Sentence structure and punctuation check.
(Check for correct construction and correct punctuation of a simple sentence, a simple sentence with compound parts, or a compound sentence.)

_____ E4. Spelling and homonym check.
(Check for misspelled words and incorrect homonym choices.)

_____ E5. Usage check.
(Check subject-verb agreement, a/an choice, double negatives, verb tenses, and contractions.)

Read each paragraph and go through the Paragraph Checkpoints below.

_____ E6. Check to see that each paragraph is indented.

_____ E7. Check each paragraph for a topic sentence.

_____ E8. Check each sentence to make sure it supports the topic of the paragraph.

_____ E9. Check the content for interest and creativity.

_____ E10. Check the type and format of the writing assigned.

Notice that each checkpoint on the editing guide has a capital *E* and a number beside it. The capital *E* refers to the editing checklist (*E* for editing). The number indicates which skill area is listed beside each checkpoint. So, *E1* means you are editing the first skill area. We will call *E1* checkpoint 1. What is being checked in checkpoint 1? (**E1:** *Sentence sense check. Check for words left out or words repeated.*) What is being checked in checkpoint 2? (**E2:** *First word, capital letter check. End mark check. Any other capitalization check. Any other punctuation check.*) What is being checked in checkpoint 3? (**E3:** *Sentence structure and punctuation check. Check for correct construction and correct punctuation of a simple sentence, a simple sentence with compound parts, or a compound sentence.*)

© SHURLEY INSTRUCTIONAL MATERIALS, INC.

CHAPTER 13 LESSON 3 CONTINUED

What is being checked in checkpoint 4? (**E4:** *Spelling and homonym check. Check for misspelled words and incorrect homonym choices.*) What is being checked in checkpoint 5? (**E5:** *Usage check. Check subject-verb agreement, a/an choice, double negatives, verb tenses, and contractions.*)

These first five checkpoints will be used for each sentence as you do a sentence-by-sentence edit. The second five checkpoints are done as you check each paragraph. What are the five paragraph checkpoints? (**E6:** *Check to see that each paragraph is indented.* **E7:** *Check each paragraph for a topic sentence.* **E8:** *Check each sentence to make sure it supports the topic of the paragraph.* **E9:** *Check the content for interest and creativity.* **E10:** *Check the type and format of the writing assigned.*)

Remember, editing is a slow, careful process that works best when you use your system. Your papers are not very long at this point, and it is crucial that you get in the habit of going through each sentence five times, one time for each sentence checkpoint. You'll know your paper pretty well by the time you finish, but that's the whole idea of editing. You should know your paper well enough to have corrected every mistake in it. This editing system may take you a little longer at the beginning, but it will save you from having to redo a poor editing job due to improper editing techniques.

I will guide you through an expository essay that has been edited so you can see the editing process. Look at the bottom of Reference 43 on page 36 in your book. *(Use the reference box below as you go through the teaching script that follows. Make sure you point out that all corrections are written on the line above each mistake.) (Do not go over the rough draft and final paper sections at this time. They will be discussed in later lessons.)*

Reference 43: Editing Example

Topic: **Reasons why amusement parks are so much fun**
Three main points: **(1. Thrilling rides   2. Entertaining games   3. Tasty snacks)**

Amusement P
The Amusing Amusemant park

→   a   (.)T   reasons   so
People everywhere love to visit Amusement parks for various reasons three reason amusement parks are sew much
                (,)   (,)   offer (.)
fun are the thrilling rides the entertaining games and the tasty snacks that amusement parks offers
                                                        is   coasters
   The first reason amusement parks are so much fun are the thrilling rides. From roller costers to tilt-a-whirls, each
          variety   anyone's   no comma
park offers a wide vareity of rides to match anyones style. The second reason amusement parks are so much fun,
is   knock
Is the number of entertaining games. A couple of dollars gives you the chance to nock down a target with a baseball
            animal   is
and win a huge stuffed anamal. The third reason amusement parks are so much fun are the tasty snacks. The
                  an   lemonade   (,)
park contains a abundance of concession stands that offer fresh squeezed lemonaide, hot funnel cakes fluffy
 cotton   (.)
cotten candy, and sticky caramel apples
                        are   reasons   (,)
   In conclusion, amusement parks is entertaining for many reason. The thrilling rides, entertaining games and tasty
     no comma   an
snacks, make the amusement parks a exceptionally fun place to visit.

Total Mistakes: 31
Editing Guide: Sentence checkpoints: **E1, E2, E3, E4, E5**   Paragraph checkpoints: **E6, E7, E8, E9, E10**

© SHURLEY INSTRUCTIONAL MATERIALS, INC.

CHAPTER 13 LESSON 3 CONTINUED

1. Check the title for capitalization and spelling mistakes. (*Capitalization check—correct <u>park</u> with a capital P.* **Spelling check** *– change the second a to e in* **amusement.**)

2. **Read the first sentence.** (People everywhere love to visit Amusement parks for various reasons)

3. Are there any mistakes for checkpoint 1? *(Read checkpoint 1 and check the sentence.)* (**Sentence sense check**— *no mistakes.*)

4. Are there any mistakes for checkpoint 2? *(Read checkpoint 2 and check the sentence.)* (**First word, capital letter check**— *no mistakes.* **End mark check**— *correct with a period.* **Any other capitalization check**— *correct* **Amusement** *with a lowercase* **a.** **Any other punctuation check**— *no mistakes.*)

5. Are there any mistakes for checkpoint 3? *(Read checkpoint 3 and check the sentence.)* (**Sentence structure and punctuation check**— *no mistakes.*)

6. Are there any mistakes for checkpoint 4? *(Read checkpoint 4 and check the sentence.)* (**Spelling and homonym check**— *no mistakes.*)

7. Are there any mistakes for checkpoint 5? You have to do an individual usage-by-usage check in checkpoint 5 because there are too many different skills to check as a group. *(Read checkpoint 5 and check the sentence.)* (**Subject-verb agreement check**—*no mistakes.* **A-An check**—*no mistakes.* **Double negative check**—*no mistakes.* **Verb tense check**—*no mistakes.* **Contraction check**—*no mistakes.*)

Now, we start the checkpoints over again on the next sentence. You will make very few editing mistakes if you stick with this system until it becomes automatic. As soon as editing becomes automatic, you will go through the editing process with ease, so trust me on this. Begin.

1. **Read the second sentence.** (three reason amusement parks are sew much fun are the thrilling rides the entertaining games and the tasty snacks that amusement parks offers)

2. Are there any mistakes for checkpoint 1? *(Checkpoint 1:* **Sentence sense check**—*no mistakes.*)

3. Are there any mistakes for checkpoint 2? *(Checkpoint 2:* **First word, capital letter check**—*correct the first word with a capital* **T.** **End mark check**—*put a period after the word offers.* **Any other capitalization check**—*no mistakes.* **Any other punctuation check**—*put commas between* **rides, the** *and* **games, and.**)

4. Are there any mistakes for checkpoint 3? *(Checkpoint 3:* **Sentence structure and punctuation check**—*no mistakes.*)

5. Are there any mistakes for checkpoint 4? *(Checkpoint 4:* **Spelling and homonym check**—*correct the spelling of* **sew** *to* **so.**)

6. Are there any mistakes for checkpoint 5? *(Checkpoint 5:* **Subject-verb agreement check**—*change* **offers** *to* **offer** *and* **reason** *to* **reasons.** **A-An check**—*no mistakes.* **Double negative check**—*no mistakes.* **Verb tense check**—*no mistakes.* **Contraction check**—*no mistakes.*)

© SHURLEY INSTRUCTIONAL MATERIALS, INC.

CHAPTER 13 LESSON 3 CONTINUED

Look at the first paragraph. Now, we will do a paragraph check for the last five checkpoints.

1. Are there any mistakes for checkpoint 6? *(Read checkpoint 6 and check the first paragraph.)* *(Indent.)*
2. Are there any mistakes for checkpoint 7? *(Read checkpoint 7 and check the first paragraph.)* *(No corrections.)*
3. Are there any mistakes for checkpoint 8? *(Read checkpoint 8 and check the first paragraph.)* *(No corrections.)*
4. Are there any mistakes for checkpoint 9? *(Read checkpoint 9 and check the first paragraph.)* *(No corrections.)*
5. Are there any mistakes for checkpoint 10? *(Read checkpoint 10 and check the first paragraph.)* *(No corrections.)*

(Work through the remaining sentences in the last two paragraphs. **Make sure you take the time now to establish the editing routine that you want your students to follow.***)*

 PRACTICE TIME

Have students turn to page 74 in the Practice Section of their book and find the skill under Chapter 13, Lesson 3, Practice. Go over the directions to make sure they understand what to do. Check and discuss the Practice after students have finished. *(Chapter 13, Lesson 3, Practice key is given below.)*

Chapter 13, Lesson 3, Practice: Find each error and write the correction above it. Write the punctuation corrections where they belong.

(indent)   many   (.) (T)   obvious
Lemons and oranges have miny things in common the most obveous is that they are both fruits. Both
                     oranges   sweeter   have   on
have a tangy flavor, although orangs are sweet. Both fruits has seeds and grow in trees. Finally,
b   weather   plenty
Both need warmer whether to grow and pleanty of sunshine.

Total Mistakes: 12

(End of lesson.)

© SHURLEY INSTRUCTIONAL MATERIALS, INC.

CHAPTER 13 LESSON 4

Objectives: Jingles, Study, Test, Check, Activity, and Writing (journal).

JINGLE TIME

Have students turn to the Jingle Section in their books and recite the previously-taught jingles.

STUDY TIME

Have students study the vocabulary words in their vocabulary notebooks. Remind students that any vocabulary word in their notebooks could be on their test. Also, have students study any of the skills in the Practice Section that they need to review.

TEST TIME

Have students turn to page 109 in the Test Section of their book and find Chapter 13 Test. Students are allowed to use the Reference Section to help them remember the new information and to check the capitalization and punctuation rules while they correct capitalization and punctuation errors. Go over the directions to make sure they understand what to do. (*Chapter 13 Test key is on the next page.*)

CHECK TIME

After students have finished, check and discuss their test papers. Make sure they understand why their answers are right or wrong. (*For total points, count each required answer as a point.*)

ACTIVITY / ASSIGNMENT TIME

Students will continue to draw or trace the states and write the following questions and answers.

Kentucky	Louisiana
1. What is the state on the front of this card? **Kentucky**	1. What is the state on the front of this card? **Louisiana**
2. What is the capital of Kentucky? **Frankfort**	2. What is the capital of Louisiana? **Baton Rouge**
3. What is the postal abbreviation of Kentucky? **KY**	3. What is the postal abbreviation of Louisiana? **LA**
4. What year was Kentucky admitted to the Union? **1792**	4. What year was Louisiana admitted to the Union? **1812**

Color these states and look up an interesting fact about each state to write on the cards. Use the cards to quiz family members, friends, and relatives. You may want to time the responses to your questions. Also, along with previous suggestions, think of other ways to have fun with your United States card file.

(End of lesson.)

© SHURLEY INSTRUCTIONAL MATERIALS, INC.

Chapter 13 Test
(Student Page 109)

Exercise 1: Classify each sentence.

          A   SN   V-t   DO P PPA OP   P   A   OP

1. <u>SN V-t</u>   The farmer / feeds hay (to his cows) (during the winter). **D**

  DO P2

          HV A   Adj   SN   V-t   Adj   CDO   C   Adj   CDO

2. <u>SN V-t</u>   Did the terrible windstorm / damage tree branches and telephone lines? **Int**

  DO P2

          HV PPA SN   V-t CDO   C   CDO   P   OP

3. <u>SN V-t</u>   Does your family / eat turkey and dressing (during Thanksgiving)? **Int**

  DO P2

Exercise 2: Use Sentence 1 to underline the complete subject once and the complete predicate twice and to complete the table below.

List the Noun Used	List the Noun Job	Singular or Plural	Common or Proper	Simple Subject	Simple Predicate
1. **farmer**	2. **SN**	3. **S**	4. **C**	5. **farmer**	6. **feeds**
7. **hay**	8. **DO**	9. **S**	10. **C**		
11. **cows**	12. **OP**	13. **P**	14. **C**		
15. **winter**	16. **OP**	17. **S**	18. **C**		

Exercise 3: Identify each pair of words as synonyms or antonyms by putting parentheses ( ) around *syn* or *ant*.

1. tepid, warm	**(syn)** ant	4. support, oppose	syn **(ant)**	7. winner, victor	**(syn)** ant
2. repaired, fixed	**(syn)** ant	5. courage, fear	syn **(ant)**	8. pleasure, joy	**(syn)** ant
3. famous, obscure	syn **(ant)**	6. cover, wrap	**(syn)** ant	9. serious, frivolous	syn **(ant)**

Exercise 4: Underline the correct homonym in each sentence.

1. Can you (<u>hear</u>, here) the music on the radio?
2. We (lead, <u>led</u>) the music during service yesterday.
3. My arms felt (<u>weak</u>, week) from exhaustion.
4. The (<u>lead</u>, led) pipes made the drinking water unsafe.
5. Judy will be gone for a (weak, <u>week</u>).
6. They said (your, <u>you're</u>) from Ohio.
7. I really like (<u>your</u>, you're) new shoes.
8. Put your books over (hear, <u>here</u>).

Exercise 5: <u>For Sentences 1 and 2</u>: Write the capitalization and punctuation corrections only. <u>For Sentence 3</u>: Write the capitalization and punctuation rule numbers for each correction in bold.

  N   C J   I   M
1. nancy, is your recipe for c. j.'s famous italian herb chicken an original from milan**?**

> **Editing Guide: Capitals: 5   Commas: 1   Apostrophes: 1   Periods: 2   End Marks: 1**

  T   M   R   I   I   C   W
2. today, mrs. rhines and i visited a famous indian reservation near cheyenne, wyoming**.**

> **Editing Guide: Capitals: 7   Commas: 2   Periods: 1   End Marks: 1**

   1   10 10 7   14   14
3. **O**ur class president, **J. C. P**etty, announced this year's choir tour to **B**akersfield, **C**alifornia.

               11 17 17   11   20   7   1

> **Editing Guide: Capitals: 6   Commas: 3   Periods: 2   Apostrophes: 1   End Marks: 1**

Exercise 6: In your journal, write a paragraph summarizing what you have learned this week.

© SHURLEY INSTRUCTIONAL MATERIALS, INC.

CHAPTER 13 LESSON 4 CONTINUED

TEACHER INSTRUCTIONS

Use the Question and Answer Flows below for the sentences on the Chapter 13 Test.

Question and Answer Flow for Sentence 1: The farmer feeds hay to his cows during the winter.

1. Who feeds hay to his cows during the winter? farmer - SN
2. What is being said about farmer? farmer feeds - V
3. Farmer feeds what? hay - verify the noun
4. Does hay mean the same thing as farmer? No.
5. Hay - DO
6. Feeds - V-t
7. To - P
8. To what? cows - OP
9. Whose cows? his - PPA
10. During - P
11. During what? winter - OP
12. The - A
13. The - A
14. SN V-t DO P2 Check
15. Verb-transitive - Check again.
16. (To his cows) - Prepositional phrase
17. (During the winter) - Prepositional phrase
18. Period, statement, declarative sentence
19. Go back to the verb - divide the complete subject from the complete predicate.

Classified Sentence:

                                    A   SN   V-t   DO P PPA OP   P   A   OP

<u>SN V-t</u>   The farmer **/** feeds hay (to his cows) (during the winter). **D**
DO P2

Question and Answer Flow for Sentence 2: Did the terrible windstorm damage tree branches and telephone lines?

1. What did damage tree branches and telephone lines? windstorm - SN
2. What is being said about windstorm? windstorm did damaged - V
3. Did - HV
4. Windstorm did damage what? branches and lines - verify the nouns
5. Do branches and lines mean the same thing as windstorm? No.
6. Branches and lines - CDO, CDO (compound direct object, compound direct object)
7. Damage - V-t
8. What kind of branches? tree - Adj
9. And - C
10. What kind of lines? telephone - Adj
11. What kind of windstorm? terrible - Adj
12. The - A
13. SN V-t DO P2 Check
14. Verb-transitive - Check again.
15. No prepositional phrases.
16. Question mark, question, interrogative sentence
17. Go back to the verb - divide the complete subject from the complete predicate.

Classified Sentence:

                         HV A   Adj   SN   V-t   Adj CDO   C   Adj   CDO

<u>SN V-t</u>   Did the terrible windstorm **/** damage tree branches and telephone lines? **Int**
DO P2

Question and Answer Flow for Sentence 3: Does your family eat turkey and dressing during Thanksgiving?

1. Who does eat turkey and dressing during Thanksgiving? family - SN
2. What is being said about family? family does eat - V
3. Does - HV
4. Family does eat what? turkey and dressing - verify the nouns
5. Do turkey and dressing mean the same thing as family? No.
6. Turkey and dressing - CDO, CDO
7. Eat - V-t
8. And - C
9. During - P
10. During what? Thanksgiving - OP
11. Whose family? your - PPA
12. SN V-t DO P2 Check
13. Verb-transitive - Check again.
14. (During Thanksgiving) - Prepositional phrase
15. Question mark, question, interrogative sentence
16. Go back to the verb - divide the complete subject from the complete predicate.

Classified Sentence:

                         HV PPA SN   V-t CDO   C   CDO   P   OP

<u>SN V-t</u>   Does your family **/** eat turkey and dressing (during Thanksgiving)? **Int**
DO P2

(End of lesson.)

© SHURLEY INSTRUCTIONAL MATERIALS, INC.

CHAPTER 13   LESSON 5

Objectives: Writing Assignments #10 and #11, Bonus Option.

 WRITING TIME

TEACHING SCRIPT FOR PRACTICING DIFFERENT KINDS OF WRITING

Today, you are assigned two different kinds of writing. You will write a three-paragraph persuasive essay and a three-point expository paragraph. <u>You will revise and edit the three-paragraph persuasive essay.</u> (*Read the box below for more information about students' writing assignment.*) As you edit, make sure you use the checkpoints in the editing checklist provided in Reference 42. Remember to read through the whole essay, starting with the title, and then edit, sentence-by-sentence, using the five sentence checkpoints for each sentence. Use the paragraph checkpoints to check each paragraph. Remember, your editing is now more detailed and more comprehensive, so take your time.

Writing Assignment Box #1

Writing Assignment #10: Three-Paragraph Persuasive Essay

Remind students that the 3-paragraph essay has three parts: 1. Introduction 2. Body 3. Conclusion. Have students use their regular editing checklist to edit this assignment.

Writing topics: Why Computers Are Important   or   Why I Should Be Allowed to Decorate My Room
                        or   Why Children Should Have Play Time

---

Your second writing assignment is to write a three-point expository paragraph. (*Read the box below for more information about students' writing assignment.*) You do not have to edit this assignment with the editing checklist.

Writing Assignment Box #2

Writing Assignment #11: Three-Point Expository Paragraph

Writing topics: My Favorite Sport   or   Reasons ____ Is My Favorite Subject   or
                        Things I Like to Do During My Free Time

<u>**Bonus Option:**</u> **Do you memorize Bible verses? Do you know someone who does? Write the verses you know**
                        in your journal. From which book of the Bible have you memorized the most verses? Make a list
                        of scripture you want to memorize in the future. Record the date in your Journal to see how long
                        it takes you. Keep a record of different people who memorize Bible verses, and the verses they
                        memorize.

Read, check, and discuss Writing Assignment #10 after students have finished their final papers. Use the checklists as you check and discuss students' papers. Make sure students are using the regular editing checklist correctly. Read and discuss Writing Assignment #11 for fun and enrichment.

(End of lesson.)

© SHURLEY INSTRUCTIONAL MATERIALS, INC.

CHAPTER 14   LESSON 1

Objectives: Jingles, Grammar (Practice Sentences), Oral Skill Builder Check, Skills (identify complete sentences and sentence fragments, correcting sentence fragments), Practice Exercise, Vocabulary #1, and Activity

JINGLE TIME

Have students turn to the Jingle Section in their books and recite the previously-taught jingles.

GRAMMAR TIME

First-Year Option: Put the Practice Sentences from the box below on the board or on notebook paper. Use these sentences as you practice the concepts that have been taught. For the greatest benefit, students must participate orally with the teacher. **Second-Year Option:** Have students classify the Practice Sentences independently on paper. Check students' sentences with the answers provided below. *(If you have the CDs for Practice Sentences, have students check their sentences with the CDs.)*

Chapter 14, Practice Sentences for Lesson 1
1. _____ We planted corn and radish seeds in the garden today.   2. _____ Drew and I rode a ferry to the other side of the island.

TEACHING SCRIPT FOR PRACTICING PATTERN 2 SENTENCES

We will practice classifying Pattern 2 sentences. We will classify the sentences together. Begin. *(You might have your students write the labels above the sentences at this time.)*

Question and Answer Flow for Sentence 1: We planted corn and radish seeds in the garden today.

1. Who planted corn and radish seeds in the garden today?
   we - SP
2. What is being said about we? we planted - V
3. We planted what? seeds - verify the noun
4. Do seeds mean the same thing as we? No.
5. Seeds - DO
6. Planted - V-t
7. What kind of seeds? corn and radish - CAdj, CAdj
8. In - P
9. In what? garden - OP
10. The - A
11. Planted when? today - Adv
12. And - C
13. SN V-t DO P2 Check
14. Verb-transitive - Check again.
15. (In the garden) - Prepositional phrase
16. Period, statement, declarative sentence
17. Go back to the verb - divide the complete subject from the complete predicate.

Classified Sentence:

	SP	V-t	CAdj	C	CAdj	DO	P	A	OP	Adv
<u>SN V-t</u> DO P2	We /	planted	corn	and	radish	seeds	(in	the	garden)	today. D

© SHURLEY INSTRUCTIONAL MATERIALS, INC.

CHAPTER 14 LESSON 1 CONTINUED

Question and Answer Flow for Sentence 2: Drew and I rode a ferry to the other side of the island.

1. Who rode a ferry to the other side of the island?
   Drew and I - CSN, CSP
2. What is being said about Drew and I?
   Drew and I rode - V
3. Drew and I rode what? ferry - verify the noun
4. Does ferry mean the same thing as Drew and I? No.
5. Ferry - DO
6. Rode - V-t
7. A - A
8. To - P
9. To what? side - OP
10. Which side? other - Adj

11. The - A
12. Of - P
13. Of what? island - OP
14. The - A
15. And - C
16. SN V-t DO P2 Check
17. Verb-transitive - Check again.
18. (To the other side) - Prepositional phrase
19. (Of the island) - Prepositional phrase
20. Period, statement, declarative sentence
21. Go back to the verb - divide the complete subject
    from the complete predicate.

Classified Sentence:

```
               CSN   C CSP   V-t  A  DO   P  A   Adj  OP   P  A   OP
  SN V-t     Drew and I / rode a ferry (to the other side) (of the island). D
  DO P2
```

Use Sentences 1-2 that you just classified with your students to do an Oral Skill Builder Check. Use the guidelines below.

Oral Skill Builder Check

1. **Noun check.**
   (Say the job and then say the noun. Circle each noun.)
2. **Identify the nouns as singular or plural.**
   (Write S or P above each noun.)
3. **Identify the nouns as common or proper.**
   (Follow established procedure for oral identification.)
4. **Do a vocabulary check.**
   (Follow established procedure for oral identification.)

5. **Identify the complete subject and the complete predicate.** (Underline the complete subject once and the complete predicate twice.)
6. **Identify the simple subject and simple predicate.**
   (Underline the simple subject once and the simple predicate twice. Bold, or highlight, the lines.)
7. **Recite the irregular verb chart.**
   (Located on student page 25 and teacher page 163.)

SKILL TIME

TEACHING SCRIPT FOR IDENTIFYING COMPLETE SENTENCES AND SENTENCE FRAGMENTS

You should feel comfortable using a variety of sentences in your writing. A basic knowledge of different kinds of sentence structure is necessary for you to become a writer who is confident and effective. Today, we will learn to recognize and work with simple sentences and sentence fragments.

First, we are going to learn the difference between a complete sentence and a fragment. Most of the time you will have no trouble writing a complete sentence because you know the five rules that make a correct sentence. Let's recite the Sentence jingle again to make sure we are all focused on the same thing. (_Recite the Sentence jingle._)

© SHURLEY INSTRUCTIONAL MATERIALS, INC.

CHAPTER 14 LESSON 1 CONTINUED

When you are writing, sometimes you will put a thought down without checking the five parts. If your sentence **does not have a subject, a verb, and a complete thought**, you could have a sentence fragment. This lesson is to teach you how to recognize and prevent sentence fragments so all your sentences can be written correctly.

Next, we will learn more about the simple sentence. A **simple sentence is one complete sentence**. It is also **one complete thought**. Adjectives, adverbs, and prepositional phrases add greater meaning, more life, and more color to simple sentences, but they are not necessary for a sentence to be a complete thought. A simple or complete sentence must have **a subject, a verb, and contain a complete thought**. The abbreviation for a simple sentence is the letter **S**. A sentence fragment does not express a complete thought because it always has one or more of the core parts missing. The abbreviation for a fragment is the letter **F**.

Find Reference 44 on page 37 in your book. Let's read the directions together. (*Read and discuss the directions*.) We will identify whether each sentence is a fragment or a simple sentence. After we decide what type of sentence it is, we will put the correct abbreviation in the blank at the left of each group of words. The abbreviations that you use are found in the directions. Remember, check each group of words for the main parts that make it a sentence: a subject, a verb, and a complete thought. (*Work through sentences 1–5, showing students how to identify each type of sentence and write the abbreviation in the blank*.)

Reference 44: Complete Sentences and Sentence Fragments

PART 1: Identifying Sentences and Fragments

Identifying simple sentences and fragments: Write S for a complete sentence and F for a sentence fragment on the line beside each group of words below.

S	1.	The zebra ran swiftly.
F	2.	During the show.
S	3.	The cruiser sailed.
F	4.	Asking for our support.
F	5.	The green house on the corner.

PART 2: Sentence Fragments

Fragment Examples: (1) growled at the cat (2) the two bear cubs (3) after I fell
(4) watching the baby.

Look at the title "Sentence Fragments" under Part 2 in the reference box. I am going to read several things about a fragment. As I read each one, you will read the fragment example that illustrates that point. I'll tell you when to read by saying "read." (*Teacher reads sentences 1-4 below. After each one, the teacher says, "Read." Students will read the fragment from the box that illustrates the point just read by the teacher. You may want to do this part of the exercise again after your students realize what you are doing*.)

1. A fragment is a group of words that does not have a subject. Read fragment 1: (growled at the cat)
2. A fragment is a group of words that does not have a verb. Read fragment 2: (the two bear cubs)
3. A fragment is a group of words that does not complete a thought. Read fragment 3: (after I fell)
4. Sentence fragments should not be punctuated as complete sentences. Read fragment 4: (watching the baby.)

Remember, if a sentence is missing one of these three parts, a <u>subject</u>, a <u>verb</u>, or a <u>complete thought</u>, you probably have a sentence fragment.

© SHURLEY INSTRUCTIONAL MATERIALS, INC.

CHAPTER 14 LESSON 1 CONTINUED

TEACHING SCRIPT FOR CORRECTING SENTENCE FRAGMENTS

I want you to know how to add missing subject parts or missing predicate parts to make sentences complete. Look at the third part of Reference 44. It will help us learn how to correct fragments. Follow along as I go over it with you. These are all sentence fragments. We will make them complete sentences by adding the underlined part. (*Read the directions and work through the third part with your students. Part 3 is located below.*)

Reference 44: Complete Sentences and Sentence Fragments (continued)

PART 3: Correcting Sentence Fragments

Directions: Add the part that is underlined in parentheses to make each fragment into a complete sentence.

1. On a lily pad in the pond. (subject part, predicate part, <u>both the subject and the predicate</u>)
   (**The frog dozed** on a lily pad in the pond.)

2. The nasty storm. (subject part, <u>predicate part</u>, both the subject and the predicate)
   (The nasty storm **toppled trees in the night**.)

3. Glued a gold star on my paper. (<u>subject part</u>, predicate part, both the subject and the predicate)
   (**The teacher** glued a gold star on my paper.)

 PRACTICE TIME

Have students turn to pages 74 and 75 in the Practice Section of their book and find Chapter 14, Lesson 1, Practice (*1-2*). Go over the directions to make sure they understand what to do. Check and discuss the Practices after students have finished. (*Chapter 14, Lesson 1, Practice keys are given below.*)

Chapter 14, Lesson 1, Practice 1: On notebook paper, add the part that is underlined in the parentheses to make each fragment into a complete sentence. **(Sentences will vary.)**

1. In Jeremy's closet   (subject part, predicate part, <u>both the subject and the predicate</u>)
2. Collected and sorted the laundry   (<u>subject part</u>, predicate part, both the subject and the predicate)
3. Three wild turkeys in the yard   (subject part, <u>predicate part</u>, both the subject and the predicate)

Chapter 14, Lesson 1, Practice 2: Identify each kind of sentence by writing the abbreviation in the blank. (S, F)

S	1.	The wheel turned quickly.
F	2.	Above the couch in the living room.
S	3.	The boys sang loudly with the radio.
F	4.	Watching the television on the floor.
F	5.	The flag waving from the top of the building.

© SHURLEY INSTRUCTIONAL MATERIALS, INC.

CHAPTER 14 LESSON 1 CONTINUED

VOCABULARY TIME

Assign Chapter 14, Vocabulary Words **#1** on page 9 in the Reference Section for students to define in their Vocabulary notebooks. Tell students they may use a dictionary or thesaurus. After they write each word and its meaning, students are to write a sentence using the vocabulary word.

Chapter 14, Vocabulary Words #1
(puny, robust, illness, disease)

ACTIVITY / ASSIGNMENT TIME

This activity will be a fun reminder of careless mistakes you may make while classifying sentences. This can be used with practice and test sentences. If you miss the classification of a word in a Question and Answer Flow, you must wear the following items for a designated time as a reminder of where you went wrong today.

Classification Error	Girls' Attire	Boys' Attire
1. Subject Noun	a lady's hat	a necktie
2. Verb (*includes helping verbs*)	unmatched shoes	unmatched shoes
3. Adjective (*includes articles*)	a neck scarf	one glove
4. Adverb	one earring	shirt on backwards
5. Preposition	curlers in your hair	a pair of overshoes
6. Object of a Preposition	an apron	a ball cap on backwards
7. Conjunction or Interjection	a pair of overshoes	4 garbage bags tied on your belt

(End of lesson.)

CHAPTER 14   LESSON 2
Objectives: Jingles, Grammar (Practice Sentences), Pattern 2 Practice Sentence, Skills (simple sentence with compound parts, run-on sentence), Practice Exercise, and Vocabulary #2.

 **JINGLE TIME**

Have students turn to the Jingle Section in their books and recite the previously-taught jingles.

 GRAMMAR TIME

First-Year Option: Put the Practice Sentences from the box below on the board or on notebook paper. Use these sentences as you practice the concepts that have been taught. For the greatest benefit, students must participate orally with the teacher. **Second-Year Option:** Have students classify the Practice Sentences independently on paper. Check students' sentences with the answers provided below. (*If you have the CDs for Practice Sentences, have students check their sentences with the CDs.*)

Chapter 14, Practice Sentences for Lesson 2
1. _____ Clay filled his pail with sand and water.
2. _____ My class wrote a letter to our city mayor.

TEACHING SCRIPT FOR PRACTICING PATTERN 2 SENTENCES

We will practice classifying Pattern 2 sentences. We will classify the sentences together. Begin. (*You might have your students write the labels above the sentences at this time.*)

Question and Answer Flow for Sentence 1: Clay filled his pail with sand and water.

1. Who filled his pail with sand and water? Clay - SN
2. What is being said about Clay? Clay filled - V
3. Clay filled what? pail - verify the noun
4. Does pail mean the same thing as Clay? No.
5. Pail - DO
6. Filled - V-t
7. Whose pail? his - PPA
8. With - P

9. With what? sand and water - COP, COP
10. And - C
11. SN V-t DO P2 Check
12. Verb-transitive - Check again.
13. (With sand and water) - Prepositional phrase
14. Period, statement, declarative sentence
15. Go back to the verb - divide the complete subject from the complete predicate.

Classified Sentence:

                    SN   V-t PPA DO   P   COP C   COP
         SN V-t   Clay / filled his pail (with sand and water). **D**
         DO P2

© SHURLEY INSTRUCTIONAL MATERIALS, INC.

CHAPTER 14 LESSON 2 CONTINUED

Question and Answer Flow for Sentence 2: My class wrote a letter to our city mayor.	
1. Who wrote a letter to our city mayor? class - SN	10. What kind of mayor? city - Adj
2. What is being said about class? class wrote - V	11. Whose mayor? our - PPA
3. Class wrote what? letter - verify the noun	12. Whose class? my - PPA
4. Does letter mean the same thing as class? No.	13. SN V-t DO P2 Check
5. Letter - DO	14. Verb-transitive - Check again.
6. Wrote - V-t	15. (To our city mayor) - Prepositional phrase
7. A - A	16. Period, statement, declarative sentence
8. To - P	17. Go back to the verb - divide the complete subject
9. To whom? mayor - OP	from the complete predicate.

Classified Sentence:

                    PPA SN   V-t   A DO   P PPA Adj OP

      <u>SN V-t</u>   My class **/** wrote a letter (to our city mayor). **D**

      DO P2

TEACHER INSTRUCTIONS FOR A PATTERN 2 SENTENCE

Tell students that their sentence writing assignment today is to write a Pattern 2 sentence. They are to follow the same procedure used in the previous lessons. They should decide on their labels, arrange them in a selected order, write their sentences, and edit their sentences for improved word choices. (*Students do not have to write an Improved Sentence at this point unless you feel they need more one-on-one word choice writing practice.*) Check and discuss the Pattern 2 sentence after students have finished.

SKILL TIME

TEACHING SCRIPT FOR A SIMPLE SENTENCE WITH COMPOUND PARTS

In the previous lesson, we learned about the three main parts that make a complete sentence. What are the three main parts? (*subject, verb, complete sense*) We also learned that the abbreviation for a simple sentence is the letter **S** and the abbreviation for a fragment is the letter **F**.

Turn to Reference 45 on page 37 in your Reference Section. (*Reference 45 is located on the next page.*) Look at Example 1. This is an example of a simple sentence. Let's read the simple sentence together: **The red ball bounced slowly down the hill.** (S) (*Do not read the (S) on the end.*) The (S) abbreviation in parentheses at the end is an identification symbol that indicates it is a simple sentence.

A simple sentence may have **compound parts, such as a compound subject or a compound verb**, even though it expresses only one complete thought. The abbreviation for a simple sentence with a compound subject is **SCS** (*simple sentence, compound subject*). The abbreviation for a simple sentence with a compound verb is **SCV** (*simple sentence, compound verb*).

Let's read Examples 2 and 3 together. Notice that the abbreviation at the end tells us what kind of sentence it is. (*Read the two sentences with your students.*) Example 2: **Julie and Amanda work at the restaurant.** (SCS) Example 3: **Alex painted and decorated the birdhouse.** (SCV)

© SHURLEY INSTRUCTIONAL MATERIALS, INC.

CHAPTER 14 LESSON 2 CONTINUED

Reference 45: Simple Sentences, Compound Parts, and Fragments

Example 1: The red ball bounced slowly down the hill. (S)
Example 2: <u>Julie and Amanda</u> work at the restaurant. (SCS)
Example 3: Alex <u>painted and decorated</u> the birdhouse. (SCV)

Part 2: Identify each kind of sentence by writing the abbreviation in the blank. (S, SS, F, SCS, SCV)

<u>SCV</u> 1. The children laughed and cheered for the magician.
<u>SCS</u> 2. The pen and pencil were left on the desk.
<u>F</u> 3. Before we move to Atlanta.
<u>S</u> 4. The birds made their nests in the trees.
<u>SS</u> 5. I turned on the oven. It heated up the cold room.

Part 3: Put a slash to separate each run-on sentence below. Then, correct the run-on sentences by rewriting them as indicated by the labels in parentheses at the end of each sentence.

1. The young woman was walking **/** her car ran out of gas. (SS)
   The young woman was walking. Her car ran out of gas.
2. The picture is on the mantel **/** the clock is on the mantel. (SCS)
   The picture and the clock are on the mantel.
3. The toddler rolled in the snow **/** she played in the snow for hours. (SCV)
   The toddler rolled and played in the snow for hours.

Look at Part 2. We will identify whether each sentence is a fragment, a simple sentence, a simple sentence with a compound subject, or a simple sentence with a compound verb. After we decide what type of sentence it is, we will discuss the correct abbreviation in the blank at the left of each sentence. The abbreviations are found at the end of the directions. (*Read the directions and work through sentences 1–5, showing students how to identify each type of sentence.*)

TEACHING SCRIPT FOR A RUN-ON SENTENCE

If two sentences are written together as one sentence without being punctuated correctly, the result is a <u>run-on sentence</u>. Go to Part 3 in your reference box and look at number 1: **The young woman was walking her car ran out of gas. (SS)**. Is the first part of the sentence "The young woman was walking" a complete thought? (*yes*) Is the second part of the sentence "her car ran out of gas" a complete thought? (*yes*) The two complete thoughts are run together because they are written as one sentence.

There are several ways to correct a run-on sentence. First, we will put a slash between the two thoughts that are run together so we can see each sentence clearly. (*The young woman was walking / her car ran out of gas.*) Next, we will look at the abbreviation in parentheses at the end of number 1 to see how we are to correct this run-on sentence. Look at the end of number 1.

The **(SS)** in parentheses tells us to correct the run-on sentence by making it two simple sentences. After we correct the run-on sentence, we will check the punctuation. (*The first word of each sentence must be capitalized, and each sentence must have end mark punctuation. Read the two simple sentences:* **The young woman was walking. Her car ran out of gas.**)

© SHURLEY INSTRUCTIONAL MATERIALS, INC.

CHAPTER 14 LESSON 2 CONTINUED

We will now look at a second way to correct a run-on sentence. Look at number 2: **The picture is on the mantel the clock is on the mantel.** (**SCS**) This is a run-on sentence that needs to be corrected. First, we will put a slash between the two thoughts that are run together so we can see each sentence clearly. (*The picture is on the mantel / the clock is on the mantel.*)

Next, we will look at the abbreviation in parentheses at the end of number 2 to see how we are to correct the run-on sentence. Look at the end of number 2. The **(SCS)** in parentheses tells us to correct the run-on sentence by writing a simple sentence with a compound subject. When each sentence has a different subject, join the two subjects together with the conjunction *AND*. That will make a compound subject. If the subjects have additional subject words, include them as you write the compound subjects. (**The picture and the clock**)

Since both sentences have the same verb, the verb will stay the same except for one change. This change is a subject-verb agreement change. When the words *picture* and *clock* were used as singular subjects, they each used the singular verb *is*. Now that the words *picture* and *clock* have become a compound subject, the singular verb *is* <u>MUST</u> be changed to the plural verb *are* because a compound subject requires a plural verb form. This new sentence is called a simple sentence with a compound subject. (**The picture and the clock are on the mantel.**)

Now, we will look at a third way to correct a run-on sentence. Look at number 3: **The toddler rolled in the snow she played in the snow for hours**. (**SCV**) This is a run-on sentence that needs to be corrected. First, we will put a slash between the two thoughts that are run together so we can see each sentence clearly. (*The toddler rolled in the snow / she played in the snow for hours.*)

Next, we will look at the abbreviation in parentheses at the end of number 3 to see how we are to correct the run-on sentence. Look at the end of number 3. The **(SCV)** in parentheses tells us to correct the run-on sentence by writing a simple sentence with a compound verb. Since both sentences have the same subject (***toddler*** *and* ***she*** *are the same person*), the subject noun *toddler* is used.

Finally, we will look at the verbs. Since each sentence has a different verb, the two verbs are joined together with the conjunction *AND*. Joining the verbs together with a conjunction makes a compound verb. If the verbs have additional predicate words, the predicate words are always included as the compound verbs are written. (**rolled and played in the snow for hours**) This new sentence is called a simple sentence with a compound verb. (**The toddler rolled and played in the snow for hours.**)

© SHURLEY INSTRUCTIONAL MATERIALS, INC.

CHAPTER 14 LESSON 2 CONTINUED

 PRACTICE TIME

Have students turn to page 75 in the Practice Section of their book and find Chapter 14, Lesson 2, Practice (*1-2*). Go over the directions to make sure they understand what to do. Check and discuss the Practices after students have finished. (*Chapter 14, Lesson 2, Practice keys are given below.*)

Chapter 14, Lesson 2, Practice 1: Put a slash to separate each run-on sentence below. Then, correct the run-on sentences by rewriting them as indicated by the labels in parentheses at the end of each sentence.

1. Samantha earned extra money **/** she spent it on makeup. (SCV)
   Samantha earned extra money and spent it on makeup.
2. I am going to the store **/** Jonathan is going to the store. (SCS)
   Jonathan and I are going to the store.
3. My little brother is adorable **/** he likes to play games with me. (SS)
   My little brother is adorable. He likes to play games with me.

Chapter 14, Lesson 2, Practice 2: Identify each kind of sentence by writing the abbreviation in the blank. (S, SS, F, SCS, SCV)

F	1.	Whenever the vegetables are ripe.
SCV	2.	My aunt planned the party and invited the guests.
SCS	3.	Hot dogs and mustard are good together.
SS	4.	The cat ran away. Dad searched for it.
S	5.	The pictures were developed in the photo lab.

 VOCABULARY TIME

Assign Chapter 14, Vocabulary Words **#2** on page 9 in the Reference Section for students to define in their Vocabulary notebooks. Tell students they are to use a dictionary or thesaurus to look up the meanings of the vocabulary words. After they write each word and its meaning, students are to write a sentence using the vocabulary word.

Chapter 14, Vocabulary Words #2
(smart, intelligent, consistent, irregular)

(End of lesson.)

© SHURLEY INSTRUCTIONAL MATERIALS, INC.

CHAPTER 14 LESSON 3

Objectives: Jingles, Grammar (Practice Sentences), Skills (compound sentence, and run-on sentence), Practice Exercise, and Activity.

 **JINGLE TIME**

Have students turn to the Jingle Section in their books and recite the previously-taught jingles.

 GRAMMAR TIME

First-Year Option: Put the Practice Sentences from the box below on the board or on notebook paper. Use these sentences as you practice the concepts that have been taught. For the greatest benefit, students must participate orally with the teacher. **Second-Year Option:** Have students classify the Practice Sentences independently on paper. Check students' sentences with the answers provided below. (*If you have the CDs for Practice Sentences, have students check their sentences with the CDs.*)

Chapter 14, Practice Sentences for Lesson 3
1. _____ We built a scarecrow for our grandfather's garden.
2. _____ Ouch! Jim smashed his finger in the car door!

TEACHING SCRIPT FOR PRACTICING PATTERN 2 SENTENCES

We will practice classifying Pattern 2 sentences. We will classify the sentences together. Begin. (*You might have your students write the labels above the sentences at this time.*)

Question and Answer Flow for Sentence 1: We built a scarecrow for our grandfather's garden.
1. Who built a scarecrow for our grandfather's garden? we - SP
2. What is being said about we? we built - V
3. We built what? scarecrow - verify the noun
4. Does scarecrow mean the same thing as we? No.
5. Scarecrow - DO
6. Built - V-t
7. A - A
8. For - P
9. For what? garden - OP
10. Whose garden? grandfather's - PNA
11. Whose grandfather? our - PPA
12. SN V-t DO P2 Check
13. Verb-transitive - Check again.
14. (For our grandfather's garden) - Prepositional phrase
15. Period, statement, declarative sentence
16. Go back to the verb - divide the complete subject from the complete predicate.

Classified Sentence:

```
                    SP   V-t A    DO     P PPA    PNA      OP
        SN  V-t    We / built a scarecrow (for our grandfather's garden).  D
        DO  P2
```

CHAPTER 14 LESSON 3 CONTINUED

Question and Answer Flow for Sentence 2: Ouch! Jim smashed his finger in the car door!

1. Who smashed his finger in the car door? Jim - SN
2. What is being said about Jim?
   Jim smashed - V
3. Jim smashed what? finger - verify the noun
4. Does finger mean the same thing as Jim? No.
5. Finger - DO
6. Smashed - V-t
7. Whose finger? his - PPA
8. In - P
9. In what? door - OP
10. What kind of door? car - Adj
11. The - A
12. Ouch - I
13. SN V-t DO P2 Check
14. Verb-transitive - Check again.
15. (In the car door) - Prepositional phrase
16. Exclamation point, strong feeling, exclamatory sentence
17. Go back to the verb - divide the complete subject
    from the complete predicate.

Classified Sentence:

I   SN   V-t   PPA DO   P   A   Adj OP

SN V-t   Ouch! Jim / smashed his finger (in the car door)! E

DO P2

SKILL TIME

TEACHING SCRIPT FOR COMPOUND SENTENCES

Another kind of sentence you need to recognize and write is the compound sentence. Look at the information about the compound sentence in Reference 46 on page 38 in your book. Pay special attention to the ways you can correctly join the parts of a compound sentence. (*Read the information about a compound sentence with your students. This information is reproduced for you.*) As you can see in the example, the labels in parentheses at the end of the sentence give directions on how to correct the run-on sentences.

Reference 46: The Compound Sentence

1. Compound means two. A compound sentence is two complete sentences joined together correctly with a comma and a conjunction. The abbreviation for a compound sentence is **CD**.

2. One way to join two sentences and make a compound sentence is to use a comma and a conjunction. The formula for you to follow will always be given at the end of the sentence. The formula gives the abbreviation for the compound sentence and lists the conjunction to use (**CD, and**). (The three most commonly-used conjunctions are **and, but, or**.) Remember to place the comma BEFORE the conjunction.
   Example: We picked vegetables from the **garden, and** we ate them for dinner. (CD, and)

3. Compound sentences should be closely related in thought and importance.
   Correct: We picked vegetables from the **garden, and** we ate them for dinner.
   Incorrect: We picked vegetables from the **garden, and** my baby brother doesn't like cheese.

Now, we will review what you have just learned. First, compound sentences can be correctly joined with conjunctions and commas. You must know how to use commas and conjunctions when you join two sentences together to make a compound sentence. The three most commonly used conjunctions are **and**, **or**, and **but**. Second, conjunctions are used to join words together to make compound subjects, compound verbs, or other compound parts.

© SHURLEY INSTRUCTIONAL MATERIALS, INC.

CHAPTER 14 LESSON 3 CONTINUED

The most important thing to remember is how to recognize the difference between a sentence with compound parts, such as compound subjects or compound verbs, and a compound sentence. The easiest way to do this is to find another subject and verb after the conjunction. Remember, a compound sentence is two separate sentences joined together with a comma and a conjunction.

TEACHING SCRIPT FOR DIFFERENT WAYS TO CORRECT RUN-ON SENTENCES

Look at Reference 47 on page 38 in your book. We will now review different ways to correct run-on sentences. First, we must read the directions to be sure we know what to do. (*Read the directions for Reference 47 below. Then, follow the teaching script given for this reference.*)

Reference 47: Using SCS, SCV, and CD Correctly
Put a slash to separate the two complete thoughts in each run-on sentence. Correct the run-on sentences or fragments as indicated by the labels in parentheses at the end of each sentence.
1. Samantha loves amusement parks **/** she doesn't like the roller coasters. (CD, but)   **Samantha loves amusement parks, but she doesn't like the roller coasters.**
2. My uncle owns a pizza parlor **/** the food is delicious! (CD, and)   **My uncle owns a pizza parlor, and the food is delicious!**
3. Beth works in the church kitchen **/** Mary works in the church kitchen. (SCS)   **Beth and Mary work in the church kitchen.** *(When the subject is compound, the verb is plural.)*
4. For extra money, Susan walks dogs **/** she watches children. (SCV)   **For extra money, Susan walks dogs and watches children.**

Look at number 1. Is "Samantha loves amusement parks" a complete sentence? (*Yes, except for an end mark.*) Is "she doesn't like the roller coasters" a complete sentence? (*Yes, except for a capital letter and end mark.*) The directions tell us to put a slash between these two complete thoughts. (*Show students how the two sentences are divided with a slash.*)

Next, look at the end of number 1. The (**CD, but**) in parentheses tells us how to make these two sentences into a compound sentence. The (**CD**) stands for compound sentence, and the (**but**) tells which conjunction to use. Remember, we must also place a comma in front of the conjunction in order to punctuate the compound sentence correctly.

As you can see, the compound sentence has been written by using the information in parentheses (**CD, but**). (*Read the compound sentence: **Samantha loves amusement parks, but she doesn't like the roller coasters**.*) These two sentences are made into a compound sentence by using a comma and the conjunction *but* to join them.

© SHURLEY INSTRUCTIONAL MATERIALS, INC.

CHAPTER 14 LESSON 3 CONTINUED

TEACHER INSTRUCTIONS

Work through the rest of the Practice Sentences (2-4) in the same way. Make sure your students understand that the labels in parentheses at the end of the sentences give directions on how to correct run-on sentences or fragments.

Now, have students look at Reference 48. Read the directions and work through Parts 1 and 2. Make sure students understand how each example was done because they will be tested in each format. (*In Part 2, point out that number 7 is a compound sentence because it has two sentences joined by a comma and conjunction. Number 8 is a simple sentence with a compound verb because it is only one sentence with a conjunction connecting two verbs.*)

Reference 48: Identifying S, F, SCS, SCV, and CD
Part 1: Identify each kind of sentence by writing the abbreviation in the blank (S, F, SCS, SCV, CD).

SCV 1. The hungry pup gnawed on his bone and growled.
F 2. Only because no one bid on the property.
CD 3. He was elected senator, but he narrowly won the election.
S 4. Between acts, there was a brief intermission.
SCS 5. Lee and his wife are expecting twins.
CD 6. The fire truck arrived, and an ambulance came shortly thereafter.

Part 2: Use the ways listed below to correct this run-on sentence: **He made a mistake he did not correct it.**

7. CD, but **He made a mistake, but he did not correct it.** 8. SCV **He made a mistake but did not correct it.**

 PRACTICE TIME

Have students turn to page 76 in the Practice Section of their book and find Chapter 14, Lesson 3, Practice (*1-3*). Go over the directions to make sure they understand what to do. Check and discuss the Practices after students have finished. (*Chapter 14, Lesson 3 Practice keys are given below and on the next page.*)

Chapter 14, Lesson 3, Practice 1: Put a slash to separate each run-on sentence below. Then, correct the run-on sentences by rewriting them as indicated by the labels in parentheses at the end of each sentence.

1. He got lost in the woods / he found his way out (CD, but)
   He got lost in the woods, but he found his way out.
2. He got lost in the woods / he found his way out (CD, and)
   He got lost in the woods, and he found his way out.
3. He got lost in the woods / his brother got lost in the woods (SCS)
   He and his brother got lost in the woods.
4. He got lost in the woods / he fell in the pond. (SCV)
   He got lost in the woods and fell in the pond.

© SHURLEY INSTRUCTIONAL MATERIALS, INC.

CHAPTER 14 LESSON 3 CONTINUED

Chapter 14, Lesson 3, Practice 2: Identify each kind of sentence by writing the abbreviation in the blank. (S, F, SCS, SCV, CD)

SCV	1. The catcher slid and touched the bag.
F	2. In the railroad yard on the east end of town.
CD	3. I like peach pie, but my wife prefers apple pie.
SCS	4. The players and fans were exceptionally angry.
CD	5. You will stay awake in class, or you will leave.

Chapter 14, Lesson 3, Practice 3: On notebook paper, write two compound sentences using these labels to guide you: (CD, but) (CD, and) **(Sentences will vary)**

ACTIVITY / ASSIGNMENT TIME

Put the code below on the board. Explain the code by drawing people faces that illustrate the sample sentences below. Then, have students use the code to draw people faces that illustrate the sentences at the bottom of the box. Students could also write their own code, and they could write sentences of their own and draw people faces that illustrate their original sentences.

Code Box	
1. Noun – left eye	5. Adverb – left ear
2. Verb – nose	6. Preposition – hair
3. Pronoun – left eyebrow	7. Conjunction – right ear
4. Adjective – right eye Article Adjective – mouth	8. Interjection – right eyebrow

Sample Sentences

   Adj   SN   P A OP V   Adv   Adv
1. Twenty pigeons on the roof flew rapidly away.

Draw a round circle for the head. After classifying the above sentence, you will draw these features on the head: a right eye (adjective), a left eye (noun), hair (preposition), a mouth (article adjective), a nose (verb), and a left ear (adverb).

   I   CSN   C CSP HV   V   Adv
2. Marvelous! Clint and I are graduating tonight.

Draw a round circle for the head. After classifying the above sentence, you will draw these features on the head: a right eyebrow (interjection), a left eye (noun), a right ear (conjunction), a left eyebrow (pronoun), a nose (verb), and a left ear (adverb).

Sentences

1. Whew! Two pheasants landed in the corn field beside Kenneth's barn.
2. We went to the mall today.
3. We laughed and shouted yesterday.
4. The boys leaped across the ditch.
5. The beautiful horses ran swiftly around the track.

(End of lesson.)

© SHURLEY INSTRUCTIONAL MATERIALS, INC.

CHAPTER 14   LESSON 4

Objectives: Jingles, Study, Test, Check, Activity, and Writing (journal).

 JINGLE TIME

Have students turn to the Jingle Section in their books and recite the previously-taught jingles.

 STUDY TIME

Have students study the vocabulary words in their vocabulary notebooks. Remind students that any vocabulary word in their notebooks could be on their test. Also, have students study any of the skills in the Practice Section that they need to review.

 TEST TIME

Have students turn to page 110 in the Test Section of their book and find Chapter 14 Test. Go over the directions to make sure they understand what to do. (*The Chapter 14 Test key is on the next page.*)

 CHECK TIME

After students have finished, check and discuss their test papers. Make sure they understand why their answers are right or wrong. (*For total points, count each required answer as a point.*)

 ACTIVITY / ASSIGNMENT TIME

Students will continue to draw or trace the states and write the following questions and answers.

Maine	Maryland
1. What is the state on the front of this card? **Maine**	1. What is the state on the front of this card? **Maryland**
2. What is the capital of Maine? **Augusta**	2. What is the capital of Maryland? **Annapolis**
3. What is the postal abbreviation of Maine? **ME**	3. What is the postal abbreviation of Maryland? **MD**
4. What year was Maine admitted to the Union? **1820**	4. What year was Maryland admitted to the Union? **1788**

Color these states and look up an interesting fact about each state to write on the cards. Use the cards to quiz family members, friends, and relatives. You may want to time the responses to your questions. Also, along with previous suggestions, think of other ways to have fun with your United States card file.

(End of lesson.)

Level 3 Homeschool Teacher's Manual

© SHURLEY INSTRUCTIONAL MATERIALS, INC.

Chapter 14 Test
(Student Page 110)

Exercise 1: Classify each sentence.

```
         A      SN     V-t  A  Adj    DO   P  A    OP      P  PPA  OP
```
1. __SN V-t__   The campers / built a cooking fire (in the middle) (of their camp). **D**
   __DO P2__

```
           SN     V-t   Adj  Adj   DO      P    A  PNA    Adj    OP
```
2. __SN V-t__   Mark / found some great bargains (during the store's blowout sale). **D**
   __DO P2__

Exercise 2: Use Sentence 2 to underline the complete subject once and the complete predicate twice and to complete the table below.

List the Noun Used	List the Noun Job	Singular or Plural	Common or Proper	Simple Subject	Simple Predicate
1. **Mark**	2. **SN**	3. **S**	4. **P**	5. **Mark**	6. **found**
7. **bargains**	8. **DO**	9. **P**	10. **C**		
11. **sale**	12. **OP**	13. **S**	14. **C**		

Exercise 3: Identify each pair of words as synonyms or antonyms by putting parentheses ( ) around *syn* or *ant*.

1. droop, wilt	**(syn)** ant	4. depart, stay	syn **(ant)**	7. consistent, irregular	syn **(ant)**
2. puny, robust	syn **(ant)**	5. evade, avoid	**(syn)** ant	8. smart, intelligent	**(syn)** ant
3. disease, illness	**(syn)** ant	6. pleasure, joy	**(syn)** ant	9. intentional, unintended	syn **(ant)**

Exercise 4: Put a slash to separate each run-on sentence below. Then, correct the run-on sentences by rewriting them on notebook paper as indicated by the labels in parentheses at the end of each sentence.

1. Daisies are blooming / they cover the fields. (CD, and)
   Daisies are blooming, and they cover the fields.
2. Johnny painted a picture / Debbie painted a picture. (SCS)
   Johnny and Debbie painted a picture.
3. The boys hung up a hammock / they slept outside. (SCV)
   The boys hung up a hammock and slept outside.
4. My brother washed the dog / he did not clean up the bathroom. (CD, but)
   My brother washed the dog, but he did not clean up the bathroom.
5. Timothy painted the fence / Justin helped him. (SCS)
   Timothy and Justin painted the fence.
6. She laughed loudly / she giggled loudly. (SCV)
   She laughed and giggled loudly.

Exercise 5: Identify each kind of sentence by writing the abbreviation in the blank. (S, F, SCS, SCV, CD).

__SCS__	1.	Apples and pears are my favorite fruits.
__CD__	2.	The engine sputtered, and the lawnmower ran out of gas.
__F__	3.	Walking through the city on a frigid winter morning.
__SCV__	4.	The electrician switched off the breaker and repaired the broken wires.
__CD__	5.	The tiny baby tried to walk, but he toppled to the ground.
__S__	6.	The detour around the construction site was very long.
__CD__	7.	I know her sister, but I can't remember her name.

Exercise 6: On notebook paper, write two sentences, using these labels to guide you: (SCV) (CD, and). **(Answers will vary.)**

Exercise 7: In your journal, write a paragraph summarizing what you have learned this week.

© SHURLEY INSTRUCTIONAL MATERIALS, INC.

CHAPTER 14 LESSON 4 CONTINUED

TEACHER INSTRUCTIONS

Use the Question and Answer Flows below for the sentences on the Chapter 14 Test.

Question and Answer Flow for Sentence 1: The campers built a cooking fire in the middle of their camp.

1. Who built a cooking fire in the middle of their camp? campers - SN
2. What is being said about campers? campers built - V
3. Campers built what? fire - verify the noun
4. Does fire mean the same thing as campers? No.
5. Fire - DO
6. Built - V-t
7. What kind of fire? cooking - Adj
8. A - A
9. In - P
10. In what? middle - OP
11. The - A
12. Of - P
13. Of what? camp - OP
14. Whose camp? their - PPA
15. The - A
16. SN V-t DO P2 Check
17. Verb-transitive - Check again.
18. (In the middle) - Prepositional phrase
19. (Of their camp) - Prepositional phrase
20. Period, statement, declarative sentence
21. Go back to the verb - divide the complete subject from the complete predicate.

Classified Sentence:

A	SN	V-t	A	Adj	DO	P	A	OP	P	PPA	OP

SN V-t / DO P2   The campers / built a cooking fire (in the middle) (of their camp). **D**

Question and Answer Flow for Sentence 2: Mark found some great bargains during the store's blowout sale.

1. Who found some great bargains during the store's blowout sale? Mark - SN
2. What is being said about Mark? Mark found - V
3. Mark found what? bargains - verify the noun
4. Do bargains mean the same thing as Mark? No.
5. Bargains - DO
6. Found - V-t
7. What kind of bargains? great - Adj
8. How many bargains? some - Adj
9. During - P
10. During what? sale - OP
11. What kind of sale? blowout - Adj
12. Whose sale? store's - PNA
13. The - A
14. SN V-t DO P2 Check
15. Verb-transitive - Check again.
16. (During the store's blowout sale) - Prepositional phrase
17. Period, statement, declarative sentence
18. Go back to the verb - divide the complete subject from the complete predicate.

Classified Sentence:

SN	V-t	Adj	Adj	DO	P	A	PNA	Adj	OP

SN V-t / DO P2   Mark / found some great bargains (during the store's blowout sale). **D**

© SHURLEY INSTRUCTIONAL MATERIALS, INC.

CHAPTER 14   LESSON 5

Objectives: Writing Assignments #12 and #13.

WRITING TIME

TEACHING SCRIPT FOR PRACTICING DIFFERENT KINDS OF WRITING

Today, you are assigned two different kinds of writing. You will write a three-paragraph expository essay and a three-point persuasive paragraph. <u>You will revise and edit the three-paragraph expository essay</u>. (_Read the box below for more information about students' writing assignment._) As you edit, make sure you use the checkpoints in the editing checklist provided in Reference 42. Remember to read through the whole essay, starting with the title, and then edit, sentence-by-sentence, using the five sentence checkpoints for each sentence. Use the paragraph checkpoints to check each paragraph. After you are satisfied with your revising and editing, you will write a final paper, using the Final Paper Checklist in Reference 13.

Writing Assignment Box #1

Writing Assignment #12: Three-Paragraph Expository Essay

Remind students that the 3-paragraph essay has three parts: 1. Introduction 2. Body 3. Conclusion. Have students use their regular editing checklist to edit this assignment.

Writing topic: Ways Exercise Can Be Fun   or My Favorite Automobile   or Three States I Would Like To Visit

---

Your second writing assignment is to write a three-point persuasive paragraph. (_Read the box below for more information about the students' writing assignment._) You do not have to edit this assignment with the editing checklist.

Writing Assignment Box #2

Writing Assignment #13: Three-Point Persuasive Paragraph

Writing topic: Why We Need A Bigger/Smaller Yard   or   Why I Should/Should Not Have a Phone in My Room
                    or   Why Good Listening Skills Are Important

---

Read, check, and discuss Writing Assignment #12 after students have finished their final papers. Use the checklists as you check and discuss students' papers. Make sure students are using the regular editing checklist correctly. Read and discuss Writing Assignment #13 for fun and enrichment.

(End of lesson.)

© SHURLEY INSTRUCTIONAL MATERIALS, INC.

CHAPTER 15 LESSON 1

Objectives: Jingles, Grammar (Practice Sentences), Oral Skill Builder Check, Skills (contractions), Practice Exercise, and Vocabulary #1.

 JINGLE TIME

Have students turn to the Jingle Section in their books and recite the previously-taught jingles.

 GRAMMAR TIME

First-Year Option: Put the Practice Sentences from the box below on the board or on notebook paper. Use these sentences as you practice the concepts that have been taught. For the greatest benefit, students must participate orally with the teacher. **Second-Year Option:** Have students classify the Practice Sentences independently on paper. Check students' sentences with the answers provided below. *(If you have the CDs for Practice Sentences, have students check their sentences with the CDs.)*

Chapter 15, Practice Sentences for Lesson 1
1. _____ Mom keeps a flashlight in the car for emergencies.
2. _____ We flew our kites in the park on Saturday.

TEACHING SCRIPT FOR PRACTICING PATTERN 2 SENTENCES

We will practice classifying Pattern 2 sentences. We will classify the sentences together. Begin. (*You might have your students write the labels above the sentences at this time.*)

Question and Answer Flow for Sentence 1: Mom keeps a flashlight in the car for emergencies.

1. Who keeps a flashlight in the car for emergencies?
   Mom - SN
2. What is being said about Mom? Mom keeps - V
3. Mom keeps what? flashlight - verify the noun
4. Does flashlight mean the same thing as Mom? No.
5. Flashlight - DO
6. Keeps - V-t
7. A - A
8. In - P
9. In what? car - OP

10. The - A
11. For - P
12. For what? emergencies - OP
13. SN V-t DO P2 Check
14. Verb-transitive - Check again.
15. (In the car) - Prepositional phrase
16. (For emergencies) - Prepositional phrase
17. Period, statement, declarative sentence
18. Go back to the verb - divide the complete subject from the complete predicate.

Classified Sentence:

      SN   V-t A   DO   P A OP P   OP
 SN V-t   Mom / keeps a flashlight (in the car) (for emergencies). **D**
 DO P2

© SHURLEY INSTRUCTIONAL MATERIALS, INC.

CHAPTER 15 LESSON 1 CONTINUED

Question and Answer Flow for Sentence 2: We flew our kites in the park on Saturday.

1. Who flew our kites in the park on Saturday? we - SP
2. What is being said about we? we flew - V
3. We flew what? kites - verify the noun
4. Do kites mean the same thing as we? No.
5. Kites - DO
6. Flew - V-t
7. Whose kites? our - PPA
8. In - P
9. In what? park - OP
10. The - A
11. On - P
12. On what? Saturday - OP
13. SN V-t DO P2 Check
14. Verb-transitive - Check again.
15. (In the park) - Prepositional phrase
16. (On Saturday) - Prepositional phrase
17. Period, statement, declarative sentence
18. Go back to the verb - divide the complete subject from the complete predicate.

Classified Sentence:

```
                        SP   V-t  PPA DO   P  A   OP    P    OP
              SN V-t    We / flew our kites (in the park) (on Saturday).  D
              DO P2
```

Use Sentences 1-2 that you just classified with your students to do an Oral Skill Builder Check. Use the guidelines below.

Oral Skill Builder Check

1. Noun check. (Say the job and then say the noun. Circle each noun.)
2. Identify the nouns as singular or plural. (Write S or P above each noun.)
3. Identify the nouns as common or proper. (Follow established procedure for oral identification.)
4. Do a vocabulary check. (Follow established procedure for oral identification.)

5. Identify the complete subject and the complete predicate. (Underline the complete subject once and the complete predicate twice.)
6. Identify the simple subject and simple predicate. (Underline the simple subject once and the simple predicate twice. Bold, or highlight, the lines.)
7. Recite the irregular verb chart. (Located on student page 25 and teacher page 163.)

SKILL TIME

TEACHING SCRIPT FOR INTRODUCING CONTRACTIONS

A contraction is two words shortened into one word, and the new word always has an apostrophe. The apostrophe takes the place of the letters that have been left out. When we worked with homonyms, you learned how important it was to choose the correct word. You had to constantly be aware of the spelling of certain words and their meanings. This will still be important as you work with contractions. You must know how to spell contractions correctly and which contraction is correct. And, of course, some contractions can be confused with possessive pronouns, so you must always be aware of the right choices.

Look at Reference 49 on page 39. I want you to repeat with me the words from which the contraction is made and then repeat the contraction. (*Go over all the contractions in this manner. This will help your students see them, say them, and hear them correctly. Develop a singsong chant that has enough rhythm to sound good and to be fun at the same time. The contraction chart is reproduced for you on the next page.*)

© SHURLEY INSTRUCTIONAL MATERIALS, INC.

CHAPTER 15 LESSON 1 CONTINUED

Reference 49: Contraction Chart				Pronoun	Contraction
AM		HAS			
I am — I'm		has not — hasn't		**its**	**it's**
		he has — he's		(owns)	(it is)
IS		she has — she's		*its coat*	*it's cute*
is not — isn't					
he is — he's		HAVE			
she is — she's		have not — haven't		**your**	**you're**
it is — it's		I have — I've		(owns)	(you are)
who is — who's		you have — you've		*your car*	*you're right*
that is — that's		we have — we've			
what is — what's		they have — they've			
there is — there's				**their**	**they're**
		HAD		(owns)	(they are)
ARE		had not — hadn't		*their house*	*they're gone*
are not — aren't		I had — I'd			
you are — you're		he had — he'd			
we are — we're		she had — she'd		**whose**	**who's**
they are — they're		you had — you'd		(owns)	(who is)
		we had — we'd		*whose cat*	*who's going*
WAS, WERE		they had — they'd			
was not — wasn't					
were not — weren't		WILL, SHALL			
		will not — won't			
DO, DOES, DID		I will — I'll			
do not — don't		he will — he'll			
does not — doesn't		she will — she'll			
did not — didn't		you will — you'll			
		we will — we'll			
CAN		they will — they'll			
cannot — can't					
		WOULD			
LET		would not — wouldn't			
let us — let's		I would — I'd			
		he would — he'd			
		she would — she'd			
		you would — you'd			
		we would — we'd			
		they would — they'd			
		SHOULD, COULD			
		should not — shouldn't			
		could not — couldn't			

© SHURLEY INSTRUCTIONAL MATERIALS, INC.

CHAPTER 15 LESSON 1 CONTINUED

 PRACTICE TIME

Have students turn to pages 76 and 77 in the Practice Section of their book and find Chapter 15, Lesson 1, Practice (*1-3*). Go over the directions to make sure they understand what to do. Check and discuss the Practices after students have finished. (*Use the contraction chart on page 262 to help students check their assignments. Chapter 15, Lesson 1, Practice keys are given below.*)

Chapter 15, Lesson 1, Practice 1: Copy the following words on another sheet of paper. Write the correct contraction beside each word. **Key: can't, let's, don't, wasn't, they're, aren't, hadn't, isn't, she's, who's, you're, didn't, it's, we're, weren't, doesn't, hasn't, I'm, I've, I'd, won't, I'll, wouldn't, I'd, shouldn't, couldn't, they'd.**
Words: cannot, let us, do not, was not, they are, are not, had not, is not, she is, who is, you are, did not, it is, we are, were not, does not, has not, I am, I have, I had, will not, I will, would not, I would, should not, could not, they would.

Chapter 15, Lesson 1, Practice 2: Put a slash to separate each run-on sentence below. Then, correct the run-on sentences by rewriting them as indicated by the labels in parentheses at the end of each sentence.

1. The dog dug a hole in the ground / he buried his bone. (SCV)
   The dog dug a hole in the ground and buried his bone.
2. The dog dug a hole in the ground / he buried his bone. (CD, and)
   The dog dug a hole in the ground, and he buried his bone.
3. The dog chewed on a bone / the cat chewed on a bone. (SCS)
   The dog and the cat chewed on a bone.

Chapter 15, Lesson 1, Practice 3: Identify each kind of sentence by writing the abbreviation in the blank. (S, F, SCS, SCV, CD)

   SCV 1. The boy tripped and fell on the playground.
   CD 2. Patsy baked the casserole, and Jean set the table.
   SCS 3. His mom and dad are in the air force.
   F 4. Made in factories all across the United States.
   CD 5. I like squash, and my brother likes okra.

 VOCABULARY TIME

Assign Chapter 15, Vocabulary Words **#1** on page 9 in the Reference Section for students to define in their Vocabulary notebooks. Tell students they are to use a dictionary or thesaurus to look up the meanings of the vocabulary words. After they write each word and its meaning, students are to write a sentence using the vocabulary word.

Chapter 15, Vocabulary Words #1
(occupied, vacant, hidden, concealed)

(End of lesson.)

CHAPTER 15   LESSON 2

Objectives: Jingles, Grammar (Practice Sentences), Pattern 2 Practice Sentence, Oral Contraction Review, Practice Exercise, Vocabulary #2, and Activity.

JINGLE TIME

Have students turn to the Jingle Section in their books and recite the previously-taught jingles.

GRAMMAR TIME

First-Year Option: Put the Practice Sentences from the box below on the board or on notebook paper. Use these sentences as you practice the concepts that have been taught. For the greatest benefit, students must participate orally with the teacher. **Second-Year Option:** Have students classify the Practice Sentences independently on paper. Check students' sentences with the answers provided below. (*If you have the CDs for Practice Sentences, have students check their sentences with the CDs.*)

Chapter 15, Practice Sentences for Lesson 2
1. _____ My dad bought milk and bread at the convenience store today.
2. _____ Larry played a grand piano during the music recital.

TEACHING SCRIPT FOR PRACTICING PATTERN 2 SENTENCES

We will practice classifying Pattern 2 sentences. We will classify the sentences together. Begin. (*You might have your students write the labels above the sentences at this time.*)

Question and Answer Flow for Sentence 1: My dad bought milk and bread at the convenience store today.

1. Who bought milk and bread at the convenience store today? dad - SN
2. What is being said about dad? dad bought - V
3. Dad bought what? milk and bread - verify the nouns
4. Do milk and bread mean the same thing as dad? No.
5. Milk and bread - CDO, CDO
6. Bought - V-t
7. And - C
8. At - P
9. At what? store - OP
10. What kind of store? convenience - Adj
11. The - A
12. Bought when? today - Adv
13. Whose dad? my - PPA
14. SN V-t DO P2 Check
15. Verb-transitive - Check again.
16. (At the convenience store) - Prepositional phrase
17. Period, statement, declarative sentence
18. Go back to the verb - divide the complete subject from the complete predicate.

Classified Sentence:

<pre>
                    PPA SN   V-t   CDO C CDO P A   Adj   OP   Adv
          SN V-t   My dad / bought milk and bread (at the convenience store) today. D
          DO P2
</pre>

© SHURLEY INSTRUCTIONAL MATERIALS, INC.

CHAPTER 15 LESSON 2 CONTINUED

Question and Answer Flow for Sentence 2: Larry played a grand piano during the music recital.

1. Who played a grand piano during the music recital?
   Larry - SN
2. What is being said about Larry? Larry played - V
3. Larry played what? piano - verify the noun
4. Does piano mean the same thing as Larry? No.
5. Piano - DO
6. Played - V-t
7. What kind of piano? grand - Adj
8. A - A
9. During - P

10. During what? recital - OP
11. What kind of recital? music - Adj
12. The - A
13. SN V-t DO P2 Check
14. Verb-transitive - Check again.
15. (During the music recital) - Prepositional phrase
16. Period, statement, declarative sentence
17. Go back to the verb - divide the complete subject
    from the complete predicate.

Classified Sentence:

SN   V-t   A   Adj   DO   P   A   Adj   OP
<u>SN V-t</u>   Larry / played a grand piano (during the music recital). D
<u>DO P2</u>

TEACHER INSTRUCTIONS FOR A PATTERN 2 SENTENCE

Tell students that their sentence writing assignment today is to write a Pattern 2 sentence. They are to follow the same procedure used in the previous lessons. They should decide on their labels, arrange them in a selected order, write their sentence, and edit the sentence for improved word choices. (*Students do not have to write an Improved Sentence at this point unless you feel they need more one-on-one word choice writing practice.*) Check and discuss the Pattern 2 sentence after students have finished.

Oral Contraction Review

To develop listening skills, give students a review of contractions orally. In the first chart, repeat the contractions in bold and have students respond with the correct words that stand for each contraction. In the second chart, repeat the words and have students respond with the correct contractions.

Chart 1:

shouldn't - should not	**wasn't** - was not	**we're** - we are	**wouldn't** - would not
can't - cannot	**doesn't** - does not	**haven't** - have not	**I've** - I have
I'm - I am	**let's** - let us	**you've** - you have	**won't** - will not

Chart 2:

did not - didn't	**they would** - they'd	**were not** - weren't	**they had** - they'd
I will - I'll	**we have** - we've	**she will** - she'll	**they are** - they're
what is - what's	**you will** - you'll	**he would** - he'd	**he had** - he'd

 PRACTICE TIME

Have students turn to pages 77 and 78 in the Practice Section of their book and find Chapter 15, Lesson 2, Practice (*1-3*). Go over the directions to make sure they understand what to do. Check and discuss the Practices after students have finished. (*Chapter 15, Lesson 2, Practice keys are given on the next page.*)

© SHURLEY INSTRUCTIONAL MATERIALS, INC.

CHAPTER 15 LESSON 2 CONTINUED

Chapter 15, Lesson 2, Practice 1: Copy the following contractions on another sheet of paper. Write the correct word beside each contraction. **Key: cannot, let us, do not, was not, they are, are not, had not, is not, she is or she has, who is, you are, did not, it is, we are, were not, does not, has not, I am, I have, I had or I would, will not, I will, would not, should not, could not, they had or they would.**

<u>Contractions</u>: can't, let's, don't, wasn't, they're, aren't, hadn't, isn't, she's, who's, you're, didn't, it's, we're, weren't, doesn't, hasn't, I'm, I've, I'd, won't, I'll, wouldn't, shouldn't, couldn't, they'd.

Chapter 15, Lesson 2, Practice 2: Put a slash to separate each run-on sentence below. Then, correct the run-on sentences by rewriting them as indicated by the labels in parentheses at the end of each sentence.

1. The robins gathered twigs **/** they built a nest. (SCV)
   The robins gathered twigs and built a nest.
2. The robins gathered twigs **/** they searched for worms also. (CD, but)
   The robins gathered twigs, but they searched for worms also.
3. The robins searched for worms **/** the chickens searched for worms. (SCS)
   The robins and chickens searched for worms.

Chapter 15, Lesson 2, Practice 3: Identify each kind of sentence by writing the abbreviation in the blank. (S, F, SCS, SCV, CD)

   SCV 1. The actors danced and sang during the musical.
   CD 2. Travis watched the children, and Donna went to the mall.
   SCS 3. My aunt and uncle are missionaries in Russia.
   F 4. Moved to the north side of the city.
   CD 5. He likes to vacuum, and she likes to dust the furniture.

 VOCABULARY TIME

Assign Chapter 15, Vocabulary Words **#2** on page 9 in the Reference Section for students to define in their Vocabulary notebooks. Tell students they are to use a dictionary or thesaurus to look up the meanings of the vocabulary words. After they write each word and its meaning, students are to write a sentence using the vocabulary word.

Chapter 15, Vocabulary Words #2
(distant, remote, censor, permit)

© SHURLEY INSTRUCTIONAL MATERIALS, INC.

CHAPTER 15 LESSON 2 CONTINUED

ACTIVITY / ASSIGNMENT TIME

Have students use the directions below to create a **personality poem** that uses parts of speech. Have students create a **personality poem** for themselves and one for each family member and for a friend or other relative. (*Write the directions and the example below on the board for your students.*)

Directions for each line of a personality poem:

1. Write your first name.
2. Write two adjectives that describe your personality.
3. Write four words that describe your appearance.
   (*adjective, noun, adjective, noun*)
4. Write five nouns naming things you enjoy.
5. Write any descriptive word you choose about yourself.

Example:

Michelle
Bright, brainy
Brown eyes, beautiful smile
Tennis, biking, beaches, friends, jokes
Loveable

(End of lesson.)

© SHURLEY INSTRUCTIONAL MATERIALS, INC.

CHAPTER 15   LESSON 3

Objectives: Jingles, Grammar (Practice Sentences), Oral Contraction Review, Practice Exercise, and Activity.

 JINGLE TIME

Have students turn to the Jingle Section in their books and recite the previously-taught jingles.

 GRAMMAR TIME

First-Year Option: Put the Practice Sentences from the box below on the board or on notebook paper. Use these sentences as you practice the concepts that have been taught. For the greatest benefit, students must participate orally with the teacher. **Second-Year Option:** Have students classify the Practice Sentences independently on paper. Check students' sentences with the answers provided below. (*If you have the CDs for Practice Sentences, have students check their sentences with the CDs.*)

Chapter 15, Practice Sentences for Lesson 3
1. _____ Jennifer saved two seats in the movie theatre for her friends.
2. _____ My dad fixed the broken radio in his garage yesterday.

TEACHING SCRIPT FOR PRACTICING PATTERN 2 SENTENCES

We will practice classifying Pattern 2 sentences. We will classify the sentences together. Begin. (*You might have your students write the labels above the sentences at this time.*)

Question and Answer Flow for Sentence 1: Jennifer saved two seats in the movie theatre for her friends.

1. Who saved two seats in the movie theatre for her friends? Jennifer - SN
2. What is being said about Jennifer? Jennifer saved - V
3. Jennifer saved what? seats - verify the noun
4. Do seats mean the same thing as Jennifer? No.
5. Seats - DO
6. Saved - V-t
7. How many seats? two - Adj
8. In - P
9. In what? theatre - OP
10. What kind of theatre? movie - Adj
11. The - A
12. For - P
13. For whom? friends - OP
14. Whose friends? her - PPA
15. SN V-t DO P2 Check
16. Verb-transitive - Check again.
17. (In the movie theatre) - Prepositional phrase
18. (For her friends) - Prepositional phrase
19. Period, statement, declarative sentence
20. Go back to the verb - divide the complete subject from the complete predicate.

Classified Sentence:

SN   V-t   Adj DO   P A   Adj   OP   P PPA OP
SN V-t   Jennifer / saved two seats (in the movie theatre) (for her friends). **D**
DO P2

© SHURLEY INSTRUCTIONAL MATERIALS, INC.

CHAPTER 15 LESSON 3 CONTINUED

Question and Answer Flow for Sentence 2: My dad fixed the broken radio in his garage yesterday.

1. Who fixed the broken radio in his garage yesterday?
   dad - SN
2. What is being said about dad? dad fixed - V
3. Dad fixed what? radio - verify the noun
4. Does radio mean the same thing as dad? No.
5. Radio - DO
6. Fixed - V-t
7. What kind of radio? broken - Adj
8. The - A
9. In – P

10. In what? garage - OP
11. Whose garage? his - PPA
12. Fixed when? yesterday - Adv
13. Whose dad? my - PPA
14. SN V-t DO P2 Check
15. Verb-transitive - Check again.
16. (In his garage) - Prepositional phrase
17. Period, statement, declarative sentence
18. Go back to the verb - divide the complete subject from the complete predicate.

Classified Sentence:

```
                        PPA SN      V-t   A   Adj    DO   P PPA  OP        Adv
            SN  V-t     My  dad  /  fixed the broken radio (in his garage) yesterday.  D
            DO  P2
```

Oral Contraction Review

To develop listening skills, give students a review of contractions orally. In the first chart, repeat the contractions in bold and have students respond with the correct words that stand for each contraction. In the second chart, repeat the words and have students respond with the correct contractions.

Chart 1:

isn't - is not	**it's** - it is	**he's** - he is or he has	**they've** - they have
don't - do not	**hasn't** - has not	**aren't** - are not	**hadn't** - had not
who's - who is	**they'll** - they will	**we'll** - we will	**you're** - you are

Chart 2:

did not - didn't	**you would** - you'd	**they are** - they're	**we had** - we'd
I will - I'll	**could not** - couldn't	**she has** - she's	**she is** - she's
we would - we'd	**I would** - I'd	**that is** - that's	**you had** - you'd

 PRACTICE TIME

Have students turn to page 78 in the Practice Section of their book and find Chapter 15, Lesson 3, Practice (1-3). Go over the directions to make sure they understand what to do. Check and discuss the Practices after students have finished. (*Chapter 15, Lesson 3, Practice keys are given below and on the next page.*)

Chapter 15, Lesson 3, Practice 1: Copy the following words on another sheet of paper. Write the correct contraction beside each word. **Key: I'm, he's, it's, that's, there's, you're, they're, weren't, doesn't, can't, hasn't, she's, haven't, you've, they've, I'd, he'd, you'd, they'd, I'll, she'll, we'll, we'd, shouldn't, couldn't.**

Words: I am, he is, it is, that is, there is, you are, they are, were not, does not, cannot, has not, she has, have not, you have, they have, I would, he had, you had, they had, I will, she will, we will, we would, should not, could not.

© SHURLEY INSTRUCTIONAL MATERIALS, INC.

CHAPTER 15 LESSON 3 CONTINUED

Chapter 15, Lesson 3, Practice 2: Put a slash to separate each run-on sentence below. Then, correct the run-on sentences by rewriting them as indicated by the labels in parentheses at the end of each sentence.

1. Tyler tripped on the power cord / he bruised both of his knees. (SCV)
   Tyler tripped on the power cord and bruised both of his knees.
2. Tyler tripped on the power cord / he didn't turn over the television. (CD, but)
   Tyler tripped on the power cord, but he didn't turn over the television.
3. Tyler tripped on the power cord / Ginger tripped on the power cord. (SCS)
   Tyler and Ginger tripped on the power cord.

Chapter 15, Lesson 3, Practice 3: Identify each kind of sentence by writing the abbreviation in the blank. (S, F, SCS, SCV, CD)

   SCV 1. The raccoon ducked and dodged the highway traffic.
   CD 2. Jeremy raked the leaves, and Henry mowed the lawn.
   SCS 3. Julie's brother and sister are twins.
   F 4. Watched as the clouds floated by.
   CD 5. I like chocolate, and Rebecca likes vanilla.

ACTIVITY / ASSIGNMENT TIME

The **limerick** is a popular type of rhymed poem consisting of five lines. It was popularized in the United States by the poet Ogden Nash. The intent of the **limerick** is to evoke a smile or chuckle in the reader. Almost all **limericks** are humorous and are fun to write. The rules are simple. The first, second, and fifth lines contain three accents and rhyme with each other. The third and fourth lines contain two accents and rhyme with each other. Read and discuss the example below. Have students write their own limerick and then share it with others.

> When Arnold forgot his math,
> It aroused his mother's wrath.
> She fed him clam chowder;
> He complained even louder,
> So she sent him upstairs for a bath.

(End of lesson.)

© SHURLEY INSTRUCTIONAL MATERIALS, INC.

CHAPTER 15   LESSON 4

Objectives: Jingles, Study, Test, Check, Activity, and Writing (journal).

JINGLE TIME

Have students turn to the Jingle Section in their books and recite the previously-taught jingles.

STUDY TIME

Have students study the vocabulary words in their vocabulary notebooks. Remind students that any vocabulary word in their notebooks could be on their test. Also, have students study any of the skills in the Practice Section that they need to review.

TEST TIME

Have students turn to page 111 in the Test Section of their book and find Chapter 15 Test. Go over the directions to make sure they understand what to do. (*Chapter 15 Test key is on the next page.*)

CHECK TIME

After students have finished, check and discuss their test papers. Make sure they understand why their answers are right or wrong. (*For total points, count each required answer as a point.*)

ACTIVITY / ASSIGNMENT TIME

Students will continue to draw or trace the states and write the following questions and answers.

Massachusetts	Michigan
1. What is the state on the front of this card? **Massachusetts**	1. What is the state on the front of this card? **Michigan**
2. What is the capital of Massachusetts? **Boston**	2. What is the capital of Michigan? **Lansing**
3. What is the postal abbreviation of Massachusetts? **MA**	3. What is the postal abbreviation of Michigan? **MI**
4. What year was Massachusetts admitted to the Union? **1788**	4. What year was Michigan admitted to the Union? **1837**

Color these states and look up an interesting fact about each state to write on the cards. Use the cards to quiz family members, friends, and relatives. You may want to time the responses to your questions. Also, along with previous suggestions, think of other ways to have fun with your United States card file.

(End of lesson.)

© SHURLEY INSTRUCTIONAL MATERIALS, INC.

Chapter 15 Test
(Student Page 111)

Exercise 1: Classify each sentence.

```
         CSN   C   CSN   HV   V-t   A   DO   Adv   P  A    OP    P   A    OP
1. SN V-t      Tommy and Daniel / have landed the plane safely (on the runway) (at the airport).  D
   DO P2
   (You) SP       V-t  A   CDO   C   CDO   P  OP
2. SN V-t      / Pass the peanuts and popcorn (to me).  Imp
   DO P2
```

Exercise 2: Use Sentence 2 to underline the complete subject once and the complete predicate twice and to complete the table below.

List the Noun Used	List the Noun Job	Singular or Plural	Common or Proper	Simple Subject	Simple Predicate
1. peanuts	2. CDO	3. P	4. C	5. you	6. pass
7. popcorn	8. CDO	9. S	10. C		

Exercise 3: Identify each pair of words as synonyms or antonyms by putting parentheses ( ) around *syn* or *ant*.

1. disease, illness	**(syn)** ant	4. cover, wrap	**(syn)** ant	7. smart, intelligent	**(syn)** ant
2. censor, permit	syn **(ant)**	5. distant, remote	**(syn)** ant	8. hidden, concealed	**(syn)** ant
3. famous, obscure	syn **(ant)**	6. occupied, vacant	syn **(ant)**	9. gorgeous, unsightly	syn **(ant)**

Exercise 4: Put a slash to separate each run-on sentence below. Then, correct the run-on sentences by rewriting them on notebook paper as indicated by the labels in parentheses at the end of each sentence.

1. The birds are flying south / they cover the sky. (CD, and)
   The birds are flying south, and they cover the sky.
2. Erin studied for the exam / Jack studied for the exam. (SCS)
   Erin and Jack studied for the exam.
3. The girls sat at the kitchen table / they ate banana splits. (SCV)
   The girls sat at the kitchen table and ate banana splits.
4. The artist made many sculptures / he did not sell them at the market. (CD, but)
   The artist made many sculptures, but did not sell them at the market.

Exercise 5: Identify each kind of sentence by writing the abbreviation in the blank. (S, F, SCS, SCV, CD).

SCS	1.	Tina and Jerry ran to catch the bus.
SCV	2.	The car put on its blinker and turned off the highway.
F	3.	Wading in the creek behind my grandmother's house.
SCV	4.	The customers waited in line and paid their bills.
CD	5.	The young lady carried her briefcase, but she forgot her keys.
S	6.	The frog jumped onto the lily pad.
CD	7.	Joe quickly went to the bank, and he made a large deposit for his company.

Exercise 6: Copy the following words on notebook paper. Write the correct contraction beside each word. **Key: can't, let's, don't, wasn't, they're, aren't, hadn't, isn't, she's, who's, you're, didn't, it's, we're, weren't, doesn't, hasn't, I'm, I've, I'd, won't, I'll, wouldn't, I'd, shouldn't, couldn't, they'd.**
Words: cannot, let us, do not, was not, they are, are not, had not, is not, she is, who is, you are, did not, it is, we are, were not, does not, has not, I am, I have, I had, will not, I will, would not, I would, should not, could not, they would.

Exercise 7: In your journal, write a paragraph summarizing what you have learned this week.

© SHURLEY INSTRUCTIONAL MATERIALS, INC.

CHAPTER 15 LESSON 4 CONTINUED

TEACHER INSTRUCTIONS

Use the Question and Answer Flows below for the sentences on the Chapter 15 Test.

Question and Answer Flow for Sentence 1: Tommy and Daniel have landed the plane safely on the runway at the airport.

1. Who have landed the plane safely on the runway at the airport? Tommy and Daniel - CSN, CSN
2. What is being said about Tommy and Daniel? Tommy and Daniel have landed - V
3. Have - HV
4. Tommy and Daniel have landed what? plane - verify the noun
5. Does plane mean the same thing as Tommy and Daniel? No.
6. Plane - DO
7. Landed - V-t
8. The - A
9. Landed how? safely - Adv
10. On - P
11. On what? runway - OP
12. The - A
13. At - P
14. At what? airport - OP
15. The - A
16. And - C
17. SN V-t DO P2 Check
18. Verb-transitive - Check again.
19. (On the runway) - Prepositional phrase
20. (At the airport) - Prepositional phrase
21. Period, statement, declarative sentence
22. Go back to the verb - divide the complete subject from the complete predicate.

Classified Sentence:		CSN	C	CSN	HV	V-t	A	DO	Adv	P	A	OP	P	A	OP
SN V-t **DO P2**	Tommy and Daniel **/** have landed the plane safely (on the runway) (at the airport). **D**

Question and Answer Flow for Sentence 2: Pass the peanuts and popcorn to me.

1. Who pass the peanuts and popcorn to me? you - SP (understood subject pronoun)
2. What is being said about you? you pass - V
3. You pass what? peanuts and popcorn - verify the nouns
4. Do peanuts and popcorn mean the same thing as you? No.
5. Peanuts and popcorn - CDO, CDO
6. Pass - V-t
7. The - A
8. And - C
9. To - P
10. To whom? me - OP
11. SN V-t DO P2 Check
12. Verb-transitive - Check again.
13. (To me) - Prepositional phrase
14. Period, command, imperative sentence
15. Go back to the verb - divide the complete subject from the complete predicate.

Classified Sentence:	(You) SP	V-t	A	CDO	C	CDO	P	OP
SN V-t **DO P2**	**/** Pass the peanuts and popcorn (to me). **Imp**

© SHURLEY INSTRUCTIONAL MATERIALS, INC.

CHAPTER 15   LESSON 5

Objectives: Writing Assignments #14 and #15, Bonus Option.

 WRITING TIME

TEACHING SCRIPT FOR PRACTICING DIFFERENT KINDS OF WRITING

Today, you are assigned two different kinds of writing. You will write a three-paragraph persuasive essay and a three-point expository paragraph. <u>You will revise and edit the three-paragraph persuasive essay</u>. (*Read the box below for more information about students' writing assignment*.) As you edit, make sure you use the checkpoints in the editing checklist provided in Reference 42. Remember to read through the whole essay, starting with the title, and then edit, sentence-by-sentence, using the five-sentence checkpoints for each sentence. Use the paragraph checkpoints to check each paragraph.

Writing Assignment Box #1

Writing Assignment #14: Three-Paragraph Persuasive Essay

Remind students that the 3-paragraph essay has three parts: 1. Introduction 2. Body 3. Conclusion. Have students use their regular editing checklist to edit this assignment.

Writing topics: Why Everyone Should Have A Pet or **Why You Should Keep Promises** or
       Why Memorizing Bible Verses Is Important

Your second writing assignment is to write a three-point expository paragraph. (*Read the box below for more information about students' writing assignment*.) You do not have to edit this assignment with the editing checklist.

Writing Assignment Box #2

Writing Assignment #15: Three-Point Expository Paragraph

Writing topics: Big Events In My Life or **Reptiles I Dislike** or   **Why Cheating Does Not Pay**

<u>**Bonus Option:**</u> **How many books are in the Old Testament? Look up all the books of the Old Testament and list them in your Journal. Next, create a word search that contains all the books of the Old Testament. Be careful to spell all the names correctly. Give the word search to a family member to complete. Make a key so you can check the finished word search. (Show students how to do a word search if they do not know how.)**

Read, check, and discuss Writing Assignment #14 after students have finished their final papers. Use the checklists as you check and discuss students' papers. Make sure students are using the regular editing checklist correctly. Read and discuss Writing Assignment #15 for fun and enrichment.

Bonus Option Answer: *There are 39 books in the Old Testament.*

(End of lesson.)

© SHURLEY INSTRUCTIONAL MATERIALS, INC.

CHAPTER 16   LESSON 1

Objectives: Jingles, Grammar (Practice Sentences), Oral Skill Builder Check, Skill (linking verbs), Practice Exercise, and Vocabulary #1.

 JINGLE TIME

Have students turn to the Jingle Section in their books and recite the previously-taught jingles.

 GRAMMAR TIME

First-Year Option: Put the Practice Sentences from the box below on the board or on notebook paper. Use these sentences as you practice the concepts that have been taught. For the greatest benefit, students must participate orally with the teacher. **Second-Year Option:** Have students classify the Practice Sentences independently on paper. Check students' sentences with the answers provided below. (*If you have the CDs for Practice Sentences, have students check their sentences with the CDs.*)

Chapter 16, Practice Sentences for Lesson 1
1. _____ The evil pirates buried the treasure chest on an unknown island.
2. _____ The clever thief stole a television from the store.

TEACHING SCRIPT FOR PRACTICING PATTERN 2 SENTENCES

We will practice classifying Pattern 2 sentences. We will classify the sentences together. Begin. (*You might have your child write the labels above the sentences at this time.*)

Question and Answer Flow for Sentence 1: The evil pirates buried the treasure chest on an unknown island.

1. Who buried the treasure chest on an unknown island? pirates - SN
2. What is being said about pirates? pirates buried - V
3. Pirates buried what? chest - verify the noun
4. Does chest mean the same thing as pirates? No.
5. Chest - DO
6. Buried - V-t
7. What kind of chest? treasure - Adj
8. The - A
9. On - P
10. On what? island - OP
11. What kind of island? unknown - Adj
12. An - A
13. What kind of pirates? evil - Adj
14. The - A
15. SN V-t DO P2 Check
16. Verb-transitive - Check again.
17. (On an unknown island) - Prepositional phrase
18. Period, statement, declarative sentence
19. Go back to the verb - divide the complete subject from the complete predicate.

Classified Sentence:

```
                    A   Adj  SN      V-t  A   Adj    DO   P  A   Adj     OP
          SN  V-t   The evil pirates / buried the treasure chest (on an unknown island).  D
          DO  P2
```

© SHURLEY INSTRUCTIONAL MATERIALS, INC.

CHAPTER 16 LESSON 1 CONTINUED

Question and Answer Flow for Sentence 2: The clever thief stole a television from the store.	
1. Who stole a television from the store? thief - SN	10. The - A
2. What is being said about thief? thief stole - V	11. What kind of thief? clever - Adj
3. Thief stole what? television - verify the noun	12. The - A
4. Does television mean the same thing as thief? No.	13. SN V-t DO P2 Check
5. Television - DO	14. Verb-transitive - Check again.
6. Stole - V-t	15. (From the store) - Prepositional phrase
7. A - A	16. Period, statement, declarative sentence
8. From - P	17. Go back to the verb - divide the complete subject
9. From what? store - OP	from the complete predicate.

Classified Sentence:

```
                              A   Adj  SN   V-t  A   DO      P   A   OP
          SN  V-t     The clever thief / stole a television (from the store).  D
          DO  P2
```

Use Sentences 1-2 that you just classified with your students to do an Oral Skill Builder Check. Use the guidelines below.

Oral Skill Builder Check	
1. **Noun check.** (Say the job and then say the noun. Circle each noun.)	5. **Identify the complete subject and the complete predicate.** (Underline the complete subject once and the complete predicate twice.)
2. **Identify the nouns as singular or plural.** (Write S or P above each noun.)	
3. **Identify the nouns as common or proper.** (Follow established procedure for oral identification.)	6. **Identify the simple subject and simple predicate.** (Underline the simple subject once and the simple predicate twice. Bold, or highlight, the lines.)
4. **Do a vocabulary check.** (Follow established procedure for oral identification.)	7. **Recite the irregular verb chart.** (Located on student page 25 and teacher page 163.)

SKILL TIME

TEACHING SCRIPT FOR LINKING VERBS

The verbs that you have studied in Patterns 1-2 are action verbs because they show what the subjects do. Today, you will study a new kind of verb called a linking verb. This verb does not show action. The linking verb does exactly what its name says it does: it links, or connects, a word in the predicate to the subject of the sentence. Turn to Reference 50 on page 40 in the Reference Section of your book. Follow along as I read about how to identify linking verbs. (*Reference 50 is located on the next page.*)

© SHURLEY INSTRUCTIONAL MATERIALS, INC.

CHAPTER 16 LESSON 1 CONTINUED

Reference 50: Linking Verbs

An action verb shows action. It tells what the subject does. A linking verb does not show action. It does not tell what the subject does. A linking verb is called a state of being verb because it tells **what the subject is or is like**. A **linking verb** is identified with the abbreviation **LV**. To decide if a verb is linking or action, remember these two things:

1. A linking verb connects the subject to a noun in the predicate that means the same thing as the subject.

A predicate noun is a noun in the predicate that means the same thing as the subject. The subject and predicate noun are connected by a linking verb. A **predicate noun** is identified with the abbreviation **PrN**.

(Mrs. Land is the <u>teacher</u>.)   *(<u>They</u> are the <u>actors</u>.)*   *(<u>Sue</u> is the <u>friend</u>.)*   *(<u>Uncle</u> is the <u>mayor</u>.)*

SN   LV   PrN   SP LV   PrN   SN LV   PrN   SN LV   PrN
<u>Mrs. Land</u> **is** my (teacher).   <u>They</u> **are** famous (actors).   <u>Sue</u> **is** my new (friend).   My <u>uncle</u> **is** the town (mayor).

2. A linking verb connects the subject to an adjective in the predicate that describes the subject.

A predicate adjective is an adjective in the predicate that describes the subject. The subject and predicate adjective are connected by a linking verb. A **predicate adjective** is identified with the abbreviation **PA**.

(What kind of tree? tall)   *(What kind of Kay? thirsty)* *(What kind of apple? red)*   *(What kind of they? envious)*

SN LV PA   SN LV   PA   SN LV PA   SP   LV   PA
The <u>tree</u> **is** (tall).   <u>Kay</u> **was** (thirsty).   The <u>apple</u> **is** (red).   <u>They</u> **were** very (envious).

These are the <u>most common</u> linking verbs: *am, is, are, was, were, be, been, seem, become.*
These <u>sensory verbs</u> can be linking or action: *taste, sound, smell, feel, look.*

A good rule to follow:
If a sentence has a predicate noun (PrN) or a predicate adjective (PA), it has a linking verb.
If a sentence <u>does not have</u> a predicate noun (PrN) or a predicate adjective (PA), it probably has an action verb.

Example: Underline each subject and fill in each column according to the title.

	List each Verb	Write PrN, PA, or None	Write L or A
1. The <u>roads</u> are wet.	are	PA	L
2. The <u>train</u> moves quickly down the rails.	moves	None	A
3. <u>Terra</u> is my new roommate.	is	PrN	L
4. The <u>gnat</u> is buzzing my ear.	is buzzing	None	A

PRACTICE TIME

Have students turn to page 79 in the Practice Section of their book and find the instructions under Chapter 16, Lesson 1, Practice *(1-2)*. Go over the directions to make sure they understand what to do. If students need a review, have them study the information in the Reference Section of their books. Check and discuss the Practices after students have finished. *(Chapter 16, Lesson 1, Practice keys are on the next page.)*

© SHURLEY INSTRUCTIONAL MATERIALS, INC.

Chapter 16, Lesson 1, Practice 1: Underline each subject and fill in each column according to the title.

	List each Verb	Write PrN, PA, or None	Write L or A
1. Those <u>lemons</u> are sour.	are	PA	L
2. My new <u>car</u> is beautiful.	is	PA	L
3. <u>They</u> listened to the presenter.	listened	None	A
4. <u>Tigers</u> are fierce creatures.	are	PrN	L
5. <u>She</u> is our new mayor.	is	PrN	L
6. All the <u>dishes</u> are dirty.	are	PA	L
7. That <u>song</u> was very popular.	was	PA	L
8. <u>Sally</u> marched in the parade.	marched	None	A
9. <u>They</u> visited the new stadium.	visited	None	A
10. <u>Patrick</u> is a good athlete.	is	PrN	L'
11. My <u>sister</u> is mowing the lawn.	is mowing	None	A
12. <u>Denver</u> is a very large city.	is	PrN	L
13. The <u>river</u> was beautiful.	was	PA	L
14. <u>Kelly</u> is the youngest child.	is	PrN	L
15. <u>Oliver</u> is my pet iguana.	is	PrN	L

Chapter 16, Lesson 1, Practice 2: Copy the following words on another sheet of paper. Write the correct contraction beside each word. **Key: shouldn't, they'll, won't, we'd, haven't, I've, she's, let's, can't, don't, we're, what's, it's, isn't, I'm.**
<u>Words</u>: Should not, they will, will not, we had, have not, I have, she is, let us, cannot, do not, we are, what is, it is, is not, I am.

VOCABULARY TIME

Assign Chapter 16, Vocabulary Words **#1** on page 9 in the Reference Section for students to define in their Vocabulary notebooks. Tell students they are to use a dictionary or thesaurus to look up the meanings of the vocabulary words. After they write each word and its meaning, students are to write a sentence using the vocabulary word.

Chapter 16, Vocabulary Words #1
(pretend, imagine, plentiful, sparse)

(End of lesson.)

Level 3 Homeschool Teacher's Manual

© SHURLEY INSTRUCTIONAL MATERIALS, INC.

<table><tr><td colspan="2">CHAPTER 16   LESSON 2</td></tr>
<tr><td colspan="2">Objectives: Jingles, Grammar (Practice Sentences), Skills (similes and metaphors), Bonus Option, Practice Exercise, and Vocabulary #2.</td></tr></table>

JINGLE TIME

Have students turn to the Jingle Section in their books and recite the previously-taught jingles.

GRAMMAR TIME

Put the Practice Sentences from the box below on the board. Use these sentences as you practice the concepts that have been taught. For the greatest benefit, students must participate orally with the teacher. (*You might put the Practice Sentences on notebook paper if you are doing one-on-one instruction with your child.*)

Chapter 16, Practice Sentences for Lesson 2
1. _____ Would you like a thin slice of cheese on your sandwich?
2. _____ Wow! He drank two glasses of water in thirty seconds!

TEACHING SCRIPT FOR PRACTICING PATTERN 2 SENTENCES

We will practice classifying Pattern 2 sentences. We will classify the sentences together. Begin. (*You might have your child write the labels above the sentences at this time.*)

Question and Answer Flow for Sentence 1: Would you like a thin slice of cheese on your sandwich?	
1. Who would like a thin slice of cheese on your sandwich? you - SP	11. Of what? cheese - OP
2. What is being said about you? you would like - V	12. On - P
3. Would - HV	13. On what? sandwich - OP
4. You would like what? slice - verify the noun	14. Whose sandwich? your - PPA
5. Does slice mean the same thing as you? No.	15. SN V-t DO P2 Check
6. Slice - DO	16. Verb-transitive - Check again.
7. Like - V-t	17. (Of cheese) - Prepositional phrase
8. What kind of slice? thin - Adj	18. (On your sandwich) - Prepositional phrase
9. A - A	19. Question mark, question, interrogative sentence
10. Of - P	20. Go back to the verb - divide the complete subject from the complete predicate.

Classified Sentence:

```
              HV  SP  V-t A Adj DO   P   OP    P PPA  OP
    SN V-t    Would you / like a thin slice (of cheese) (on your sandwich)? Int
    DO P2
```

CHAPTER 16 LESSON 2 CONTINUED

Question and Answer Flow for Sentence 2: Wow! He drank two glasses of water in thirty seconds!

1. Who drank two glasses of water in thirty seconds? he - SP
2. What is being said about he? he drank - V
3. He drank what? glasses - verify the noun
4. Do glasses mean the same thing as he? No.
5. Glasses - DO
6. Drank - V-t
7. How many glasses? two - Adj
8. Of - P
9. Of what? water - OP
10. In - P
11. In what? seconds - OP
12. How many seconds? thirty - Adj
13. Wow - I
14. SN V-t DO P2 Check
15. Verb-transitive - Check again.
16. (Of water) - Prepositional phrase
17. (In thirty seconds) - Prepositional phrase
18. Exclamation point, strong feeling, exclamatory sentence
19. Go back to the verb - divide the complete subject from the complete predicate.

Classified Sentence:

                               I   SP   V-t Adj   DO   P   OP   P Adj   OP

<u> SN V-t </u>   Wow! He / drank two glasses (of water) (in thirty seconds)! **E**

  DO P2

SKILL TIME

TEACHING SCRIPT FOR SIMILES AND METAPHORS

Today, we will learn about similes and metaphors. Look at Reference 51 on page 41 in the Reference Section of your book. (*Read and discuss the following information about similes and metaphors.*)

Reference 51: Similes and Metaphors

When a writer uses words to draw a picture of two things that he is comparing, it is called a figure of speech. Two figures of speech that writers use most often are **simile** and **metaphor**.

<u>A simile</u> draws a picture by comparing one noun to another noun in the sentence using "like" or "as."

         Examples: Regina's glare was as cold as ice. Her smile was as bright as the sun.
                          His hands shook like leaves. The boys swing from the branches like monkeys.

<u>A metaphor</u> draws a picture by showing how two very different things can be alike. It will use linking verbs (*am, is, are, was, were*) to connect the noun in the predicate to the subject.

         Examples: Her homemade chili was fire that burned in my stomach.
                          The snow is a blanket on our lawn.

TEACHER INSTRUCTIONS

Guide students in the practice exercises. **Bonus Option:** Write and share a short story using similes and metaphors.

© SHURLEY INSTRUCTIONAL MATERIALS, INC.

CHAPTER 16 LESSON 2 CONTINUED

PRACTICE TIME

Have students turn to pages 79 and 80 in the Practice Section of their book and find the instructions under Chapter 16, Lesson 2, Practice (*1-3*). Go over the directions to make sure they understand what to do. Check and discuss the Practices after students have finished. (*Chapter 16, Lesson 2, Practice keys are below*.)

Chapter 16, Lesson 2, Practice 1: Tell whether each sentence is an example of a simile or a metaphor by writing *like* or *as* in the Simile column or by writing the noun in the predicate that renames the subject in the Metaphor column.

	Simile	Metaphor
1. My stomach fluttered like butterflies.	like	
2. The strong linebacker was a bulldozer.		bulldozer
3. Her voice was as sweet as sugar.	as	
4. The young American swimmer was a fish.		fish
5. We were so hungry that we ate like pigs.	like	

Chapter 16, Lesson 2, Practice 2: Underline each subject and fill in each column according to the title.

	List each Verb	Write PrN, PA, or None	Write L or A
1. My <u>brother</u> rode his bike to town.	rode	None	A
2. Her <u>essay</u> was exciting.	was	PA	L
3. My <u>mother</u> is an artist.	is	PrN	L
4. <u>Samantha</u> is my cousin.	is	PrN	L
5. The autumn <u>leaves</u> are yellow.	are	PA	L
6. My <u>brother</u> sold his guitar.	sold	None	A
7. We <u>went</u> to the mall yesterday.	went	None	A

Chapter 16, Lesson 2, Practice 3: Copy the following contractions on another sheet of paper. Write the correct word beside each contraction. **Key: has not, he is or he has, I have, they have, she had or she would, will not, she will, you will, could not, let us, cannot, does not, do not, were not, you are, there is, what is, who is, is not, I am.**
<u>Contractions</u>: hasn't, he's, I've, they've, she'd, won't, she'll, you'll, couldn't, let's, can't, doesn't, don't, weren't, you're, there's, what's, who's, isn't, I'm.

VOCABULARY TIME

Assign Chapter 16, Vocabulary Words **#2** on page 9 in the Reference Section for students to define in their Vocabulary notebooks. After they write each word and its meaning, students are to write a sentence using the vocabulary word. Have students study the vocabulary words when they have finished.

Chapter 16, Vocabulary Words #2
(sorrow, bliss, volunteer, offer)

(End of lesson.)

© SHURLEY INSTRUCTIONAL MATERIALS, INC.

CHAPTER 16   LESSON 3

Objectives: Jingles, Grammar (Practice Sentences), Oral Contraction Review, Practice Exercise, and Activity.

 **JINGLE TIME**

Have students turn to the Jingle Section in their books and recite the previously-taught jingles.

 GRAMMAR TIME

First-Year Option: Put the Practice Sentences from the box below on the board or on notebook paper. Use these sentences as you practice the concepts that have been taught. For the greatest benefit, students must participate orally with the teacher. **Second-Year Option:** Have students classify the Practice Sentences independently on paper. Check students' sentences with the answers provided below. (*If you have the CDs for Practice Sentences, have students check their sentences with the CDs.*)

Chapter 16, Practice Sentences for Lesson 3

1. _____ Martha and Jason will win the contest without a doubt.
2. _____ Can Karen reach the table easily with the new booster seat?

TEACHING SCRIPT FOR PRACTICING PATTERN 2 SENTENCES

We will practice classifying Pattern 2 sentences. We will classify the sentences together. Begin. (*You might have your students write the labels above the sentences at this time.*)

Question and Answer Flow for Sentence 1:   Martha and Jason will win the contest without a doubt.

1. Who will win the contest without a doubt?
   Martha and Jason - CSN, CSN
2. What is being said about Martha and Jason?
   Martha and Jason will win - V
3. Will - HV
4. Martha and Jason will win what? contest - verify the noun
5. Does contest mean the same thing as Martha and Jason?
   No.
6. Contest - DO
7. Win - V-t
8. The - A

9. Without - P
10. Without what? doubt - OP
11. A - A
12. And - C
13. SN V-t DO P2 Check
14. Verb-transitive - Check again.
15. (Without a doubt) - Prepositional phrase
16. Period, statement, declarative sentence
17. Go back to the verb - divide the complete subject
    from the complete predicate.

Classified Sentence:

                  CSN   C   CSN   HV V-t A   DO   P   A OP

<u> SN V-t </u> Martha and Jason / will win the contest (without a doubt). **D**

  DO P2

© SHURLEY INSTRUCTIONAL MATERIALS, INC.

Question and Answer Flow for Sentence 2: Can Karen reach the table easily with the new booster seat?

1. Who can reach the table easily with the new booster seat? Karen - SN
2. What is being said about Karen? Karen can reach - V
3. Can - HV
4. Karen can reach what? table - verify the noun
5. Does table mean the same thing as Karen? No.
6. Table - DO
7. Reach - V-t
8. The - A
9. Reach how? easily - Adv
10. With - P
11. With what? seat - OP
12. What kind of seat? booster - Adj
13. What kind of seat? new - Adj
14. The - A
15. SN V-t DO P2 Check
16. Verb-transitive - Check again.
17. (With the new booster seat) - Prepositional phrase
18. Question mark, question, interrogative sentence
19. Go back to the verb - divide the complete subject from the complete predicate.

Classified Sentence:

	HV	SN	V-t	A	DO	Adv	P	A	Adj	Adj	OP

SN V-t / Can Karen / reach the table easily (with the new booster seat)? Int
DO P2

Oral Contraction Review

To develop listening skills, give students a review of contractions orally. In the first chart, repeat the contractions in bold and have students respond with the correct words that stand for each contraction. In the second chart, repeat the words and have students respond with the correct contractions.

Chart 1:

won't - will not	**weren't** - were not	**can't** - cannot	**haven't** - have not
you're - you are	**what's** - what is	**let's** - let us	**she'll** - she will
don't - do not	**I'm** - I am	**hasn't** - has not	**shouldn't** - should not

Chart 2:

they would - they'd	**would not** - wouldn't	**we had** - we'd	**are not** - aren't
I will - I'll	**who is** - who's	**they had** - they'd	**does not** - doesn't
it is - it's	**was not** - wasn't	**is not** - isn't	**we would** - we'd

 PRACTICE TIME

Have students turn to pages 80 and 81 in the Practice Section of their book and find the instructions under Chapter 16, Lesson 3, Practice (*1-3*). Go over the directions to make sure they understand what to do. Check and discuss the Practices after students have finished. (*Chapter 16, Lesson 3, Practice keys are below and on the next page.*)

Chapter 16, Lesson 3, Practice 1: Copy the following words on another sheet of paper. Write the correct contraction beside each word. **Key: let's, doesn't, don't, wasn't, aren't, there's, that's, it's, isn't, shouldn't, wouldn't, you'd, they'd, hadn't, they've, haven't, hasn't, he's, you're, who's.**
Words: let us, does not, do not, was not, are not, there is, that is, it is, is not, should not, would not, you would, they had, had not, they have, have not, has not, he has, you are, who is.

CHAPTER 16 LESSON 3 CONTINUED

Chapter 16, Lesson 3, Practice 2: Tell whether each sentence is an example of a simile or a metaphor by writing *like* or *as* in the Simile column or by writing the noun in the predicate that renames the subject in the Metaphor column.

	Simile	Metaphor
1. Kindness is the fruit of human understanding.		fruit
2. His patience wore as thin as gift wrap.	as	
3. The storm clouds came like a thief in the night.	like	
4. My neighbor's baby is a little angel.		angel
5. The climber scaled the slope like a mountain goat.	like	

Chapter 16, Lesson 3, Practice 3: Underline each subject and fill in each column according to the title.

	List each Verb	Write PrN, PA, or None	Write L or A
1. The <u>vegetables</u> are fresh.	are	PA	L
2. His <u>hometown</u> is small.	is	PA	L
3. <u>They</u> passed by the new shops.	passed	None	A
4. <u>Bats</u> are my favorite animal.	are	PrN	L
5. <u>He</u> is my youngest brother.	is	PrN	L
6. Some of the <u>pieces</u> are missing.	are	PA	L
7. <u>I</u> watched my favorite movie.	watched	None	A

 ACTIVITY / ASSIGNMENT TIME

Read and discuss the example below of a color poem containing similes with your students. Have them follow the directions given to write their own color poem. (*Write the sample poem and directions on the board.*)

1. Choose a color for a title.
2. Write similes using *like* or *as*. Write one line for each of the five senses below:
   sight
   smell
   taste
   hearing
   touch

Orange

Looks like jack-o-lanterns on windowsills
Smells like a freshly-baked pumpkin pie
Tastes as sweet as Caramel apples
Sounds like the whisper of autumn leaves
And feels as bright as a morning sun.

(End of lesson.)

© SHURLEY INSTRUCTIONAL MATERIALS, INC.

CHAPTER 16   LESSON 4

Objectives: Jingles, Study, Test, Check, Activity and Writing (journal).

JINGLE TIME

Have students turn to the Jingle Section in their books and recite the previously-taught jingles.

STUDY TIME

Have students study the vocabulary words in their vocabulary notebooks. Remind students that any vocabulary word in their notebooks could be on their test. Also, have students study any of the skills in the Practice Section that they need to review.

TEST TIME

Have students turn to page 112 in the Test Section of their book and find Chapter 16 Test. Go over the directions to make sure they understand what to do. (*Chapter 16 Test key is on the next page.*)

CHECK TIME

After students have finished, check and discuss their test papers. Make sure they understand why their answers are right or wrong. (*For total points, count each required answer as a point.*)

ACTIVITY / ASSIGNMENT TIME

Students will continue to draw or trace the states and write the following questions and answers.

Minnesota	Mississippi
1. What is the state on the front of this card? **Minnesota**	1. What is the state on the front of this card? **Mississippi**
2. What is the capital of Minnesota? **St. Paul**	2. What is the capital of Mississippi? **Jackson**
3. What is the postal abbreviation of Minnesota? **MN**	3. What is the postal abbreviation of Mississippi? **MS**
4. What year was Minnesota admitted to the Union? **1858**	4. What year was Mississippi admitted to the Union? **1817**

Color these states and look up an interesting fact about each state to write on the cards. Use the cards to quiz family members, friends, and relatives. You may want to time the responses to your questions. Also, along with previous suggestions, think of other ways to have fun with your United States card file.

(End of lesson.)

© SHURLEY INSTRUCTIONAL MATERIALS, INC.

Chapter 16 Test
(Student Page 112)

Exercise 1: Classify each sentence.

```
           I   A   Adj   Adj    SN      V-t   PPA   Adj   DO    P  A    Adj      OP
1. SN V-t   Yikes! The three ferocious beasts / showed their sharp fangs (to the dangerous cougar)!  E
   ──────
   DO P2

           SP  HV  V-t  CAdj  C  CAdj   DO    P  A  OP
2. SN V-t   We / are taking ham and cheese sandwiches (on the picnic).  D
   ──────
   DO P2
```

Exercise 2: Use Sentence 1 to underline the complete subject once and the complete predicate twice and to complete the table below.

List the Noun Used	List the Noun Job	Singular or Plural	Common or Proper	Simple Subject	Simple Predicate
1. **beasts**	2. **SN**	3. **P**	4. **C**	5. **beasts**	6. **showed**
7. **fangs**	8. **DO**	9. **P**	10. **C**		
11. **cougar**	12. **OP**	13. **S**	14. **C**		

Exercise 3: Identify each pair of words as synonyms or antonyms by putting parentheses ( ) around *syn* or *ant*.

1. offer, volunteer	**(syn)** ant	4. pretend, imagine	**(syn)** ant	7. sparse, plentiful	syn	**(ant)**
2. distant, remote	**(syn)** ant	5. fear, courage	syn **(ant)**	8. consistent, irregular	syn	**(ant)**
3. sorrow, bliss	syn **(ant)**	6. hidden, concealed	**(syn)** ant	9. occupied, vacant	syn	**(ant)**

Exercise 4: Tell whether each sentence contains a simile or a metaphor by writing *like* or *as* in the Simile column or by writing the noun in the predicate that renames the subject in the Metaphor column.

	Simile	Metaphor
1. My uncle is as unpredictable as the weather.	**as**	
2. My cousin is a walking encyclopedia.		**encyclopedia**
3. My father is a bear before his morning coffee.		**bear**
4. Shelly looked like an angel in the morning light.	**like**	
5. My brother stood as still as a statue.	**as**	

Exercise 5: Underline each subject and fill in each column according to the title.

	List each Verb	Write PrN, PA, or None	Write L or A
1. <u>Bats</u> are mammals.	**are**	**PrN**	**L**
2. <u>Sirens</u> screamed across town.	**screamed**	**None**	**A**
3. Our <u>daughter</u> is the class treasurer.	**is**	**PrN**	**L**
4. His new <u>shirt</u> is torn.	**is**	**PA**	**L**
5. The <u>mailman</u> was friendly yesterday.	**was**	**PA**	**L**
6. Her <u>hair</u> is too curly.	**is**	**PA**	**L**

Exercise 6: On notebook paper, write one sentence for each of these labels: (SCS), (SCV), (CD). **(Answers will vary.)**

Exercise 7: In your journal, write a paragraph summarizing what you have learned this week.

© SHURLEY INSTRUCTIONAL MATERIALS, INC.

CHAPTER 16 LESSON 4 CONTINUED

TEACHER INSTRUCTIONS

Use the Question and Answer Flows below for the sentences on the Chapter 16 Test.

Question and Answer Flow for Sentence 1: Yikes! The three ferocious beasts showed their sharp fangs to the dangerous cougar!

1. Who showed their sharp fangs to the dangerous cougar? beasts - SN
2. What is being said about beasts? beasts showed - V
3. Beasts showed what? fangs - verify the noun
4. Do fangs mean the same thing as beasts? No.
5. Fangs - DO
6. Showed - V-t
7. What kind of fangs? sharp - Adj
8. Whose fangs? their - PPA
9. To - P
10. To what? cougar - OP
11. What kind of cougar? dangerous - Adj
12. The - A
13. What kind of beasts? ferocious - Adj
14. How many beasts? three - Adj
15. The - A
16. Yikes - I
17. SN V-t DO P2 Check
18. Verb-transitive - Check again.
19. (To the dangerous cougar) - Prepositional phrase
20. Exclamation point, strong feeling, exclamatory sentence
21. Go back to the verb - divide the complete subject from the complete predicate.

Classified Sentence:

| | I | A | Adj | Adj | SN | V-t | PPA | Adj | DO | P | A | Adj | OP |

SN V-t / DO P2   Yikes! The three ferocious beasts **/** showed their sharp fangs (to the dangerous cougar)! **E**

Question and Answer Flow for Sentence 2: We are taking ham and cheese sandwiches on the picnic.

1. Who are taking ham and cheese sandwiches on the picnic? we - SP
2. What is being said about we? we are taking - V
3. Are - HV
4. We are taking what? sandwiches - verify the noun
5. Do sandwiches mean the same thing as we? No.
6. Sandwiches - DO
7. Taking - V-t
8. What kind of sandwiches? ham and cheese - CAdj, CAdj
9. And - C
10. On - P
11. On what? picnic - OP
12. The - A
13. SN V-t DO P2 Check
14. Verb-transitive - Check again.
15. (On the picnic) - Prepositional phrase
16. Period, statement, declarative sentence
17. Go back to the verb - divide the complete subject from the complete predicate.

Classified Sentence:

| SP | HV | V-t | CAdj | C | CAdj | DO | P | A | OP |

SN V-t / DO P2   We **/** are taking ham and cheese sandwiches (on the picnic). **D**

CHAPTER 16   LESSON 5

Objectives: Writing Assignments #16 and #17, Bonus Option.

 WRITING TIME

TEACHING SCRIPT FOR PRACTICING DIFFERENT KINDS OF WRITING

Today, you are assigned two different kinds of writing. You will write a three-paragraph persuasive essay and a three-point expository paragraph. <u>You will revise and edit the three-paragraph persuasive essay.</u> (*Read the box below for more information about students' writing assignment.*) As you edit, make sure you use the checkpoints in the editing checklist provided in Reference 42. Remember to read through the whole essay, starting with the title, and then edit, sentence-by-sentence, using the five-sentence checkpoints for each sentence. Use the paragraph checkpoints to check each paragraph.

Writing Assignment Box #1

Writing Assignment #16: Three-Paragraph Persuasive Essay
Remind students that the 3-paragraph essay has three parts: 1. Introduction 2. Body 3. Conclusion. Have students use their regular editing checklist to edit this assignment.

Writing topics: Why I Should/Should Not Stay Home Alone or **Why I Should Have My Own Room** or
                   Reasons People Should Visit My State

Your second writing assignment is to write a three-point expository paragraph. (*Read the box below for more information about students' writing assignment.*) You do not have to edit this assignment with the editing checklist.

Writing Assignment Box #2

Writing Assignment #17: Three-Point Expository Paragraph

Writing topics: Three Important Things to Take Camping or **Things Money Cannot Buy** or **Favorite Books**

<u>Bonus Option</u>: The Bible uses similes and metaphors. Write the following verses. Tell whether each verse is an example of a simile or metaphor by writing S or M after each one. Find other examples and add them to your list.
    1. Psalms 119:105(KJV)   2. II Samuel 22:2(KJV)   3. Revelation 4:7(KJV)   4. Peter 1:24(KJV)

Read, check, and discuss Writing Assignment #16 after students have finished their final papers. Use the checklists as you check and discuss students' papers. Make sure students are using the regular editing checklist correctly. Read and discuss Writing Assignment #17 for fun and enrichment.

Bonus Option Answers: (1) Metaphor   (2) Metaphor   (3) Simile   (4) Simile

(End of lesson.)

© SHURLEY INSTRUCTIONAL MATERIALS, INC.

CHAPTER 17   LESSON 1
Objectives: Jingles, Grammar (Introductory Sentences), Oral Skill Builder Check, Skills (beginning quotes, ending quotes), Practice Exercise, and Vocabulary #1.

JINGLE TIME

Have students turn to the Jingle Section in their books and recite the previously-taught jingles.

GRAMMAR TIME

Put the introductory sentences from the box below on the board. Use these sentences as you go through each new concept covered in your teaching script. (*You might put the introductory sentences on notebook paper if you are doing one-on-one instruction with your students.*)

Chapter 17, Introductory Sentences for Lesson 1
1. _____ Go to the supermarket with Billy and me.
2. _____ That car did not stop at the traffic light.
3. _____ Yummy! Mother has cooked our favorite dinner tonight!

TEACHING SCRIPT FOR INTRODUCING MIXED PATTERNS

You have studied Pattern 1 and Pattern 2 separately. Today, we will mix up the patterns in a set of sentences. You must decide if a sentence is a Pattern 1 or a Pattern 2 and write the correct pattern in the blank after you classify the sentence. We will classify three sentences to practice identifying the different sentence patterns. Begin. (*You might have your students write the labels above the sentences at this time.*)

Question and Answer Flow for Sentence 1: Go to the supermarket with Billy and me.	
1. Who go to the supermarket with Billy and me? you - SP (understood subject pronoun)	8. And - C
	9. SN V P1 Check
2. What is being said about you? you go - V	10. (To the supermarket) - Prepositional phrase
3. To - P	11. (With Billy and me) - Prepositional phrase
4. To what? supermarket - OP	12. Period, command, imperative sentence
5. The - A	13. Go back to the verb - divide the complete subject
6. With - P	from the complete predicate.
7. With whom? Billy and me - COP, COP	

Classified Sentence:　　(You) SP　　V　P　A　　OP　　　P　COP C COP
　　　　　　　　　　　　　　SN　V　　／ Go (to the supermarket) (with Billy and me). **Imp**
　　　　　　　　　　　　　　P1

© SHURLEY INSTRUCTIONAL MATERIALS, INC.

CHAPTER 17 LESSON 1 CONTINUED

Question and Answer Flow for Sentence 2: That car did not stop at the traffic light.

1. What did not stop at the traffic light? car - SN
2. What is being said about car? car did stop - V
3. Did - HV
4. Did stop how? not - Adv
5. At - P
6. At what? light - OP
7. What kind of light? traffic - Adj

8. The - A
9. Which car? that - Adj
10. SN V P1 Check
11. (At the traffic light) - Prepositional phrase
12. Period, statement, declarative sentence
13. Go back to the verb - divide the complete subject from the complete predicate.

Classified Sentence:

			Adj	SN	HV	Adv	V	P	A	Adj	OP
SN	V		That	car /	did	not	stop	(at	the	traffic	light). **D**
P1											

Question and Answer Flow for Sentence 3: Yummy! Mother has cooked our favorite dinner tonight!

1. Who has cooked our favorite dinner tonight? Mother - SN
2. What is being said about Mother? Mother has cooked - V
3. Has - HV
4. Mother has cooked what? dinner - verify the noun
5. Does dinner mean the same thing as Mother? No.
6. Dinner - DO
7. Cooked - V-t
8. What kind of dinner? favorite - Adj
9. Whose dinner? our - PPA

10. Has cooked when? tonight - Adv
11. Yummy - I
12. SN V-t DO P2 Check
13. Verb-transitive - Check again.
14. No prepositional phrases.
15. Exclamation point, strong feeling, exclamatory sentence
16. Go back to the verb - divide the complete subject from the complete predicate.

Classified Sentence:

			I	SN	HV	V-t	PPA	Adj	DO	Adv
SN	V-t		Yummy!	Mother /	has	cooked	our	favorite	dinner	tonight! **E**
DO	P2									

Use Sentences 1-3 that you just classified with your students to do an Oral Skill Builder Check. Use the guidelines below.

Oral Skill Builder Check

1. **Noun check.**
   (Say the job and then say the noun. Circle each noun.)

2. **Identify the nouns as singular or plural.**
   (Write S or P above each noun.)

3. **Identify the nouns as common or proper.**
   (Follow established procedure for oral identification.)

4. **Do a vocabulary check.**
   (Follow established procedure for oral identification.)

5. **Identify the complete subject and the complete predicate.** (Underline the complete subject once and the complete predicate twice.)

6. **Identify the simple subject and simple predicate.**
   (Underline the simple subject once and the simple predicate twice. Bold, or highlight, the lines.)

7. **Recite the irregular verb chart.**
   (Located on student page 25 and teacher page 163.)

© SHURLEY INSTRUCTIONAL MATERIALS, INC.

CHAPTER 17 LESSON 1 CONTINUED

SKILL TIME

TEACHING SCRIPT FOR BEGINNING QUOTES

I am going to read you two short stories. They are the same story, but they are written two different ways. When I am finished, I want you to tell me if you enjoyed Story 1 or Story 2 the best.

Story 1

Janet and Kara scrambled to get ready for their trip to the mall. Aunt Lisa would be by to pick them up in only a few minutes, and she was never late. Janet looked for her favorite sweater while Kara tried to iron her pants. The girls looked frantically at the time and moved even faster. Aunt Lisa arrived before they were completely ready. They quickly finished and rushed out the door in a wave of excitement.

Story 2

"Have you seen my red sweater?" Janet asked as she pulled on her boots. Kara shook her head as she concentrated on ironing her black pants. Janet rummaged through the dresser drawers and started humming a tune.

"Can't you sing a different song?" Kara complained. "That one is getting so old."

Janet just smiled and changed the subject. "When did Aunt Lisa say she'd pick us up to go to the mall?" she asked Kara.

Kara sighed as she tried to remember the phone conversation she had with her aunt earlier that morning. "Three o'clock, I think. Oh my goodness! It's time!" Kara yelled as she glanced at her watch. The girls scrambled frantically, trying to get dressed. Their aunt was never late.

Just then the girls heard a car honk in the driveway. They quickly finished getting ready and rushed out to the car, beaming with excitement.

Did you enjoy Story 1 or Story 2 the best? (*Discuss reasons your students give for their preferences.*) Quotations are used to make your writing come alive and to make your readers believe that they are right in the middle of the action. Quotations help build pictures for your readers as the story unfolds. In Story 2, the action was direct, vigorous, and strong. In Story 1, the action was indirect and a little weak, even though the meanings of the two stories were almost identical. You will use quotations more if you understand how to write them correctly. Quotations are fun to use, but, as all good writers know, to learn the basic rules requires a little effort.

Quotations are words spoken by someone, and quotation marks are used to set off the exact words that are spoken. The words set off by quotation marks are usually called a direct quotation. In your writing, you will often find it necessary to tell what someone has said, and you will need to know several rules of punctuation in order to write quotations.

© SHURLEY INSTRUCTIONAL MATERIALS, INC.

CHAPTER 17 LESSON 1 CONTINUED

We will start with how to punctuate beginning quotes. Look at Reference 52 on page 41 in the Reference Section of your book. We will go through each rule as we punctuate the guided sample sentence in the rule box for beginning quotes. (*It would be best to put the guided sentence on the board so students can follow each step as you write it. Read the step-by-step teaching script for beginning quotes below and on the next page.*)

Reference 52: Quotation Rules for Beginning Quotes
1. **Pattern:** "**C** -quote- **(,!?)** " <u>explanatory words</u> **(.)** (Quotation marks, capital letter, quote, end punctuation choice, quotation marks closed, explanatory words, period)
2. Underline **end explanatory words** and use a period at the end.
3. You should see the **beginning quote** – Use quotation marks at the beginning and end of what is said. Then, put a comma, question mark, or exclamation point (no period) after the quote but in front of the quotation mark.
4. **Capitalize** the first word of the quote, any proper nouns, or the pronoun I.
5. **Punctuate** the rest of the sentence by checking for any apostrophes, periods, or commas that may be needed within the sentence.
Guided Practice
Sentence: the space shuttle will land a day late capt walker stated
1. Pattern: "**C** -quote- **(,!?)** " <u>explanatory words</u> **(.)**
2. the space shuttle will land a day late **capt walker stated**(.)
3. "the space shuttle will land a day late," <u>capt walker stated</u>.
4. "**T**he space shuttle will land a day late," **Capt W**alker <u>stated</u>.
5. "The space shuttle will land a day late," <u>Capt**.** Walker stated</u>.
6. **Corrected Sentence:** "The space shuttle will land a day late," Capt. Walker stated.

You will never have trouble punctuating beginning quotations if you follow these simple quotation rules because they tell you exactly what to do to the whole sentence. Look at the sentence under the Guided Practice and read the sentence with me: (*the space shuttle will land a day late capt walker stated*). We will break it up into sections, and then we will punctuate each section.

First, you always write a pattern to follow, so we will write the pattern for a beginning quote. That's number one under your rules. Let's read what the pattern says: "***C** -quote- **(,!?)** " <u>explanatory words</u> **(.)**. I will translate the pattern for you: quotation marks, capital letter to begin a quote, the quote itself, a choice of end mark (,!?), quotation marks, explanatory words, and a period. You will understand it better as I explain each part to you.

Look at Rule 2. Rule 2 says to underline *end explanatory words* and use a period at the end. Explanatory words are the words that explain who is talking but are not part of the actual quote. Any time you have a beginning quote, your explanatory words will be at the end. What are the explanatory words at the end of this sentence? (*capt walker stated*) (*Underline these explanatory words and put a period at the end.*)

Look at Rule 3. Rule 3 says, for beginning quotes, use quotation marks at the beginning and end of what is said. Which words need quotation marks at the beginning and end? (*"the space shuttle will land a day late"*) (*Put quotation marks around these words.*) Rule 3 also says to put a comma, question mark, or exclamation point (but no period) after the quote but in front of the quotation mark. Which punctuation mark would you use and why? (*Use a comma because the sentence is a statement, not a question or an exclamation.*) (*Put a comma after **late** but in front of the quotation marks.*)

© SHURLEY INSTRUCTIONAL MATERIALS, INC.

Look at Rule 4. Rule 4 says to capitalize the beginning of the quote, any proper nouns, or the pronoun *I*. Which words would be capitalized in this sentence? (*The, Capt, Walker*) (*Capitalize these words.*)

Look at Rule 5. Rule 5 says to punctuate the rest of the sentence by checking for any apostrophes, periods, or commas that may be needed within the sentence. What punctuation is needed in this sentence? (*A period is needed after **Capt.** because it is a person's title.*) (*Punctuate this abbreviation.*)

Now, we have a corrected sentence. Wasn't that easy? For a final check, I will go through the corrected sentence using the quotation pattern only. You will still have to remember to capitalize and punctuate the rest of the sentence, but this pattern will help you remember how to punctuate a beginning quote correctly. (*As you read each part of the quotation pattern, point out that part in the corrected sentence.*) **"C** -quote- **(,!?) "** *explanatory words* **(.)**

TEACHING SCRIPT FOR ENDING QUOTES

Look at Reference 53 for end quotes on page 42. We will go through each rule as we punctuate the guided sample sentence in the rule box for end quotes. (*It would be best to put the guided sentence on the board so students can follow each step as you write it. Read the step-by-step teaching script for end quotes on the next page.*)

Reference 53: Quotation Rules for End Quotes

1. **Pattern:** <u>C - explanatory words</u>**(,)** **"C** -quote- **(.!?) "**
   (Capital letter, explanatory words, comma, quotation marks, capital letter, quote, end punctuation choice, quotation marks closed)
2. Underline **beginning explanatory words** and use a comma after them.
3. You should see the **end quote** – Use quotation marks at the beginning and end of what is said. Then, put a period, question mark, or exclamation point (no comma) after the quote, but in front of the quotation marks.
4. **Capitalize** the first of the explanatory words at the beginning of a sentence, the first word of the quote, and any proper nouns or the pronoun *I*.
5. **Punctuate** the rest of the sentence by checking for any apostrophes, periods, or commas that may be needed within the sentence.

Guided Practice

Sentence: capt walker stated the space shuttle will land a day late

1. Pattern: <u>C -explanatory words</u>**(,)** **"C** -quote- **(.!?) "**

2. <u>**capt walker stated**</u>**(,)** the space shuttle will land a day late

3. <u>capt walker stated</u>, "the space shuttle will land a day late**. "**

4. <u>**C**apt **W**alker stated</u>, "**T**he space shuttle will land a day late."

5. <u>**C**apt. Walker stated</u>, "The space shuttle will land a day late."

6. **Corrected Sentence:** Capt. Walker stated, "The space shuttle will land a day late."

© SHURLEY INSTRUCTIONAL MATERIALS, INC.

CHAPTER 17 LESSON 1 CONTINUED

You will never have trouble punctuating end quotations if you follow these simple rules because they tell you exactly what to do to the whole sentence. Look at the sentence under the Guided Practice and read the sentence with me: *(capt walker stated the space shuttle will land a day late)*. We will break it up into sections, and then we will punctuate each section.

First, you always write a pattern to follow, so we will write the pattern for an end quote. That's number one under your rules. Let's read what the pattern says: ***C* -explanatory words(,) "*C* -quote- (.!?) "**. I will translate the pattern for you: capital letter to begin the explanatory words, the explanatory words, comma, quotation marks, capital letter to begin the quotation, the quote itself, a choice of end marks (.!?), and quotation marks.

Look at Rule 2. Rule 2 says to underline *beginning explanatory words* and use a comma after them. Remember, explanatory words are the words that explain who is talking but are not part of the actual quote. What are the explanatory words at the beginning of this sentence? *(capt walker stated)* *(Underline these explanatory words and put a comma after **stated**.)*

Look at Rule 3. Rule 3 says, for end quotes, use quotation marks at the beginning and end of what is said. What words need quotation marks around them? *("the space shuttle will land a day late")* *(Put quotation marks around these words.)* Rule 3 also says to put a period, question mark, or exclamation point (but no comma) after the quote, but in front of the quotation marks. Which punctuation mark would you use and why? *(Use a period because the sentence is a statement, not a question or an exclamation.)* *(Put a period after **late** but in front of the quotation marks.)*

Look at Rule 4. Rule 4 says to capitalize the first of the explanatory words at the beginning of a sentence, the beginning of the quote, any proper nouns, or the pronoun *I*. Which words would be capitalized in this sentence? *(Capt, Walker, The)* *(Capitalize these words.)*

Look at Rule 5. Rule 5 says to punctuate the rest of the sentence by checking for any apostrophes, periods, or commas that may be needed within the sentence. What punctuation is needed in this sentence? *(A period is needed after **Capt.** because it is a person's title.)* *(Punctuate this abbreviation.)*

Now, we have a corrected sentence. For a final check, I will go through the corrected sentence using the quotation pattern only. You will still have to remember to capitalize and punctuate the rest of the sentence, but this pattern will help you remember how to punctuate end quotes correctly. *(As you read each part of the quotation pattern, point out that part in the corrected sentence.)*
***C* -explanatory words(,) "*C* -quote- (.!?) "**

© SHURLEY INSTRUCTIONAL MATERIALS, INC.

CHAPTER 17 LESSON 1 CONTINUED

 PRACTICE TIME

Have students turn to page 81 in the Practice Section of their book and find Chapter 17, Lesson 1, Practice. Go over the directions to make sure they understand what to do. Guide students closely as they do the practice exercise for the first time. (*Students may use the Reference section in their books to help them remember the new information.*) Check and discuss the Practice after students have finished. (*Chapter 17, Lesson 1, Practice key is given below.*)

Chapter 17, Lesson 1, Practice: Use the Quotation Rules to help punctuate the quotations below. Underline the explanatory words.

```
     M   S           T
1.  ms. smith said, "thank you for your help."

     T                   M   S
2.  "thank you for your help," ms. smith said.

     A               I       M   I
3.  after football practice i gasped, "mom, i'm starving!"

     M   I               I
4.  "mom, i'm starving!" i gasped after football practice.

     P   T           T                   S
5.  pastor thomas replied, "the church picnic will be next sunday."

     T                   S       P   T
6.  "the church picnic will be next sunday," pastor thomas replied.

     I                           L
7.  i screamed during the scary movie, "look out!"

     L       I
8.  "look out!" i screamed during the scary movie.
```

 VOCABULARY TIME

Assign Chapter 17, Vocabulary Words **#1** on page 9 in the Reference Section for students to define in their Vocabulary notebooks. After they write each word and its meaning, students are to write a sentence using the vocabulary word.

Chapter 17, Vocabulary Words #1
(identical, alike, unprotected, guarded)

(End of lesson.)

© SHURLEY INSTRUCTIONAL MATERIALS, INC.

CHAPTER 17   LESSON 2

Objectives: Jingles, Grammar (Practice Sentences), Pattern 2 Practice Sentence, Practice Exercise, and Vocabulary #2.

JINGLE TIME

Have students turn to the Jingle Section in their books and recite the previously-taught jingles.

GRAMMAR TIME

First-Year Option: Put the Practice Sentences from the box below on the board or on notebook paper. Use these sentences as you practice the concepts that have been taught. For the greatest benefit, students must participate orally with the teacher. **Second-Year Option:** Have students classify the Practice Sentences independently on paper. Check students' sentences with the answers provided below. *(If you have the CDs for Practice Sentences, have students check their sentences with the CDs.)*

Chapter 17, Practice Sentences for Lesson 2
1. _____ Jerry tore his pants on a sharp nail in the barn.
2. _____ Can you swim across the pool?

TEACHING SCRIPT FOR PRACTICING MIXED PATTERNS

We will practice classifying Mixed Patterns. We will classify the sentences together. Begin. *(You might have your students write the labels above the sentences at this time.)*

Question and Answer Flow for Sentence 1: Jerry tore his pants on a sharp nail in the barn.

1. Who tore his pants on a sharp nail in the barn?
   Jerry - SN
2. What is being said about Jerry?   Jerry tore - V
3. Jerry tore what? pants - verify the noun
4. Do pants mean the same thing as Jerry? No.
5. Pants - DO
6. Tore - V-t
7. Whose pants? his - PPA
8. On - P
9. On what? nail - OP
10. What kind of nail? sharp - Adj

11. A - A
12. In - P
13. In what? barn - OP
14. The - A
15. SN V-t DO P2 Check
16. Verb-transitive - Check again.
17. (On a sharp nail) - Prepositional phrase
18. (In the barn) - Prepositional phrase
19. Period, statement, declarative sentence
20. Go back to the verb - divide the complete subject from the complete predicate.

Classified Sentence:

```
                        SN    V-t PPA DO    P  A  Adj OP  P  A   OP
        SN V-t          Jerry / tore his pants (on a sharp nail) (in the barn). D
        DO P2
```

© SHURLEY INSTRUCTIONAL MATERIALS, INC.

CHAPTER 17 LESSON 2 CONTINUED

Question and Answer Flow for Sentence 2: Can you swim across the pool?

1. Who can swim across the pool? you - SP
2. What is being said about you? you can swim - V
3. Can - HV
4. Across - P
5. Across what? pool - OP
6. The - A

7. SN V P1 Check
8. (Across the pool) - Prepositional phrase
9. Question mark, question, interrogative sentence
10. Go back to the verb - divide the complete subject from the complete predicate.

Classified Sentence:

                                HV SP   V   P   A   OP
       <u>SN V</u>   Can you / swim (across the pool)? **Int**
       P1

TEACHER INSTRUCTIONS FOR A PATTERN 2 PRACTICE SENTENCE

Tell students that their sentence writing assignment today is to write a Pattern 2 Practice Sentence. They are to follow the same procedure used in the previous lessons. They should decide on their labels, arrange them in a selected order, write their sentence, and edit the sentence for improved word choices. (*Students do not have to write an Improved Sentence at this point unless you feel they need more one-on-one word choice writing practice.*) Check and discuss the Pattern 2 Practice Sentence after students have finished.

 PRACTICE TIME

Students will continue punctuating direct quotations. Have students turn to pages 82 and 83 in the Practice Section of their book and find Chapter 17, Lesson 2, Practice (*1-4*). Go over the directions to make sure they understand what to do. Check and discuss the Practices after students have finished. (*Chapter 17, Lesson 2, Practice keys are given below and on the next page.*)

Chapter 17, Lesson 2, Practice 1: Tell whether each sentence is an example of a simile or a metaphor by writing *like* or *as* in the Simile column or by writing the noun in the predicate that renames the subject in the Metaphor column.

1. The frightened horse ran like a bolt of lightning.

2. The sun was a blazing round ball.

3. Our goat is as tame as a kitten.

Simile	Metaphor
like	
	ball
as	

Chapter 17, Lesson 2, Practice 2: Copy the following words on another sheet of paper. Write the correct contraction beside each word. **Key: can't, let's, don't, wasn't, they're, aren't, hadn't, isn't, she's, who's, you're, didn't, it's, we're, weren't, doesn't, hasn't, I'm, I've, I'd, won't, I'll, wouldn't, shouldn't, couldn't, they'd.**
Words: cannot, let us, do not, was not, they are, are not, had not, is not, she is, who is, you are, did not, it is, we are, were not, does not, has not, I am, I have, I had, will not, I will, would not, should not, could not, they would.

© SHURLEY INSTRUCTIONAL MATERIALS, INC.

CHAPTER 17 LESSON 2 CONTINUED

Chapter 17, Lesson 2, Practice 3: Underline each subject and fill in each column according to the title.

	List each Verb	Write PrN, PA, or None	Write L or A
1. My <u>brother</u> ate forty marshmallows.	ate	None	A
2. That <u>movie</u> is funny.	is	PA	L
3. Those <u>flowers</u> are roses.	are	PrN	L
4. Her <u>dress</u> is pretty.	is	PA	L
5. <u>He</u> is our new pastor.	is	PrN	L

Chapter 17, Lesson 2, Practice 4: Use the Quotation Rules to help punctuate the quotations below. Underline the explanatory words.

    T   W

1. <u>the patient asked</u>, "why does my head hurt**?**"

    W

2. "why does my head hurt**?**" <u>asked the patient</u>**.**

    D   T

3. <u>dad yelled</u>, "there's a cow in our pool**!**"

    W   J

4. "will you go to the park with me**?**" <u>james asked</u>**.**

    Y   M

5. "you can have an apple before dinner," <u>mother replied</u>**.**

    D   I   M C

6. <u>daniel said</u>, "i wrote a poem for mrs. clark**.**"

 VOCABULARY TIME

Assign Chapter 17, Vocabulary Words **#2** on page 9 in the Reference Section for students to define in their Vocabulary notebooks. Tell students they are to use a dictionary or thesaurus to look up the meanings of the vocabulary words. After they write each word and its meaning, students are to write a sentence using the vocabulary word.

Chapter 17, Vocabulary Words #2
(tidy, cluttered, slope, incline)

(End of lesson.)

© SHURLEY INSTRUCTIONAL MATERIALS, INC.

CHAPTER 17   LESSON 3

Objectives: Jingles, Grammar (Practice Sentences), and Practice Exercise.

 JINGLE TIME

Have students turn to the Jingle Section in their books and recite the previously-taught jingles.

 GRAMMAR TIME

First-Year Option: Put the Practice Sentences from the box below on the board or on notebook paper. Use these sentences as you practice the concepts that have been taught. For the greatest benefit, students must participate orally with the teacher. **Second-Year Option:** Have students classify the Practice Sentences independently on paper. Check students' sentences with the answers provided below. (*If you have the CDs for Practice Sentences, have students check their sentences with the CDs.*)

Chapter 17, Practice Sentences for Lesson 3

1. _____ Brian wrote a letter to his aunt in Ireland.
2. _____ Have your grandmother's tulips bloomed in her yard yet?

TEACHING SCRIPT FOR PRACTICING MIXED PATTERNS

We will practice classifying Mixed Patterns together. We will classify the sentences together. Begin. (*You might have your students write the labels above the sentences at this time.*)

Question and Answer Flow for Sentence 1: Brian wrote a letter to his aunt in Ireland.

1. Who wrote a letter to his aunt in Ireland? Brian - SN
2. What is being said about Brian? Brian wrote - V
3. Brian wrote what? letter - verify the noun
4. Does letter mean the same thing as Brian? No.
5. Letter - DO
6. Wrote - V-t
7. A - A
8. To - P
9. To whom? aunt - OP
10. Whose aunt? his - PPA
11. In - P
12. In what? Ireland - OP
13. SN V-t DO P2 Check
14. Verb-transitive - Check again.
15. (To his aunt) - Prepositional phrase
16. (In Ireland) - Prepositional phrase
17. Period, statement, declarative sentence
18. Go back to the verb - divide the complete subject from the complete predicate.

Classified Sentence:

SN   V-t   A   DO   P PPA OP P   OP
SN V-t   Brian / wrote a letter (to his aunt) (in Ireland). **D**
DO P2

© SHURLEY INSTRUCTIONAL MATERIALS, INC.

CHAPTER 17 LESSON 3 CONTINUED

Question and Answer Flow for Sentence 2: Have your grandmother's tulips bloomed in her yard yet?

1. What have bloomed in her yard yet? tulips - SN
2. What is being said about tulips?
   tulips have bloomed - V
3. Have - HV
4. In - P
5. In what? yard - OP
6. Whose yard? her - PPA
7. Have bloomed when? yet - Adv

8. Whose tulips? grandmother's - PNA
9. Whose grandmother? your - PPA
10. SN V P1 Check
11. (In her yard) - Prepositional phrase
12. Question mark, question, interrogative sentence
13. Go back to the verb - divide the complete subject
    from the complete predicate.

Classified Sentence:

		HV	PPA	PNA	SN	V	P PPA OP Adv

SN V   Have your grandmother's tulips / bloomed (in her yard) yet? **Int**

P1

PRACTICE TIME

Students will continue punctuating direct quotations. Have students turn to page 83 in the Practice Section of their book and find Chapter 17, Lesson 3, Practice *(1-3)*. Go over the directions to make sure they understand what to do. Check and discuss the Practices after students have finished. *(Chapter 17, Lesson 3, Practice keys are given below.)*

Chapter 17, Lesson 3, Practice 1: Use the Quotation Rules to help punctuate the quotations below. Underline the explanatory words.

    I   T   C   M L
1. "i have no doubt you will enjoy hearing the trinity choir in concert," <u>said mr. lawrence</u>.

  M L   I   T   C
2. <u>mr. lawrence said</u>, "I have no doubt you will enjoy hearing the trinity choir in concert."

   W   A   B   B   I   H
3. "will you visit aunt betty in boise, idaho this fall?" <u>asked heather</u>.

  H   W   A   B   B   I
4. <u>heather asked</u>, "will you visit aunt betty in boise, idaho this fall?"

  S   I   M   P
5. <u>susan stated</u>, "i didn't know that mrs. peterson wore glasses."

Chapter 17, Lesson 3, Practice 2: On notebook paper, write a sentence demonstrating a beginning quote and a sentence demonstrating an end quote. **(Answers will vary.)**

Chapter 17, Lesson 3, Practice 3: On notebook paper, write one sentence for each of these labels:
(SCS) (SCV) (CD). **(Answers will vary.)**

(End of lesson.)

© SHURLEY INSTRUCTIONAL MATERIALS, INC.

CHAPTER 17   LESSON 4

Objectives: Jingles, Study, Test, Check, Activity and Writing (journal).

JINGLE TIME

Have students turn to the Jingle Section in their books and recite the previously-taught jingles.

STUDY TIME

Have students study the vocabulary words in their vocabulary notebooks. Remind students that any vocabulary word in their notebooks could be on their test. Also, have students study any of the skills in the Practice Section that they need to review.

TEST TIME

Have students turn to page 113 in the Test Section of their books and find Chapter 17 Test. Go over the directions to make sure they understand what to do. (*Chapter 17 Test key is on the next page.*)

CHECK TIME

After students have finished, check and discuss their test papers. Make sure they understand why their answers are right or wrong. (*For total points, count each required answer as a point.*)

ACTIVITY / ASSIGNMENT TIME

Students will continue to draw or trace the states and write the following questions and answers.

Missouri	Montana
1. What is the state on the front of this card? **Missouri**	1. What is the state on the front of this card? **Montana**
2. What is the capital of Missouri? **Jefferson City**	2. What is the capital of Montana? **Helena**
3. What is the postal abbreviation of Missouri? **MO**	3. What is the postal abbreviation of Montana? **MT**
4. What year was Missouri admitted to the Union? **1821**	4. What year was Montana admitted to the Union? **1889**

Color these states and look up an interesting fact about each state to write on the cards. Use the cards to quiz family members, friends, and relatives. You may want to time the responses to your questions. Also, along with previous suggestions, think of other ways to have fun with your United States card file.

(End of lesson.)

Chapter 17 Test
(Student Page 113)

Exercise 1: Classify each sentence.

               PNA   Adj   SN   V-t A Adj DO   P PPA OP

1. **SN V-t**   Cindy's baby boy **/** had a red rash **(**on his skin**).** **D**
   DO P2

             A   Adj   SN   V   P A Adj Adj   OP

2. **SN V**   The young seal **/** splashed **(**into the cold ocean water**).** **D**
   P1

Exercise 2: Use Sentence 2 to underline the complete subject once and the complete predicate twice and to complete the table below.

List the Noun Used	List the Noun Job	Singular or Plural	Common or Proper	Simple Subject	Simple Predicate
1. **seal**	2. **SN**	3. **S**	4. **C**	5. **seal**	6. **splashed**
7. **water**	8. **OP**	9. **S**	10. **C**		

Exercise 3: Identify each pair of words as synonyms or antonyms by putting parentheses ( ) around *syn* or *ant*.

1. alike, identical	**(syn)** ant	4. slope, incline	**(syn)** ant	7. offer, volunteer	**(syn)** ant
2. tidy, cluttered	syn **(ant)**	5. puny, robust	syn **(ant)**	8. guarded, unprotected	syn **(ant)**
3. censor, permit	syn **(ant)**	6. pretend, imagine	**(syn)** ant	9. plentiful, sparse	syn **(ant)**

Exercise 4: Use the Quotation Rules to help punctuate the quotations below. Underline the explanatory words.

     W   **I**   **B**

1. "where did you find those earrings**?**" <u>i asked beth</u>**.**

     B   **M**   **M**   **R**   **G** **S**   **P**   **S**

2. <u>beth answered</u>**,** "mrs. matthews got these for me at ralph's gift store on prince street."

     T   **I**

3. "they are absolutely gorgeous**!**" <u>i exclaimed</u>**.**

     B   **I**   **M**   **M**

4. <u>beth smiled and said</u>**,** "i'll be sure to tell mrs. matthews that you like them."

Exercise 5: Copy the following contractions on notebook paper. Write the correct word beside each contraction.
Key: cannot, let us, do not, was not, they are, are not, had not, is not, she is or she has, who is, you are, did not, it is, we are.
<u>Contractions:</u> can't, let's, don't, wasn't, they're, aren't, hadn't, isn't, she's, who's, you're, didn't, it's, we're.

Exercise 6: On notebook paper, write one sentence for each of these labels: (SCS) (SCV) (CD, and).
(Answers will vary.)

Exercise 7: On notebook paper, write a sentence demonstrating a beginning quote and a sentence demonstrating an end quote. **(Answers will vary.)**

Exercise 8: In your journal, write a paragraph summarizing what you have learned this week.

                               Level 3 Homeschool Teacher's Manual

© SHURLEY INSTRUCTIONAL MATERIALS, INC.

CHAPTER 17 LESSON 4 CONTINUED

TEACHER INSTRUCTIONS

Use the Question and Answer Flows below for the sentences on the Chapter 17 Test.

Question and Answer Flow for Sentence 1: Cindy's baby boy had a red rash on his skin.

1. Who had a red rash on his skin? boy - SN
2. What is being said about boy? boy had - V
3. Boy had what? rash - verify the noun
4. Does rash mean the same thing as boy? No.
5. Rash - DO
6. Had - V-t
7. What kind of rash? red - Adj
8. A - A
9. On - P
10. On what? skin - OP
11. Whose skin? his - PPA
12. What kind of boy? baby - Adj
13. Whose boy? Cindy's - PNA
14. SN V-t DO P2 Check
15. Verb-transitive - Check again.
16. (On his skin) - Prepositional phrase
17. Period, statement, declarative sentence
18. Go back to the verb - divide the complete subject from the complete predicate.

Classified Sentence:

```
                          PNA    Adj   SN    V-t  A Adj  DO   P PPA  OP
             SN  V-t      Cindy's baby boy / had a red rash (on his skin).  D
             DO  P2
```

Question and Answer Flow for Sentence 2: The young seal splashed into the cold ocean water.

1. What splashed into the cold ocean water? seal - SN
2. What is being said about seal? seal splashed - V
3. Into - P
4. Into what? water - OP
5. What kind of water? ocean - Adj
6. What kind of water? cold - Adj
7. The - A
8. What kind of seal? young - Adj
9. The - A
10. SN V P1 Check
11. (Into the cold ocean water) - Prepositional phrase
12. Period, statement, declarative sentence
13. Go back to the verb - divide the complete subject from the complete predicate.

Classified Sentence:

```
                      A   Adj   SN      V      P   A  Adj  Adj   OP
          SN  V       The young seal / splashed (into the cold ocean water).  D
          P1
```

© SHURLEY INSTRUCTIONAL MATERIALS, INC.

CHAPTER 17   LESSON 5

Objectives: Writing (narrative, writing with dialogue and without dialogue) and Writing Assignments #18 and #19.

 WRITING TIME

TEACHING SCRIPT FOR INTRODUCING NARRATIVE WRITING

Narrative writing is simply the telling of a story. When you compose stories, you are actually writing what professional writers call narratives, or short stories. Short stories have certain characteristics that make them different from other types of writing. You will study five characteristics known as Story Elements. These Story Elements are main idea, setting, characters, plot, and ending. Your narrative writing skills will be developed through the use of the Story Elements. Narrative writing will have a beginning, a middle, and an end.

You will now learn how to use the five Story Elements – main idea, setting, characters, plot, and ending – to make a Story Elements outline. This outline will help keep your writing focused and help you choose details and events that support the main idea of your story. Before you begin every story writing assignment, you will complete a Story Elements outline like the one in Reference 54 on page 43. (_Have students go to Reference 54 on student page 43. Read and discuss the story elements and sample story with them._)

Reference 54: Story Elements Outline

1. **Main Idea (Tell the problem or situation that needs a solution.)**
   Allen is waiting on his little brother so they can play baseball.
2. **Setting (Tell when and where the story takes place, either clearly stated or implied.)**
   When – The story takes place in the afternoon. Where – The story takes place at the Marshall's house.
3. **Characters (Tell whom or what the story is about.)**
   The main characters are Allen and Calvin Marshall.
4. **Plot (Tell what the characters in the story do and what happens to them.)**
   The story is about a boy's frustrating experience with a younger sibling.
5. **Ending (Use a strong ending that will bring the story to a close.)**
   The story ends with Allen leaving ahead of his brother to go to the ball field.

Big Brother

Following an afternoon snack, the Marshall brothers, Allen and Calvin, prepared to leave the house to play baseball in the schoolyard. Allen quickly gathered his baseball gear and waited patiently for his brother on the front porch. He tossed his bat onto his shoulders and began to whistle a tune.

Meanwhile, Calvin rushed around the house looking for his shoes and his lucky baseball cap. He grabbed a couple of worn-out baseballs; then, he darted onto the front porch without his shoes. He quickly dropped the baseballs and his cap on the front steps and rushed back into the house for his shoes.

Allen just rolled his eyes and sighed. He had already waited on his little brother for ten minutes. He impatiently looked at his watch and began the long journey to the schoolyard. He knew his brother would eventually catch up with him.

© SHURLEY INSTRUCTIONAL MATERIALS, INC.

CHAPTER 17 LESSON 5 CONTINUED

You will make a Story Elements outline when you get ready to write. I want to tell you about another special element that makes narrative writing especially interesting, and that is conversation. Remember, another word for conversation is **dialogue**. Writers use dialogue, or conversation, in their short stories because it helps move the plot along, and it helps the reader understand the characters better.

Dialogue "shows" instead of "tells" in narratives. It also "shows" what a character is like. It is much better than the writer's "telling" what a character is like. A character's personal quotations show the readers a great deal about the character.

Listen as I review the main punctuation rules to observe when working with dialogue.

1. Dialogue is always placed in quotation marks. This placement will separate dialogue from any explanatory words or other words that develop the plot of the story.
2. Periods, commas, question marks, and exclamation marks that punctuate dialogue always go INSIDE the quotation marks. You will follow the rules for punctuating quotations that you have already learned.
3. If more than one character is speaking, you must indent and create a new paragraph each time a different character speaks.

TEACHING SCRIPT FOR WRITING WITH DIALOGUE AND WITHOUT DIALOGUE

You will do two narrative writing assignments. The first narrative writing assignment will be a story without dialogue. The second narrative writing assignment will be the same story with dialogue. Both rough drafts will go through the revision and editing stages. (*Read the boxes below for more information about students' writing assignment.*)

Writing Assignment Box #1

Writing Assignment #18: A Narrative without dialogue
Remind students to make a Story Elements outline.

Writing topics: The Secret Passage or The Mystery Gift or
　　　　　　　　Choose a story from the Bible or another favorite story and write it without dialogue.

Writing Assignment Box #2

Writing Assignment #19: A Narrative with dialogue
Students will use the same Story Elements outline from Writing Assignment #18.

Writing topics: The Secret Passage or The Mystery Gift or
　　　　　　　　Choose a story from the Bible or another favorite story and write it with dialogue.

Read, check, and discuss Writing Assignments #18 and #19 after students have finished their final papers. Use the checklists as you check and discuss students' papers. Make sure students are using the regular editing checklist and quotation rules correctly.

(End of lesson.)

© SHURLEY INSTRUCTIONAL MATERIALS, INC.

CHAPTER 18   LESSON 1

Objectives: Jingles, Grammar (Practice Sentences), Oral Skill Builder Check, Skills (regular and irregular verbs), Practice Exercise, and Vocabulary #1

JINGLE TIME

Have students turn to the Jingle Section in their books and recite the previously-taught jingles.

GRAMMAR TIME

First-Year Option: Put the Practice Sentences from the box below on the board or on notebook paper. Use these sentences as you practice the concepts that have been taught. For the greatest benefit, students must participate orally with the teacher. **Second-Year Option:** Have students classify the Practice Sentences independently on paper. Check students' sentences with the answers provided below. (*If you have the CDs for Practice Sentences, have students check their sentences with the CDs.*)

Chapter 18, Practice Sentences for Lesson 1
1. _____   May I taste your homemade chicken soup?
2. _____   The concert piano player sat on a comfortable bench.

TEACHING SCRIPT FOR PRACTICING MIXED PATTERNS

We will practice classifying Mixed Patterns. We will classify the sentences together. Begin. (*You might have your students write the labels above the sentences at this time.*)

Question and Answer Flow for Sentence 1: May I taste your homemade chicken soup?

1. Who may taste your homemade chicken soup? I - SP
2. What is being said about I? I may taste - V
3. May - HV
4. I may taste what? soup - verify the noun
5. Does soup mean the same thing as I? No.
6. Soup - DO
7. Taste - V-t
8. What kind of soup? chicken - Adj
9. What kind of soup? homemade - Adj
10. Whose soup? your - PPA
11. SN V-t DO P2 Check
12. Verb-transitive - Check again.
13. No prepositional phrases.
14. Question mark, question, interrogative sentence
15. Go back to the verb - divide the complete subject from the complete predicate.

Classified Sentence:

		HV	SP	V-t	PPA	Adj	Adj	DO
SN V-t		May	I /	taste	your	homemade	chicken	soup? Int
DO P2								

CHAPTER 18 LESSON 1 CONTINUED

Question and Answer Flow for Sentence 2: The concert piano player sat on a comfortable bench.	
1. Who sat on a comfortable bench? player - SN	8. What kind of player? concert - Adj
2. What is being said about player? player sat - V	9. The - A
3. On - P	10. SN V P1 Check
4. On what? bench - OP	11. (On a comfortable bench) - Prepositional phrase
5. What kind of bench? comfortable - Adj	12. Period, statement, declarative sentence
6. A - A	13. Go back to the verb - divide the complete subject
7. What kind of player? piano - Adj	from the complete predicate.

Classified Sentence:

<u>SN V</u>
P1

A   Adj   Adj   SN   V   P A   Adj   OP
The concert piano player / sat (on a comfortable bench). **D**

Use Sentences 1-2 that you just classified with your students to do an Oral Skill Builder Check.

Oral Skill Builder Check	
1. **Noun check.** (Say the job and then say the noun. Circle each noun.)	5. **Identify the complete subject and the complete predicate.** (Underline the complete subject once and the complete predicate twice.)
2. **Identify the nouns as singular or plural.** (Write S or P above each noun.)	
3. **Identify the nouns as common or proper.** (Follow established procedure for oral identification.)	6. **Identify the simple subject and simple predicate.** (Underline the simple subject once and the simple predicate twice. Bold, or highlight, the lines.)
4. **Do a vocabulary check.** (Follow established procedure for oral identification.)	7. **Recite the irregular verb chart.** (Located on student page 25 and teacher page 163.)

SKILL TIME

TEACHING SCRIPT FOR IDENTIFYING REGULAR AND IRREGULAR VERBS

You are going to learn three interesting things about verbs that will help you make correct verb choices when you speak and write. You will learn how to identify regular and irregular verbs, how to identify the simple verb tenses, and how to identify the tenses of helping verbs. Turn to page 44 and look at Reference 55. Follow along as I go over this important information with you. (_Read the information to your students and work through the guided examples provided for each concept. This information and the guided examples are reproduced for you on the next page._)

CHAPTER 18 LESSON 1 CONTINUED

Reference 55: Regular and Irregular Verbs

Most verbs are **regular verbs**. This means that they form the past tense merely by adding **-ed**, **-d**, or **-t** to the main verb: *race, raced*. This simple procedure makes regular verbs easy to identify. Some verbs, however, do not form their past tense this way. For that reason, they are called **irregular verbs**. Most irregular verbs form the past tense by having a **vowel spelling change** in the word. For example: *br<u>ea</u>k, br<u>o</u>ke, br<u>o</u>ken* or *s<u>i</u>ng, s<u>a</u>ng, s<u>u</u>ng*.

To decide if a verb is regular or irregular, remember these two things:

1. Look only at the main verb. If the main verb is made past tense with an *-ed, -d, or -t* ending, it is a regular verb. (*trace, traced, traced*)
2. Look only at the main verb. If the main verb is made past tense with a vowel spelling change, it is an irregular verb. (*sink, sank, sunk*)

A partial listing of the most common irregular verbs is on the irregular verb chart located in Reference 31 on page 25 in the student book. *(Page 163 in the Teacher's Manual.)* Refer to this chart whenever necessary.

Identify each verb as regular or irregular and put R or I in the blank. Then, write the past tense form.

fly	I	flew	move	R	moved	tell	I	told
build	R	built	freeze	I	froze	enjoy	R	enjoyed

PRACTICE TIME

Have students turn to page 84 in the Practice Section of their book and find Chapter 18, Lesson 1, Practice. Go over the directions to make sure they understand what to do. Check and discuss the Practice after students have finished. *(Chapter 18, Lesson 1, Practice key is given below.)*

Chapter 18, Lesson 1, Practice: Identify each verb as regular or irregular by writing R or I in the first blank and the past tense form in the second blank. Also, underline each verb or verb phrase in Sentences 6-10.

Verb	R or I	Past Tense	Underline the Verb	R or I	Past Tense
1. come	I	came	6. Heidi <u>gives</u> instructions to Phil.	I	gave
2. push	R	pushed	7. Dawn <u>reached</u> for her purse.	R	reached
3. prove	R	proved	8. Margie <u>is sitting</u> in the corner.	I	sat
4. write	I	wrote	9. Turner <u>wrote</u> the article.	I	wrote
5. blow	I	blew	10. Dana <u>likes</u> her baby cousin.	R	liked

VOCABULARY TIME

Assign Chapter 18, Vocabulary Words **#1** on page 9 in the Reference Section for students to define in their Vocabulary notebooks. After they write each word and its meaning, students are to write a sentence using the vocabulary word.

Chapter 18, Vocabulary Words #1
(allow, thwart, unusual, strange)

(End of lesson.)

© SHURLEY INSTRUCTIONAL MATERIALS, INC.

CHAPTER 18 LESSON 2

Objectives: Jingles, Grammar (Practice Sentences), Skills (simple verb tenses, tenses of helping verbs), Practice Exercise, and Vocabulary #2.

JINGLE TIME

Have students turn to the Jingle Section in their books and recite the previously-taught jingles.

GRAMMAR TIME

First-Year Option: Put the Practice Sentences from the box below on the board or on notebook paper. Use these sentences as you practice the concepts that have been taught. For the greatest benefit, students must participate orally with the teacher. **Second-Year Option:** Have students classify the Practice Sentences independently on paper. Check students' sentences with the answers provided below. (*If you have the CDs for Practice Sentences, have students check their sentences with the CDs.*)

Chapter 18, Practice Sentences for Lesson 2
1. _____ Stop and wait at the corner for the bus.
2. _____ Look out! Someone has spilled water on the tile floor!

TEACHING SCRIPT FOR PRACTICING MIXED PATTERNS

We will practice classifying Mixed Patterns. We will classify the sentences together. Begin. (*You might have your students write the labels above the sentences at this time.*)

Question and Answer Flow for Sentence 1: Stop and wait at the corner for the bus.

1. Who stop and wait at the corner for the bus?
   you - SP (understood subject pronoun)
2. What is being said about you?
   you stop and wait - CV, CV
3. At - P
4. At what? corner - OP
5. The - A
6. For - P
7. For what? bus - OP

8. The - A
9. And - C
10. SN V P1 Check
11. (At the corner) - Prepositional phrase
12. (For the bus) - Prepositional phrase
13. Period, command, imperative sentence
14. Go back to the verb - divide the complete subject from the complete predicate.

Classified Sentence:

            (You) SP   CV   C CV   P A   OP   P A OP
            <u>SN V   </u>   / Stop and wait (at the corner) (for the bus). **Imp**
            <u>P1</u>

© SHURLEY INSTRUCTIONAL MATERIALS, INC.

CHAPTER 18 LESSON 2 CONTINUED

Question and Answer Flow for Sentence 2: Look out! Someone has spilled water on the tile floor!

1. Who has spilled water on the tile floor? someone - SN
2. What is being said about someone? someone has spilled - V
3. Has - HV
4. Someone has spilled what? water - verify the noun
5. Does water mean the same thing as someone? No.
6. Water - DO
7. Spilled - V-t
8. On - P
9. On what? floor - OP

10. What kind of floor? tile - Adj
11. The - A
12. Look out - I
13. SN V-t DO P2 Check
14. Verb-transitive - Check again.
15. (On the tile floor) - Prepositional phrase
16. Exclamation point, strong feeling, exclamatory sentence
17. Go back to the verb - divide the complete subject from the complete predicate.

Classified Sentence:

<u>SN V-t</u>   I   SN   HV   V-t   DO   P A Adj OP
DO P2   Look out! Someone / has spilled water (on the tile floor)! E

SKILL TIME

TEACHING SCRIPT FOR IDENTIFYING SIMPLE VERB TENSES

You are going to learn more about verbs to help you better understand how verbs function. Look at Reference 56 while I go over this important information with you. (*Read the information to your students and work through the guided examples provided.*)

Reference 56: Simple Verb Tenses

When you are writing paragraphs, you must use verbs that are in the same tense. Tense means time. The tense of a verb shows the time of the action. There are three basic tenses that show when an action takes place. They are **present tense, past tense,** and **future tense**. These tenses are known as the simple tenses.

1. The **simple present tense** shows that something is happening now, in the present. The present tense form usually ends in *s, es,* or in a *plain ending*.
   (Regular present tense form: cover, covers) (Irregular present tense form: swim, swims)
   (**Examples:** Piles of snow <u>cover</u> the sidewalk. Jeff <u>swims</u> in the lake everyday.)

2. The **simple past tense** shows that something has happened sometime in the past. The regular past tense form usually ends in *-ed, -d,* or *-t.* Most irregular past tense forms should be memorized.
   (Regular past tense form: covered) (Irregular past tense form: swam)
   (**Examples:** Piles of snow <u>covered</u> the sidewalk. Jeff <u>swam</u> in the lake everyday.)

3. The **future tense** shows that something will happen sometime in the future. The future tense form always has the helping verb *will* or *shall* before the main verb.
   (Regular future tense form: will cover) (Irregular future tense form: will swim)
   (**Examples:** Piles of snow <u>will cover</u> the sidewalk. Jeff <u>will swim</u> in the lake everyday.)

Simple Present Tense	Simple Past Tense	Simple Future Tense
What to look for: **one verb** with s, es, or plain ending.	What to look for: **one verb** with -ed, -d, -t, or irr spelling change.	What to look for: **will** or **shall** with a main verb.
1. He <u>moves</u> to the inside.	1. He <u>moved</u> to the inside.	1. He <u>will move</u> to the inside.
2. He <u>does</u> electrical work.	2. He <u>did</u> electrical work.	2. He <u>will do</u> electrical work.

Level 3 Homeschool Teacher's Manual

© SHURLEY INSTRUCTIONAL MATERIALS, INC.

CHAPTER 18 LESSON 2 CONTINUED

TEACHING SCRIPT FOR IDENTIFYING THE TENSES OF HELPING VERBS

Next, you will learn about the tenses of helping verbs to help you better understand how verbs function. This is a very important concept, so I want you to pay close attention as we go over the information in the reference box. Look at Reference 57 while I go over the information with you. (*Read the information to your students and work through the guided examples provided.*)

Reference 57: Tenses of Helping Verbs

1. If there is only a main verb in a sentence, the tense is determined by the main verb and will be either present tense or past tense.
2. If there is a helping verb with a main verb, the tense of both verbs will be determined by the helping verb, not the main verb.

Since the helping verb determines a verb's tense, it is important to learn the tenses of the 14 helping verbs you will be using. You should memorize the list below so you will never have trouble with tenses.

> **Present tense helping verbs: am, is, are, has, have, does, do**
> **Past tense helping verbs: was, were, had, did, been**
> **Future tense helping verbs: will, shall**

If you use a present tense helping verb, it is considered present tense even though the main verb has an -*ed* ending, and it doesn't sound like present tense. (*I have walked - present tense.*) In later grades, you will learn that certain helping verbs help form other tenses called the perfect tenses.

Example 1: Underline each verb or verb phrase. Identify the verb tense by writing a number 1 for present tense, a number 2 for past tense, and a number 3 for future tense. Write the past tense form and R or I for Regular or Irregular.

Verb Tense		Main Verb Past Tense Form	R or I
1	1. My parents <u>have gone</u> to the store.	went	I
2	2. She <u>had walked</u> several miles.	walked	R
3	3. The theater <u>will open</u> next week.	opened	R

Example 2: List the present tense and past tense helping verbs below.

Present tense:	1. **am**	2. **is**	3. **are**	4. **has**	5. **have**	6. **does**	7. **do**
Past tense:	8. **was**	9. **were**	10. **had**	11. **did**	12. **been**		

© SHURLEY INSTRUCTIONAL MATERIALS, INC.

CHAPTER 18 LESSON 2 CONTINUED

PRACTICE TIME

Have students turn to page 84 in the Practice Section of their book and find Chapter 18, Lesson 2, Practice. Go over the directions to make sure they understand what to do. Check and discuss the Practice after students have finished. (*Chapter 18, Lesson 2, Practice key is given below.*)

Chapter 18, Lesson 2, Practice: Underline each verb or verb phrase. Identify the verb tense by writing a number 1 for present tense, a number 2 for past tense, and a number 3 for future tense. Write the past tense form and R or I for Regular or Irregular.

Verb Tense		Main Verb Past Tense Form	R or I
2	1. Those acorns <u>did fall</u> from our tree.	fell	I
1	2. That ship <u>is sailing</u> tomorrow.	sailed	R
1	3. They <u>are eating</u> pizza in the lunchroom.	ate	I
3	4. Tonight, I <u>will clean</u> my room.	cleaned	R
1	5. Mary <u>does work</u> at the local hospital.	worked	R
3	6. Doug <u>will wear</u> purple shoes to school.	wore	I
2	7. Kevin <u>had sold</u> all his candy.	sold	I
2	8. Mom <u>was exercising</u> at the gym.	exercised	R
1	9. I <u>have grown</u> three inches.	grew	I
3	10. I <u>will work</u> for Mr. Green next week.	worked	R

VOCABULARY TIME

Assign Chapter 18, Vocabulary Words **#2** on page 9 in the Reference Section for students to define in their Vocabulary notebooks. Tell students they are to use a dictionary or thesaurus to look up the meanings of the vocabulary words. After they write each word and its meaning, students are to write a sentence using the vocabulary word.

Chapter 18, Vocabulary Words #2
(crevice, crack, defeat, victory)

(End of lesson.)

© SHURLEY INSTRUCTIONAL MATERIALS, INC.

CHAPTER 18   LESSON 3

Objectives: Jingles, Grammar (Practice Sentences), Skills (changing verbs to different tenses in a paragraph), Practice Exercise.

JINGLE TIME

Have students turn to the Jingle Section in their books and recite the previously-taught jingles.

GRAMMAR TIME

First-Year Option: Put the Practice Sentences from the box below on the board or on notebook paper. Use these sentences as you practice the concepts that have been taught. For the greatest benefit, students must participate orally with the teacher. **Second-Year Option:** Have students classify the Practice Sentences independently on paper. Check students' sentences with the answers provided below. (*If you have the CDs for Practice Sentences, have students check their sentences with the CDs.*)

Chapter 18, Practice Sentences for Lesson 3
1. _____ My dad's motorcycle was parked under our tree.
2. _____ Did you buy envelopes and stationery at the supermarket today?

TEACHING SCRIPT FOR PRACTICING MIXED PATTERNS

We will practice classifying Mixed Patterns. We will classify the sentences together. Begin. (*You might have your students write the labels above the sentences at this time.*)

Question and Answer Flow for Sentence 1: My dad's motorcycle was parked under our tree.

1. What was parked under our tree? motorcycle - SN
2. What is being said about motorcycle? motorcycle was parked - V
3. Was - HV
4. Under - P
5. Under what? tree - OP
6. Whose tree? our - PPA
7. Whose motorcycle? dad's - PNA

8. Whose dad? my - PPA
9. SN V P1 Check
10. (Under our tree) - Prepositional phrase
11. Period, statement, declarative sentence
12. Go back to the verb - divide the complete subject from the complete predicate.

Classified Sentence:

```
                           PPA PNA     SN      HV   V     P    PPA OP
   SN  V                   My  dad's  motorcycle / was parked (under our  tree). D
   P1
```

© SHURLEY INSTRUCTIONAL MATERIALS, INC.

CHAPTER 18 LESSON 3 CONTINUED

Question and Answer Flow for Sentence 2: Did you buy envelopes and stationery at the supermarket today?

1. Who did buy envelopes and stationery at the supermarket today? you - SP
2. What is being said about you? you did buy - V
3. Did - HV
4. You did buy what? envelopes and stationery - verify the nouns
5. Do envelopes and stationery mean the same thing as you? No.
6. Envelopes and stationery - CDO, CDO
7. Buy - V-t
8. And - C

9. At - P
10. At what? supermarket - OP
11. The - A
12. Did buy when? today - Adv
13. SN V-t DO P2 Check
14. Verb-transitive - Check again.
15. (At the supermarket) - Prepositional phrase
16. Question mark, question, interrogative sentence
17. Go back to the verb - divide the complete subject from the complete predicate.

Classified Sentence:

	HV SP	V-t	CDO	C	CDO	P A	OP	Adv
SN V-t	Did you / buy	envelopes	and	stationery	(at the	supermarket)	today? Int
DO P2							

SKILL TIME

TEACHING SCRIPT FOR CHANGING VERBS TO DIFFERENT TENSES IN A PARAGRAPH

It is very important to study verb tenses because you will use what you learn in your writing. Remember, verb tenses in sentences are used to tell the reader the time period an event takes place. In writing, one of the most common mistakes students make is mixing present tense and past tense verbs. Mixing verb tenses can make your writing awkward and confusing to your reader. Look at this example. (_Put the example on the board._) Example: **The magician <u>smiles</u> and <u>waved</u> to the children as he <u>walks</u> around the auditorium.**

In this sentence, _waved_ is past tense, and _smiles_ and _walks_ are present tense. The shift from present to past and back to present leaves your reader wondering about the time these actions take place. To make your writing clear and effective, choose a verb tense, or time, for your writing and stick to it.

We will now work with verb tenses in a paragraph format. We will do several things to help you understand how the different tenses are used. First, we will identify the tense used in a sample paragraph as either present tense or past tense. Next, we will change from one tense to another tense in a paragraph. Then, we will work with mixed tenses. This means that a paragraph has a mixture of present and past tense verbs. Since past tense and present tense are usually not used together in the same paragraph, we will change all the mixed verbs to the tense indicated.

As I read the sample paragraph to you, listen very carefully to the verbs. After I have finished, I will ask you the tense of the paragraph. (_Read the sample paragraph in Reference 58 on the next page to your students. Do not allow them to look at the paragraph in their books, yet._) What is the tense of the paragraph? (_present tense_) We will now change the paragraph to past tense. To do this, we must change each verb to past tense, one at a time. After we have finished, I will read both paragraphs again so you can train your ear to hear the difference between present tense and past tense. (_Have students go to the first guided example in Reference 58 on page 46 and follow along as you show them how to change each present tense verb to a past tense verb._)

© SHURLEY INSTRUCTIONAL MATERIALS, INC.

Reference 58: Changing Tenses in Paragraphs

Guided Example 1: Change the underlined present tense verbs in Paragraph 1 to past tense verbs in Paragraph 2.

Paragraph 1: Present Tense

Annie **rides** her bike every afternoon. She **is** very careful, and she **watches** eagerly for her grandmother. At the end of the block, her grandmother **is waiting** for her and **waves** happily. Together, they **sit** on the porch and **munch** several of Grandma's homemade cookies.

Paragraph 2: Past Tense

Annie **rode** her bike every afternoon. She **was** very careful, and she **watched** eagerly for her grandmother. At the end of the block, her grandmother **was waiting** for her and **waved** happily. Together, they **sat** on the porch and **munched** several of Grandma's homemade cookies.

Guided Example 2: Change the underlined mixed tense verbs in Paragraph 3 to present tense verbs in Paragraph 4.

Paragraph 3: Mixed Tenses

Dimples **was** the name of my cat. She **loved** to sleep behind the pillows on our couch. Whenever I **opened** the door, she **dashes** outside and **chased** leaves. Dimples **loves** adventure!

Paragraph 4: Present Tense

Dimples **is** the name of my cat. She **loves** to sleep behind the pillows on our couch. Whenever I **open** the door, she **dashes** outside and **chases** leaves. Dimples **loves** adventure!

 PRACTICE TIME

Students will continue their practice of verb tenses. Have students turn to pages 84 and 85 in the Practice Section of their books and find Chapter 18, Lesson 3, Practice (*1-4*). Go over the directions to make sure they understand what to do. Check and discuss the Practices after students have finished. (*Chapter 18, Lesson 3, Practice keys are given below and on the next page.*)

Chapter 18, Lesson 3, Practice 1: Underline each verb or verb phrase. Identify the verb tense by writing a number 1 for present tense, a number 2 for past tense, and a number 3 for future tense. Write the past tense form and R or I for Regular or Irregular.

Verb Tense			Main Verb Past Tense Form	R or I
2	1.	I <u>did</u> <u>ride</u> the brown and white pony.	rode	I
3	2.	<u>Shall</u> I <u>bring</u> money for the trip?	brought	I
3	3.	Beth <u>will</u> <u>grade</u> papers for Ms. Cook.	graded	R
1	4.	I <u>am</u> <u>decorating</u> cupcakes for the party.	decorated	R

© SHURLEY INSTRUCTIONAL MATERIALS, INC.

CHAPTER 18 LESSON 3 CONTINUED

Chapter 18, Lesson 3, Practice 2: Change the underlined present tense verbs in Paragraph 1 to past tense verbs in Paragraph 2.

Paragraph 1: Present Tense

My family **is** well organized for camping trips. Mom **plans** the meals and **packs** the food. I **gather** and **load** the camping gear. My dad **locates** the fishing gear and **places** it in the boat. He **checks** all the supplies carefully. We never **leave** for a camping trip without the necessary food and gear!

Paragraph 2: Past Tense

My family **was** well organized for camping trips. Mom **planned** the meals and **packed** the food. I **gathered** and **loaded** the camping gear. My dad **located** the fishing gear and **placed** it in the boat. He **checked** all the supplies carefully. We never **left** for a camping trip without the necessary food and gear!

Chapter 18, Lesson 3, Practice 3: On notebook paper, write the seven present tense helping verbs, the five past tense helping verbs, and the two future tense helping verbs. **(The order of answers may vary.)** (Present: **am, is, are, has, have, do, does**;   Past: **was, were, had, did, been**; Future: **will, shall**)

Chapter 18, Lesson 3, Practice 4: Change the underlined mixed tense verbs in Paragraph 1 to present tense verbs in Paragraph 2.

Paragraph 1: Mixed Tenses

My family **ate** dinner at Grandmother's house every Sunday. She always **cooks** a gigantic feast! Grandmother **fried** chicken in a big black skillet. It always **looks** and **smelled** delicious! Her vegetables often **tasted** fresh from the vine. Grandmother also **baked** fresh bread and pastries. Sunday afternoons at Grandmother's house **is filled** with love, food, and family.

Paragraph 2: Present Tense

My family **eats** dinner at Grandmother's house every Sunday. She always **cooks** a gigantic feast! Grandmother **fries** chicken in a big black skillet. It always **looks** and **smells** delicious! Her vegetables often **taste** fresh from the vine. Grandmother also **bakes** fresh bread and pastries. Sunday afternoons at Grandmother's house **is filled** with love, food, and family.

(End of lesson.)

© SHURLEY INSTRUCTIONAL MATERIALS, INC.

CHAPTER 18   LESSON 4

Objectives: Jingles, Study, Test, Check, Activity, and Writing (journal).

JINGLE TIME

Have students turn to the Jingle Section in their books and recite the previously-taught jingles.

STUDY TIME

Have students study the vocabulary words in their vocabulary notebooks. Remind students that any vocabulary word in their notebooks could be on their test. Also, have students study any of the skills in the Practice Section that they need to review.

TEST TIME

Have students turn to pages 114 and 115 in the Test Section of their books and find Chapter 18 Tests A and B. Go over the directions to make sure they understand what to do. (*Chapter 18 Test A and B keys are on the next two pages.*)

CHECK TIME

After students have finished, check and discuss their test papers. Make sure they understand why their answers are right or wrong. (*For total points, count each required answer as a point.*)

ACTIVITY / ASSIGNMENT TIME

Students will continue to draw or trace the states and write the following questions and answers.

Nebraska	Nevada
1. What is the state on the front of this card? **Nebraska**	1. What is the state on the front of this card? **Nevada**
2. What is the capital of Nebraska? **Lincoln**	2. What is the capital of Nevada? **Carson City**
3. What is the postal abbreviation of Nebraska? **NE**	3. What is the postal abbreviation of Nevada? **NV**
4. What year was Nebraska admitted to the Union? **1867**	4. What year was Nevada admitted to the Union? **1864**

Color these states and look up an interesting fact about each state to write on the cards. Use the cards to quiz family members, friends, and relatives. You may want to time the responses to your questions. Also, along with previous suggestions, think of other ways to have fun with your United States card file.

(End of lesson.)

© SHURLEY INSTRUCTIONAL MATERIALS, INC.

Chapter 18 Test A
(Student Page 114)

Exercise 1: Classify each sentence.

```
                    HV   A    SN   P   A    OP        V  CAdv C CAdv    P   Adj    OP
1. SN V    Does the liquid (in a thermometer) / go up or down (during cold weather)? Int
   P1
                    I   PPA  SN      V   PPA  Adj      DO   P  A  Adj  OP
2. SN V    Oh no!  My brother / found his birthday present (in the hall closet)!  E
   P1
```

Exercise 2: Use Sentence 2 to underline the complete subject once and the complete predicate twice and to complete the table below.

List the Noun Used	List the Noun Job	Singular or Plural	Common or Proper	Simple Subject	Simple Predicate
1. **stomach**	2. **SN**	3. **S**	4. **C**	5. **stomach**	6. **is hurting**
7. **meal**	8. **OP**	9. **S**	10. **C**		

Exercise 3: Identify each pair of words as synonyms or antonyms by putting parentheses ( ) around *syn* or *ant*.

1. strange, unusual	**(syn)** ant	4. crack, crevice	**(syn)** ant	7. identical, alike	**(syn)** ant
2. sorrow, bliss	syn **(ant)**	5. defeat, victory	syn **(ant)**	8. guarded, unprotected	syn **(ant)**
3. allow, thwart	syn **(ant)**	6. censor, permit	syn **(ant)**	9. concealed, hidden	**(syn)** ant

Exercise 4: Underline each verb or verb phrase. Identify the verb tense by writing a number 1 for present tense, a number 2 for past tense, and a number 3 for future tense. Write the past tense form and R or I for Regular or Irregular.

Verb Tense		Main Verb Past Tense Form	R or I
1	1. He is traveling to Europe.	traveled	R
3	2. The students will make our lunch.	made	I
2	3. Was she searching for the recipe?	searched	R
1	4. The ducks are flying south for the winter.	flew	I
2	5. The principal had called his mother.	called	R
3	6. Debby will slice the apples.	sliced	R
2	7. Cody talked to the counselor.	talked	R
1	8. We have sold all the tickets.	sold	I
1	9. Jacob is swimming in our pool.	swam	I
2	10. Katy was throwing the baseball.	threw	I

Exercise 5: Identify each kind of sentence by writing the abbreviation in the blank. (S, F, SCS, SCV, CD).

CD   1. She picked the apples, and her mother baked them.
SCV   2. We mowed the lawn and watered the flowers.
SCS   3. Fruits and vegetables should be eaten every day.
F   4. During the contest.
CD   5. He called his grandmother, and they talked for hours.

© SHURLEY INSTRUCTIONAL MATERIALS, INC.

Chapter 18 Test B
(Student Page 115)

Exercise 6: Change the underlined present tense verbs in Paragraph 1 to past tense verbs in Paragraph 2.

Paragraph 1: Present Tense

Mr. Chang **performs** many jobs at his restaurant. First, he **buys** fresh meats and vegetables. He **selects** only the finest ingredients to be prepared. Later, he **helps** out in the kitchen. Mr. Chang **dices** vegetables into small pieces for the cooks. He also **greets** his customers with a smile. He always **checks** for customer satisfaction. Mr. Chang **wears** many hats at his restaurant.

Paragraph 2: Past Tense

Mr. Chang **performed** many jobs at his restaurant. First, he **bought** fresh meats and vegetables. He **selected** only the finest ingredients to be prepared. Later, he **helped** out in the kitchen. Mr. Chang **diced** vegetables into small pieces for the cooks. He also **greeted** his customers with a smile. He always **checked** for customer satisfaction. Mr. Chang **wore** many hats at his restaurant.

Exercise 7: Change the underlined mixed tense verbs in Paragraph 1 to present tense verbs in Paragraph 2.

Paragraph 1: Mixed Tense

My sister and I **went** to the park every weekend. We **laugh** and **played** for hours on the swings. She **pushes** me high into the sky, and I **screamed** loudly! Sometimes, I **push** her on the merry-go-round. She always **begged** me to slow down. My sister and I **run** and **played** happily at the park every weekend.

Paragraph 2: Present Tense

My sister and I **go** to the park every weekend. We **laugh** and **play** for hours on the swings. She **pushes** me high into the sky, and I **scream** loudly! Sometimes, I **push** her on the merry-go-round. She always **begs** me to slow down. My sister and I **run** and **play** happily at the park every weekend.

Exercise 8: On notebook paper, write the seven present tense helping verbs, the five past tense helping verbs, and the two future tense helping verbs. **(The order of answers may vary.)** (Present: **am, is, are, has, have, do, does;** Past: **was, were, had, did, been;** Future: **will, shall**)

Exercise 9: In your journal, write a paragraph summarizing what you have learned this week.

© SHURLEY INSTRUCTIONAL MATERIALS, INC.

CHAPTER 18 LESSON 4 CONTINUED

TEACHER INSTRUCTIONS

Use the Question and Answer Flows below for the sentences on the Chapter 18 Test A.

Question and Answer Flow for Sentence 1: Does the liquid in a thermometer go up or down during cold weather?

1. What does go up or down during cold weather? liquid - SN
2. What is being said about liquid? liquid does go - V
3. Does - HV
4. Does go how? up or down - CAdv, CAdv
5. Or - C
6. During - P
7. During what? weather - OP
8. What kind of weather? cold - Adj
9. In - P

10. In what? thermometer - OP
11. A - A
12. The - A
13. SN V P1 Check
14. (In a thermometer) - Prepositional phrase
15. (During cold weather) - Prepositional phrase
16. Question mark, question, interrogative sentence
17. Go back to the verb - divide the complete subject from the complete predicate.

Classified Sentence:

		HV	A	SN	P	A	OP		V	CAdv	C	CAdv	P	Adj	OP	
SN V	Does	the	liquid	(in	a	thermometer)	/	go	up	or	down	(during	cold	weather)?	**Int**
P1															

Question and Answer Flow for Sentence 2: Oh no! My brother found his birthday present in the hall closet!

1. Who found his birthday present in the hall closet? brother - SN
2. What is being said about brother? brother found - V
3. Brother found what? present - verify the noun
4. Does present mean the same thing as brother? No.
5. Present - DO
6. Found - V-t
7. What kind of present? birthday - Adj
8. Whose present? his - PPA
9. In - P

10. In what? closet - OP
11. Which closet? hall - Adj
12. The - A
13. Whose brother? my - PPA
14. Oh no - I
15. SN V DO P2 Check
16. Verb transitive - Check again
17. (In the hall closet) - Prepositional phrase
18. Exclamation point, strong feeling, exclamatory sentence
19. Go back to the verb - divide the complete subject from the complete predicate.

Classified Sentence:

		I	PPA	SN		V-t	PPA	Adj	DO	P	A	Adj	OP	
SN V	Oh no!	My	brother	/	found	his	birthday	present	(in	the	hall	closet)!	**E**
DO P2													

© SHURLEY INSTRUCTIONAL MATERIALS, INC.

CHAPTER 18   LESSON 5

Objectives: Writing Assignments #20 and #21, Bonus Option.

 **WRITING TIME**

TEACHING SCRIPT FOR NARRATIVE WRITING ASSIGNMENTS

You will do two narrative writing assignments. The first narrative writing assignment will be a story without dialogue. The second narrative writing assignment will be a _different story_ with dialogue. You will make a Story Elements outline for both stories. Both rough drafts will go through the revision and editing process. (_Read the boxes below for more information about the students' writing assignment._)

Writing Assignment Box #1

Writing Assignment #20: Narrative Essay <u>Without</u> Dialogue

Remind students to make a Story Elements Outline.

Writing topics: My Magic Shoes/Hat   or   My Narrow Escape   or   My Hero

---

Writing Assignment Box #2

Writing Assignment #21: Narrative Essay <u>With</u> Dialogue

Remind students to make a Story Elements Outline.

Writing topics: The Computer Mystery   or   Escape From the Zoo   or   A Spooky Night

<u>Bonus Option:</u> **How many books are in the New Testament? Look up all the books of the New Testament and list them in your Journal. Next, create a word search that contains all the books of the New Testament. Be careful to spell all the names correctly. Give the word search to a family member to complete. Make a key so you can check the finished word search.**

TEACHER INSTRUCTIONS FOR CHECKING WRITING ASSIGNMENTS #20 AND #21

Read, check, and discuss Writing Assignments #20 and #21 after students have finished their final papers. Use the editing checklist as you check and discuss students' papers. Make sure students are using the editing checklist correctly.

Bonus Option Answer: _There are 27 books in the New Testament._

(End of lesson.)

© SHURLEY INSTRUCTIONAL MATERIALS, INC.

CHAPTER 19   LESSON 1

Objectives: Jingles, Grammar (Practice Sentences), Oral Skill Builder Check, Skill (double negatives), Practice Exercise, and Vocabulary #1.

 JINGLE TIME

Have students turn to the Jingle Section in their books and recite the previously-taught jingles.

 GRAMMAR TIME

First-Year Option: Put the Practice Sentences from the box below on the board or on notebook paper. Use these sentences as you practice the concepts that have been taught. For the greatest benefit, students must participate orally with the teacher. **Second-Year Option:** Have students classify the Practice Sentences independently on paper. Check students' sentences with the answers provided below. *(If you have the CDs for Practice Sentences, have students check their sentences with the CDs.)*

Chapter 19, Practice Sentences for Lesson 1
1. _____ Does your new digital camera take quality pictures?
2. _____ The perceptive teacher tapped on the student's desk for his attention.
3. _____ Stone can be carved into many different shapes.

Question and Answer Flow for Sentence 1: Does your new digital camera take quality pictures?

1. What does take quality pictures? camera - SN
2. What is being said about camera? camera does take - V
3. Does - HV
4. Camera does take what? pictures - verify the noun
5. Do pictures mean the same thing as camera? No.
6. Pictures - DO
7. Take - V-t
8. What kind of pictures? quality - Adj
9. What kind of camera? digital - Adj
10. What kind of camera? new - Adj
11. Whose camera? your - PPA
12. SN V-t DO P2 Check
13. Verb-transitive - Check again.
14. No prepositional phrases.
15. Question mark, question, interrogative sentence
16. Go back to the verb - divide the complete subject from the complete predicate.

Classified Sentence:

	HV PPA Adj Adj SN V-t Adj DO
SN V-t	Does your new digital camera / take quality pictures? Int
DO P2	

© SHURLEY INSTRUCTIONAL MATERIALS, INC.

CHAPTER 19 LESSON 1 CONTINUED

Question and Answer Flow for Sentence 2: The perceptive teacher tapped on the student's desk for his attention.

1. Who tapped on the student's desk for his attention?
   teacher - SN
2. What is being said about teacher? teacher tapped - V
3. On - P
4. On what? desk - OP
5. Whose desk? student's - PNA
6. The - A
7. For - P
8. For what? attention - OP
9. Whose attention? his - PPA

10. What kind of teacher? perceptive - Adj
11. The - A
12. SN V P1 Check
13. (On the student's desk) - Prepositional phrase
14. (For his attention) - Prepositional phrase
15. Period, statement, declarative sentence
16. Go back to the verb - divide the complete subject
    from the complete predicate.

Classified Sentence:

| | | A | Adj | SN | V | P | A | PNA | OP | P | PPA | OP |

<u>SN V</u> The perceptive teacher **/** tapped **(**on the student's desk**) (**for his attention**).** **D**
P1

Question and Answer Flow for Sentence 3: Stone can be carved into many different shapes.

1. What can be carved into many different shapes?
   stone - SN
2. What is being said about stone? stone can be carved - V
3. Can - HV
4. Be - HV
5. Into - P
6. Into what? shapes - OP
7. What kind of shapes? different - Adj

8. How many shapes? many - Adj
9. SN V P1 Check
10. (Into many different shapes) - Prepositional phrase
11. Period, statement, declarative sentence
12. Go back to the verb - divide the complete subject
    from the complete predicate.

Classified Sentence:

| | SN | HV HV | V | P | Adj | Adj | OP |

<u>SN V</u> Stone **/** can be carved **(**into many different shapes**).** **D**
P1

Use Sentences 1-3 that you just classified with your students to do an Oral Skill Builder Check.

Oral Skill Builder Check

1. Noun check. (Say the job and then say the noun. Circle each noun.) **2. Identify the nouns as singular or plural.** (Write S or P above each noun.) **3. Identify the nouns as common or proper.** (Follow established procedure for oral identification.) **4. Do a vocabulary check.** (Follow established procedure for oral identification.)	**5. Identify the complete subject and the complete predicate.** (Underline the complete subject once and the complete predicate twice.) **6. Identify the simple subject and simple predicate.** (Underline the simple subject once and the simple predicate twice. Bold, or highlight, the lines.) **7. Recite the irregular verb chart.** (Located on student page 25 and teacher page 163.)

© SHURLEY INSTRUCTIONAL MATERIALS, INC.

CHAPTER 19 LESSON 1 CONTINUED

SKILL TIME

TEACHING SCRIPT FOR DOUBLE NEGATIVES

Today, we are going to learn how to correct double negative mistakes in writing. The first thing we need to know is what it means to have a double negative mistake. Double means TWO, and negative means NOT. We have a **double negative** mistake when we use two negative words that both mean NOT in the same sentence. Most negative words begin with the letter *n*. Other negative words do not begin with the letter *n* but are negative in meaning. There are also some prefixes that give words a negative meaning.

Look at Reference 59 on page 47 in your book. First, we will go over the most commonly-used negative words and prefixes. Then, we'll learn three ways to correct double negative mistakes, and, finally, we'll see different ways to change negative words to positive words. (*Read and discuss the information in Reference 59 below with your students.*)

Reference 59: Double Negatives		
Negative Words That Begin With *N*	**Other Negative Words**	**Negative Prefixes**
neither no no one not (n't) nowhere never nobody none nothing	barely, hardly, scarcely	dis, non, un

Three Ways to Correct a Double Negative
Rule 1: **Change** the second negative to a positive: Wrong: We **couldn't** find **no** money.   Right: We **couldn't** find **any** money.
Rule 2: **Take out** the negative part of a contraction: Wrong: We **couldn't** find **no** money.   Right: We **could** find **no** money.
Rule 3: **Remove** the first negative word (possibility of a verb change):   Wrong: We **couldn't** find **no** money.   Right: We **found no** money.

Changing Negative Words to Positive Words
1. Change *no* or *none* to *any*.   4. Change *nothing* to *anything*.   7. Change *neither* to *either*. 2. Change *nobody* to *anybody*.   5. Change *nowhere* to *anywhere*.   8. Remove the *n't* from a contraction. 3. Change *no one* to *anyone*.   6. Change *never* to *ever*.

Examples: Underline the negative words in each sentence. Rewrite each sentence and correct the double-negative mistake as indicated by the rule number in parentheses at the end of the sentence.
 	
    1. He <u>didn't</u> have <u>no</u> homework. (Rule 3) **He had no homework.**
    2. The children <u>couldn't</u> <u>hardly</u> wait for the party. (Rule 2) **The children could hardly wait for the party.**
    3. She <u>didn't</u> order <u>nothing</u> for dessert. (Rule 1) **She didn't order anything for dessert.**

Go through the guided examples with your students. Make sure students know how to make the double-negative correction according to the rule provided at the end of each sentence. (*Remember, the reference answers are keyed to give students guided examples.*)

© SHURLEY INSTRUCTIONAL MATERIALS, INC.

CHAPTER 19 LESSON 1 CONTINUED

PRACTICE TIME

Have students turn to page 86 in the Practice Section of their book and find Chapter 19, Lesson 1, Practice (*1-2*). Go over the directions to make sure they understand what to do. Check and discuss the Practices after students have finished. (*Chapter 19, Lesson 1, Practice keys are given below.*)

Chapter 19, Lesson 1, Practice 1: Underline the negative words in each sentence. Rewrite each sentence on notebook paper and correct the double negative mistake as indicated by the rule number in parentheses at the end of the sentence.

Rule 1	Rule 2	Rule 3
Change the second negative to a positive.	Take out the negative part of a contraction.	Remove the first negative word (verb change).

1. Danny <u>doesn't</u> have <u>no</u> money. (Rule 3)
   Danny has no money.
2. Our old truck <u>doesn't</u> <u>never</u> start. (Rule 1)
   Our old truck doesn't ever start.
3. Maria <u>wouldn't</u> <u>never</u> say that. (Rule 2)
   Maria would never say that.
4. The hunters <u>didn't</u> have <u>no</u> license. (Rule 1)
   The hunter didn't have any license.
5. Our house <u>doesn't</u> have <u>no</u> shutters. (Rule 3)
   Our house has no shutters.
6. The volunteers <u>didn't</u> want <u>no</u> pay. (Rule 3)
   The volunteers wanted no pay.
7. He <u>wouldn't</u> do <u>no</u> wrong. (Rule 2)
   He would do no wrong.
8. There <u>isn't</u> <u>no</u> milk in the refrigerator. (Rule 1)
   There isn't any milk in the refrigerator.

Chapter 19, Lesson 1, Practice 2: Underline each verb or verb phrase. Identify the verb tense by writing a number 1 for present tense, a number 2 for past tense, and a number 3 for future tense. Write the past tense form and R or I for Regular or Irregular.

Verb Tense		Main Verb Past Tense Form	R or I
1	1. He <u>is</u> <u>swimming</u> in deep water.	swam	I
3	2. <u>Will</u> he <u>search</u> for the lost diamond?	searched	R
2	3. Jody <u>ate</u> her dessert first.	ate	I
1	4. <u>Has</u> he <u>signed</u> the checks yet?	signed	R
2	5. <u>Did</u> he <u>shoot</u> the wild pheasant?	shot	I

VOCABULARY TIME

Assign Chapter 19, Vocabulary Words **#1** on page 9 in the Reference Section for students to define in their Vocabulary notebooks. Tell students they are to use a dictionary or thesaurus to look up the meanings of the vocabulary words. After they write each word and its meaning, students are to write a sentence using the vocabulary word.

Chapter 19, Vocabulary Words #1
(destroy, construct, insightful, perceptive)

(End of lesson.)

CHAPTER 19   LESSON 2

Objectives: Jingles, Grammar (Practice Sentences), Practice Exercise, and Vocabulary #2.

 **JINGLE TIME**

Have students turn to the Jingle Section in their books and recite the previously-taught jingles.

 GRAMMAR TIME

First-Year Option: Put the Practice Sentences from the box below on the board or on notebook paper. Use these sentences as you practice the concepts that have been taught. For the greatest benefit, students must participate orally with the teacher. **Second-Year Option:** Have students classify the Practice Sentences independently on paper. Check students' sentences with the answers provided below. (*If you have the CDs for Practice Sentences, have students check their sentences with the CDs.*)

Chapter 19, Practice Sentences for Lesson 2
1. _____ Tim and I walked up the stairs to the third floor.
2. _____ Will the band play their new songs at the concert?
3. _____ Look out! The parrot has escaped from its cage!

TEACHING SCRIPT FOR PRACTICING MIXED PATTERNS

We will practice classifying Mixed Patterns. We will classify the sentences together. Begin. (*You might have your students write the labels above the sentences at this time.*)

Question and Answer Flow for Sentence 1: Tim and I walked up the stairs to the third floor.	
1. Who walked up the stairs to the third floor? Tim and I - CSN, CSP	8. Which floor? third - Adj
	9. The - A
2. What is being said about Tim and I? Tim and I walked - V	10. And - C
	11. SN V P1 Check
3. Up - P	12. (Up the stairs) - Prepositional phrase
4. Up what? stairs - OP	13. (To the third floor) - Prepositional phrase
5. The - A	14. Period, statement, declarative sentence
6. To - P	15. Go back to the verb - divide the complete subject
7. To what? floor - OP	from the complete predicate.

Classified Sentence:

```
                        CSN  C CSP    V      P   A   OP     P   A   Adj   OP
        SN  V           Tim and I / walked (up the stairs) (to the third floor).  D
        P1
```

© SHURLEY INSTRUCTIONAL MATERIALS, INC.

CHAPTER 19 LESSON 2 CONTINUED

Question and Answer Flow for Sentence 2: Will the band play their new songs at the concert?

1. Who will play their new songs at the concert? band - SN
2. What is being said about band? band will play - V
3. Will - HV
4. Band will play what? songs - verify the noun
5. Do songs mean the same thing as band? No.
6. Songs - DO
7. Play - V-t
8. What kind of songs? new - Adj
9. Whose songs? their - PPA
10. At - P
11. At what? concert - OP
12. The - A
13. The - A
14. SN V-t DO P2 Check
15. Verb-transitive - Check again.
16. (At the concert) - Prepositional phrase
17. Question mark, question, interrogative sentence
18. Go back to the verb - divide the complete subject from the complete predicate.

Classified Sentence:

<pre>
                    HV   A   SN   V-t PPA Adj DO   P   A   OP
   SN V-t   Will the band / play their new songs (at the concert)? Int
   DO P2
</pre>

Question and Answer Flow for Sentence 3: Look out! The parrot has escaped from its cage!

1. What has escaped from its cage? parrot - SN
2. What is being said about parrot? parrot has escaped - V
3. Has - HV
4. From - P
5. From what? cage - OP
6. Whose cage? its - PPA
7. The - A
8. Look out - I
9. SN V P1 Check
10. (From its cage) - Prepositional phrase
11. Exclamation point, strong feeling, exclamatory sentence
12. Go back to the verb - divide the complete subject from the complete predicate.

Classified Sentence:

<pre>
                 I   A   SN   HV   V   P PPA OP
   SN V   Look out! The parrot / has escaped (from its cage)! E
   P1
</pre>

 PRACTICE TIME

Have students turn to pages 86 and 87 in the Practice Section of their book and find Chapter 19, Lesson 2, Practice (*1-4*). Go over the directions to make sure they understand what to do. Check and discuss the Practices after students have finished. (*Chapter 19, Lesson 2, Practice keys are given below and on the next page.*)

Chapter 19, Lesson 2, Practice 1: Underline the negative words in each sentence. Rewrite each sentence on notebook paper and correct the double negative mistake as indicated by the rule number in parentheses at the end of the sentence.

Rule 1	Rule 2	Rule 3
Change the second negative to a positive.	Take out the negative part of a contraction.	Remove the first negative word (verb change).

1. He <u>didn't</u> believe <u>nothing</u> I said. (Rule 1)
   He didn't believe anything I said.
2. <u>Don't</u> <u>never</u> pay with cash. (Rule 1)
   Don't ever pay with cash.
3. I <u>wouldn't</u> <u>never</u> eat spinach. (Rule 2)
   I would never eat spinach.
4. Mark <u>hadn't</u> <u>never</u> owned a dog. (Rule 2)
   Mark had never owned a dog.

5. The fisherman <u>didn't</u> catch <u>no</u> fish. (Rule 3)
   The fisherman caught no fish.
6. We <u>didn't</u> find <u>no</u> arrowheads in the cave. (Rule 3)
   We found no arrowheads in the cave.
7. She <u>couldn't</u> find <u>nothing</u> she liked. (Rule 1)
   She couldn't find anything she liked.
8. We <u>haven't</u> received <u>no</u> payment. (Rule 2)
   We have received no payment.

© SHURLEY INSTRUCTIONAL MATERIALS, INC.

CHAPTER 19 LESSON 2 CONTINUED

Chapter 19, Lesson 2, Practice 2: Underline each verb or verb phrase. Identify the verb tense by writing a number 1 for present tense, a number 2 for past tense, and a number 3 for future tense. Write the past tense form and R or I for Regular or Irregular.

Verb Tense	
3	1. We <u>will</u> <u>be</u> <u>staying</u> in Des Moines.
2	2. <u>Did</u> he really <u>win</u> the jackpot?
2	3. He <u>fell</u> from the edge of the cliff.
1	4. Chris <u>is</u> <u>studying</u> for his algebra test.

Past Tense	R or I
stayed	R
won	I
fell	I
studied	R

Chapter 19, Lesson 2, Practice 3: Change the underlined present tense verbs in Paragraph 1 to past tense verbs in Paragraph 2.

Paragraph 1: Present Tense

   Paul **delivers** newspapers after school. He **wants** to earn enough money for summer camp. He **has** a route that **covers** ten city blocks. He always **throws** the papers on the driveway, and his faithful customers **think** he **does** a great job.

Paragraph 2: Past Tense

   Paul **delivered** newspapers after school. He **wanted** to earn enough money for summer camp. He **had** a route that **covered** ten city blocks. He always **threw** the papers on the driveway, and his faithful customers **thought** he **did** a great job.

Chapter 19, Lesson 2, Practice 4: On notebook paper, write the seven present tense helping verbs, the five past tense helping verbs, and the two future tense helping verbs. **(The order of answers may vary.)** (Present: **am, is, are, has, have, do, does**;   Past: **was, were, had, did, been**; Future: **will, shall**)

 VOCABULARY TIME

Assign Chapter 19, Vocabulary Words #2 on page 9 in the Reference Section for students to define in their Vocabulary notebooks. After they write each word and its meaning, students are to write a sentence using the vocabulary word.

Chapter 19, Vocabulary Words #2
(rejoice, celebrate, private, public)

(End of lesson.)

Level 3 Homeschool Teacher's Manual
© SHURLEY INSTRUCTIONAL MATERIALS, INC.

CHAPTER 19 LESSON 3

Objectives: Jingles, Grammar (Practice Sentences), and Practice Exercise.

 **JINGLE TIME**

Have students turn to the Jingle Section in their books and recite the previously-taught jingles.

 GRAMMAR TIME

First-Year Option: Put the Practice Sentences from the box below on the board or on notebook paper. Use these sentences as you practice the concepts that have been taught. For the greatest benefit, students must participate orally with the teacher. **Second-Year Option:** Have students classify the Practice Sentences independently on paper. Check students' sentences with the answers provided below. (*If you have the CDs for Practice Sentences, have students check their sentences with the CDs.*)

Chapter 19, Practice Sentences for Lesson 3
1. _____ Squeeze a glass of fresh juice from those oranges for breakfast.
2. _____ The wheels of the bus spun in the mud.
3. _____ Will our football team play the championship game on Friday night?

TEACHING SCRIPT FOR PRACTICING MIXED PATTERNS

We will practice classifying Mixed Patterns. We will classify the sentences together. Begin. (*You might have your students write the labels above the sentences at this time.*)

Question and Answer Flow for Sentence 1: Squeeze a glass of fresh juice from those oranges for breakfast.

1. Who squeeze some fresh juice from those oranges for breakfast? you - SP (understood subject pronoun)
2. What is being said about you? you squeeze - V
3. You squeeze what? glass - verify the noun
4. Does glass mean the same thing as you? No.
5. Glass - DO
6. Squeeze - V-t
7. A - A
8. Of - P
9. Of what? juice - OP
10. What kind of juice? fresh - Adj
11. From - P
12. From what? oranges - OP
13. Which oranges? those - Adj
14. For - P
15. For what? breakfast - OP
16. SN V-t DO P2 Check
17. (From those oranges) - Prepositional phrase
18. (For breakfast) - Prepositional phrase
19. Period, command, imperative sentence
20. Go back to the verb - divide the complete subject from the complete predicate.

Classified Sentence:

	(You) SP		V-t	A	DO	P	Adj	OP	P	Adj	OP	P	OP
	SN V-t	/ Squeeze	a	glass	of	fresh	juice	(from	those	oranges)	(for	breakfast).	Imp
	DO P2												

CHAPTER 19 LESSON 3 CONTINUED

Question and Answer Flow for Sentence 2: The wheels of the bus spun in the mud.

1. What spun in the mud? wheels - SN
2. What is being said about wheels? wheels spun - V
3. In - P
4. In what? mud - OP
5. The - A
6. Of - P
7. Of what? bus - OP
8. The -A

9. The - A
10. SN V P1 Check
11. (Of the bus) - Prepositional phrase
12. (In the mud) - Prepositional phrase
13. Period, statement, declarative sentence
14. Go back to the verb - divide the complete subject from the complete predicate.

Classified Sentence:

<pre>
                      A   SN   P A OP   V   P A OP
      SN V   The wheels (of the bus) / spun (in the mud). D
      P1
</pre>

Question and Answer Flow for Sentence 3: Will our football team play the championship game on Friday night?

1. Who will play the championship game on Friday night? team - SN
2. What is being said about team? team will play - V
3. Will - HV
4. Team will play what? game - verify the noun
5. Does game mean the same thing as team? No.
6. Game - DO
7. Play - V-t
8. What kind of game? championship - Adj
9. The - A
10. On - P

11. On what? night - OP
12. Which night? Friday - Adj
13. What kind of team? football - Adj
14. Whose team? our - PPA
15. SN V-t DO P2 Check
16. Verb-transitive - Check again.
17. (On Friday night) - Prepositional phrase
18. Question mark, question, interrogative sentence
19. Go back to the verb - divide the complete subject from the complete predicate.

Classified Sentence:

<pre>
                        HV PPA Adj   SN   V-t A   Adj   DO   P Adj   OP
      SN V-t   Will our football team / play the championship game (on Friday night)? Int
      DO P2
</pre>

 PRACTICE TIME

Have students turn to pages 87 and 88 in the Practice Section of their book and find Chapter 19, Lesson 3, Practice (*1-3*). Go over the directions to make sure they understand what to do. Check and discuss the Practices after students have finished. (*Chapter 19, Lesson 3, Practice keys are given below and on the next page.*)

Chapter 19, Lesson 3, Practice 1: Copy the following words on notebook paper. Write the correct contraction beside each word. **Key: can't, let's, don't, wasn't, they're, aren't, hadn't, isn't, she's, who's, you're, didn't, it's, we're, weren't, doesn't.** <u>Words:</u> cannot, let us, do not, was not, they are, are not, had not, is not, she is, who is, you are, did not, it is, we are, were not, does not.

© SHURLEY INSTRUCTIONAL MATERIALS, INC.

CHAPTER 19 LESSON 3 CONTINUED

Chapter 19, Lesson 3, Practice 2: Underline the negative words in each sentence. Rewrite each sentence on notebook paper and correct the double negative mistake as indicated by the rule number in parentheses at the end of the sentence.

Rule 1	Rule 2	Rule 3
Change the second negative to a positive.	Take out the negative part of a contraction.	Remove the first negative word (verb change).

1. He <u>didn't</u> want <u>nothing</u> in return. (Rule 3)
   He wanted nothing in return.
2. I <u>don't</u> have <u>no</u> fever today. (Rule 1)
   I don't have any fever today.
3. She <u>can't</u> <u>never</u> find her glasses. (Rule 2)
   She can never find her glasses.

4. Gary <u>doesn't</u> have <u>no</u> brothers. (Rule 1)
   Gary doesn't have any brothers.
5. <u>Don't</u> <u>never</u> leave your car unlocked. (Rule 1)
   Don't ever leave your car unlocked.
6. There <u>wasn't</u> <u>no</u> dessert left. (Rule 2)
   There was no dessert left.

Chapter 19, Lesson 3, Practice 3: Change the underlined mixed tense verbs in Paragraph 1 to present tense verbs in Paragraph 2.

Paragraph 1: Mixed Tenses

Jill **grabs** her blanket out of the car and **climbed** up the steps to the stadium. She **bought** her ticket at the ticket booth and **walks** through the gate. She **found** a seat in the bleachers next to her friends and **spreads** out her blanket. Soon, the game **begins**, and she **cheers** for the home team.

Paragraph 2: Present Tense

Jill **grabs** her blanket out of the car and **climbs** up the steps to the stadium. She **buys** her ticket at the ticket booth and **walks** through the gate. She **finds** a seat in the bleachers next to her friends and **spreads** out her blanket. Soon, the game **begins**, and she **cheers** for the home team.

(End of lesson.)

© SHURLEY INSTRUCTIONAL MATERIALS, INC.

CHAPTER 19   LESSON 4

Objectives: Jingles, Study, Test, Check, Activity and Writing (journal).

 JINGLE TIME

Have students turn to the Jingle Section in their books and recite the previously-taught jingles.

 STUDY TIME

Have students study the vocabulary words in their vocabulary notebooks. Remind students that any vocabulary word in their notebooks could be on their test. Also, have students study any of the skills in the Practice Section that they need to review.

 TEST TIME

Have students turn to page 116 in the Test Section of their book and find Chapter 19 Test. Go over the directions to make sure they understand what to do. (*Chapter 19 Test key is on the next page.*)

 CHECK TIME

After students have finished, check and discuss their test papers. Make sure they understand why their answers are right or wrong. (*For total points, count each required answer as a point.*)

 ACTIVITY / ASSIGNMENT TIME

Students will continue to draw or trace the states and write the following questions and answers.

New Hampshire	New Jersey
1. What is the state on the front of this card? **New Hampshire**	1. What is the state on the front of this card? **New Jersey**
2. What is the capital of New Hampshire? **Concord**	2. What is the capital of New Jersey? **Trenton**
3. What is the postal abbreviation of New Hampshire? **NH**	3. What is the postal abbreviation of New Jersey? **NJ**
4. What year was New Hampshire admitted to the Union? **1788**	4. What year was New Jersey admitted to the Union? **1787**

Color these states and look up an interesting fact about each state to write on the cards. Use the cards to quiz family members, friends, and relatives. You may want to time the responses to your questions. Also, along with previous suggestions, think of other ways to have fun with your United States card file.

(End of lesson.)

© SHURLEY INSTRUCTIONAL MATERIALS, INC.

Chapter 19 Test
(Student Page 116)

Exercise 1: Classify each sentence.

```
              I    PNA   SN    HV  HV    V      P  A   OP      P  Adj  OP
1.  SN  V        Wow!  Bill's brother / has been running (in the marathon) (for two hours)!  E
    P1
```

```
              HV  SP   V-t  A    DO    P   A   Adj    OP
2.  SN  V-t       Did you / spill the cereal (on the kitchen floor)?  Int
    DO  P2
```

```
              SN       V-t  A  Adj   DO   P   A    Adj    OP
3.  SN  V-t       Henry / sorted the dirty clothes (in the laundry basket).  D
    DO  P2
```

Exercise 2: Identify each pair of words as synonyms or antonyms by putting parentheses ( ) around *syn* or *ant.*

1. incline, slope	**(syn)** ant	4. perceptive, insightful	**(syn)** ant	7. thwart, allow	syn **(ant)**
2. public, private	syn **(ant)**	5. construct, destroy	syn **(ant)**	8. cluttered, tidy	syn **(ant)**
3. crack, crevice	**(syn)** ant	6. rejoice, celebrate	**(syn)** ant	9. victory, defeat	syn **(ant)**

Exercise 3: Change the underlined mixed tense verbs in Paragraph 1 to past tense verbs in Paragraph 2.

Paragraph 1: Mixed Tenses

Yesterday, Jerry and I **went** to the zoo. Jerry **loves** the monkey cages, so we **walked** to them first. He **imitated** the monkeys' calls, and we both **laugh**. When the day **was** almost over, we **walk** back to the car and **left**.

Paragraph 2: Past Tense

Yesterday, Jerry and I **went** to the zoo. Jerry **loved** the monkey cages, so we **walked** to them first. He **imitated** the monkeys' calls, and we both **laughed**. When the day **was** almost over, we **walked** back to the car and **left**.

Exercise 4: Underline the negative words in each sentence. Rewrite each sentence on notebook paper and correct the double negative mistake as indicated by the rule number in parentheses at the end of the sentence.

Rule 1	Rule 2	Rule 3
Change the second negative to a positive.	Take out the negative part of a contraction.	Remove the first negative word (verb change).

1. Barry <u>doesn't</u> have <u>no</u> razors. (Rule 1)
   Barry doesn't have any razors.
2. I <u>can't</u> <u>never</u> find any toothbrush. (Rule 2)
   I can never find any toothbrush.
3. My dad <u>doesn't</u> have <u>no</u> neckties. (Rule 3)
   My dad has no neckties.
4. He <u>isn't</u> <u>never</u> home. (Rule 2)
   He is never home.

Exercise 5: Copy the following words on notebook paper. Write the correct contraction beside each word. **(Key: you've, there's, isn't, they'll, won't, it's, he'll, let's, we'd, I'll.)**
<u>Words:</u> you have, there is, is not, they will, will not, it is, he will, let us, we would, I will.

Exercise 6: Copy the following contractions on notebook paper. Write the correct word beside each contraction. **(Key: they are, he is or he has, you are, has not, you had or you would, we have, does not, had not, cannot, I had or I would, do not.)**
<u>Contractions:</u> they're, he's, you're, hasn't, you'd, we've, doesn't, hadn't, can't, I'd, don't.

Exercise 7: In your journal, write a paragraph summarizing what you have learned this week.

© SHURLEY INSTRUCTIONAL MATERIALS, INC.

CHAPTER 19 LESSON 4 CONTINUED

TEACHER INSTRUCTIONS

Use the Question and Answer Flows below for the sentences on the Chapter 19 Test.

Question and Answer Flow for Sentence 1: Wow! Bill's brother has been running in the marathon for two hours!

1. Who has been running in the marathon for two hours? brother - SN
2. What is being said about brother? has been running - V
3. Has - HV
4. Been - HV
5. In - P
6. In what? marathon - OP
7. The - A
8. For - P
9. For what? hours - OP
10. How many hours? two - Adj
11. Whose brother? Bill's - PNA
12. Wow - I
13. SN V P1 Check
14. (In the marathon) - Prepositional phrase
15. (For two hours) - Prepositional phrase
16. Exclamation point, strong feeling, exclamatory sentence
17. Go back to the verb - divide the complete subject from the complete predicate.

Classified Sentence:

```
              I   PNA  SN    HV HV   V    P A   OP    P  Adj  OP
  SN  V    Wow!  Bill's brother / has been running (in the marathon) (for two hours)!  E
  P1
```

Question and Answer Flow for Sentence 2: Did you spill the cereal on the kitchen floor?

1. Who did spill the cereal on the kitchen floor? you - SP
2. What is being said about you? you did spill - V
3. Did - HV
4. You did spill what? cereal - verify the noun
5. Does cereal mean the same thing as you? No.
6. Cereal - DO
7. Spill - V-t
8. The - A
9. On - P
10. On what? floor - OP
11. What kind of floor? kitchen - Adj
12. The - A
13. SN V-t DO P2 Check
14. Verb-transitive - Check again.
15. (On the kitchen floor) - Prepositional phrase
16. Question mark, question, interrogative sentence
17. Go back to the verb - divide the complete subject from the complete predicate.

Classified Sentence:

```
                HV  SP   V-t A   DO   P A   Adj   OP
  SN  V-t    Did you / spill the cereal (on the kitchen floor)?  Int
  DO  P2
```

Question and Answer Flow for Sentence 3: Henry sorted the dirty clothes in the laundry basket.

1. Who sorted the dirty clothes in the laundry basket? Henry - SN
2. What is being said about Henry? Henry sorted - V
3. Henry sorted what? clothes - verify the noun
4. Do clothes mean the same thing as Henry? No.
5. Clothes - DO
6. Sorted - V-t
7. What kind of clothes? dirty - Adj
8. The - A
9. In - P
10. In what? basket - OP
11. What kind of basket? laundry - Adj
12. The - A
13. SN V-t DO P2 Check
14. Verb-transitive - Check again.
15. (In the laundry basket) - Prepositional phrase
16. Period, statement, declarative sentence
17. Go back to the verb - divide the complete subject from the complete predicate.

Classified Sentence:

```
                SN     V-t  A  Adj   DO   P A   Adj   OP
  SN  V-t    Henry / sorted the dirty clothes (in the laundry basket).  D
  DO  P2
```

© SHURLEY INSTRUCTIONAL MATERIALS, INC.

CHAPTER 19   LESSON 5

Objectives: Writing Assignments #22 and #23, and Bonus Option.

 **WRITING TIME**

TEACHING SCRIPT FOR WRITING ASSIGNMENTS

You will do two writing assignments. The first writing assignment will be a narrative essay with or without dialogue. It's your choice. The second writing assignment will be an expository paragraph or essay. Again, it's your choice. You should make a Story Elements outline for the narrative writing. Both rough drafts will go through the revision and editing stages. As you revise and edit, make sure you use the checkpoints in the Regular Editing Checklist provided in Reference 42. (*Read the boxes below for more information about students' writing assignment.*)

Writing Assignment Box #1

Writing Assignment #22: Narrative Essay <u>With or Without</u> Dialogue

Remind students to make a Story Elements outline for their story.

Writing topic choices: The Castle Mystery   or   **The Time Traveler**   or   **My Life As A . . .**

Writing Assignment Box #2

Writing Assignment #23: Expository Paragraph or Essay

Writing topic choices: Three Animals That Live In the Ocean   or   **Dangers of Playing With Fire**   or
Things That Run on Batteries

<u>**Bonus Option:**</u> **Find the Lord's Prayer in the Book of Matthew. Write down the chapter and verse number; then write the Lord's Prayer in your Journal. Last, write a prayer of your own. It can be a prayer of thanks, praise, forgiveness, needs, or a combination of whatever you choose . You can express happiness, sadness, concern, or fear in prayer.**

Read, check, and discuss Writing Assignments #22 and #23 after students have finished their final papers. Use the editing checklist as you check and discuss students' papers.

Bonus Option Answer: *Matthew 6:9-13*

(End of lesson.)

© SHURLEY INSTRUCTIONAL MATERIALS, INC.

CHAPTER 20   LESSON 1
Objectives: Jingles, Grammar (Practice Sentences), Oral Skill Builder Check, Skill (form the plurals of nouns with different endings), Practice Exercise, and Vocabulary #1.

 **JINGLE TIME**

Have students turn to the Jingle Section in their books and recite the previously-taught jingles.

 GRAMMAR TIME

First-Year Option: Put the Practice Sentences from the box below on the board or on notebook paper. Use these sentences as you practice the concepts that have been taught. For the greatest benefit, students must participate orally with the teacher. **Second-Year Option:** Have students classify the Practice Sentences independently on paper. Check students' sentences with the answers provided below. *(If you have the CDs for Practice Sentences, have students check their sentences with the CDs.)*

Chapter 20, Practice Sentences for Lesson 1
1. _____ They searched around the crime scene for several hours.
2. _____ Look! Robert is holding the zookeeper's pet snake!

TEACHING SCRIPT FOR PRACTICING MIXED PATTERNS

We will practice classifying Mixed Patterns. We will classify the sentences together. Begin. *(You might have your students write the labels above the sentences at this time.)*

Question and Answer Flow for Sentence 1: They searched around the crime scene for several hours.	
1. Who searched around the crime scene for several hours? they - SP	8. For what? hours - OP
2. What is being said about they? they searched - V	9. How many hours? several - Adj
3. Around - P	10. SN V P1 Check
4. Around what? scene - OP	11. (Around the crime scene) - Prepositional phrase
5. What kind of scene? crime - Adj	12. (For several hours) - Prepositional phrase
6. The - A	13. Period, statement, declarative sentence
7. For - P	14. Go back to the verb - divide the complete subject from the complete predicate.

Classified Sentence:

```
                       SP     V       P    A  Adj  OP    P  Adj   OP
         SN  V     They / searched (around the crime scene) (for several hours).  D
         P1
```

© SHURLEY INSTRUCTIONAL MATERIALS, INC.

CHAPTER 20 LESSON 1 CONTINUED

Question and Answer Flow for Sentence 2: Look! Robert is holding the zookeeper's pet snake!

1. Who is holding the zookeeper's pet snake? Robert - SN
2. What is being said about Robert? Robert is holding - V
3. Is - HV
4. Robert is holding what? snake - verify the noun
5. Does snake mean the same thing as Robert? No.
6. Snake - DO
7. Holding - V-t
8. What kind of snake? pet - Adj
9. Whose snake? zookeeper's - PNA

10. The - A
11. Look - I
12. SN V-t DO P2 Check
13. Verb-transitive - Check again.
14. No prepositional phrases.
15. Exclamation point, strong feeling, exclamatory sentence
16. Go back to the verb - divide the complete subject from the complete predicate.

Classified Sentence:

                  I   SN HV V-t A PNA   Adj DO

<u>SN V-t</u>   Look! Robert / is holding the zookeeper's pet snake! **E**
<u>DO P2</u>

Use Sentences 1-2 that you just classified with your students to do an Oral Skill Builder Check. Use the guidelines below.

Oral Skill Builder Check

1. **Noun check.**
   (Say the job and then say the noun. Circle each noun.)
2. **Identify the nouns as singular or plural.**
   (Write S or P above each noun.)
3. **Identify the nouns as common or proper.**
   (Follow established procedure for oral identification.)
4. **Do a vocabulary check.**
   (Follow established procedure for oral identification.)

5. **Identify the complete subject and the complete predicate.** (Underline the complete subject once and the complete predicate twice.)
6. **Identify the simple subject and simple predicate.** (Underline the simple subject once and the simple predicate twice. Bold, or highlight, the lines.)
7. **Recite the irregular verb chart.**
   (Located on student page 25 and teacher page 163.)

SKILL TIME

TEACHING SCRIPT FOR HOW TO FORM THE PLURALS OF NOUNS WITH DIFFERENT ENDINGS

Today, we will learn how to form the plurals of nouns with different endings. Look at Reference 60 on page 47. This is a box of rules that will make it a little easier to form the plurals of nouns with different endings. Let's read the rules and discuss how each one is used. (*Read and discuss the rules in the reference box on the next page.*)

© SHURLEY INSTRUCTIONAL MATERIALS, INC.

CHAPTER 20 LESSON 1 CONTINUED

Reference 60: Rules for the Plurals of Nouns with Different Endings	
1. "ch, sh, z, s, ss, x" – add "es."	6. "f" or "ff," add "s."
2. a vowel plus "y," add an "s."	7. a vowel plus "o," add "s."
3. a consonant plus "y," change "y" to "i" and add "es."	8. a consonant plus "o," add "es."
4. "f" or "fe," change the "f" or "fe" to "v" and add "es."	9. stays the same for S and P.
5. irregular nouns – change spellings completely.	10. regular nouns – add "s."

Use the rules above to write the correct plural form of these nouns:

	Rule	Plural Form			Rule	Plural Form
1. key	2	keys	3.	roof	6	roofs
2. shelf	4	shelves	4.	fish	1 or 9	fish or fishes

After reading the rules, we know 3 things:

1. Which rule you choose will usually depend on the last two letters of a word.

2. You will have to decide whether some letters are vowels or consonants before you can choose a rule.

3. There are some plurals that you will just have to memorize if you don't want to look them up in a dictionary.

I am going to show you how to form the plurals of nouns by using the words in your reference box so you can see how the rules are used. Look at the first word in your reference box. It is the word **key**. What are the two letters at the end of **key**? *(ey)* Is the 'e' a consonant or vowel? *(vowel)* What is the number of the rule that tells you what to do when you have a vowel plus 'y'? *(Rule 2)*

As you can see, the number 2 is written in the blank beside **key** and under the **Rule** title. Now, we will read Rule 2 to find out how to make **key** plural. What does Rule 2 tell you to do to make **key** plural? *(add an s)* How do you spell the plural of **key**? *(k-e-y-s)* Notice that the correct plural spelling is written in the blank beside **key** and under the **Plural Form** title.

Look at the next two words on your sheet. They are **shelf** and **roof**. What is the letter at the end of each of these words? *(f)* What two rules deal with the letter 'f'? *(Rules 4 and 6)* By reading these two rules, can you tell how to make **shelf** and **roof** plural? *(no)*

The only time you know for sure you can use Rule 4 is when you have a word that ends in "fe" *(like knife - knives)*. The only time you know for sure you can use Rule 6 is when you have a word that ends in "ff" *(like cuff - cuffs)* Words that end only in "f" *(like elf and proof)* must be looked up in the dictionary if you do not already know how to form their plurals. The correct spelling for words like **shelf** and **roof** that do not follow a definite rule will have to be memorized.

TEACHER INSTRUCTIONS: At this point, either look up **shelf** and **roof** in the dictionary or ask your students to spell these plurals orally. Write them on the board for the students to see. Encourage the students to use the dictionary when they are not sure of the spellings. *(You could even allow them to use a dictionary on their test; it will help them remember the words they do not know.)* Then, have students study the rules and the correct plural spellings for **shelf** and **roof** in the reference box. Make sure students know how to use the rules to help them spell the plural words correctly.

© SHURLEY INSTRUCTIONAL MATERIALS, INC.

CHAPTER 20 LESSON 1 CONTINUED

Finally, I want you to look at the last word to correct in your reference box. It is the word **fish**. What is the letter at the end of the word **fish**? *(sh)* Which two rules deal with the word fish? *(Rules 1 and 9)* By reading these two rules, we can tell how to make **fish** plural. *(At this point, have students look up the word **fish** in a dictionary. Discuss the two plural spellings and how each rule applies.)*

 PRACTICE TIME

Have students turn to pages 88 and 89 in the Practice Section of their book and find Chapter 20, Lesson 1, Practice *(1-2)*. Go over the directions to make sure they understand what to do. Check and discuss the Practices after students have finished. *(Chapter 20, Lesson 1, Practice keys are given below.)*

Chapter 20, Lesson 1, Practice 1: Write the rule number from Reference 60 and the correct plural form of the nouns below.

		Rule	Plural Form			Rule	Plural Form
1.	day	2	days	6.	match	1	matches
2.	knife	4	knives	7.	patio	7	patios
3.	puff	6	puffs	8.	tomato	8	tomatoes
4.	deer	9	deer	9.	star	10	stars
5.	man	5	men	10.	spy	3	spies

Chapter 20, Lesson 1, Practice 2: On notebook paper, write the seven present tense helping verbs, the five past tense helping verbs, and the two future tense helping verbs. **(The order of answers may vary.)** (Present: **am, is, are, has, have, do, does**; Past: **was, were, had, did, been**; Future: **will, shall**)

 VOCABULARY TIME

Assign Chapter 20, Vocabulary Words **#1** on page 9 in the Reference Section for students to define in their Vocabulary notebooks. After they write each word and its meaning, students are to write a sentence using the vocabulary word.

Chapter 20, Vocabulary Words #1
(pause, hesitate, delete, insert)

(End of lesson.)

© SHURLEY INSTRUCTIONAL MATERIALS, INC.

CHAPTER 20   LESSON 2

Objectives: Jingles, Grammar (Practice Sentences), Practice Exercise, Vocabulary #2, Activity, and Bonus Option.

 JINGLE TIME

Have students turn to the Jingle Section in their books and recite the previously-taught jingles.

 GRAMMAR TIME

First-Year Option: Put the Practice Sentences from the box below on the board or on notebook paper. Use these sentences as you practice the concepts that have been taught. For the greatest benefit, students must participate orally with the teacher. **Second-Year Option:** Have students classify the Practice Sentences independently on paper. Check students' sentences with the answers provided below. (*If you have the CDs for Practice Sentences, have students check their sentences with the CDs.*)

Chapter 20, Practice Sentences for Lesson 2
1. _____ My sister and I played a game of solitaire.
2. _____ Did you sleep with your new stuffed bear?

TEACHING SCRIPT FOR PRACTICING MIXED PATTERNS

We will practice classifying Mixed Patterns. We will classify the sentences together. Begin. (*You might have your students write the labels above the sentences at this time.*)

Question and Answer Flow for Sentence 1: My sister and I played a game of solitaire.

1. Who played a game of solitaire? sister and I - CSN, CSP
2. What is being said about sister and I? sister and I played - V
3. Sister and I played what? game - verify the noun
4. Does game mean the same thing as sister and I? No.
5. Game - DO
6. Played - V-t
7. A - A
8. Of - P
9. Of what? solitaire - OP
10. And - C
11. Whose sister? my - PPA
12. SN V-t DO P2 Check
13. Verb-transitive - Check again.
14. (Of solitaire) - Prepositional phrase
15. Period, statement, declarative sentence
16. Go back to the verb - divide the complete subject from the complete predicate.

Classified Sentence:

```
                    PPA  CSN   C  CSP   V-t  A   DO    P    OP
          SN V-t    My  sister and  I / played  a  game (of solitaire). D
          DO P2
```

© SHURLEY INSTRUCTIONAL MATERIALS, INC.

CHAPTER 20 LESSON 2 CONTINUED

Question and Answer Flow for Sentence 2: Did you sleep with your new stuffed bear?

1. Who did sleep with your new stuffed bear?
   you - SP
2. What is being said about you? you did sleep - V
3. Did - HV
4. With - P
5. With what? bear - OP
6. What kind of bear? stuffed - Adj
7. What kind of bear? new - Adj
8. Whose bear? your - PPA
9. SN V P1 Check
10. (With your new stuffed bear) - Prepositional phrase
11. Question mark, question, interrogative sentence
12. Go back to the verb - divide the complete subject from the complete predicate.

Classified Sentence:

	HV SP	V	P	PPA	Adj	Adj	OP
SN V	Did you /	sleep	(with	your	new	stuffed	bear)? Int
P1							

PRACTICE TIME

Have students turn to page 89 in the Practice Section of their book and find Chapter 20, Lesson 2, Practice (1-2). Go over the directions to make sure they understand what to do. Check and discuss the Practices after students have finished. (*Chapter 20, Lesson 2, Practice keys are given below.*)

Chapter 20, Lesson 2, Practice 1: Write the rule number from Reference 60 and the correct plural form of the nouns below.

		Rule	Plural Form				Rule	Plural Form
1.	journey	2	journeys		6.	church	1	churches
2.	leaf	4	leaves		7.	video	7	videos
3.	gulf	6	gulfs		8.	volcano	8	volcanoes
4.	sheep	9	sheep		9.	car	10	cars
5.	mouse	5	mice		10.	party	3	parties

Chapter 20, Lesson 2, Practice 2: Underline the negative words in each sentence. Rewrite each sentence on notebook paper and correct the double negative mistake as indicated by the rule number in parentheses at the end of the sentence.

Rule 1	Rule 2	Rule 3
Change the second negative to a positive.	Take out the negative part of a contraction.	Remove the first negative word (verb change).

1. There <u>wasn't</u> <u>no</u> cake left. (Rule 1)
   There wasn't any cake left.
2. Lucy <u>doesn't</u> have <u>no</u> paper. (Rule 3)
   Lucy has no paper.
3. We <u>don't</u> see <u>nothing</u> on the table. (Rule 1)
   We don't see anything on the table.
4. Mike <u>hadn't</u> <u>never</u> bought a new car. (Rule 2)
   Mike had never bought a new car.
5. They <u>didn't</u> see <u>nothing</u> in the barn. (Rule 2)
   They did see nothing in the barn.
6. <u>Don't</u> <u>never</u> stay home alone. (Rule 1)
   Don't ever stay home alone.

© SHURLEY INSTRUCTIONAL MATERIALS, INC.

CHAPTER 20 LESSON 2 CONTINUED

VOCABULARY TIME

Assign Chapter 20, Vocabulary Words **#2** on page 9 in the Reference Section for students to define in their Vocabulary notebooks. Tell students they are to use a dictionary or thesaurus to look up the meanings of the vocabulary words. After they write each word and its meaning, students are to write a sentence using the vocabulary word.

Chapter 20, Vocabulary Words #2
(laborious, effortless, excuse, alibi)

ACTIVITY / ASSIGNMENT TIME

Write the following paragraph on the board or on notebook paper. *(Do not underline the prepositions at this time.)* Have students read it aloud and note their reactions. See if they can figure out what is wrong with the paragraph. After they have analyzed the problem, have them identify all the prepositions. There should be 16 prepositions. Then, students should rewrite the paragraph and substitute more appropriate prepositions. They may use their Preposition Flow jingle to help them. Have students read the corrected paragraph aloud. Discuss why choosing the right prepositions is so important.
Bonus Option: Have students write their own paragraph with all the prepositions used incorrectly. They can give this paragraph to others to correct.

At Days Johnny Went **Under** the River

Johnny loved to go fishing **to** his dad. Usually, they went **until** the river, **during** six miles **over** where they lived. Sometimes, they would hitch their boat **since** the back of the car and leave early **against** the morning. Occasionally, they would stop **along** a roadside restaurant **outside** breakfast. **Under** breakfast, they would stop **between** a bait shop to stock up on worms and hooks. Once **underneath** the lake, they would search **except** a shady spot where they could sit **for** the bank and wait **up** the whoppers to bite.

Answers will vary, but one sample key is given below.

On Days Johnny Went **To** the River

Johnny loved to go fishing **with** his dad. Usually, they went **to** the river, **over** six miles **from** where they lived. Sometimes, they would hitch their boat **to** the back of the car and leave early **during** the morning. Occasionally, they would stop **at** a roadside restaurant **for** breakfast. **After** breakfast, they would stop **at** a bait shop to stock up on worms and hooks. Once **at** the lake, they would search **for** a shady spot where they could sit **on** the bank and wait **for** the whoppers to bite.

(End of lesson.)

© SHURLEY INSTRUCTIONAL MATERIALS, INC.

CHAPTER 20   LESSON 3

Objectives: Jingles, Grammar (Practice Sentences), and Practice Exercise.

JINGLE TIME

Have students turn to the Jingle Section in their books and recite the previously-taught jingles.

GRAMMAR TIME

First-Year Option: Put the Practice Sentences from the box below on the board or on notebook paper. Use these sentences as you practice the concepts that have been taught. For the greatest benefit, students must participate orally with the teacher. **Second-Year Option:** Have students classify the Practice Sentences independently on paper. Check students' sentences with the answers provided below. *(If you have the CDs for Practice Sentences, have students check their sentences with the CDs.)*

Chapter 20, Practice Sentences for Lesson 3
1. _____ Were you speaking to Julie or me?
2. _____ Yippee! My parents purchased a new car today!

TEACHING SCRIPT FOR PRACTICING MIXED PATTERNS

We will practice classifying Mixed Patterns. We will classify the sentences together. Begin. (*You might have your students write the labels above the sentences at this time.*)

Question and Answer Flow for Sentence 1: Were you speaking to Julie or me?	
1. Who were speaking to Julie or me? you - SP	7. SN V P1 Check
2. What is being said about you? you were speaking - V	8. (To Julie or me) - Prepositional phrase
3. Were - HV	9. Question mark, question, interrogative sentence
4. To - P	10. Go back to the verb - divide the complete subject
5. To whom? Julie or me - COP, COP	from the complete predicate.
6. Or - C	

Classified Sentence:

```
                       HV   SP      V      P  COP C COP
          SN  V      Were  you / speaking (to Julie or me)? Int
          P1
```

© SHURLEY INSTRUCTIONAL MATERIALS, INC.

CHAPTER 20 LESSON 3 CONTINUED

Question and Answer Flow for Sentence 2: Yippee! My parents purchased a new car today!

1. Who purchased a new car today? parents - SN
2. What is being said about parents?
   parents purchased - V
3. Parents purchased what? car - verify the noun
4. Does car mean the same thing as parents? No.
5. Car - DO
6. Purchased - V-t
7. What kind of car? new - Adj
8. A - A

9. Purchased when? today - Adv
10. Whose parents? my - PPA
11. Yippee - I
12. SN V-t DO P2 Check
13. No prepositional phrases.
14. Exclamation point, strong feeling, exclamatory sentence
15. Go back to the verb - divide the complete subject
    from the complete predicate.

Classified Sentence:

<u>SN V-t</u>   I   PPA   SN   V-t   A   Adj   DO   Adv
DO P2   Yippee! My parents / purchased a new car today! **E**

PRACTICE TIME

Have students turn to pages 89 and 90 in the Practice Section of their books and find Chapter 20, Lesson 3, Practice (*1-5*). Go over the directions to make sure they understand what to do. If students need a review, have them study the information and examples in the Reference Section of their books. Check and discuss the Practices after students have finished. (*Chapter 20, Lesson 3, Practice keys are given below and on the next page.*)

Chapter 20, Lesson 3, Practice 1: Underline each subject and fill in each column according to the title.

	List each Verb	Write PrN, PA, or None	Write L or A
1. <u>Paris</u> is a beautiful city.	is	PrN	L
2. <u>He</u> worked on the car.	worked	None	A
3. The <u>papers</u> are graded.	are	PA	L
4. The <u>dog</u> barked during the night.	barked	None	A
5. Those two <u>girls</u> are sisters.	are	PrN	L
6. My <u>feet</u> are sore.	are	PA	L

© SHURLEY INSTRUCTIONAL MATERIALS, INC.

CHAPTER 20 LESSON 3 CONTINUED

Chapter 20, Lesson 3, Practice 2: Write the rule number from Reference 60 and the correct plural form of the nouns below.

		Rule	Plural Form				Rule	Plural Form
1.	alloy	2	alloys		6.	kiss	1	kisses
2.	shelf	4	shelves		7.	rodeo	7	rodeos
3.	roof	6	roofs		8.	dingo	8	dingoes
4.	moose	9	moose		9.	dinosaur	10	dinosaurs
5.	fireman	5	firemen		10.	pastry	3	pastries

Chapter 20, Lesson 3, Practice 3: Underline the negative words in each sentence. Rewrite each sentence on notebook paper and correct the double negative mistake as indicated by the rule number in parentheses at the end of the sentence.

Rule 1	Rule 2	Rule 3
Change the second negative to a positive.	Take out the negative part of a contraction.	Remove the first negative word (verb change).

1. The boys <u>didn't</u> ride <u>no</u> roller coaster. (Rule 3)
   The boys rode no roller coaster.
2. We <u>hadn't</u> <u>never</u> been to a football game. (Rule 2)
   We had never been to a football game.
3. She <u>doesn't</u> want <u>no</u> candy. (Rule 1)
   She doesn't want any candy.
4. She <u>didn't</u> see <u>nothing</u> to buy. (Rule 1)
   She didn't see anything to buy.

Chapter 20, Lesson 3, Practice 4: Underline each verb or verb phrase. Identify the verb tense by writing a number 1 for present tense, a number 2 for past tense, and a number 3 for future tense. Write the past tense form and R or I for Regular or Irregular.

Verb Tense			Main Verb Past Tense Form	R or I
2	1.	<u>Did</u> you <u>write</u> that poem?	wrote	I
3	2.	Betty <u>will</u> <u>watch</u> the children.	watched	R
3	3.	Tomorrow, he <u>will</u> <u>drive</u> to school.	drove	I
2	4.	I <u>worked</u> with a new boss.	worked	R

Chapter 20, Lesson 3, Practice 5: Copy the following words on another sheet of paper. Write the correct contraction beside each word. **Key: can't, let's, don't, wasn't, they're, aren't, hadn't, isn't, she's, who's, you're, didn't, it's, we're, weren't, doesn't.**
<u>Words</u>: cannot, let us, do not, was not, they are, are not, had not, is not, she is, who is, you are, did not, it is, we are, were not, does not.

(End of lesson.)

CHAPTER 20 LESSON 4

Objectives: Jingles, Study, Test, Check, Activity, and Writing (journal).

JINGLE TIME

Have students turn to the Jingle Section in their books and recite the previously-taught jingles.

STUDY TIME

Have students study the vocabulary words in their vocabulary notebooks. Remind students that any vocabulary word in their notebooks could be on their test. Also, have students study any of the skills in the Practice Section that they need to review.

TEST TIME

Have students turn to page 117 in the Test Section of their books and find Chapter 20 Test. Go over the directions to make sure they understand what to do. (*Chapter 20 Test key is on the next page.*)

CHECK TIME

After students have finished, check and discuss their test papers. Make sure they understand why their answers are right or wrong. (*For total points, count each required answer as a point.*)

ACTIVITY / ASSIGNMENT TIME

Students will continue to draw or trace the states and write the following questions and answers.

New Mexico	New York
1. What is the state on the front of this card? **New Mexico**	1. What is the state on the front of this card? **New York**
2. What is the capital of New Mexico? **Santa Fe**	2. What is the capital of New York? **Albany**
3. What is the postal abbreviation of New Mexico? **NM**	3. What is the postal abbreviation of New York? **NY**
4. What year was New Mexico admitted to the Union? **1912**	4. What year was New York admitted to the Union? **1788**

Color these states and look up an interesting fact about each state to write on the cards. Use the cards to quiz family members, friends, and relatives. You may want to time the responses to your questions. Also, along with previous suggestions, think of other ways to have fun with your United States card file.

(End of lesson.)

© SHURLEY INSTRUCTIONAL MATERIALS, INC.

Chapter 20 Test
(Student Page 117)

Exercise 1: Classify each sentence.

<pre>
          SP   V-t A Adj   DO   P PPA PNA   OP
1. <u>SN V-t</u>   We / built a large snowman (in our neighbor's yard). D
   <u>DO P2</u>

          A   SN   V   P PNA   OP   P A Adj   OP
2. <u>SN V</u>   The guests / sneaked (into Eve's house) (for a surprise party)! E
   <u>P1</u>
</pre>

Exercise 2: Identify each pair of words as synonyms or antonyms by putting parentheses ( ) around *syn* or *ant*.

1. sorrow, bliss	syn **(ant)**	4. unusual, strange	**(syn)** ant	7. construct, destroy	syn **(ant)**
2. excuse, alibi	**(syn)** ant	5. delete, insert	syn **(ant)**	8. insightful, perceptive	**(syn)** ant
3. public, private	syn **(ant)**	6. hesitate, pause	**(syn)** ant	9. effortless, laborious	syn **(ant)**

Exercise 3: Write the rule number from Reference 60 and the correct plural form of the nouns below.

		Rule	Plural Form				Rule	Plural Form
1.	key	2	**keys**		6.	brush	1	**brushes**
2.	pansy	3	**pansies**		7.	child	5	**children**
3.	mouse	5	**mice**		8.	moose	9	**moose**
4.	cameo	7	**cameos**		9.	wolf	4	**wolves**
5.	knife	4	**knives**		10.	whiff	6	**whiffs**

Exercise 4: Underline the negative words in each sentence. Rewrite each sentence on notebook paper and correct the double negative mistake as indicated by the rule number in parentheses at the end of the sentence.

Rule 1	Rule 2	Rule 3
Change the second negative to a positive.	Take out the negative part of a contraction.	Remove the first negative word (verb change).

1. The car <u>doesn't</u> have <u>no</u> gas. (Rule 3)
   The car has no gas.
2. She <u>wouldn't</u> eat <u>no</u> cereal. (Rule 2)
   She would eat no cereal.
3. Sandra <u>shouldn't</u> eat <u>no</u> dessert. (Rule 1)
   Sandra shouldn't eat any dessert.
4. The teacher <u>didn't</u> <u>never</u> give the test. (Rule 3)
   The teacher never gave the test.
5. That guide <u>didn't</u> bring <u>no</u> water. (Rule 1)
   That guide didn't bring any water.
6. Scott <u>hasn't</u> <u>never</u> stayed out late. (Rule 2)
   Scott has never stayed out late.

Exercise 5: On notebook paper, write the seven present tense helping verbs, the five past tense helping verbs, and the two future tense helping verbs. **(The order of answers may vary.)** (Present: **am, is, are, has, have, do, does**; Past: **was, were, had, did, been**; Future: **will, shall**)

Exercise 6: Copy the following words on notebook paper. Write the correct contraction beside each word.
Key: can't, let's, don't, wasn't, they're, aren't, hadn't, isn't, she's, who's, you're, didn't, it's.
<u>Words</u>: cannot, let us, do not, was not, they are, are not, had not, is not, she is, who is, you are, did not, it is.

Exercise 7: In your journal, write a paragraph summarizing what you have learned this week.

CHAPTER 20 LESSON 4 CONTINUED

TEACHER INSTRUCTIONS

Use the Question and Answer Flows below for the sentences on the Chapter 20 Test.

Question and Answer Flow for Sentence 1: We built a large snowman in our neighbor's yard.

1. Who built a large snowman in our neighbor's yard? we - SP
2. What is being said about we? we built - V
3. We built what? snowman - verify the noun
4. Does snowman mean the same thing as we? No.
5. Snowman - DO
6. Built - V-t
7. What kind of snowman? large - Adj
8. A - A
9. In - P
10. In what? yard - OP
11. Whose yard? neighbor's - PNA
12. Whose neighbor? our - PPA
13. SN V-t DO P2 Check
14. Verb-transitive - Check again.
15. (In our neighbor's yard) - Prepositional phrase
16. Period, statement, declarative sentence
17. Go back to the verb - divide the complete subject from the complete predicate.

Classified Sentence:

                                 SP   V-t A Adj   DO   P PPA PNA   OP

        <u>SN V-t</u>   We / built a large snowman (in our neighbor's yard). **D**

        DO P2

Question and Answer Flow for Sentence 2: The guests sneaked into Eve's house for a surprise party!

1. Who sneaked into Eve's house for a surprise party? guests - SN
2. What is being said about guests? guests sneaked - V
3. Into - P
4. Into what? house - OP
5. Whose house? Eve's - PNA
6. For - P
7. For what? party - OP
8. What kind of party? surprise - Adj
9. A - A
10. The - A
11. SN V P1 Check
12. (Into Eve's house) - Prepositional phrase
13. (For a surprise party) - Prepositional phrase
14. Exclamation point, strong feeling, exclamatory sentence
15. Go back to the verb - divide the complete subject from the complete predicate.

Classified Sentence:

                                 A   SN   V   P PNA OP   P A Adj   OP

        <u>SN V</u>   The guests / sneaked (into Eve's house) (for a surprise party)! **E**

        P1

© SHURLEY INSTRUCTIONAL MATERIALS, INC.

CHAPTER 20   LESSON 5
Objectives: Writing (descriptive), Writing Assignment #24, and Bonus Option.

 **WRITING TIME**

TEACHING SCRIPT FOR INTRODUCING DESCRIPTIVE WRITING

An artist paints a picture on canvas with paint. A descriptive writer paints a picture on paper with words. Both the artist and writer must select what they will include in their picture. Descriptive writing **shows** the reader what is being described. It does not just **tell** him about it.

Even though you can use description in expository, narrative, and persuasive writing, sometimes you are asked to write only a descriptive piece of writing. Then, you must know that a **descriptive paragraph** gives a detailed picture of a person, place, thing, or idea.

A descriptive paragraph will usually start with an overall impression of what you are describing. That will be your topic sentence. Then, you will add supporting sentences that give details about the topic. To make a description clear and vivid, these detail sentences should include as much information as possible about how the topic looks, sounds, feels, or tastes. The sensory details that you include will depend on what you are describing. Since all the senses are not significant in all situations, the following guidelines about descriptive writing will give you the types of details that you should consider when you are describing certain topics.

Look at Reference 61 on page 48 in your Reference Section. Follow along as I read the guidelines for descriptive writing. This reference will give you ideas and help guide you as you write descriptive paragraphs. (*Read and discuss Reference 61 below with your students. You might even want to make a descriptive - guidelines poster for the wall so students can have a visual guide as they write descriptive paragraphs.*)

Reference 61: Guidelines for Descriptive Writing
1. **When describing people,** it is helpful to notice these types of details: appearance, walk, voice, manner, gestures, personality traits, any special incident related to the person being described, and any striking details that make that person stand out in your mind.
2. **When describing places or things,** it is helpful to notice these types of details: the physical features of a place or thing (color, texture, smell, shape, size, age), any unusual features, any special incident related to the place or thing being described, and whether or not the place or thing is special to you.
3. **When describing nature,** it is helpful to notice these types of details: the special features of the season, the sights, smells, sounds, colors, animals, insects, birds, and any special incident related to the scene being described.
4. **When describing an incident or an event,** it is helpful to notice these types of details: the order in which the event takes place, any specific facts that will keep the story moving from a beginning to an ending, the answers to any of the *who, what, when, where, why,* and *how* questions that the reader needs to know, and especially the details that will create a clear picture, such as how things look, sound, smell, feel, etc.

© SHURLEY INSTRUCTIONAL MATERIALS, INC.

CHAPTER 20 LESSON 5 CONTINUED

Look at Reference 62 on page 48. Follow along as I go over the steps in writing a descriptive paragraph.
(Read the samples below as students follow along in the reference box.)

♦ Writing Topic: **A Trip to the Supermarket**
♦ <u>The Title</u> - Since there are many possibilities for titles, decide if you want to leave the topic as your title or if you want to write a different phrase to tell what your paragraph is about.
   (A Trip to the Supermarket)

1. Sentence #1 - Write a topic sentence that introduces what is being described.
    (Almost every week, Mom makes a trip to the supermarket, and my little brother and I go with her.)

2. Sentences #2 - #8 -Write sentences that give a description of your topic. *(Use the descriptive writing guidelines in Reference 61 to help you.)*

    (Before we leave, Mom hurries around the kitchen making a list of all the groceries that we need. I put on my socks and shoes, and then I help Joey with his. We all pile into our mini van and travel into town. When we arrive at the supermarket, Mom puts Joey in the basket, and I walk beside her. By the time we have finished shopping, my legs are tired. The check-out line is my favorite part of the whole trip, even though the lines are always long. Mom lets Joey and me pick out our favorite treat to eat on our way home.)

3. Sentence #9 -Write a concluding (final) sentence that summarizes your paragraph or relates it back to the topic sentence. Read the topic sentence again and then restate it by using some of the same words to say the same thing in a different way.
    (After the grocer sacks all our food, we happily head out to our mini van with a smile on our face and a sweet treat in our hand.)

Reference 62: Descriptive Paragraph Guidelines

A. Sentence 1 is the topic sentence that introduces **what is being described**.
B. For sentences 2-8, use **the descriptive details** in Reference 61.
C. Sentence 9 is a concluding sentence that **restates, or relates back to, the topic sentence**.

A Trip to the Supermarket

   Almost every week, Mom makes a trip to the supermarket, and my little brother and I go with her. Before we leave, Mom hurries around the kitchen making a list of all the groceries that we need. I put on my socks and shoes, and then I help Joey with his. We all pile into our mini van and travel into town. When we arrive at the supermarket, Mom puts Joey in the basket, and I walk beside her. By the time we have finished shopping, my legs are tired. The check-out line is my favorite part of the whole trip, even though the lines are always long. Mom lets Joey and me pick out our favorite treat to eat on our way home. After the grocer sacks all our food, we happily head out to our mini van with a smile on our face and a sweet treat in our hand.

© SHURLEY INSTRUCTIONAL MATERIALS, INC.

CHAPTER 20 LESSON 5 CONTINUED

Teacher's Note: The descriptive paragraph guideline is a suggested guide to help students as they learn to write descriptive paragraphs. However, some students will be able to organize their ideas and stick to the topic without following the guideline exactly. The number of sentences may also vary.

You will write a descriptive paragraph. You should use the descriptive paragraph guidelines to help you notice and describe different types of details. <u>You will revise and edit this writing assignment</u>. (*Read the box below for more information about students' writing assignment*.) As you edit, make sure you use the checkpoints in the editing checklist provided in Reference 42. Remember to read through the whole paragraph, starting with the title, and then edit, sentence-by-sentence, using the five-sentence checkpoints for each sentence. Use the paragraph checkpoints to check each paragraph.

Writing Assignment Box

Writing Assignment #24: Descriptive Paragraph

Writing topic choices: Favorite Biblical Character or **Smells of the County Fair** or **Litter Along the Highway**
or **Two Robins Building a Nest**

<u>**Bonus Option**</u>: **Look at Psalm 23 (King James Version). What words are used to describe the following:**
1. **the pastures** 2. **the waters** 3. **the paths**

Select one of the verses in Psalm 23 and illustrate it. Be sure to write the verse at the bottom of your drawing. Tell which verse is your favorite and explain why.

Read, check, and discuss Writing Assignment #24 after students have finished their final papers. Use the editing checklist as you check and discuss students' papers. Make sure students are using the editing checklist correctly.

<u>**Bonus Option Answers**</u>:
(1) **green**
(2) **still**
(3) **righteousness**

(End of lesson.)

© SHURLEY INSTRUCTIONAL MATERIALS, INC.

CHAPTER 21   LESSON 1

Objectives: Jingles, Grammar (Practice Sentences), Skills (parts of a friendly letter, parts of an envelope), Practice Exercise, and Vocabulary #1.

JINGLE TIME

Have students turn to the Jingle Section in their books and recite the previously-taught jingles.

GRAMMAR TIME

First-Year Option: Put the Practice Sentences from the box below on the board or on notebook paper. Use these sentences as you practice the concepts that have been taught. For the greatest benefit, students must participate orally with the teacher. **Second-Year Option:** Have students classify the Practice Sentences independently on paper. Check students' sentences with the answers provided below. (*If you have the CDs for Practice Sentences, have students check their sentences with the CDs.*)

Chapter 21, Practice Sentences for Lesson 1

1. _____ I signed my name across the dotted line.
2. _____ Do not slip on the wet floor in the kitchen.

TEACHING SCRIPT FOR PRACTICING MIXED PATTERNS

We will practice classifying Mixed Patterns. We will classify the sentences together. Begin. (*You might have your students write the labels above the sentences at this time.*)

Question and Answer Flow for Sentence 1: I signed my name across the dotted line.

1. Who signed my name across the dotted line? I - SP
2. What is being said about I? I signed - V
3. I signed what? name - verify the noun
4. Does name mean the same thing as I? No.
5. Name - DO
6. Signed - V-t
7. Whose name? my - PPA
8. Across - P
9. Across what? line - OP
10. What kind of line? dotted - Adj
11. The - A
12. SN V-t DO P2 Check
13. Verb-transitive - Check again.
14. (Across the dotted line) - Prepositional phrase
15. Period, statement, declarative sentence
16. Go back to the verb - divide the complete subject from the complete predicate.

Classified Sentence:

```
                        SP  V-t  PPA  DO    P   A  Adj  OP
            SN V-t      I / signed my name (across the dotted line).  D
            ------
            DO P2
```

© SHURLEY INSTRUCTIONAL MATERIALS, INC.

Question and Answer Flow for Sentence 2: Do not slip on the wet floor in the kitchen.

1. Who do not slip on the wet floor in the kitchen?
   you - SP (understood subject pronoun)
2. What is being said about you? you do slip - V
3. Do - HV
4. Do slip how? not - Adv
5. On - P
6. On what? floor - OP
7. What kind of floor? wet - Adj
8. The - A

9. In - P
10. In what? kitchen - OP
11. The - A
12. SN V P1 Check
13. (On the wet floor) - Prepositional phrase
14. (In the kitchen) - Prepositional phrase
15. Period, command, imperative sentence
16. Go back to the verb - divide the complete subject from the complete predicate.

Classified Sentence:

	(You) SP		HV	Adv	V	P	A	Adj	OP	P	A	OP	
	SN V	/	Do	not	slip	(on	the	wet	floor)	(in	the	kitchen).	**Imp**
	P1												

SKILL TIME

TEACHING SCRIPT FOR THE PARTS OF A FRIENDLY LETTER

Close your eyes. Picture a good friend or favorite relative that you really like but don't get to see very often. Open your eyes. The memory of that favorite person in your life brought a smile to your face, didn't it? Remember, keeping in touch with favorite people brings smiles to their faces, too. Writing a letter is a great way to stay in touch with people you care about and who care about you.

A letter written to or received from friends or relatives is called a **friendly letter**. Listen carefully to some tips that will make your friendly letter interesting and enjoyable to read. (*Read and discuss the tips below. Option: You might choose to dictate the writing tips to your students to enhance their listening skills.*)

Tips for Writing Friendly Letters

Tip #1: Write as if you were talking to the person face-to-face. Share information about yourself and mutual friends. Tell stories, conversations, or jokes. Share photographs, articles, drawings, poems, etc. Avoid saying something about someone else that you'll be sorry for later.

Tip #2: If you are writing a return letter, be sure to answer any questions that were asked. Repeat the question so that your reader will know what you are writing about. (You asked about . . .)

Tip #3: End your letter in a positive way so that your reader will want to write a return letter.

© SHURLEY INSTRUCTIONAL MATERIALS, INC.

CHAPTER 21 LESSON 1 CONTINUED

Now that you know what things to write about, you must learn to put your friendly letter in the correct friendly-letter format. The friendly letter has five parts: the heading; the friendly greeting, which is also called the salutation; the body; the closing; and the signature.

Each of the parts of a friendly letter has a specific place where it should be written in order for your letter to have correct friendly-letter form. Look at the five parts of a friendly letter and the friendly letter example in Reference 63 on page 49 in your book. We will now go over each of the five parts, what information is contained in each part, and where each part is placed in a friendly-letter form. (*Go over the letter parts and the letter example reproduced below with your students.*)

Reference 63: The Five Parts of a Friendly Letter

1. Heading
1. Box or street address of writer
2. City, state, zip code of writer
3. Date letter was written
4. Placement: upper right-hand corner

2. Friendly Greeting or Salutation
1. Begins with *Dear*
2. Names person receiving the letter
3. Has comma after person's name
4. Placement: at left margin, two lines below heading

3. Body
1. Tells reason the letter was written
2. Can have one or more paragraphs
3. Has indented paragraphs
4. Is placed one line below the greeting
5. Skips one line between each paragraph

4. Closing
1. Closes letter with a personal phrase - (Your friend, With love,)
2. Capitalizes only first word
3. Is followed by a comma
4. Is placed two lines below the body
5. Begins just to the right of the middle of the letter

5. Signature
1. Tells who wrote the letter
2. Is usually signed in cursive
3. Uses first name only unless there is a question as to which friend or relative you are
4. Is placed beneath the closing

Friendly Letter Example

1. Heading
67 Edgewood Court
Madison, KY 38287
August 21, 20___

2. Friendly Greeting, (or Salutation)
Dear Tim,

3. Body (Indent Paragraphs)

Jon's team, as you may know, made it to the championship finals last weekend. The team will play in Tucson, Arizona, next weekend for the winner's trophy. We are planning to drive to the game and wondered if you'd like to go with us. If so, give me a quick call, and we'll plan to pick you up.

4. Closing,
Love,

5. Signature
Aunt Tracey

© SHURLEY INSTRUCTIONAL MATERIALS, INC.

CHAPTER 21 LESSON 1 CONTINUED

TEACHING SCRIPT FOR THE PARTS OF AN ENVELOPE

In order to address the envelope of your friendly letter correctly, you must know the parts that go on the envelope and where to write them. Look at Reference 64 on page 50 and follow along as I read the information about the parts of an envelope. Notice what information is contained in the two parts, and where each part is placed on the envelope. (*Go over the information below with your students.*)

Reference 64: Friendly Envelope Parts	
Envelope Parts	**Friendly Envelope Example**

The return address:
1. Name of the person writing the letter
2. Box or street address of the writer
3. City, state, zip code of the writer
 	
The mailing address:
1. Name of the person receiving the letter
2. Street address of the person receiving the letter
3. City, state, zip of the person receiving the letter
	Return Address
	Tracey Lang
	67 Edgewood Court
	Madison, KY 38287 Stamp
	
	                       Mailing Address
	                       Tim Tipton
	                       4007 Delaney Drive
	                       Hartsville, TN 75938

 PRACTICE TIME

Have students turn to page 91 in the Practice Section of their book and find Chapter 21, Lesson 1, Practice. Go over the directions to make sure they understand what to do. Check and discuss the Practice after students have finished. (*Chapter 21, Lesson 1, Practice instructions are given below.*)

Chapter 21, Lesson 1, Practice: Use butcher paper, large pieces of construction paper, or poster board to make a colorful wall poster identifying the five parts of a friendly letter and the parts of an envelope. Write the title and an example for each of the five parts. Illustrate your work. Then, give an oral presentation about the friendly letter and the envelope when you have finished. (*This project may take several days.*)

 VOCABULARY TIME

Assign Chapter 21, Vocabulary Words **#1** on page 9 in the Reference Section for students to define in their Vocabulary notebooks. After they write each word and its meaning, students are to write a sentence using the vocabulary word.

Chapter 21, Vocabulary Words #1
(abrupt, sudden, torrid, frigid)

(End of lesson.)

© SHURLEY INSTRUCTIONAL MATERIALS, INC.

CHAPTER 21   LESSON 2

Objectives: Jingles, Grammar (Practice Sentences), Independent Practice Sentence, Practice Exercise, and Vocabulary #2.

JINGLE TIME

Have students turn to the Jingle Section in their books and recite the previously-taught jingles.

GRAMMAR TIME

First-Year Option: Put the Practice Sentences from the box below on the board or on notebook paper. Use these sentences as you practice the concepts that have been taught. For the greatest benefit, students must participate orally with the teacher. **Second-Year Option:** Have students classify the Practice Sentences independently on paper. Check students' sentences with the answers provided below. *(If you have the CDs for Practice Sentences, have students check their sentences with the CDs.)*

Chapter 21, Practice Sentences for Lesson 2
1. _____ Can you see the moon and stars in the cloudy night sky?
2. _____ Lisa walked slowly down the aisle during the ceremony.

TEACHING SCRIPT FOR PRACTICING MIXED PATTERNS

We will practice classifying Mixed Patterns. We will classify the sentences together. Begin. *(You might have your students write the labels above the sentences at this time.)*

Question and Answer Flow for Sentence 1: Can you see the moon and stars in the cloudy night sky?

1. Who can see the moon and stars in the cloudy night sky? you - SP
2. What is being said about you? you can see - V
3. Can - HV
4. You can see what? moon and stars - verify the nouns
5. Do moon and stars mean the same thing as you? No.
6. Moon and stars - CDO, CDO
7. See - V-t
8. The - A
9. And – C
10. In - P
11. In what? sky - OP
12. What kind of sky? night - Adj
13. What kind of sky? cloudy - Adj
14. The - A
15. SN V-t DO P2 Check
16. Verb-transitive - Check again.
17. (In the cloudy night sky) - Prepositional phrase
18. Question mark, question, interrogative sentence
19. Go back to the verb - divide the complete subject from the complete predicate.

Classified Sentence:

```
                      HV  SP  V-t  A  CDO  C  CDO  P  A   Adj   Adj  OP
          SN V-t      Can you / see the moon and stars (in the cloudy night sky)?  Int
          DO P2
```

© SHURLEY INSTRUCTIONAL MATERIALS, INC.

CHAPTER 21 LESSON 2 CONTINUED

Question and Answer Flow for Sentence 2: Lisa walked slowly down the aisle during the ceremony.

1. Who walked slowly down the aisle during the ceremony? Lisa - SN
2. What is being said about Lisa? Lisa walked - V
3. Walked how? slowly - Adv
4. Down - P
5. Down what? aisle - OP
6. The - A
7. During - P

8. During what? ceremony - OP
9. The - A
10. SN V P1 Check
11. (Down the aisle) - Prepositional phrase
12. (During the ceremony) - Prepositional phrase
13. Period, statement, declarative sentence
14. Go back to the verb - divide the complete subject from the complete predicate.

Classified Sentence:	SN	V	Adv	P	A	OP	P	A	OP

SN V P1   Lisa / walked slowly (down the aisle) (during the ceremony). **D**

TEACHER INSTRUCTIONS FOR A PRACTICE SENTENCE

Tell students that their sentence writing assignment today is to write a sentence pattern of their choice. They may choose any Pattern, 1-2, for a Practice Sentence. They are to follow the same procedure used in the previous lessons. They should decide on their labels, arrange them in a selected order, write their sentences, and edit their sentences for improved word choices. (*Students do not have to write an Improved Sentence at this point unless you feel they need more one-on-one word choice writing practice.*) Check and discuss the sentence pattern chosen after students have finished.

PRACTICE TIME

Students will continue letter-writing activities. Have students turn to page 91 in the Practice Section of their book and find Chapter 21, Lesson 2, Practice. Go over the directions to make sure they understand what to do. Check and discuss the Practice after students have finished. (*Chapter 21, Lesson 2, Practice instructions are given below.*)

Chapter 21, Lesson 2, Practice: Write a friendly letter to a special friend or relative. Before you start, review the references and tips for writing friendly letters. After your letter has been edited, fold the letter and put it in an envelope. Address the envelope properly and mail it. Don't forget the stamp. (E-mail does not take the place of this assignment.)

VOCABULARY TIME

Assign Chapter 21, Vocabulary Words **#2** on page 9 in the Reference Section for students to define in their Vocabulary notebooks. They should write each word, its meaning, and a sentence using the word.

Chapter 21, Vocabulary Words #2
(link, disconnect, most, maximum)

(End of lesson.)

© SHURLEY INSTRUCTIONAL MATERIALS, INC.

CHAPTER 21 LESSON 3

Objectives: Jingles, Grammar (Practice Sentences), Practice Exercise, and Activity.

JINGLE TIME

Have students turn to the Jingle Section in their books and recite the previously-taught jingles.

GRAMMAR TIME

First-Year Option: Put the Practice Sentences from the box below on the board or on notebook paper. Use these sentences as you practice the concepts that have been taught. For the greatest benefit, students must participate orally with the teacher. **Second-Year Option:** Have students classify the Practice Sentences independently on paper. Check students' sentences with the answers provided below. (*If you have the CDs for Practice Sentences, have students check their sentences with the CDs.*)

Chapter 21, Practice Sentences for Lesson 3

1. _____ Jason and I smiled for our grandmother's camera.
2. _____ That snake can bend its body into many coils!

TEACHING SCRIPT FOR PRACTICING MIXED PATTERNS

We will practice classifying Mixed Patterns. We will classify the sentences together. Begin. (*You might have your students write the labels above the sentences at this time.*)

Question and Answer Flow for Sentence 1: Jason and I smiled for our grandmother's camera.

1. Who smiled for our grandmother's camera?
   Jason and I - CSN, CSP
2. What is being said about Jason and I?
   Jason and I smiled - V
3. For - P
4. For what? camera - OP
5. Whose camera? grandmother's - PNA
6. Whose grandmother? our - PPA

7. And - C
8. SN V P1 Check
9. (For our grandmother's camera) - Prepositional phrase
10. Period, statement, declarative sentence
11. Go back to the verb - divide the complete subject
    from the complete predicate.

Classified Sentence:

	CSN	C CSP	V	P	PPA	PNA		OP	
SN V	Jason	and I /	smiled	(for	our	grandmother's		camera).	**D**
P1									

© SHURLEY INSTRUCTIONAL MATERIALS, INC.

CHAPTER 21 LESSON 3 CONTINUED

Question and Answer Flow for Sentence 2: That snake can bend its body into many coils!

1. What can bend its body into many coils? snake - SN
2. What is being said about snake? snake can bend - V
3. Can - HV
4. Snake can bend what? body - verify the noun
5. Does body mean the same thing as snake? No.
6. Body - DO
7. Bend - V-t
8. Whose body? its - PPA
9. Into - P
10. Into what? coils - OP

11. How many coils? many - Adj
12. Which snake? that - Adj
13. SN V-t DO P2 Check
14. Verb-transitive - Check again.
15. (Into many coils) - Prepositional phrase
16. Exclamation point, strong feeling, exclamatory sentence
17. Go back to the verb - divide the complete subject from the complete predicate.

Classified Sentence:

	Adj	SN	HV	V-t	PPA	DO	P	Adj	OP
SN V-t	That	snake /	can	bend	its	body	(into	many	coils)! E
DO P2									

PRACTICE TIME

Have students turn to page 91 in the Practice Section of their books and find Chapter 21, Lesson 3, Practice (*1-2*). Go over the directions to make sure they understand what to do. Check and discuss the Practices after students have finished. (*Chapter 21, Lesson 3, Practice instructions are given below.*)

Chapter 21, Lesson 3, Practice 1: On notebook paper, identify the parts of a friendly letter and envelope by writing the titles and an example for each title. Use References 63 and 64 to help you. (**Use References 63-64 to check the parts of a friendly letter and envelope.**)

Chapter 21, Lesson 3, Practice 2: Write a friendly letter to a neighbor, nursing home resident, or relative. This person must be someone different from the person chosen in the previous lesson. Before you start, review the references and tips for writing friendly letters. After your letter has been edited, fold the letter and put it in an envelope. Address the envelope properly and mail it. Don't forget the stamp.

ACTIVITY / ASSIGNMENT TIME

Have students make a booklet and title it, "Little Known Facts About Interesting People." They should interview one person a week for several weeks and organize their facts into a pleasing format. They may want to add photographs, artwork, etc. (*This can also be done on the computer.*) Students may use the suggestions below as they compile information for their folders. Suggested people to interview: parents, grandparents, brothers, sisters, aunts, uncles, cousins, or friends. (*Some questions may not apply to all people.*)

Name: City of residence: Occupation: Birth date and place: Date of marriage: How I met my spouse: My favorite color is..., My favorite month is..., My favorite school subject was..., My favorite dessert is..., My favorite food is..., My favorite restaurant is..., My favorite room in the house is..., My favorite book is..., My favorite music/song is..., My favorite movie is..., My favorite TV show is..., My hobbies are..., My pet peeve is..., I like people who..., My best vacation was..., If I could go anywhere in the world, I'd go to..., The person who influenced me the most was..., My proudest accomplishments are..., My words of wisdom for others are....

(End of lesson.)

CHAPTER 21   LESSON 4

Objectives: Jingles, Study, Test, Check, Activity, and Writing (journal).

JINGLE TIME

Have students turn to the Jingle Section in their books and recite the previously-taught jingles.

STUDY TIME

Have students study the vocabulary words in their vocabulary notebooks. Remind students that any vocabulary word in their notebooks could be on their test. Also, have students study any of the skills in the Practice Section that they need to review.

TEST TIME

Have students turn to page 118 in the Test Section of their books and find Chapter 21 Test. Go over the directions to make sure they understand what to do. (*Chapter 21 Test key is on the next page.*)

CHECK TIME

After students have finished, check and discuss their test papers. Make sure they understand why their answers are right or wrong. (*For total points, count each required answer as a point.*)

ACTIVITY / ASSIGNMENT TIME

Students will continue to draw or trace the states and write the following questions and answers.

North Carolina	North Dakota
1. What is the state on the front of this card? **North Carolina**	1. What is the state on the front of this card? **North Dakota**
2. What is the capital of North Carolina? **Raleigh**	2. What is the capital of North Dakota? **Bismarck**
3. What is the postal abbreviation of North Carolina? **NC**	3. What is the postal abbreviation of North Dakota? **ND**
4. What year was North Carolina admitted to the Union? **1789**	4. What year was North Dakota admitted to the Union? **1889**

Color these states and look up an interesting fact about each state to write on the cards. Use the cards to quiz family members, friends, and relatives. You may want to time the responses to your questions. Also, along with previous suggestions, think of other ways to have fun with your United States card file.

(End of lesson.)

© SHURLEY INSTRUCTIONAL MATERIALS, INC.

Chapter 21 Test
(Student Page 118)

Exercise 1: Classify each sentence.

```
     (You) SP    V-t   PPA   DO    P  A     OP        P   OP     P  A     OP
1.  SN V-t      / Ride your bicycle (on the sidewalk) (in front) (of the house).  Imp
    ‾‾‾‾‾‾
    DO  P2
```

```
                 I    PPA Adj Adj SN    V    P   OP    P  A  Adj  OP   P  A     OP
2.  SN V        Oh, no!  Her new red ball / rolled (in front) (of the fast cars) (on the highway)!  E
    ‾‾‾‾‾
    P1
```

Exercise 2: Identify each pair of words as synonyms or antonyms by putting parentheses ( ) around *syn* or *ant*.

1. torrid, frigid	syn **(ant)**	4. allow, thwart	syn **(ant)**	7. hesitate, pause	**(syn)** ant
2. insert, delete	syn **(ant)**	5. most, maximum	**(syn)** ant	8. sudden, abrupt	**(syn)** ant
3. excuse, alibi	**(syn)** ant	6. link, disconnect	syn **(ant)**	9. laborious, effortless	syn **(ant)**

Exercise 3: Underline the negative words in each sentence. Rewrite each sentence on notebook paper and correct the double negative mistake as indicated by the rule number in parentheses at the end of the sentence.

Rule 1	Rule 2	Rule 3
Change the second negative to a positive.	Take out the negative part of a contraction.	Remove the first negative word (verb change).

1. Our cattle <u>won't</u> eat <u>no</u> hay. (Rule 1)
   Our cattle won't eat any hay.
2. The waitress <u>didn't</u> want <u>no</u> tip. (Rule 1)
   The waitress didn't want any tip.
3. My uncle <u>didn't</u> <u>never</u> visit us. (Rule 3)
   My uncle never visited us.
4. She <u>doesn't</u> do <u>nothing</u> after school. (Rule 3)
   She does nothing after school.
5. He <u>wouldn't</u> <u>never</u> be late for work. (Rule 2)
   He would never be late for work.
6. You <u>shouldn't</u> <u>never</u> borrow money. (Rule 2)
   You should never borrow money.

Exercise 4: Write the rule number from Reference 60 and the correct plural form of the nouns below.

		Rule	Plural Form
1.	convoy	2	**convoys**
2.	berry	3	**berries**
3.	postman	5	**postmen**
4.	rodeo	7	**rodeos**
5.	half	4	**halves**

		Rule	Plural Form
6.	tax	1	**taxes**
7.	louse	5	**lice**
8.	sheep	9	**sheep**
9.	calf	4	**calves**
10.	cliff	6	**cliffs**

Exercise 5: On notebook paper, write the seven present tense helping verbs, the five past tense helping verbs, and the two future tense helping verbs. **(The order of answers may vary.)** (Present: **am, is, are, has, have, do, does**; Past: **was, were, had, did, been**; Future: **will, shall**)

Exercise 6: Copy the following words on notebook paper. Write the correct contraction beside each word.
Key: can't, let's, don't, wasn't, they're, aren't, hadn't, isn't, she's, who's, you're, didn't, it's, we're, weren't, doesn't, hasn't, I'm, I've, I'd, won't, I'll, wouldn't, shouldn't, couldn't, they'd.
<u>Words</u>: cannot, let us, do not, was not, they are, are not, had not, is not, she is, who is, you are, did not, it is, we are, were not, does not, has not, I am, I have, I would, will not, I will, would not, should not, could not, they would.

Exercise 7: In your journal, write a paragraph summarizing what you have learned this week.

CHAPTER 21 LESSON 4 CONTINUED

TEACHER INSTRUCTIONS

Use the Question and Answer Flows below for the sentences on the Chapter 21 Test.

Question and Answer Flow for Sentence 1: Ride your bicycle on the sidewalk in front of the house.

1. Who ride your bicycle on the sidewalk in front of the house? you - SP (understood subject pronoun)
2. What is being said about you? you ride - V
3. You ride what? bicycle - verify the noun
4. Does bicycle mean the same thing as you? No.
5. Bicycle - DO
6. Ride - V-t
7. Whose bicycle? your - PPA
8. On - P
9. On what? sidewalk - OP
10. The - A
11. In - P

12. In what? front - OP
13. Of - P
14. Of what? house - OP
15. The - A
16. SN V-t DO P2 Check
17. Verb-transitive - Check again.
18. (On the sidewalk) - Prepositional phrase
19. (In front) - Prepositional phrase
20. (Of the house) - Prepositional phrase
21. Period, command, imperative sentence
22. Go back to the verb - divide the complete subject from the complete predicate.

Classified Sentence:

```
                   (You) SP    V-t  PPA  DO    P  A   OP    P  OP    P  A   OP
                    SN V-t    / Ride your bicycle (on the sidewalk) (in front) (of the house).  Imp
                    DO P2
```

Question and Answer Flow for Sentence 2: Oh, no! Her new red ball rolled in front of the fast cars on the highway!

1. What rolled in front of the fast cars on the highway? ball - SN
2. What is being said about ball? ball rolled - V
3. In - P
4. In what? front - OP
5. Of - P
6. Of what? cars - OP
7. What kind of cars? fast - Adj
8. The - A
9. On - P
10. On what? highway - OP
11. The - A

12. What kind of ball? red - Adj
13. What kind of ball? new - Adj
14. Whose ball? her - PPA
15. Oh, no - I
16. SN V P1 Check
17. (In front) - Prepositional phrase
18. (Of the fast cars) - Prepositional phrase
19. (On the highway) - Prepositional phrase
20. Exclamation point, strong feeling, exclamatory sentence
21. Go back to the verb - divide the complete subject from the complete predicate.

Classified Sentence:

```
                           I   PPA Adj Adj SN    V    P   OP    P  A  Adj OP    P  A    OP
                 SN V     Oh, no!  Her new red ball / rolled (in front) (of the fast cars) (on the highway)!  E
                  P1
```

© SHURLEY INSTRUCTIONAL MATERIALS, INC.

CHAPTER 21   LESSON 5

Objectives: Writing Assignments #25 and #26, Bonus Option.

 **WRITING TIME**

TEACHING SCRIPT FOR WRITING ASSIGNMENTS

Today, you are assigned two different kinds of writing. You will write a descriptive paragraph and a friendly letter. <u>You will revise and edit both writing assignments.</u> (*Read the box below for more information about students' writing assignment.*) As you edit, make sure you use the checkpoints in the editing checklist provided in Reference 42 Remember to read through the whole paragraph, starting with the title, and then edit, sentence by sentence, using the five-sentence checkpoints for each sentence. Use the paragraph checkpoints to check the paragraph.

Writing Assignment Box #1

Writing Assignment #25: Descriptive Paragraph
Remind students to use the descriptive guidelines to help them notice and describe different types of details. Have students use their regular editing checklist to edit this assignment.

Writing topics: Rain Storm   or   **A Trip to the Beach**   or   **Butterflies**   or
      Describe something that belongs to someone you love.

Your second writing assignment is to write a friendly letter. (*Read the box below for more information about students' writing assignment.*)

Writing Assignment Box #2

Writing Assignment #26: Write a friendly letter to a person of your choice. Before you start, review the tips for writing friendly letters and any references about friendly letters. After your letter has been edited, fold the letter and put it in an envelope. Address the envelope properly and mail it. Don't forget the stamp.

Bonus Option: Write Deuteronomy 6:5 in your Journal from memory. Then, write an essay that explains what this verse in the Bible means to you. If you do not have this verse memorized, record in your Journal how long it takes to memorize it.

Read, check, and discuss Writing Assignment #25 after students have finished their final papers. Use the checklists as you check and discuss students' papers. Make sure students are using the regular editing checklist correctly. Read and discuss Writing Assignment #26 for fun and enrichment.

(End of lesson.)

© SHURLEY INSTRUCTIONAL MATERIALS, INC.

CHAPTER 22   LESSON 1

Objectives: Jingles, Grammar (Practice Sentences), Oral Skill Builder Check, Skills (types of business letters, parts of a business letter, and parts of a business envelope), Practice Exercise, Vocabulary #1, and Activity.

JINGLE TIME

Have students turn to the Jingle Section in their books and recite the previously-taught jingles.

GRAMMAR TIME

First-Year Option: Put the Practice Sentences from the box below on the board or on notebook paper. Use these sentences as you practice the concepts that have been taught. For the greatest benefit, students must participate orally with the teacher. **Second-Year Option:** Have students classify the Practice Sentences independently on paper. Check students' sentences with the answers provided below. (*If you have the CDs for Practice Sentences, have students check their sentences with the CDs.*)

Chapter 22, Practice Sentences for Lesson 1

1. _____ Have they lived in that house for fifty years?
2. _____ I baked oatmeal cookies in the oven.

TEACHING SCRIPT FOR PRACTICING MIXED PATTERNS

We will practice classifying Mixed Patterns. We will classify the sentences together. Begin. (*You might have your students write the labels above the sentences at this time.*)

Question and Answer Flow for Sentence 1: Have they lived in that house for fifty years?

1. Who have lived in that house for fifty years? they - SP
2. What is being said about they? they have lived - V
3. Have - HV
4. In - P
5. In what? house - OP
6. Which house? that - Adj
7. For - P
8. For what? years - OP
9. How many years? fifty - Adj
10. SN V P1 Check
11. (In that house) - Prepositional phrase
12. (For fifty years) - Prepositional phrase
13. Question mark, question, interrogative sentence
14. Go back to the verb - divide the complete subject from the complete predicate.

Classified Sentence:

		HV	SP	V	P	Adj	OP	P	Adj	OP
SN V		Have	they /	lived	(in	that	house)	(for	fifty	years)? Int
P1										

© SHURLEY INSTRUCTIONAL MATERIALS, INC.

CHAPTER 22 LESSON 1 CONTINUED

Question and Answer Flow for Sentence 2: I baked oatmeal cookies in the oven.

1. Who baked oatmeal cookies in the oven? I - SP
2. What is being said about I? I baked - V
3. I baked what? cookies - verify the noun
4. Do cookies mean the same thing as I? No.
5. Cookies - DO
6. Baked - V-t
7. What kind of cookies? oatmeal - Adj
8. In - P
9. In what? oven - OP
10. The - A
11. SN V-t DO P2 Check
12. Verb-transitive - Check again.
13. (In the oven) - Prepositional phrase
14. Period, statement, declarative sentence
15. Go back to the verb - divide the complete subject from the complete predicate.

Classified Sentence:

```
                            SP  V-t      Adj      DO     P  A  OP
              SN  V-t       I / baked oatmeal cookies (in the oven).  D
              DO  P2
```

Use Sentences 1-2 that you just classified with your students to do an Oral Skill Builder Check. Use the guidelines below.

Oral Skill Builder Check

1. **Noun check.**
   (Say the job and then say the noun. Circle each noun.)

2. **Identify the nouns as singular or plural.**
   (Write S or P above each noun.)

3. **Identify the nouns as common or proper.**
   (Follow established procedure for oral identification.)

4. **Do a vocabulary check.**
   (Follow established procedure for oral identification.)

5. **Identify the complete subject and the complete predicate.** (Underline the complete subject once and the complete predicate twice.)

6. **Identify the simple subject and simple predicate.**
   (Underline the simple subject once and the simple predicate twice. Bold, or highlight, the lines.)

7. **Recite the irregular verb chart.**
   (Located on student page 25 and teacher page 163.)

SKILL TIME

TEACHING SCRIPT FOR THE FOUR TYPES OF BUSINESS LETTERS

Sharing information with a friend or relative is not the only reason to write a letter. Sometimes, you may need to write a letter to someone you do not know about something that is not personal in nature. This kind of letter is called a **business letter**. Even if you are not in business, there are several reasons why you may need to write a business letter.

We will discuss four reasons for writing business letters, and then we will study the four types of business letters and the type of information that should be included in each one. Look at Reference 65 on page 50 and follow along as I read the information about business letters. (*Reference 65 is reproduced for you on the next page.*)

© SHURLEY INSTRUCTIONAL MATERIALS, INC.

Reference 65: Four Types of Business Letters	
Four common reasons to write business letters and information about the four types:	
1. If you need to send for information - letter of inquiry. 2. If you want to order a product - letter of request or order. 3. If you want to express an opinion - letter to an editor or official. 4. If you want to complain about a product - letter of complaint.	

Letter of Inquiry	Letter of Request or Order
1. Ask for information or answers to your questions. 2. Keep the letter short and to the point. 3. Word the letter so that there can be no question as to what it is you need to know.	1. Carefully and clearly describe the product. 2. Keep the letter short and to the point. 3. Include information on how and where the product should be shipped. 4. Include information on how you will pay for the product.
Letter to an Editor or Official	**Letter of Complaint About a Product**
1. Clearly explain the problem or situation. 2. Offer your opinion of the cause and possible solutions. 3. Support your opinions with facts and examples. 4. Suggest ways to change or improve the situation.	1. Carefully and clearly describe the product. 2. Describe the problem and what may have caused it. (Don't spend too much time explaining how unhappy you are.) 3. Explain any action you have already taken to solve the problem. 4. End your letter with the action you would like the company to take to solve the problem.

The form of a business letter is like the friendly letter except that a business letter uses language that is more formal. A business letter also has an inside address above the greeting that tells who is receiving the letter. The inside address saves companies or business people time because they do not have to read the entire letter in order to know which person in the company receives the letter.

TEACHING SCRIPT FOR THE SIX PARTS OF A BUSINESS LETTER

Now that you know the different reasons to write business letters, you must learn to put your business letter into correct business letter form. The business letter has six parts: the heading; the inside address; the formal greeting, which is also called the salutation; the body; the closing; and the signature. I will briefly tell you some extra information about the new things that you will find in a business letter.

First, how you write the inside address will depend on what you know about the business or company that will receive the letter. If you know the name of a person in the company who can help you, you will use that name as part of the inside address. If you do not know the name of a person in the company who can help you, you will just use the name of the company.

Second, greetings in business letters are formal. This means that you use the title and last name of the person who is receiving the letter, followed by a colon. If you do not know the name of the person receiving the letter, you should use **sir** or **madam**. Third, when writing the signature of a business letter, you should always sign your first and last name.

© SHURLEY INSTRUCTIONAL MATERIALS, INC.

CHAPTER 22 LESSON 1 CONTINUED

Look at Reference 66 on page 51 in your book. We will now go over each of the six parts of a business letter and what information is contained in each part.

Reference 66 The Six Parts of a Business Letter

1. **Heading:** The heading for a business letter includes the writer's complete address and the full date. The heading is placed in the upper right-hand corner about an inch from the top of the page.

2. **Inside Address:** The inside address includes the name and complete address of the person and/or company you are writing. Place a person's title after his/her name. Separate the title from the name with a comma. If the title is two or more words, place the title separately on the next line. The inside address is placed two lines below the heading on the left side of the page.

3. **Formal Greeting or Salutation:** A formal greeting is placed two lines below the inside address. For a specific person, use a greeting like Dear Mr. (*last name*) or Ms. (*last name*). For a letter addressed to a person by title, use Dear Sir, Dear Madam, or Dear (*Title*). For a company or organization, use Gentlemen, Dear Sirs, or Dear (*Company name*). Place a colon at the end of a business greeting. (*Check the first line of the inside address to determine the right greeting to use.*)

4. **Body:** The information in the body of any business letter should be clearly and briefly written. Skip a line between each paragraph. The body of the business letter is placed two lines below the greeting.

5. **Closing:** Use a formal phrase for a business letter closing (*Very truly, Yours truly, Sincerely, etc.*). Place a comma at the end of the closing. The closing is placed two lines below the body of the letter, on the right.

6. **Signature:** A business letter ends by signing your name beneath the closing. If you are typing your letter, skip four lines and type your full name. Then, write your signature between the closing and your typed name.

Look at the business letter sample in Reference 67 on page 52 in your book. Each of the parts of a business letter has a specific place it should be written in order for your letter to have correct business letter form. We will now go over that form. (*Go over the sample reproduced below with your students.*)

Reference 67: Business Letter Example

1. HEADING

26 Bailey Road
Columbus, Ohio 43085
August 10, 20__

2. INSIDE ADDRESS

Mr. James Cook, Sales Manager
Barret Furniture
1062 Finley Street
Boise, Idaho 83700

3. FORMAL GREETING, (OR SALUTATION)

Dear Mr. Cook:

4. BODY (INDENT PARAGRAPHS)

   Please send us a catalog of your office furniture and accessories. We are planning to purchase new furniture and file cabinets.

5. FORMAL CLOSING,

Sincerely,

6. SIGNATURE

Donald Sinclair

© SHURLEY INSTRUCTIONAL MATERIALS, INC.

CHAPTER 22 LESSON 1 CONTINUED

TEACHING SCRIPT FOR THE PARTS OF A BUSINESS ENVELOPE

In order to address the envelope of your business letter correctly, you must know the parts that go on the envelope and where to write them. The parts of a business envelope are similar to the parts of an envelope for a friendly letter. There are two differences in the mailing address for the business envelope that you should remember.

(1) You must put the name of the person within the company to whom you are writing and his/her title (if you know it) on the first line of the mailing address. If you do not know the name of a particular person in the company who would handle your request or problem, you can just choose a department within the company (such as SALES, SHIPPING, ACCOUNTING, etc.). Then, you can write the name of the department on the first line of your mailing address, or you can leave the first line blank.

(2) You must put the name of the company on the second line of the mailing address.

Look at Reference 68 on page 52 for an example of the parts of a business envelope. (*Go over the information and example reproduced below with your students.*)

Reference 68: Business Envelope Parts	
Envelope Parts	**Business Envelope Example**
The return address: 1. Name of the person writing the letter 2. Box or street address of the writer 3. City, state, zip code of the writer	Return Address Donald Sinclair 26 Bailey Road Columbus, Ohio 43085
The mailing address: 1. Name of the person receiving the letter 2. Name of the company receiving the letter 3. Street address of the person receiving the letter 4. City, state, zip of the person receiving the letter	Mailing Address Mr. James Cook, Sales Manager Barret Furniture 1062 Finley Street Boise, Idaho 83700

 PRACTICE TIME

Have students turn to page 91 in the Practice Section of their book and find Chapter 22, Lesson 1, Practice. Go over the directions to make sure they understand what to do. Check and discuss the Practice after students have finished. (*Chapter 22, Lesson 1, Practice instructions are given below.*)

Chapter 22, Lesson 1, Practice: Use butcher paper, large pieces of construction paper, or poster board to make a colorful wall poster identifying the six parts of a business letter and the parts of a business envelope. Write the title and an example for each of the six parts of the business letter and envelope. Illustrate your work. Then, give an oral presentation about the business letter and the envelope when you have finished. (*This project may take several days.*)

© SHURLEY INSTRUCTIONAL MATERIALS, INC.

CHAPTER 22 LESSON 1 CONTINUED

Teacher's Note: You could cut apart the different parts of a business letter and have students put the parts together like a puzzle. You could also put magnets on the back of each piece so each child could arrange them on the refrigerator or white board.

VOCABULARY TIME

Assign Chapter 22, Vocabulary Words **#1** on page 9 in the Reference Section for students to define in their Vocabulary notebooks. Tell students they are to use a dictionary or thesaurus to look up the meanings of the vocabulary words. After they write each word and its meaning, students are to write a sentence using the vocabulary word.

Chapter 22, Vocabulary Words #1
(craze, fad, illiterate, educated)

ACTIVITY / ASSIGNMENT TIME

Put the scrambled words below on the board. All the words in this list have scrambled spellings. Have students use their Preposition Flow jingle to unscramble them to make prepositions. Then, have students scramble their own list of prepositions. They can give their scrambled words to friends or family to unscramble. Students need to make a key for their scrambled prepositions.

Scrambled Words	Key for Scrambled Words
1. tiniwh	1. within
2. scaros	2. across
3. bidhen	3. behind
4. logan	4. along
5. studioe	5. outside
6. elbow	6. below
7. anurod	7. around
8. awtrod	8. toward
9. hoghurt	9. through
10. robeef	10. before

(End of lesson.)

© SHURLEY INSTRUCTIONAL MATERIALS, INC.

CHAPTER 22   LESSON 2

Objectives: Jingles, Grammar (Practice Sentences), Independent Practice Sentence, Practice Exercise, and Vocabulary #2.

JINGLE TIME

Have students turn to the Jingle Section in their books and recite the previously-taught jingles.

GRAMMAR TIME

First-Year Option: Put the Practice Sentences from the box below on the board or on notebook paper. Use these sentences as you practice the concepts that have been taught. For the greatest benefit, students must participate orally with the teacher. **Second-Year Option:** Have students classify the Practice Sentences independently on paper. Check students' sentences with the answers provided below. *(If you have the CDs for Practice Sentences, have students check their sentences with the CDs.)*

Chapter 22, Practice Sentences for Lesson 2

1. _____ She slid the book across the table quietly.
2. _____ The shy little boy hid awkwardly behind his mother's skirt.

TEACHING SCRIPT FOR PRACTICING MIXED PATTERNS

We will practice classifying Mixed Patterns. We will classify the sentences together. Begin. *(You might have your students write the labels above the sentences at this time.)*

Question and Answer Flow for Sentence 1: She slid the book across the table quietly.

1. Who slid the book across the table quietly? she - SP
2. What is being said about she? she slid - V
3. She slid what? book - verify the noun
4. Does book mean the same thing as she? No.
5. Book - DO
6. Slid - V-t
7. The - A
8. Across - P
9. Across what? table - OP
10. The - A
11. Slid how? quietly - Adv
12. SN V-t DO P2 Check
13. Verb-transitive - Check again.
14. (Across the table) - Prepositional phrase
15. Period, statement, declarative sentence
16. Go back to the verb - divide the complete subject from the complete predicate.

Classified Sentence:

	SP	V-t	A	DO	P	A	OP	Adv
SN V-t	She / slid the book (across the table) quietly. **D**							
DO P2								

© SHURLEY INSTRUCTIONAL MATERIALS, INC.

CHAPTER 22 LESSON 2 CONTINUED

<table>
<tr><td colspan="2">Question and Answer Flow for Sentence 2: The shy little boy hid awkwardly behind his mother's skirt.</td></tr>
<tr><td>1. Who hid awkwardly behind his mother's skirt? boy - SN</td><td>9. What kind of boy? shy - Adj</td></tr>
<tr><td>2. What is being said about boy? boy hid - V</td><td>10. The - A</td></tr>
<tr><td>3. Hid how? awkwardly - Adv</td><td>11. SN V P1 Check</td></tr>
<tr><td>4. Behind - P</td><td>12. (Behind his mother's skirt) - Prepositional phrase</td></tr>
<tr><td>5. Behind what? skirt - OP</td><td>13. Period, statement, declarative sentence</td></tr>
<tr><td>6. Whose skirt? mother's - PNA</td><td>14. Go back to the verb - divide the complete subject</td></tr>
<tr><td>7. Whose mother? his - PPA</td><td>from the complete predicate.</td></tr>
<tr><td>8. What kind of boy? little - Adj</td><td></td></tr>
</table>

Classified   A Adj Adj SN V   Adv   P   PPA PNA   OP
Sentence: <u>SN V</u>   The shy little boy / hid awkwardly (behind his mother's skirt). **D**
         P1

TEACHER INSTRUCTIONS FOR A PRACTICE SENTENCE

Tell students that their sentence writing assignment today is to write a sentence pattern of their choice. They are to follow the same procedure used in the previous lessons. They should decide on their labels, arrange them in a selected order, write their sentences, and edit their sentences for improved word choices. (_Students do not have to write an Improved Sentence at this point unless you feel they need more one-on-one word choice writing practice._) Check and discuss the sentence pattern chosen after students have finished.

 PRACTICE TIME

Have students turn to page 91 in the Practice Section of their book and find Chapter 22, Lesson 2, Practice (_1-2_). Go over the directions to make sure they understand what to do. Check and discuss the Practices after students have finished. (_Chapter 22, Lesson 2, Practice instructions are given below._)

Chapter 22, Lesson 2, Practice 1: Write a friendly letter to a special friend or relative. Before you start, review the references and tips for writing friendly letters. After your letter has been edited, fold the letter and put it in an envelope. Address the envelope properly and mail it. Don't forget the stamp.

Chapter 22, Lesson 2, Practice 2: Write a business letter. You may invent the company and the situation for which you are writing. Before you begin, review the reasons for writing business letters and the four types of business letters (_Reference 65 on page 50_). After your letter has been edited, fold the letter and put it in an envelope. Address the envelope properly.

 VOCABULARY TIME

Assign Chapter 22, Vocabulary Words **#2** on page 9 in the Reference Section for students to define in their Vocabulary notebooks. They should write each word, its meaning, and a sentence using the word.

Chapter 22, Vocabulary Words #2
(offend, compliment, wicked, evil)

(End of lesson.)

© SHURLEY INSTRUCTIONAL MATERIALS, INC.

CHAPTER 22   LESSON 3

Objectives: Jingles, Grammar (Practice Sentences), Practice Exercise, and Activity.

JINGLE TIME

Have students turn to the Jingle Section in their books and recite the previously-taught jingles.

GRAMMAR TIME

First-Year Option: Put the Practice Sentences from the box below on the board or on notebook paper. Use these sentences as you practice the concepts that have been taught. For the greatest benefit, students must participate orally with the teacher. **Second-Year Option:** Have students classify the Practice Sentences independently on paper. Check students' sentences with the answers provided below. *(If you have the CDs for Practice Sentences, have students check their sentences with the CDs.)*

Chapter 22, Practice Sentences for Lesson 3
1. _____ My friend and I watched a show about fitness on television.
2. _____ Mom's answering machine filled with messages from her friends.

TEACHING SCRIPT FOR PRACTICING MIXED PATTERNS

We will practice classifying Mixed Patterns. We will classify the sentences together. Begin. *(You might have your students write the labels above the sentences at this time.)*

Question and Answer Flow for Sentence 1: My friend and I watched a show about fitness on television.

1. Who watched a show about fitness on television?
   friend and I - CSN, CSP
2. What is being said about friend and I?
   friend and I watched - V
3. Friend and I watched what? show - verify the noun
4. Does show mean the same thing as friend and I? No.
5. Show - DO
6. Watched - V-t
7. A - A
8. About - P
9. About what? fitness - OP

10. On - P
11. On what? television - OP
12. And - C
13. Whose friend? my - PPA
14. SN V-t DO P2 Check
15. Verb-transitive - Check again.
16. (About fitness) - Prepositional phrase
17. (On television) - Prepositional phrase
18. Period, statement, declarative sentence
19. Go back to the verb - divide the complete subject
   from the complete predicate.

Classified Sentence:

	PPA CSN	C CSP	V-t	A	DO	P	OP	P	OP
SN V-t	My friend	and I /	watched	a	show	(about	fitness)	(on	television). D
DO P2									

© SHURLEY INSTRUCTIONAL MATERIALS, INC.

CHAPTER 22 LESSON 3 CONTINUED

Question and Answer Flow for Sentence 2: Mom's answering machine filled with messages from her friends.	
1. What filled with messages from her friends? machine - SN	9. Whose machine? Mom's - PNA
2. What is being said about machine? machine filled - V	10. SN V P1 Check
3. With - P	11. (With messages) - Prepositional phrase
4. With what? messages - OP	12. (From her friends) - Prepositional phrase
5. From - P	13. Period, statement, declarative sentence
6. From whom? friends - OP	14. Go back to the verb - divide the complete subject
7. Whose friends? her - PPA	from the complete predicate.
8. What kind of machine? answering - Adj	

Classified	PNA Adj SN V P OP P PPA OP
Sentence: ___SN V___	Mom's answering machine / filled (with messages) (from her friends). **D**
P1	

PRACTICE TIME

Have students turn to page 92 in the Practice Section of their books and find the instructions under Chapter 22, Lesson 3, Practice. Go over the directions to make sure they understand what to do. Check and discuss the Practice after students have finished. (*Chapter 22, Lesson 3, Practice instructions are given below.*)

Chapter 22, Lesson 3, Practice: Choose a city that you would like to visit. Write several letters requesting information about the city you have chosen. (*You may need to research the different places to send the letters.*) Next, you are to use encyclopedias, newspapers, magazines, and even the Internet to find out about the interesting sites that you would like to see in your chosen city. (*This project could take several weeks.*)

ACTIVITY / ASSIGNMENT TIME

The **Parts-of-Speech Poem** is a directional poem in which one employs various parts of speech, following a prescribed formula. Teachers or students can design their own formulas to create different effects. Read and discuss the example below. Have students write their own **Parts-of-Speech Poem** using the directions below. Have them share their poems with others.

Line 1 - Write one noun (*the topic of your poem*).	Clowns,
Line 2 - Write two adjectives to describe the noun.	Funny and colorful,
Line 3 - Write one verb and one prepositional phrase.	Waves at the children
Line 4 - Write two adverbs describing the verb.	Enthusiastically and cheerfully.
Line 5 - Write a sentence about the noun.	Clowns make everyone laugh.

(End of lesson.)

© SHURLEY INSTRUCTIONAL MATERIALS, INC.

CHAPTER 22   LESSON 4

Objectives: Jingles, Study, Test, Check, Activity and Writing (journal).

JINGLE TIME

Have students turn to the Jingle Section in their books and recite the previously-taught jingles.

STUDY TIME

Have students study the vocabulary words in their vocabulary notebooks. Remind students that any vocabulary word in their notebooks could be on their test. Also, have students study any of the skills in the Practice Section that they need to review.

TEST TIME

Have students turn to page 119 in the Test Section of their books and find Chapter 22 Test. Go over the directions to make sure they understand what to do. (*Chapter 22 Test key is on the next page.*)

CHECK TIME

After students have finished, check and discuss their test papers. Make sure they understand why their answers are right or wrong. (*For total points, count each required answer as a point.*)

ACTIVITY / ASSIGNMENT TIME

Students will continue to draw or trace the states and write the following questions and answers.

Ohio	Oklahoma
1. What is the state on the front of this card? **Ohio**	1. What is the state on the front of this card? **Oklahoma**
2. What is the capital of Ohio? **Columbus**	2. What is the capital of Oklahoma? **Oklahoma City**
3. What is the postal abbreviation of Ohio? **OH**	3. What is the postal abbreviation of Oklahoma? **OK**
4. What year was Ohio admitted to the Union? **1803**	4. What year was Oklahoma admitted to the Union? **1907**

Color these states and look up an interesting fact about each state to write on the cards. Use the cards to quiz family members, friends, and relatives. You may want to time the responses to your questions. Also, along with previous suggestions, think of other ways to have fun with your United States card file.

(End of lesson.)

© SHURLEY INSTRUCTIONAL MATERIALS, INC.

Chapter 22 Test
(Student Page 119)

Exercise 1: Classify each sentence.

```
                    HV     Adj        SN     V-t  A DO  P    OP
1.  SN  V-t     Do kindergarten children / take a nap (after lunch)?  Int
    ────
    DO  P2
                    CSN   C  CSN     V-t    A   DO    P  A    OP      Adv
2.  SN  V-t     Lillian and Bryan / shoveled the snow (off the driveway) yesterday.  D
    ────
    DO  P2
```

Exercise 2: Identify each pair of words as synonyms or antonyms by putting parentheses ( ) around *syn* or *ant*.

1. fad, craze	**(syn)** ant	4. link, disconnect	syn **(ant)**	7. rejoice, celebrate	**(syn)** ant
2. torrid, frigid	syn **(ant)**	5. most, maximum	**(syn)** ant	8. abrupt, sudden	**(syn)** ant
3. evil, wicked	**(syn)** ant	6. offend, compliment	syn **(ant)**	9. educated, illiterate	syn **(ant)**

Exercise 3: Use the Quotation Rules to help punctuate the quotations below. Underline the explanatory words.

```
        D                          M        C         I
1.   "donna, would you like to eat at morrison's cafeteria?" i asked.
```

```
     D                     A        D      L
2.   denise shouted loudly to adam and daniel, "look out for that car!"
```

```
     I              M    T              J
3.   "i would like to visit mrs. thompson today," jessica said to her mother.
```

```
     T                      I                      M  J
4.   the shy girl spoke softly, "i haven't finished my book report, mr. jones."
```

```
     T                              P
5.   "that alligator was ten feet long!" gasped patrick to his brother.
```

Exercise 4: On notebook paper, tell what you have learned about the business letter and the business letter envelope.
(Answers will vary.)

Exercise 5: On notebook paper, tell what you have learned about the friendly letter and the friendly letter envelope.
(Answers will vary.)

Exercise 6: In your journal, write a paragraph summarizing what you have learned this week.

© SHURLEY INSTRUCTIONAL MATERIALS, INC.

CHAPTER 22 LESSON 4 CONTINUED

TEACHER INSTRUCTIONS

Use the Question and Answer Flows below for the sentences on the Chapter 22 Test.

Question and Answer Flow for Sentence 1: Do kindergarten children take a nap after lunch?

1. Who do take a nap after lunch? children - SN
2. What is being said about children? children do take - V
3. Do - HV
4. Children do take what? nap - verify the noun
5. Does nap mean the same thing as children? No.
6. Nap - DO
7. Take - V-t
8. A - A
9. After - P
10. After what? lunch - OP
11. What kind of children? kindergarten - Adj
12. SN V-t DO P2 Check
13. (After lunch) - Prepositional phrase
14. Question mark, question, interrogative sentence
15. Go back to the verb - divide the complete subject from the complete predicate.

Classified Sentence:

	HV	Adj	SN	V-t	A DO	P	OP

SN V-t / DO P2   Do kindergarten children / take a nap (after lunch)? **Int**

Question and Answer Flow for Sentence 2: Lillian and Bryan shoveled the snow off the driveway yesterday.

1. Who shoveled the snow off the driveway yesterday?
   Lillian and Bryan - CSN, CSN
2. What is being said about Lillian and Bryan?
   Lillian and Bryan shoveled - V
3. Lillian and Bryan shoveled what? snow - verify the noun
4. Does snow mean the same thing as Lillian and Bryan? No.
5. Snow - DO
6. Shoveled - V-t
7. The - A
8. Off - P
9. Off what? driveway - OP
10. The - A
11. Shoveled when? yesterday - Adv
12. And - C
13. SN V-t DO P2 Check
14. Verb-transitive - Check again.
15. (Off the driveway) - Prepositional phrase
16. Period, statement, declarative sentence
17. Go back to the verb - divide the complete subject from the complete predicate.

Classified Sentence:

CSN	C	CSN	V-t	A	DO	P A	OP	Adv

SN V-t / DO P2   Lillian and Bryan / shoveled the snow (off the driveway) yesterday. **D**

© SHURLEY INSTRUCTIONAL MATERIALS, INC.

CHAPTER 22   LESSON 5

Objectives: Writing Assignments #27 and #28, and Bonus Option.

 WRITING TIME

TEACHING SCRIPT FOR WRITING ASSIGNMENTS

Today, you are assigned two different kinds of writing. You will write a descriptive paragraph and a business letter. <u>You will revise and edit both writing assignments.</u> (*Read the box below for more information about the students' writing assignment.*) As you edit, make sure you use the checkpoints in the editing checklist provided in Reference 42. Remember to read through the whole paragraph, starting with the title, and then edit, sentence-by-sentence, using the five-sentence checkpoints for each sentence. Use the paragraph checkpoints to check the paragraph.

Writing Assignment Box #1

Writing Assignment #27: Descriptive Paragraph

Writing topic choices: The Most Interesting Bible Character or **A Snowy Day** or **The Mysterious Stranger** or **Choose your own topic.**

Your second writing assignment is to write a business letter. (*Read the box below for more information about students' writing assignment.*)

Writing Assignment Box #2

Writing Assignment #28: Continue working on your city project. Write business letters requesting various information about the city you have chosen. Make sure you edit your letters very carefully and address the envelopes properly. Remember to research your city to find out about the interesting and unique things that your city has to offer.

Bonus Option: Read these scriptures: Matthew 14:13-21; Mark 6:30-44; Luke 9:10-17; John 6:1-15 to answer the questions below. (King James Version)

1. What story is told in the different scriptures listed above?
2. What kind of food was shared with the multitudes?
3. Which scripture tells who had the food?
4. Which verse in each book tells how many baskets of food were left?
5. Which scripture tells that women and children were also present?
6. Which verse in each book tells where the multitudes sat?
7. How did Mark 6:34 describe the multitudes?
8. Which book had the story version that you liked best?
9. Write your favorite version in your own words in your journal.

Read, check, and discuss Writing Assignments #27 and #28 after students have finished their final papers. Use the editing checklist as you check and discuss students' papers. Make sure students are using the editing checklist correctly.

Bonus Option Answers:

1. The story of the feeding of the five thousand.	5. Matthew 14:21
2. 5 barley loaves and two small fishes.	6. Matthew 14:19, Mark 6:39, Luke 9:14-15, and John 6:10
3. John 6:9	7. ...they were as sheep not having a shepherd...
4. Matthew 14:20, Mark 6:43, Luke 9:17, John 6:13	8. and 9. Answers will vary.

(End of lesson.)

© SHURLEY INSTRUCTIONAL MATERIALS, INC.

CHAPTER 23   LESSON 1

Objectives: Jingles, Grammar (Practice Sentences), Skill (thank-you notes), and Practice Exercise.

 JINGLE TIME

Have students turn to the Jingle Section in their books and recite the previously-taught jingles.

 GRAMMAR TIME

First-Year Option : Put the Practice Sentences from the box below on the board or on notebook paper. Use these sentences as you practice the concepts that have been taught. For the greatest benefit, students must participate orally with the teacher. **Second-Year Option:** Have students classify the Practice Sentences independently on paper. Check students' sentences with the answers provided below. (*If you have the CDs for Practice Sentences, have students check their sentences with the CDs.*)

Chapter 23, Practice Sentences for Lesson 1

1. _____ Patty and he went to the pet shop after work yesterday.
2. _____ Did you buy a tent and sleeping bag for the camping trip?

TEACHING SCRIPT FOR PRACTICING MIXED PATTERNS

We will practice classifying Mixed Patterns. We will classify the sentences together. Begin. (*You might have your students write the labels above the sentences at this time.*)

Question and Answer Flow for Sentence 1: Patty and he went to the pet shop after work yesterday.

1. Who went to the pet shop after work yesterday?
   Patty and he - CSN, CSP
2. What is being said about Patty and he?
   Patty and he went - V
3. To - P
4. To what? shop - OP
5. What kind of shop? pet - Adj
6. The - A
7. After - P
8. After what? work - OP

9. Went when? yesterday - Adv
10. And - C
11. SN V P1 Check
12. (To the pet shop) - Prepositional phrase
13. (After work) - Prepositional phrase
14. Period, statement, declarative sentence
15. Go back to the verb - divide the complete subject from the complete predicate.

Classified Sentence:

		CSN	C	CSP	V		P	A	Adj	OP		P	OP		Adv	
SN V		Patty and he / went (to the pet shop) (after work) yesterday. D
P1

© SHURLEY INSTRUCTIONAL MATERIALS, INC.

CHAPTER 23 LESSON 1 CONTINUED

Question and Answer Flow for Sentence 2: Did you buy a tent and sleeping bag for the camping trip?

1. Who did buy a tent and sleeping bag for the camping trip? you - SP
2. What is being said about you? you did buy - V
3. Did - HV
4. You did buy what? tent and bag - verify the nouns
5. Do tent and bag mean the same thing as you? No.
6. Tent and bag - CDO, CDO
7. Buy - V-t
8. A - A
9. And - C
10. What kind of bag? sleeping - Adj
11. For - P
12. For what? trip - OP
13. What kind of trip? camping - Adj
14. The - A
15. SN V-t DO P2 Check
16. Verb-transitive - Check again.
17. (For the camping trip) - Prepositional phrase
18. Question mark, question, interrogative sentence
19. Go back to the verb - divide the complete subject from the complete predicate.

		HV	SP		V-t	A	CDO	C	Adj	CDO	P	A	Adj	OP	
Classified Sentence:	SN V-t	Did	you	/	buy	a	tent	and	sleeping	bag	(for	the	camping	trip)?	Int
	DO P2														

SKILL TIME

TEACHING SCRIPT FOR THANK-YOU NOTES

Close your eyes. Relax and clear your mind of clutter. Now, think of a person who has done something nice for you or has given you a gift. Sometimes, a person even gives a gift of time, so a gift does not always mean a "physical" gift. After you have thought of someone, open your eyes. That person deserves a thank-you note from you after such a nice gesture. Therefore, it is time we learn about thank-you notes.

You usually write thank-you notes to thank someone for a gift or for doing something nice. In either case, a thank-you note should include at least three statements.

1. **You should tell the person <u>what</u> you are thanking him/her for.**
2. **You should tell the person <u>how the gift was used</u> or <u>how it helped</u>.**
3. **You should tell the person <u>how much you appreciated the gift or action</u>.**

A thank-you note should follow the same form as a friendly letter: heading, greeting, body, closing, and signature. Look at Reference 69 on page 53 and follow along as I read the information about thank-you notes. (*Go over the information and examples reproduced on the next page with your students.*)

© SHURLEY INSTRUCTIONAL MATERIALS, INC.

CHAPTER 23 LESSON 1 CONTINUED

Reference 69: Thank-You Notes			
For a Gift		**For an Action**	
What -	Thank you for... (tell color, kind, and item)	**What -**	Thank you for... (tell action)
Use -	Tell how the gift is used.	**Helped -**	Tell how the action helped.
Thanks -	I appreciate your remembering me with this special gift.	**Thanks -**	I appreciate your thinking of me at this time.

Example 1: Gift

62 Palmetto Drive
Orlando, Florida 12478
April 23, 20___

Dear Brad,

   Do I ever like those awesome binoculars you sent me for my birthday! I've already watched two launches at the Kennedy Space Center. Through the binoculars, it was an amazing sight. Thanks so much.

Your cousin,
Tyler

Example 2: Action

6156 Turquoise Lane
Phoenix, Arizona 46145
June 4, 20___

Dear Jeffrey,

   Thanks so much for volunteering to flag traffic while the city workers installed a new flagpole in the village green. The concrete mixers could never have gotten in and out without your help. I look forward to returning the kindness.

Most sincerely,
Marty

PRACTICE TIME

Have students turn to page 92 in the Practice Section of their book and find Chapter 23, Lesson 1, Practice. Go over the directions to make sure they understand what to do. Check and discuss the Practice after students have finished. (*Chapter 23, Lesson 1, Practice instructions are given below.*)

Chapter 23, Lesson 1, Practice: Write your own thank-you note. First, think of a person who has done something nice for you or has given you a gift (even the gift of time). Next, write that person a thank-you note, using the information in the Reference Section as a guide. (*Check and discuss students' thank-you notes after they are finished.*)

VOCABULARY TIME

Students will no longer have assigned Vocabulary Words. As they find new or interesting words, have students add them to their list in their Vocabulary notebook.

(End of lesson.)

© SHURLEY INSTRUCTIONAL MATERIALS, INC.

CHAPTER 23   LESSON 2

Objectives: Jingles, Grammar (Practice Sentences), Skill (parts of a book), and Practice Exercise.

JINGLE TIME

Have students turn to the Jingle Section in their books and recite the previously-taught jingles.

GRAMMAR TIME

First-Year Option : Put the Practice Sentences from the box below on the board or on notebook paper. Use these sentences as you practice the concepts that have been taught. For the greatest benefit, students must participate orally with the teacher. **Second-Year Option:** Have students classify the Practice Sentences independently on paper. Check students' sentences with the answers provided below. (*If you have the CDs for Practice Sentences, have students check their sentences with the CDs.*)

Chapter 23, Practice Sentences for Lesson 2

1. _____ That cute little toddler is sharing her food with the stuffed animals.
2. _____ The trail led through the mountains.

TEACHING SCRIPT FOR PRACTICING MIXED PATTERNS

We will practice classifying Mixed Patterns. We will classify the sentences together. Begin. (*You might have your students write the labels above the sentences at this time.*)

Question and Answer Flow for Sentence 1: That cute little toddler is sharing her food with the stuffed animals.

1. Who is sharing her food with the stuffed animals?
   toddler - SN
2. What is being said about toddler? toddler is sharing - V
3. Is - HV
4. Toddler is sharing what? food - verify the noun
5. Does food mean the same thing as toddler? No.
6. Food - DO
7. Sharing - V-t
8. Whose food? her - PPA
9. With - P
10. With what? animals - OP
11. What kind of animals? stuffed - Adj

12. The - A
13. What kind of toddler? little - Adj
14. What kind of toddler? cute - Adj
15. Which toddler? That - Adj
16. SN V-t DO P2 Check
17. Verb-transitive - Check again.
18. (With the stuffed animals) - Prepositional phrase
19. Period, statement, declarative sentence
20. Go back to the verb - divide the complete subject
   from the complete predicate.

Classified Sentence:

<u>SN V-t</u>
DO P2

Adj Adj Adj SN   HV V-t PPA DO   P A Adj   OP
That cute little toddler **/** is sharing her food (with the stuffed animals). **D**

© SHURLEY INSTRUCTIONAL MATERIALS, INC.

CHAPTER 23 LESSON 2 CONTINUED

Question and Answer Flow for Sentence 2: The trail led through the mountains.

1. What led through the mountains? trail - SN
2. What is being said about trail? trail led - V
3. Through - P
4. Through what? mountains - OP
5. The - A
6. The - A

7. SN V P1 Check
8. (Through the mountains) - Prepositional phrase
9. Period, statement, declarative sentence
10. Go back to the verb - divide the complete subject from the complete predicate.

Classified Sentence:

$$\underline{\text{SN \quad V}}_{\text{P1}} \qquad \overset{\text{A \quad SN \quad V \quad P \quad A \quad OP}}{\text{The trail / led (through the mountains). D}}$$

SKILL TIME

TEACHING SCRIPT FOR INTRODUCING PARTS OF A BOOK

Do you know the parts of a book? Let's see how many we can name. (*Ask students to name the parts they know. See the parts below and on the next page.*) Actually, the parts of a book can be divided into the front part and back part. We will learn the front parts of a book, and then we will learn the back parts. Anytime you use a nonfiction book to help you with an assignment, it is necessary to understand how to use that book efficiently.

Knowing the parts of a book will help you make full use of the special features that are sometimes found in nonfiction books. I will now give you a brief description of each of the features that could appear in a book. We will start with the front parts of a book. Look at Reference 70 on page 54 in the Reference Section of your book. (*Read and discuss the parts of a book in Reference 70 with your students.*)

Reference 70: Parts of a Book

AT THE FRONT:

1. **Title Page.** This page has the full title of the book, the author's name, the illustrator's name, the name of the publishing company, and the city where the book was published.

2. **Copyright Page.** This page is right after the title page and tells the year in which the book was published and who owns the copyright. If the book has an ISBN number (International Standard Book Number), it is listed here.

3. **Preface** (also called **introduction**). If a book has this page, it will come before the table of contents and will usually tell briefly why the book was written and what it is about.

4. **Table of Contents.** This section lists the major divisions of the book by units or chapters and tells their page numbers.

5. **Body.** This is the main section, or text, of the book.

© SHURLEY INSTRUCTIONAL MATERIALS, INC.

Reference 70: Parts of a Book (continued)

AT THE BACK:

6. **Appendix.** This section includes extra informative material such as maps, charts, tables, diagrams, letters, etc. It is always wise to find out what is in the appendix, since it may contain supplementary material that you could otherwise find only by going to the library.

7. **Glossary.** This section is like a dictionary and gives the meanings of some of the important words in the book.

8. **Bibliography.** This section includes a list of books used by the author. It could serve as a guide for further reading on a topic.

9. **Index.** This will probably be your most useful section. The purpose of the index is to help you quickly locate information about the topics in the book. It has an alphabetical list of specific topics and tells on which page that information can be found. It is similar to the table of contents, but it is much more detailed.

 PRACTICE TIME

Have students turn to page 92 in the Practice Section of their book and find the instructions under Chapter 23, Lesson 2, Practice (*1-2*). Go over the directions to make sure they understand what to do. If students need a review, have them study the information and examples in the Reference Section of their books. Check and discuss the Practices after students have finished. (*Chapter 23, Lesson 2, Practice keys are below.*)

Chapter 23, Lesson 2, Practice 1: Match each part of a book listed below with the type of information it may give you. Write the appropriate letter in the blank. You may use each letter only once.

A. Body	B. Preface	C. Bibliography	D. Index	E. Copyright page	F. Appendix

1. __D__ Exact page numbers for a particular topic and used to locate topics quickly

2. __A__ Text of the book

3. __B__ Reason the book was written

4. __C__ Books listed for finding more information

5. __E__ ISBN number

6. __F__ Extra maps in a book

Chapter 23, Lesson 2, Practice 2: Write the nine parts of a book on a poster and write a description beside each part. Illustrate and color the nine parts. **(Title Page, Copyright Page, Preface, Table of Contents, Body, Appendix, Glossary, Bibliography, Index)** (*Check and discuss students' definitions and illustrations after they have finished. Note: Students may use their reference pages to help them.*)

(End of lesson.)

CHAPTER 23   LESSON 3

Objectives: Skills (introduce main parts of the library), Practice Exercise, and Activity.

SKILL TIME

TEACHING SCRIPT FOR INTRODUCING MAIN PARTS OF THE LIBRARY

A library is a good place to find information. In order to make the library an easy and fun experience, you will need to know about some of the major sections in the library and the most common materials found in the library. As we study the different sections, we can put the information on different colored construction paper. Look at Reference 71 on page 55 as we study the main parts of the library.

Teacher's Notes: Make cards from large sheets of different colored construction paper. Write these titles on them: _Fiction Section, Nonfiction Section, Reference Section, Dictionary, Encyclopedia, Atlas, Almanac, The Readers' Guide to Periodical Literature_, and the _Card Catalog_. Under each title, write the information provided below. You and your students might also illustrate and laminate the cards.

Reference 71: Main Parts of the Library

Fiction Section
Fiction books contain stories about people, places, or things that are not true. Fiction books are arranged on the shelves in alphabetical order according to the authors' last names. Since fiction stories are made-up, they cannot be used when you research your report topic.

Non-Fiction Section
Non-Fiction books contain information and stories that are true.

Reference Section
The Reference Section is designed to help you find information on many topics. The Reference Section contains many different kinds of reference books and materials. Some of the ones that you need to know about are listed below.

- **Dictionary** (Reference Book)
  The dictionary gives the definition, spelling, pronunciation, and correct usage of words and tells briefly about famous people and places.

- **Encyclopedia** (Reference Book)
  The encyclopedia gives concise, accurate information about persons, places, and events of world-wide interest.

- **Atlas** (Reference Book)
  The atlas is primarily a book of maps, but it often contains facts about oceans, lakes, mountains, areas, population, products, and climates of every part of the world.

Level 3 Homeschool Teacher's Manual

© SHURLEY INSTRUCTIONAL MATERIALS, INC.

CHAPTER 23 LESSON 3 CONTINUED

Reference 71: Main Parts of the Library (continued)

- **Almanac** (Reference Book)
  Both *The World Almanac* and the *Information Please Almanac* are published once a year and contain brief, up-to-date information on a variety of topics.

- ***The Readers' Guide to Periodical Literature*** (Reference Book)
  The Readers' Guide to Periodical Literature is an index for magazines. It is a monthly booklet that lists the titles of articles, stories, and poems published in all leading magazines. These titles are listed under topics that are arranged alphabetically. The monthly issues of *The Readers' Guide to Periodical Literature* are bound together in a single volume once a year and filed in the library. By using the *Readers' Guide*, a person researching a topic can know which back issues of magazines might be helpful.

- **Card Catalog** (Reference File)
  The card catalog is a file of cards, arranged alphabetically, and usually placed in the drawers of a cabinet called the card catalog. It is an index to the library. Some libraries now have computer terminals that show the same information as the card catalog, but the information is stored in a computer. Often, the computer listing will also tell whether or not the book is currently on loan from the library.

 PRACTICE TIME

Have students turn to page 93 in the Practice Section of their book and find Chapter 23, Lesson 3, Practice. Go over the directions to make sure they understand what to do. Check and discuss the Practice after students have finished. (*Chapter 23, Lesson 3, Practice key is given below.*)

Chapter 23, Lesson 3, Practice: Underline the correct answers.

1. The main reference book that is primarily a book of maps is the
   (**encyclopedia, dictionary, <u>atlas</u>, almanac**).
2. What would you find by going to *The Readers' Guide to Periodical Literature*?
   (**newspaper articles, <u>magazine articles</u>, encyclopedia articles**)
3. Fiction books contain information and stories that are (**true, <u>not true</u>**).
4. The main reference book that is published once a year with a variety of up-to-date information is the
   (**encyclopedia, dictionary, atlas, <u>almanac</u>**).
5. The main reference book that gives the definition, spelling, and pronunciation of words is the
   (**encyclopedia, <u>dictionary</u>, atlas, almanac**).
6. Nonfiction books contain information and stories that are (**<u>true</u>, not true**).

 ACTIVITY / ASSIGNMENT TIME

Take students on a field trip to visit their local library. Have them take pencils and notebooks to take notes and draw a diagram of the library. After they return home, have students design a library and put it on poster board. They are to label and illustrate as many areas in the library as possible. Finally, have students write a report about their study of the library. After students have finished their library illustrations and reports, have students read and discuss them with family members and/or friends. (*This project may take several days.*)

(End of lesson.)

© SHURLEY INSTRUCTIONAL MATERIALS, INC.

CHAPTER 23   LESSON 4

Objectives: Jingles, Study, Test, Check, Activity, and Writing (journal).

JINGLE TIME

Have students turn to the Jingle Section in their books and recite the previously-taught jingles.

STUDY TIME

Have students study the vocabulary words in their vocabulary notebooks. Remind students that any vocabulary word in their notebooks could be on their test. Also, have students study any of the skills in the Practice Section that they need to review.

TEST TIME

Have students turn to page 120 in the Test Section of their books and find Chapter 23 Test. Go over the directions to make sure they understand what to do. (*Chapter 23 Test key is on the next page.*)

CHECK TIME

After students have finished, check and discuss the test. Make sure they understand why their test questions and answers are right or wrong. (*For total points, count each required answer as a point.*)

ACTIVITY / ASSIGNMENT TIME

Students will continue to draw or trace the states and write the following questions and answers.

Oregon	Pennsylvania
1. What is the state on the front of this card? **Oregon**	1. What is the state on the front of this card? **Pennsylvania**
2. What is the capital of Oregon? **Salem**	2. What is the capital of Pennsylvania? **Harrisburg**
3. What is the postal abbreviation of Oregon? **OR**	3. What is the postal abbreviation of Pennsylvania? **PA**
4. What year was Oregon admitted to the Union? **1859**	4. What year was Pennsylvania admitted to the Union? **1787**

Color these states and look up an interesting fact about each state to write on the cards. Use the cards to quiz family members, friends, and relatives. You may want to time the responses to your questions. Also, along with previous suggestions, think of other ways to have fun with your United States card file.

(End of lesson.)

© SHURLEY INSTRUCTIONAL MATERIALS, INC.

Chapter 23 Test
(Student Page 120)

Exercise 1: Classify each sentence.

```
    (You) SP    V-t   A    DO       P PPA  OP    P    OP
1.  SN  V-t     / Ship the package (to my home) (in Florida).  Imp
    DO  P2
```

```
                  I     A    SN    HV  V-t  A  Adj   DO   P  A  OP
2.  SN  V-t     Look!  The policeman / is firing a warning shot (in the air)!  E
    DO  P2
```

Exercise 2: Match each part of a book listed below with the type of information it may give you. Write the appropriate letter in the blank. You may use each letter only once.

| A. Body | B. Preface | C. Bibliography | D. Index | E. Copyright page | F. Title Page | G. Appendix |

1. __D_ Exact page numbers for a particular topic and used to locate topics quickly

2. __A_ Text of the book

3. __B_ Reason the book was written

4. __C_ Books listed for finding more information

5. __E_ ISBN number

6. __F_ Publisher's name and city where the book was published

7. __G_ Extra maps in a book

Exercise 3: Underline the correct answers.

1. Nonfiction books contain information and stories that are (**true**, **not true**).
2. Fiction books contain information and stories that are (**true**, **not true**).
3. The main reference book that is primarily a book of maps is the
   (**encyclopedia, dictionary, atlas, almanac**).
4. The main reference book that gives the definition, spelling, and pronunciation of words is the
   (**encyclopedia, dictionary, atlas, almanac**).
5. The main reference book that is published once a year with a variety of up-to-date information is the
   (**encyclopedia, dictionary, atlas, almanac**).
6. What would you find by going to *The Readers' Guide to Periodical Literature*?
   (**newspaper articles, magazine articles, encyclopedia articles**)

Exercise 4: On notebook paper, write the five parts found at the front of a book. (**Title Page, Copyright Page, Preface, Table of Contents, Body**) (**The order of answers may vary.**)

Exercise 5: On notebook paper, write the four parts found at the back of a book. (**Appendix, Glossary, Bibliography, Index**) (**The order of answers may vary.**)

Exercise 6: In your journal, write a paragraph summarizing what you have learned this week.

© SHURLEY INSTRUCTIONAL MATERIALS, INC.

CHAPTER 23 LESSON 4 CONTINUED

TEACHER INSTRUCTIONS

Use the Question and Answer Flows below for the sentences on the Chapter 23 Test.

Question and Answer Flow for Sentence 1: Ship the package to my home in Florida.

1. Who ship the package to my home in Florida?
   you - SP (understood subject pronoun)
2. What is being said about you? you ship - V
3. You ship what? package - verify the noun
4. Does package mean the same as you? No.
5. Package - DO
6. Ship - V-t
7. The - A
8. To - P
9. To what? home - OP

10. Whose home? my - PPA
11. In - P
12. In what? Florida - OP
13. SN V-t DO P2 Check
14. Verb-transitive - Check again.
15. (To my home) - Prepositional phrase
16. (In Florida) - Prepositional phrase
17. Period, command, imperative sentence
18. Go back to the verb - divide the complete subject
    from the complete predicate.

Classified Sentence: (You) SP   V-t A   DO   P PPA OP   P   OP
            SN V-t   / Ship the package (to my home) (in Florida). **Imp**
            DO P2

Question and Answer Flow for Sentence 2: Look! The policeman is firing a warning shot in the air!

1. Who is firing a warning shot in the air? policeman - SN
2. What is being said about policeman?
   policeman is firing - V
3. Is - HV
4. Policeman is firing what? shot - verify the noun
5. Does shot mean the same thing as policeman? No.
6. Shot - DO
7. Firing - V-t
8. What kind of shot? warning - Adj
9. A - A
10. In - P

11. In what? air - OP
12. The - A
13. The - A
14. Look - I
15. SN V-t DO P2 Check
16. Verb-transitive - Check again.
17. (In the air) - Prepositional phrase
18. Exclamation point, strong feeling, exclamatory
    sentence
19. Go back to the verb - divide the complete subject
    from the complete predicate.

Classified Sentence: I   A   SN   HV V-t A   Adj   DO   P A OP
            SN V-t   Look! The policeman / is firing a warning shot (in the air)! **E**
            DO P2

© SHURLEY INSTRUCTIONAL MATERIALS, INC.

CHAPTER 23   LESSON 5

Objectives: Writing Assignments #29 and #30, Bonus Option.

 WRITING TIME

TEACHING SCRIPT FOR WRITING ASSIGNMENTS

Today, you are assigned two different kinds of writing. You will write a business letter for the first writing assignment. For the second writing assignment, you will have a choice of topics. This assignment will require a title that will accurately reflect the content of your paragraph or essay. You will revise and edit both writing assignments. (*Read the boxes below for more information about students' writing assignment.*) As you edit, make sure you use the checkpoints in the editing checklist provided in Reference 42

Writing Assignment Box #1

Writing Assignment #29: Write a business letter. You may invent a company and a situation for which you are writing. Before you begin, review the reasons for writing business letters and the four types of business letters (Reference 65 on page 50). This business must be different from the businesses chosen in the previous lessons. After your letter has been edited, fold the letter and put it in an envelope. Address the envelope properly.

Writing Assignment Box #2

Writing Assignment #30: Your choice

Writing choices: (1) **Expository**   (2) **Persuasive**   (3) **Narrative**   (4) **Descriptive**

<u>Bonus Option</u>: **Think about several scriptures in the Bible that would make good topics for a Bible story. Write a Bible story in your Journal, using the scripture you have chosen. Read your Bible story to family members and friends. As time goes by, you could write other Bible stories. Keep your Bible and refer to them when you are an adult. You could also show them to your children.**

Read, check, and discuss Writing Assignments #29 and #30 after students have finished their final papers. Use the editing checklist as you check and discuss students' papers. Make sure students are using the editing checklist correctly.

(End of lesson.)

© SHURLEY INSTRUCTIONAL MATERIALS, INC.

CHAPTER 24   LESSON 1

Objectives: Skills (introduce alphabetizing), and Practice Exercise.

SKILL TIME

TEACHING SCRIPT FOR INTRODUCING ALPHABETIZING

Sometimes studying involves looking words up in a dictionary. You may need to see if you have spelled a word correctly, or you may want to check a word's meaning. A dictionary gives you the correct spelling, pronunciation, meanings, and usage of words. Today, we are going to learn about alphabetizing because words are arranged in alphabetical order in a dictionary. The best way to learn alphabetizing is to alphabetize words for practice. Look at Reference 72 on page 56 in your Reference section.

There is a simple way to put words in alphabetical order. When the first letter of the words to be alphabetized is different, you only have to look at the first letter to put words in alphabetical order. Let's read the directions for the example. (_Read the directions._) Look at the two words under the title "Music Words." In the words _saxophone_ and _flute_, the first letters, _s_ and _f,_ are different. Since _f_ comes before _s_ in the alphabet, _flute_ comes before _saxophone_. A number _1_ has been written in the blank in front of _flute_ and a number _2_ has been written in the blank in front of _saxophone_ as demonstrated in the example.

Reference 72: Alphabetical Order									
Example: Put each group of words in alphabetical order. Use numbers to show the order in each column.									
Music Words		**"B" Words**		**Math Words**		**Science Words**		**"T" Words**	
2	1. saxophone	1	3. Bible	2	5. fractions	2	7. cell	1	9. task
1	2. flute	2	4. bike	1	6. division	1	8. atom	2	10. time

© SHURLEY INSTRUCTIONAL MATERIALS, INC.

CHAPTER 24 LESSON 1 CONTINUED

When the first letters of words to be alphabetized are the same, you only have to look at the second or third letters to put them in alphabetical order. Now, look at the two words *Bible* and *bike* under "B Words." In the words *Bible* and *bike*, the first two letters are the same. Go to the third letter in each word. Since *b* comes before *k* in the alphabet, *Bible* comes before *bike*. A number *1* has been written in the blank in front of *Bible* and a number *2* has been written in the blank in front of *bike*, demonstrated in the example. (*Call on students to demonstrate this process orally, with the rest of the sample words.*)

 PRACTICE TIME

Have students turn to page 93 in the Practice Section of their book and find Chapter 24, Lesson 1, Practice. Go over the directions to make sure they understand what to do. If students need a review, have them study the information and examples in the Reference Section of their books. Check and discuss the Practice after students have finished. (*Chapter 24, Lesson 1, Practice key is given below.*)

Chapter 24, Lesson 1, Practice: Put each group of words in alphabetical order. Write numbers in the blanks to show the order in each column.

School Words	Birthday Words	"C" Words	Garden Words	"P" Words
3 1. recess	2 7. cake	1 13. cave	3 19. plant	1 25. paddle
5 2. teacher	3 8. candles	6 14. cymbal	1 20. fertilizer	3 26. penny
4 3. student	1 9. balloons	2 15. channel	4 21. seeds	6 27. powder
2 4. homework	5 10. party	3 16. cigar	6 22. weeds	2 28. paint
1 5. books	6 11. presents	5 17. cross	2 23. hoe	4 29. pioneer
6 6. test	4 12. games	4 18. cricket	5 24. water	5 30. pipe

(End of lesson.)

CHAPTER 24   LESSON 2

Objectives: Skills (introduce guide words), and Practice Exercise.

SKILL TIME

TEACHING SCRIPT FOR INTRODUCING GUIDE WORDS

When you are looking a word up in the dictionary, you look first under the first letter of the word. After you have found that letter in the dictionary, you can use special words, called **guide words**, which are found at the top of the dictionary pages, to keep you from having to look at every word on every page until you find your word. When you are looking a word up in the dictionary, you need to know how to use guide words.

Guide words are the two words listed at the top of each dictionary page. Guide words tell the first and last words on the page. When you are looking up a word in the dictionary, you can save yourself time by using the guide words to help you see if the word you want to look up is on a particular page. To do this, see if your word comes between the guide words in an alphabetical order check. If it does, then your word is found on that page.

Look at Reference 73 on page 56 in the Reference Section of your book. Let's do the example to learn how to use guide words. Look at number 1. If you want to find the word _capital_ in the dictionary, there is a process you go through. Usually, this process is automatic. Now, you will decide if the word _capital_ is located on page 164 or on page 165.

1. First, you look at the guide words _canyon_ and _capitalist_ at the top of page 164.
2. Next, you decide if _capital_ is on page 164 by putting _canyon, capitalist,_ and _capital_ in alphabetical order. (_Write the example on the board:_ __1__ canyon __2__ capital __3__ capitalist)
3. Now, you know that _capital_ is found on page 164 because it comes between the two guide words listed on that page. The page number _164_ is written in the blank beside _capital_.

Reference 73: Guide Words		
Example: Below are the tops of two dictionary pages. Write the page number on which each word listed would appear.		

canyon (first word)	Page 164	**capitalist** (last word)		**capitalistic** (first word)	Page 165	**captain** (last word)

Page

164   1.   capital

165   2.   capsule

© SHURLEY INSTRUCTIONAL MATERIALS, INC.

CHAPTER 24 LESSON 2 CONTINUED

Next, you will decide if the word *capsule* is located on page 164 or on page 165. You start the process all over again.

1. First, you look at the guide words, *canyon* and *capitalist*, at the top of page 164
2. Next, you decide if *capsule* is on page 164 by putting *canyon, capitalist,* and *capsule* in alphabetical order. *(Write the example on the board:* __1__ *canyon* __2__ *capitalist* __3__ *capsule.)*
3. Now, you know that *capsule* is not found on page 164 because it does not come between the two guide words listed on that page. *Capsule* comes **after** *capitalist*. So, you go to the next page and check the guide words to see if *capsule* comes between them. Now, you start the process all over again, using the guide words on page 165.

1. First, you look at the guide words, *capitalistic* and *captain*, at the top of page 165.
2. Next, you decide if *capsule* is on page 165 by putting *capitalistic, captain,* and *capsule* in alphabetical order. *(Write the example on the board:* __1__ *capitalistic* __2__ *capsule* __3__ *captain.)*
3. Now, you know that *capsule* is found on page 165 because it comes between the two guide words listed on that page. The page number *165* is written in the blank beside *capsule*.

 PRACTICE TIME

Have students turn to page 93 in the Practice Section of their book and find Chapter 24, Lesson 2, Practice. Go over the directions to make sure they understand what to do. If students need a review, have them study the information and examples in the Reference Section of their books. Check and discuss the Practice after students have finished. *(Chapter 24, Lesson 2, Practice key is given below.)*

Chapter 24, Lesson 2, Practice: Below are the tops of two dictionary pages. Write the page number on which each word listed would appear.

freighter	Page	**friendly**
(first word)	300	(last word)

friendship	Page	**front**
(first word)	301	(last word)

Page

__301__ 1. fright

__300__ 2. fried

Page

__301__ 3. fringe

__301__ 4. frog

Page

__300__ 5. friction

__301__ 6. from

Page

__301__ 7. frisky

__300__ 8. fresh

(End of lesson.)

© SHURLEY INSTRUCTIONAL MATERIALS, INC.

CHAPTER 24   LESSON 3
Objectives: Skills (introduce the dictionary and entry words), and Practice Exercise

SKILL TIME

TEACHING SCRIPT FOR INTRODUCING THE DICTIONARY AND ENTRY WORDS

Today, we will learn about the dictionary and dictionary entry words. A dictionary gives many kinds of information. Look at Reference 74 on page 57. Follow along as I read the information about the dictionary and the parts of a dictionary entry word to you. *(Read and discuss Reference 74 below.)*

Reference 74: The Dictionary

1. The words listed in a dictionary are called <u>entry words</u> and are in bold-face type.
2. The <u>entry words</u> are listed in alphabetical order (ABC order).
3. The dictionary tells how to spell the word and how to pronounce the word.
4. The dictionary tells what the word means and gives an example to explain the meaning.
5. The dictionary tells how to use the word and gives the part of speech for the word.

Entry Words

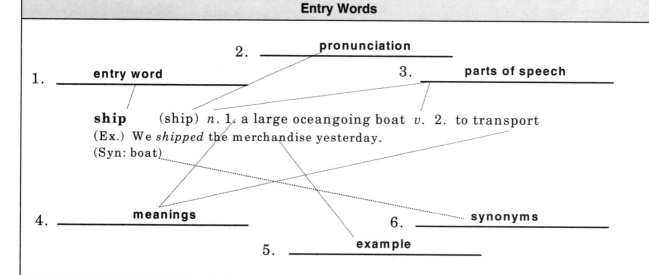

Parts of a Dictionary Entry

1. <u>The entry word</u> – gives correct spelling and divides the word into syllables.
2. <u>Pronunciation</u> – tells how to pronounce a word. It is usually put in parentheses.
3. <u>Part of speech</u> – uses small *n.* for noun, small *v.* for verb, *adj.* for adjective, etc.
4. <u>Meanings</u> – are numbered definitions listed according to the part of speech.
5. <u>Example</u> – a sentence using the entry word to illustrate a meaning. Shown as (Ex.)
6. <u>Synonyms</u> – words that have similar meanings to the entry word. Shown as (Syn:)

© SHURLEY INSTRUCTIONAL MATERIALS, INC.

CHAPTER 24 LESSON 3 CONTINUED

 PRACTICE TIME

Have students turn to page 94 in the Practice Section of their book and find Chapter 24, Lesson 3, Practice (*1-2*). Go over the directions to make sure they understand what to do. Check and discuss the Practices after students have finished. (*Chapter 24, Lesson 3, Practice keys are given below.*)

Chapter 24, Lesson 3, Practice 1: Match the definitions of the parts of a dictionary entry below. Write the correct letter of the word beside each definition.

E	1. small *n.* for noun, small *v.* for verb, *adj.* for adjective, etc.	A.	pronunciation
F	2. sentences using the entry word to illustrate a meaning	B.	meanings
D	3. words that have similar meanings to the entry word	C.	entry word
A	4. shows how to pronounce a word, usually put in parentheses	D.	synonyms
C	5. correct spelling and divides the word into syllables	E.	parts of speech
B	6. numbered definitions listed according to the part of speech	F.	examples

Chapter 24, Lesson 3, Practice 2: Label each part of the dictionary entry below. Use the definitions in the matching exercise to help you.

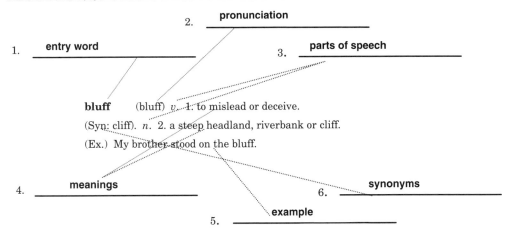

(End of lesson.)

© SHURLEY INSTRUCTIONAL MATERIALS, INC.

CHAPTER 24   LESSON 4

Objectives: Jingles, Study, Test, Check, Activity and Writing (journal).

 JINGLE TIME

Have students turn to the Jingle Section in their books and recite the previously-taught jingles.

 STUDY TIME

Have students study any of the skills in the Practice Section that they need to review.

 TEST TIME

Have students turn to page 121 in the Test Section of their books and find Chapter 24 test. Go over the directions to make sure they understand what to do. (*Chapter 24 test key is on the next page.*)

 CHECK TIME

After students have finished, check and discuss the test. Make sure they understand why their test questions and answers are right or wrong. (*For total points, count each required answer as a point.*)

 ACTIVITY / ASSIGNMENT TIME

Students will continue to draw or trace the states and write the following questions and answers.

Rhode Island	South Carolina
1. What is the state on the front of this card? **Rhode Island**	1. What is the state on the front of this card? **South Carolina**
2. What is the capital of Rhode Island? **Providence**	2. What is the capital of South Carolina? **Columbia**
3. What is the postal abbreviation of Rhode Island? **RI**	3. What is the postal abbreviation of South Carolina? **SC**
4. What year was Rhode Island admitted to the Union? **1790**	4. What year was South Carolina admitted to the Union? **1788**

Color these states and look up an interesting fact about each state to write on the cards. Use the cards to quiz family members, friends, and relatives. You may want to time the responses to your questions. Also, along with previous suggestions, think of other ways to have fun with your United States card file.

(End of lesson.)

© SHURLEY INSTRUCTIONAL MATERIALS, INC.

Chapter 24 Test
(Student Page 121)

Exercise 1: Classify each sentence.

　　　　　　　　HV PPA SN　V-t　Adj　　DO　　P A　OP
1. **SN V-t**　　Did your dad / build those shelves (in the den)?　**Int**
　DO P2

　　　　　　　　PNA　SN　　V　　P PPA OP　　P A　OP
2. **SN V**　　Sue's sister / drove (with her cousin) (to the museum).　**D**
　P1

Exercise 2: Put each group of words in alphabetical order. Use numbers to show the order in each column.

Winter Words	Picnic Words	"D" Words	Kitchen Words	"G" Words
3 1. ice	3 5. food	1 9. date	3 13. sink	1 17. gang
1 2. cold	2 6. blanket	4 10. dull	1 14. dishes	4 18. ground
4 3. snow	1 7. ants	2 11. deep	4 15. table	3 19. germ
2 4. freeze	4 8. summer	3 12. defend	2 16. oven	2 20. gas

Exercise 3: Below are the tops of two dictionary pages. Write the page number on which each word listed would appear.

kingly (first word)	Page 398	knew (last word)		knife (first word)	Page 399	knot (last word)

Page		Page		Page		Page	
398 1. kiss		399 3. knit		398 5. knee		399 7. knock	
399 2. knight		398 4. kite		398 6. kit		398 8. kitten	

Exercise 4: Match the definitions of the parts of a dictionary entry below. Write the correct letter of the word beside each definition.

C 1. gives correct spelling and divides the word into syllables
F 2. sentences using the entry word to illustrate a meaning
B 3. numbered definitions listed according to the part of speech
A 4. shows how to pronounce a word, usually put in parentheses
E 5. small *n.* for noun, small *v.* for verb, *adj.* for adjective, etc.
D 6. words that have similar meanings to the entry word

A. pronunciation
B. meanings
C. entry word
D. synonyms
E. parts of speech
F. examples

Exercise 5: In your journal, write a paragraph summarizing what you have learned this week.

© SHURLEY INSTRUCTIONAL MATERIALS, INC.

CHAPTER 24 LESSON 4 CONTINUED

TEACHER INSTRUCTIONS

Use the Question and Answer Flows below for the sentences on the Chapter 24 Test.

Question and Answer Flow for Sentence 1: Did your dad build those shelves in the den?

1. Who did build those shelves in the den? dad - SN
2. What is being said about dad? dad did build - V
3. Did - HV
4. Dad did build what? shelves - verify the noun
5. Do shelves mean the same thing as dad? No.
6. Shelves - DO
7. Build - V-t
8. Which shelves? those - Adj
9. In - P
10. In what? den - OP
11. The - A
12. Whose dad? your - PPA
13. SN V-t DO P2 Check
14. Verb-transitive - Check again.
15. (In the den) - Prepositional phrase
16. Question mark, question, interrogative sentence
17. Go back to the verb - divide the complete subject from the complete predicate.

Classified Sentence:

	HV PPA SN	V-t Adj	DO	P A OP
SN V-t	Did your dad /	build those shelves	(in the den)?	**Int**
DO P2				

Question and Answer Flow for Sentence 2: Sue's sister drove with her cousin to the museum.

1. Who drove with her cousin to the museum? sister - SN
2. What is being said about sister? sister drove - V
3. With - P
4. With whom? cousin - OP
5. Whose cousin? her - PPA
6. To - P
7. To what? museum - OP
8. The - A
9. Whose sister? Sue's - PNA
10. SN V P1 Check
11. (With her cousin) - Prepositional phrase
12. (To the museum) - Prepositional phrase
13. Period, statement, declarative sentence
14. Go back to the verb - divide the complete subject from the complete predicate.

Classified Sentence:

	PNA SN	V	P PPA OP	P A OP
SN V	Sue's sister /	drove	(with her cousin)	(to the museum). **D**
P1				

© SHURLEY INSTRUCTIONAL MATERIALS, INC.

CHAPTER 24   LESSON 5

Objectives: Writing Assignment #31 and Activity.

 WRITING TIME

TEACHING SCRIPT FOR TALL TALES

A tall tale is a humorous story that has great exaggeration, but it also includes believable events and situations. Choose a topic for a tall tale and make an opening sentence that will immediately capture the reader's interest. Build your story up to a fantastic ending. You can use a big lie, a surprise, something funny, something clever, something unexpected, or something that leaves the reader guessing. *(Give students a list of the words below to help them think of good words to use for exaggeration.)* Read and discuss Writing Assignment #31 for fun and enrichment.

Writing Assignment Box

Exaggeration Words: extraordinary, never before, unbelievable, outlandish, worst, biggest, horrendous, million, faster than, impossible, tremendous, meanest, longest, heaviest, terrible, cleverest, most unexpected.

Writing Assignment #31: Tall Tales

Writing choices:

1 **The Fastest Mouth in Town**	4. **The Homework Computer**
2. **The Smartest Cat I've Ever Seen**	5. **The Funniest Person in My Family**
3. **The Wildest Ride in the World**	6. **Make your own tall-tale title.**

 ACTIVITY / ASSIGNMENT TIME

Students will continue to draw or trace the states and write the following questions and answers.

South Dakota	Tennessee
1. What is the state on the front of this card? **South Dakota**	1. What is the state on the front of this card? **Tennessee**
2. What is the capital of South Dakota? **Pierre**	2. What is the capital of Tennessee? **Nashville**
3. What is the postal abbreviation of South Dakota? **SD**	3. What is the postal abbreviation of Tennessee? **TN**
4. What year was South Dakota admitted to the Union? **1889**	4. What year was Tennessee admitted to the Union? **1796**

Color these states and look up an interesting fact about each state to write on the cards. Use the cards to quiz family members, friends, and relatives. You may want to time the responses to your questions. Also, along with previous suggestions, think of other ways to have fun with your United States card file.

(End of lesson.)

© SHURLEY INSTRUCTIONAL MATERIALS, INC.

CHAPTER 25   LESSON 1

Objectives: Writing (Story Card 1) and Activity.

 WRITING TIME

TEACHING SCRIPT FOR STORY CARD 1

Have students make the story card listed below on a note card. They can illustrate the note card if they wish. Read the words from the story card together. Have students use the words from the story card to orally compose sentences. This will build their understanding of the words on the card. Discuss any word the students do not know.

Next, students will write a story or paragraph for the story card. Make sure they include a title for their story or paragraph. They should use the words on the card to help them as they write. They do not need to use all the words, and they can also add words of their own. Students could type their story on the computer, using the spell check to help check for spelling mistakes. Have students illustrate their story. Finally, have students put their finished story in a folder. They should write a title for the folder and illustrate the cover. Have students present their story and illustrations to family members and/or friends.

Story Card #1

Autumn, school, Halloween, costumes, Thanksgiving, pilgrims, colorful trees, crisp weather, raking leaves, football games, sweaters, jackets, scarecrow, hayride, harvest, pumpkins, apples, hay

---

 ACTIVITY / ASSIGNMENT TIME

Students will continue to draw or trace the states and write the following questions and answers.

Texas	Utah
1. What is the state on the front of this card? **Texas**	1. What is the state on the front of this card? **Utah**
2. What is the capital of Texas? **Austin**	2. What is the capital of Utah? **Salt Lake City**
3. What is the postal abbreviation of Texas? **TX**	3. What is the postal abbreviation of Utah? **UT**
4. What year was Texas admitted to the Union? **1845**	4. What year was Utah admitted to the Union? **1896**

Color these states and look up an interesting fact about each state to write on the cards. Use the cards to quiz family members, friends, and relatives. You may want to time the responses to your questions. Also, along with previous suggestions, think of other ways to have fun with your United States card file.

(End of lesson.)

© SHURLEY INSTRUCTIONAL MATERIALS, INC.

CHAPTER 25   LESSON 2

Objectives: Writing (Story Card 2) and Activity.

 WRITING TIME

TEACHING SCRIPT FOR STORY CARD 2

Have students make the story card listed below on a note card. They can illustrate the note card if they wish. Read the words from the story card together. Have students use the words from the story card to orally compose sentences. This will build their understanding of the words on the card. Discuss any word the students do not know.

Next, students will write a story or paragraph for the story card. Make sure they include a title for their story or paragraph. They should use the words on the card to help them as they write. They do not need to use all the words, and they can also add words of their own. Students could type their story on the computer, using the spell check to help check for spelling mistakes. Have students illustrate their story. Finally, have students put their finished story in a folder. They should write a title for the folder and illustrate the cover. Have students present their story and illustrations to family members and/or friends.

Story Card #2

Winter, cold, snow, ice, bare trees, snowmen, parka, coat, mittens, gloves, hat, sled, shovel, blizzard, boots, Christmas, Valentine's Day, Hanukkah, New Year's Day

---

 ACTIVITY / ASSIGNMENT TIME

Students will continue to draw or trace the states and write the following questions and answers.

Vermont	Virginia
1. What is the state on the front of this card? **Vermont**	1. What is the state on the front of this card? **Virginia**
2. What is the capital of Vermont? **Montpelier**	2. What is the capital of Virginia? **Richmond**
3. What is the postal abbreviation of Vermont? **VT**	3. What is the postal abbreviation of Virginia? **VA**
4. What year was Vermont admitted to the Union?**1791**	4. What year was Virginia admitted to the Union? **1788**

Color these states and look up an interesting fact about each state to write on the cards. Use the cards to quiz family members, friends, and relatives. You may want to time the responses to your questions. Also, along with previous suggestions, think of other ways to have fun with your United States card file.

(End of lesson.)

© SHURLEY INSTRUCTIONAL MATERIALS, INC.

CHAPTER 25   LESSON 3

Objectives: Writing (Story Card 3) and Activity.

 WRITING TIME

TEACHING SCRIPT FOR STORY CARD 3

Have students make the story card listed below on a note card. They can illustrate the note card if they wish. Read the words from the story card together. Have students use the words from the story card to orally compose sentences. This will build their understanding of the words on the card. Discuss any word the students do not know.

Next, students will write a story or paragraph for the story card. Make sure they include a title for their story or paragraph. They should use the words on the card to help them as they write. They do not need to use all the words, and they can also add words of their own. Students could type their story on the computer, using the spell check to help check for spelling mistakes. Have students illustrate their story. Finally, have students put their finished story in a folder. They should write a title for the folder and illustrate the cover. Have students present their story and illustrations to family members and/or friends.

Story Card #3

Spring, March, windy, green, flowers, kites, cool, string, clouds, rain, Easter, rabbits, umbrellas, butterflies, birds, baby animals, green grass, green trees, fishing, rainbows, St. Patrick, shamrocks

---

 ACTIVITY / ASSIGNMENT TIME

Students will continue to draw or trace the states and write the following questions and answers.

Washington	West Virginia
1. What is the state on the front of this card? **Washington**	1. What is the state on the front of this card? **West Virginia**
2. What is the capital of Washington? **Olympia**	2. What is the capital of West Virginia? **Charleston**
3. What is the postal abbreviation of Washington? **WA**	3. What is the postal abbreviation of West Virginia? **WV**
4. What year was Washington admitted to the Union? **1889**	4. What year was West Virginia admitted to the Union? **1863**

Color these states and look up an interesting fact about each state to write on the cards. Use the cards to quiz family members, friends, and relatives. You may want to time the responses to your questions. Also, along with previous suggestions, think of other ways to have fun with your United States card file.

(End of lesson.)

© SHURLEY INSTRUCTIONAL MATERIALS, INC.

CHAPTER 25   LESSON 4

Objectives: Writing (Story Card 4) and Activity.

 WRITING TIME

TEACHING SCRIPT FOR STORY CARD 4

Have students make the story card listed below on a note card. They can illustrate the note card if they wish. Read the words from the story card together. Have students use the words from the story card to orally compose sentences. This will build their understanding of the words on the card. Discuss any word the students do not know.

Next, students will write a story or paragraph for the story card. Make sure they include a title for their story or paragraph. They should use the words on the card to help them as they write. They do not need to use all the words, and they can also add words of their own. Students could type their story on the computer, using the spell check to help check for spelling mistakes. Have students illustrate their story. Finally, have students put their finished story in a folder. They should write a title for the folder and illustrate the cover. Have students present their story and illustrations to family members and/or friends.

Story Card #4

Summer, July, vacation, lazy, camp, picnic, chores, baseball, swimming, lake, playing, fireworks, grandparents, friends, bicycle, boating, bathing suits, family, hot, dry, fish, warm, sun, blister, tan, relax

---

 ACTIVITY / ASSIGNMENT TIME

Students will continue to draw or trace the states and write the following questions and answers.

Wisconsin	Wyoming
1. What is the state on the front of this card? **Wisconsin**	1. What is the state on the front of this card? **Wyoming**
2. What is the capital of Wisconsin? **Madison**	2. What is the capital of Wyoming? **Cheyenne**
3. What is the postal abbreviation of Wisconsin? **WI**	3. What is the postal abbreviation of Wyoming? **WY**
4. What year was Wisconsin admitted to the Union? **1848**	4. What year was Wyoming admitted to the Union? **1890**

Color these states and look up an interesting fact about each state to write on the cards. Use the cards to quiz family members, friends, and relatives. You may want to time the responses to your questions. Also, along with previous suggestions, think of other ways to have fun with your United States card file.

(End of lesson.)

© SHURLEY INSTRUCTIONAL MATERIALS, INC.

CHAPTER 25 LESSON 5

Objectives: Writing (Story Card 5) and Activity.

 WRITING TIME

TEACHING SCRIPT FOR STORY CARD 5

Have students make the story card listed below on a note card. They can illustrate the note card if they wish. Read the words from the story card together. Have students use the words from the story card to orally compose sentences. This will build their understanding of the words on the card. Discuss any word the students do not know.

Next, students will write a story or paragraph for the story card. Make sure they include a title for their story or paragraph. They should use the words on the card to help them as they write. They do not need to use all the words, and they can also add words of their own. Students could type their story on the computer, using the spell check to help check for spelling mistakes. Have students illustrate their story. Finally, have students put their finished story in a folder. They should write a title for the folder and illustrate the cover. Have students present their story and illustrations to family members and/or friends.

Story Card #5

famous, American, leader, courageous, caring, strong, character, Abe Lincoln, George Washington, Martin Luther King, Clara Barton, Susan Anthony, Thomas Jefferson, patriotic

---

 ACTIVITY / ASSIGNMENT TIME

To conclude their study of the fifty states, have students draw and color a flag of the United States. Discuss the importance of a national flag. If possible, make a salt dough map or clay map of the United States. *(See the sample recipe below You might also look up salt dough recipes on the internet or use recipes you may have in your files.)* Make sure students are able to locate Washington D.C. Then, have students name and locate the bodies of water around the United States. Finally, have students write what they have learned from this project.

Salt and Flour Dough Recipe
Uncooked: One part flour, one part salt. You might also try one part flour, two parts salt. Dough is a creamy white color unless food coloring is added. Moisten with water until desired consistency is reached. Add only a small amount of water at a time. For color, you can use food coloring in the dough or paint the map with poster paints after it dries.

(End of lesson.)

© SHURLEY INSTRUCTIONAL MATERIALS, INC.

CHAPTER 26   LESSON 1

Objectives: Activity (Shurley English Writing Blocks & Bible Memory Markers).

ACTIVITY / ASSIGNMENT TIME

Read and discuss the Shurley English Writing Blocks below. *(Put the examples below on the board or on notebook paper.)* Next, have students write six sentences, using the format presented below. Students should use the same subject and verb and then demonstrate expanded sentences by following the labels. For additional expression, have students to write a seventh sentence using more parts of speech. This could include different pronouns, possessive nouns, and helping verbs. This is a great activity for students to see the importance of grammar in sentence structure.

The Shurley English Writing Blocks
SN   V 1. Boys sat.
SN   V   Adv 2. Boys sat quietly.
Adj   SN   V   Adv 3. Little boys sat quietly.
Adj   Adj   SN   V   Adv 4. Four little boys sat quietly.
A   Adj   Adj   SN   V   Adv 5. The four little boys sat quietly.
A   Adj   Adj   SN   V   Adv   P   A   OP 6. The four little boys sat quietly under the tree.
A   Adj   Adj   Adj   SN   HV   V   Adv   P   A   Adj   Adj   OP   P   PNA   OP 7. The four little tired boys are sitting quietly under the big oak tree in Jeff's backyard.

ACTIVITY / ASSIGNMENT TIME

BIBLE MEMORY MARKERS FOR NEW TESTAMENT BOOKS

You will begin making Bible Memory Markers for the books of the New Testament. Cut a piece of colored construction paper into a strip. Make the strip as wide and as long as you want your bookmarker to be. At the top of the strip, write the name of Matthew, the first book of the New Testament. Underneath the name, write New Testament. Illustrate your Memory Marker.

For the rest of this lesson and for the next lesson, you will continue making Memory Markers for each book in the New Testament. When you have finished creating all 27 Memory Markers, store the strips in a handy box. As you study different books of the Bible, use the appropriate marker. You may have several markers in your Bible at any given time. On the back of each marker, record the chapter and verses that you have memorized. Don't forget to put the date.

(End of lesson.)

© SHURLEY INSTRUCTIONAL MATERIALS, INC.

CHAPTER 26   LESSON 2

Objectives: Activity (Bible Memory Markers, continued).

ACTIVITY / ASSIGNMENT TIME

BIBLE MEMORY MARKERS FOR NEW TESTAMENT BOOKS

You will finish making the Memory Markers for each book in the New Testament today. Remember, when you have finished creating all 27 Memory Markers, store the strips in a handy box. As you study different books of the Bible, use the appropriate marker. Don't forget to record the chapter and verses that you have memorized on the back of each marker. Don't forget to put the date.

(End of lesson.)

CHAPTER 26   LESSON 3

Objectives: Activity (Bible Memory Markers, continued).

ACTIVITY / ASSIGNMENT TIME

BIBLE MEMORY MARKERS FOR OLD TESTAMENT BOOKS

You will begin making Bible Memory Markers for the books of the Old Testament. You will follow the same procedure that you used for the New Testament markers. Directions: Cut a piece of colored construction paper into a strip. Make the strip as wide and as long as you want your bookmarker to be. At the top of the strip, write the name of Genesis, the first book of the Old Testament. Underneath the name, write Old Testament. Illustrate your Memory Marker.

For the rest of this lesson and for the next two lessons, you will continue making Memory Markers for each book in the Old Testament. When you have finished creating all 39 Memory Markers, store the strips in the same box as the New Testament markers or make a new box for the Old Testament markers. As you study different books of the Bible, use the appropriate marker. You may have several markers in your Bible at any given time. On the back of each marker, record the chapter and verses that you have memorized. Don't forget to put the date.

(End of lesson.)

© SHURLEY INSTRUCTIONAL MATERIALS, INC.

CHAPTER 26   LESSON 4

Objectives: Activity (Bible Memory Markers, continued).

ACTIVITY / ASSIGNMENT TIME

BIBLE MEMORY MARKERS FOR OLD TESTAMENT BOOKS

You will continue making the Memory Markers for each book in the Old Testament today. Remember, when you have finished creating all 39 Memory Markers, store the strips in a handy box. As you study different books of the Bible, use the appropriate marker. Don't forget to record the chapter and verses that you have memorized on the back of each marker. Don't forget to put the date.

(End of lesson.)

CHAPTER 26   LESSON 5

Objectives: Activity (Bible Memory Markers, continued).

ACTIVITY / ASSIGNMENT TIME

BIBLE MEMORY MARKERS FOR OLD TESTAMENT BOOKS

You should finish making the Memory Markers for each book in the Old Testament today. If your schedule did not permit you to finish, just continue several more days until the project is finished. Remember, when you have finished creating all 39 Memory Markers, store the strips in a handy box. As you study different books of the Bible, use the appropriate marker. Don't forget to record the chapter and verses that you have memorized on the back of each marker.

After you have finished making all the markers, write what you have learned from this activity. Here are some questions to guide you. (*Use the questions below to help students evaluate this activity.*)

1. Did you write or print neatly?
2. Did you have fun choosing just the right colors?
3. Did you cut the strips straight?
4. Did you spell all the books of the Bible correctly?
5. Did you take pride in a job well done?
6. Did you put up your materials and clean your work area each day?
7. Did you do everything that was required in the project?
8. Would you consider making markers for someone else?
9. What did you learn from this project?

(End of lesson.)

© SHURLEY INSTRUCTIONAL MATERIALS, INC.

Level 3
Jingles & Introductory Sentences

Shurley Instructional Materials, Inc.
366 SIM Drive
Cabot, AR 72023

© 2001 SHURLEY INSTRUCTIONAL MATERIALS INC. AND ITS LICENSORS
ALL RIGHTS RESERVED
ISBN 1-58561-041-0